Entrepreneurship, Management, and the Structure of Payoffs

William J. Baumol

The MIT Press
Cambridge, Massachusetts
London, England

© 1993 Massachusetts Institute of Technology

This book was set in Palatino by Asco Trade Typesetting Ltd., Hong Kong and was printed and bound in the United States of America.

Library of Congress Cataloging-in-Publication Data

Baumol, William J.
  Entrepreneurship, management, and the structure of payoffs / William J. Baumol.
    p.   cm.
  Includes bibliographical references (p.   ) and index.
  ISBN 0-262-02360-1
  1. Entrepreneurship. 2. Industrial productivity. 3. Profit. I. Title.
HB615.B39   1993
658.4'21—dc20

93-4456
CIP

To Harold Price

A true entrepreneur, a true gentleman, and a true friend

Contents

Preface

Ever since I became interested in economics, more than half a century ago, I have been intrigued by the entrepreneur. This, surely, is the one heroic figure produced by the capitalist mechanism. The market does not present us with nations composed only of shopkeepers. It also brings upon the stage figures larger than life—and many of them, while not always the epitome of virtue, clearly engage in activities highly beneficial to society. But stories cannot hold our interest if they contain no villains. And my first loves in the cast of economic players were the enterprising buccaneers, the Goulds, Fisks, Drews, and Vanderbilts, of whom I could read tirelessly, for their stories have plots more unlikely than any writer of fiction would dare to employ. It is said that Milton's devil is the character who really engages our interest and emerges as the principal in *Paradise Lost*. When I was young, the enterprising rent seekers held a similar place for me.

But if there are villainous as well as virtuous entrepreneurs—all major characters in the drama of growth—why is so little said about the latter, and virtually nothing about the former, in the literature of economic theory? For more than fifty years this puzzle must have been pondered in my subconscious, occasionally emerging in a brief note on entrepreneurship. But finally the time came to bring it to the surface. This book is the result.

Its subject is the entrepreneur as an *allocable resource*, whose allocation, like that of the less legendary inputs, is determined by the price mechanism—the structure of the economic payoffs to the different activities in which the entrepreneur can engage. My fundamental hypothesis is that the allocation of entrepreneurs between virtue and villainy, or to put it more dispassionately, between productive and unproductive activities, is of the utmost importance for an economy's growth performance, and is not a matter of happenstance of little significance for the economy. The structure of payoffs also affects the allocation of entrepreneurs among the productive activities that compete for their time, notably, the allocation between innovation and dissemination of new technology, with the latter a much under-rated activity.

The subject matter seems to have forced me to produce a book that is somewhat episodic and offers no linear narrative proceeding with inexorable logic from premises to conclusion. Moreover, the subject did not permit uniformity in method. The approaches I felt myself forced to employ range from bits of mathematics to bits of history, and the heterogeneity of the chapters that follow, in terms of approach, subject matter, and readability, is the consequence.

Since both as historian and game theorist I have a good deal to be modest about, the list of my debts is unusually large, particularly in these fields. Nathan Rosenberg rose well above the call of duty and went over the manuscript, chapter by chapter, and provided invaluable advice. Other historians to whom I owe enormous gratitude include Stefano Fenoaltea, Joel Mokyr, Moses Abramovitz, Paul David, Lawrence Stone, Constance Berman, Claudia Goldin, William Jordan, and Theodore Rabb. Rescue on game-theoretic matters came from Dilip Abreu, Zsuzsanna Fluck, and Maria Luisa Petit. Help on the misuse of antitrust to subvert competition, particularly in the compilation of a list of pertinent cases, came from Jonathan M. Jacobson of the Coudert Brothers law firm. Howard G. Figueroa of IBM and W. D. Lewis of United Technologies were exceedingly generous in providing invaluable information on interfirm technology transfer, and the materials were supplemented in conversations with Colby H. Chandler, then chairman of the board of Eastman Kodak, Ernest Gallo of Gallo Vineyards, and a number of other industrialists. Andrei Shleifer and my partner in crime, Edward Wolff, both also went over much of the manuscript and contributed their considerable wisdom. Louis Lowenstein helped greatly with the discussion of takeovers, and Janusz Ordover with the material on technology-sharing firms. Very valuable comments and suggestions were contributed by Barbara Blumenthal, Partha Dasgupta, Avinash Dixit, Ralph Gomory, and Burt Malkiel. Obviously, I could not have hoped for a better brain trust.

Generous support of the research was contributed, at different times, by the Price Institute for Entrepreneurial Studies, the Alfred P. Sloan Foundation, the Division of Information Science and Technology of the National Science Foundation, and last but hardly least, the C. V. Starr Center for Applied Economics at New York University. I am, of course, deeply grateful to all of them.

My greatest personal gratitude, however, goes to my co-workers. As always, or at least for a long and delightful period of association, there is

Sue Anne Batey Blackman, second to none, who carried out research on the work of inventors and on other critical portions of the book, and who admonished me whenever I did violence to the language, showing me how to do better. During the early part of the work both research and graphics were caringly supplied by Vacharee Devakula who, unfortunately, has abandoned me to return to her native Thailand. Finally, the last stages of the work had the capable and intelligent help of Janeece Roderick who, continues to work with me while making her considerable contributions to the performing arts.

Luquillo, Puerto Rico
January 1993

1 The Entrepreneur in Economic Theory

... he was ... the entrepreneur extraordinaire, with all the requisite traits for the role: nerve, persistence, dynamic energy, a talent for propaganda, a capacity for deception, imagination.

A description of Ferdinand de Lesseps in McCullough (1977, p. 53)

It is, as a business proposition, a matter of indifference to the man of large affairs whether the disturbances which his transactions set up in the industrial system help or hinder the system at large, except in so far as he has ulterior strategic ends to serve.

Veblen (1904, pp. 29–30)

The objective of this book is to help in reviving the theory of the entrepreneur-leader, and to point out ways in which one can resume the study of that individual's role in economic growth. In short, the book is an attempt to provide a contribution to the arena I once labeled the "magnificent dynamics." Here the place of the entrepreneur is well recognized and generally accepted. In a word, the entrepreneur's productive contribution is *innovation*. But it will be argued here that this credits him or her with too little, and also with too much.

One of the central arguments of the book is that the entrepreneur often makes no productive contribution at all, and in some cases plays a destructive role, engaging in what Veblen described as "systematic sabotage" of production. This does not happen fortuitously, but occurs when the structure of payoffs in an economy is such as to make unproductive activities such as rent seeking (and worse) more profitable than activities that are productive.

The other side of the matter is that the term *innovation* does not give productive entrepreneurs sufficient credit for their contributions to technological progress and growth. Technological progress has at least two dimensions, one of which is widely ignored in the literature. It depends both on the rate of flow of pertinent new ideas *and on the speed with which they are disseminated and adopted throughout the productive activities of the world.* Where products are differentiated (as is true of most "high-tech" activities) or where commodities are consumed and produced locally, goods can be supplied by many sources using different technology and different product specifications. If only one of the many producers of some good uses a valuable innovation, obviously productivity will benefit far less than if the innovation is adopted universally. Thus the greater the speed of dissemination of new technology, the more it contributes to productivity. That much seems obvious. But what is not obvious about the proposition are two associated observations that will be explored later. First, reasons will be offered suggesting that, despite its more limited glamour, speed of dissemination plays a role in its influence on productivity growth fully comparable to that of rate of innovation. Second, it will be argued that the speed of dissemination of new ideas is not a matter of happenstance, but is heavily influenced by market forces acting through the agency of the entrepreneur. Indeed, the entrepreneur plays as important a role in dissemination as in innovation. Thus several chapters are devoted to the dissemination of technology and the entrepreneur's role in the process.

1.1 Different Roles: Entrepreneurs and Managers

The entrepreneur is at once one of the most intriguing and one of the most elusive in the cast of characters that constitutes the subject of economic analysis. Long recognized as the apex of the hierarchy that determines the evolving behavior of the firm, the entrepreneur is thereby assigned a heavy responsibility for the vitality of the free-enterprise society. In the writings of the classical economists the appearance of this important figure was frequent, but shadowy, without clearly defined form and function. In the literature of formal theory, at least until very recently, only Joseph Schumpeter and, to some degree, Frank Knight succeeded in infusing this character with life and assigning to him or her a specific area of activity to any extent commensurate with his acknowledged importance. But to do so, they were forced to sacrifice analytic tractability and even substantive mathematical representation. In more recent years, although economic events continue to underscore the significance of his role, the entrepreneur has nonetheless virtually disappeared from the theoretical literature. And as we will see, while some recent theoretical writings seem at first glance to offer a convenient place for an analysis of entrepreneurial activities, closer inspection indicates that matters have not really improved substantially on this score.

This chapter focuses on three issues. First, it reviews briefly the reasons why entrepreneurship should concern us. Second, it seeks to explain why economic theory has failed to provide an illuminating formal analysis of the decision process of the entrepreneur and concludes that it is also unlikely to be able to do so in the future. Finally, it suggests ways in which theory may be able to say a great deal that is highly relevant to the subject of entrepreneurship, even if it fails to provide a rigorous analysis of the *behavior* of the entrepreneur or of the supply of entrepreneurial *ability*.

But before proceeding with the discussion, it is helpful to propose a semantic distinction that is somewhat artificial but nevertheless important. It will be useful for our purposes to differentiate between the entrepreneurial and the managerial functions, though, as Schumpeter emphasized, the same persons at different times are likely to go from the one type of activity to the other (1936, p. 78). We may define the manager as the individual who oversees the ongoing efficiency of continuing processes. It is the manager's task to see that available processes and techniques are combined in proportions appropriate for current output levels and for the future outputs already in prospect. The manager sees to it that inputs are not wasted, that schedules and contracts are met, that routine pricing and advertising outlay decisions are made, that simple growth processes entailing no novel procedures take place, and so on. In sum, the manager takes charge of the activities and decisions encompassed in the traditional models of the firm.

The preceding description is not intended to denigrate the importance of managerial activity or to imply that it is without significant difficulties. Harvey Leibenstein and Carl Kaysen, among others, have suggested that in practice most firms do not operate at maximal efficiency—in economist's terms, they occupy positions well inside their production frontiers—and one of their most challenging tasks is to find ways of approaching those loci more closely, that is, of increasing their efficiency even within the limits of known technology and familiar practice. This is presumably part of the job of the manager, who is constantly on the lookout for ways to save a little here and to squeeze out a bit more there. But though the standard theoretical models usually proceed on the assumption that the firm is able to arrive at decisions that serve its purposes optimally and, hence, efficiently, for many purposes these models would appear to provide a useful and analytically tractable description of the functions of the manager. Once aware of an arrangement that calculation, experience, or judgment indicate constitute something close to the current optimum, the manager must see that this arrangement is in fact instituted to a reasonable degree of approximation.

The entrepreneur (whether or not she also doubles as a manager) has a different role. It is her job to locate new ideas and to put them into effect. She must lead, perhaps even inspire; she cannot allow things to get into a rut and, for her, today's practice is never good enough for tomorrow. In short, she is the Schumpeterian innovator and more. She is the individual who exercises what is called "leadership" in the business literature. And it is she who is virtually absent from the received theory of the firm.

1.2 On the Significance of the Entrepreneur

If we are interested in explaining what Trygve Haavelmo has described as the "really big dissimilarities in economic life," we must be prepared to concern ourselves with entrepreneurship. For the really big differences are usually those that correspond to historical developments over long periods of time or to the comparative states of various economies, notably those of the developed and the less developed areas. They encompass contrasting developments such as the meteoric rise of some economies, like that of Japan, the fall from leadership position by others, and the prospects for still other economies whose future relative position appears to hang in the balance.

It has long been recognized that the entrepreneurial function is a vital component in the process of growth of output and productivity. Recent empirical evidence and the lessons of experience both seem to confirm this view. For example, most empirical studies on the nature of the production function have concluded that sheer capital accumulation and expansion of the labor force leave unexplained a substantial proportion of the historical growth of the nation's output. Thus, in a well-known paper, Solow (1957, p. 320) has suggested on the basis of American data for the period 1909–1949 that "gross output per man-hour doubled over the interval, with 87.5 percent of the increase attributable to technical change and the remaining 12.5 percent to increase in the use of capital."[1] But any such innovation, whether it is purely technological or constitutes a modification in the way in which an industry is organized, will require entrepreneurial initiative in its introduction. Thus we are driven to the view that by ignoring the entrepreneur we are prevented from accounting fully for a very substantial proportion of our historic growth.

Those who have concerned themselves with development policy have apparently been driven to similar conclusions. If we seek to explain the success of those economies that have managed to grow significantly, compared with those that have remained relatively stagnant, we find it difficult to do so without taking into consideration differences in the availability of entrepreneurial talent and in the motivational mechanisms that drive them on. A substantial portion of the energies of those who design plans to stimulate development has been devoted to the provision of the means whereby entrepreneurs can be trained and encouraged.

The entrepreneur also has a prominent place in institutional and applied discussions in a number of other economic areas. For example, his absence is sometimes cited as a significant source of the difficulties of a declining industry, and a balance-of-payments crisis is sometimes discussed in similar terms. Thus, analyses of both macroeconomic problems and microeconomic problems offer a substantial place for him. Whether or not he is assigned the starring role, he would appear to be no minor character.

1.3   The Schumpeterian Model: Brief Recapitulation

Since Schumpeter's model is the one analytical construct that deals directly with entrepreneurship as it is interpreted here, and since it comes up repeatedly throughout the book, a brief summary may not be redundant. It need hardly be said that a condensation inevitably excludes many of the subtleties and nuances of his original discussion, sometimes driving us to the verge of misrepresentation. Of course, those thoroughly familiar with the original will gain little from this section.

To bring out the workings of a world in which entrepreneurship plays its role, Schumpeter starts off, as contrast, with a static scenario which he calls "a circular flow," a world of routine in which every day is very much like the one that preceded it. In this model all decisions have already been made, and all the alternatives have been explored and compared, so that for every matter that was to be decided, the optimal choice has been adopted. Clearly, no economy has ever been like this—even the Dark Ages experienced innovation, as will be noted in somewhat more detail in Chapter 2, and even then, the relatively stationary economy can hardly be said to have elicited behavior that invariably attained anything like an ideal economic efficiency. Rather, the circular flow model is a useful analytical construct employed in Walrasian analysis and elsewhere to show what careful rational calculation can achieve in a world without uncertainty or change.

In Schumpeter's analysis, the entrepreneur intrudes into this eventless world, seeking opportunities to stir things up. She seeks opportunities for profit by exploiting situations that invite change. New products or new techniques for the production of goods and services previously available immediately come to mind as examples. But the opportunities for what

Schumpeter calls "new combinations" go well beyond those two. They include the adoption of new and better (or cheaper) sources of input supplies, the opening of new markets, and the introduction of more profitable forms of business organization (even for the sake of acquisition of monopoly power). Anything that was not done before and that contributes to profit is within the domain of the entrepreneur.

Schumpeter thus defines the entrepreneur as the innovator, and in the process, carefully distinguishes the entrepreneur from either the inventor or the capitalist. Innovation is the act of putting a novel idea into operation—of bringing it from the drawing board into fruitful activity in the marketplace. Schumpeter wrote:

Economic leadership in particular must hence be distinguished from "invention." As long as they are not carried into practice, inventions are economically irrelevant. And to carry any improvement into effect is a task entirely different from the inventing of it, and a task, moreover, requiring entirely different kinds of aptitudes. Although entrepreneurs of course *may* be inventors, just as they may be capitalists, they are inventors not by nature of their function but by coincidence and vice versa. Besides, the innovations which it is the function of entrepreneurs to carry out need not necessarily be any inventions at all. It is, therefore, not advisable, and it may be misleading, to stress the element of invention as much as many writers do   (1936, pp. 88–89).

Because Schumpeter's innovator is also not the capitalist, "The entrepreneur is never the risk bearer.... The one who gives the credit comes to grief if the undertaking fails" (1936, p. 137). In this, Schumpeter's vision differs sharply from that of other students of the subject, who have frequently emphasized the important role of the entrepreneur as an taker of risk and confronter of uncertainty. But whatever the insight contributed by such an interpretation, it is not the vision of Schumpeter, who reiterates, "Risk-taking is in no case an element of the entrepreneurial function. Even though he may risk his reputation, the direct economic responsibilty of failure never falls on him" (loc. cit.). Risk bearing is the task of Schumpeter's capitalist, and compensation for risk bearing is a significant component of the capitalist's reward.

The entrepreneur's profit is the key to economic growth in Schumpeter's model. By being the first to introduce a "new combination," the entrepreneur obtains temporary monopoly power. Lower costs may give her profits higher than those of her rivals, who must continue to sell at prices that cover their higher expenses. Or a superior product may permit a price above that charged by other firms. The same idea clearly fits all forms of successful innovation. But the heart of the growth mechanism is the fact that those profits are always temporary unless innovation recurs . This is clearly so if the market is competitive, because rivals will be faced with cumulative loss of market share if they ignore an innovation. They will be forced to find some way to *imitate* the innovation or to come up with an effective substitute. When they finally succeed in doing so, the entrepreneur's differential advantage will come to an end.

Even if the entrepreneur succeeds in establishing a monopoly whose returns continue indefinitely, Schumpeter argues that, as a matter of definition, the flow of gains to the entrepreneur *in her entrepreneurial* role must be very temporary. For as the flow of monopoly earnings becomes expectable and routine it is transformed into monopoly rent rather than entrepreneurial profit: "The carrying out of the monopolistic organization is an entrepreneurial act and its 'product' is expressed in profit. Once it is running smoothly the concern in this case goes on earning a surplus, which henceforth, however, must be imputed to those natural or social forces upon which the monopoly position rests" (1934, p. 152). The argument becomes very clear if we envision sale of the entrepreneur's interest in the firm to others at a price that corresponds fully to the expected earnings stream. For the new owners will then have paid a price for their asset so high that they can expect to earn only a zero economic profit, unless they, in turn, succeed in carrying out another innovation.

The upshot is that the entrepreneur who wants to continue to earn profits can never afford to rest on her laurels. She must follow the first innovation with a second and the second with a third, because otherwise the stream of profits will dry up as imitators succeed in bringing them to an end, or as the process of imputation transforms them into mere rents. Thus, by forcing the entrepreneur to run without respite in order to stand still, the pursuit of a continuing stream of profits serves as the powerful engine that injects a flow of changes into the workings of the economy. It is, in sum, the engine of growth.

1.4   The Entrepreneur: Definition, Classification, and Role

Any attempt at rigid definition of the term *entrepreneur* will be avoided assiduously here, because whatever attributes are selected, they are sure to prove excessively restrictive, ruling out some feature, activity, or accomplishment of this inherently subtle and elusive character. Rather, I will use the term to describe any member of the economy whose activities are in some manner novel, and entail the use of imagination, boldness, ingenuity, leadership, persistence, and determination in the pursuit of wealth, power, and position, though not necessarily in that order. In other words, the term is meant to encompass all *nonroutine* activities by those who direct the economic activities of larger or smaller groups or organizations. Because measures that are not obvious or tried and true are that person's domain, innovation must indeed belong to that territory.

One is tempted to consider the entrepreneur's role in economic activity to be like that of the bold strategist in military ventures, the analog of Alexander the Great, Genghis Khan, the Duke of Marlborough, or Napoleon Bonaparte. Yet such a view is misleading, as Nathan Rosenberg has argued so cogently on the basis of systematic historical evidence (see, for example, 1976, essay 4). Rosenberg warns against excessive "stress upon that charismatic figure, the entrepreneur, who posess[es] the character, courage and, above all, vision, to depart *sharply* from accepted routines and practices.... [As a result] inventive activity itself is never examined as a *continuing* activity ... and the stages through which inventions proceed on the way to full commercial application and exploitation, never emerge" (p. 67, my emphasis). The point is that both invention and innovation typically involve considerable periods of time and the participation of many individuals, a number in entrepreneurial roles, varying in dramatic scale, in the process that takes place between the initial idea and the first commercially viable products. Rosenberg's writings are filled with convincing examples, but one will suffice to bring out the point. The well-known tale of the flash of inspiration that paved the way to James Watt's improvements on Newcomen's steam engine may or may not have some element of truth. But it is certainly misleading. It took more then a decade, and the assistance of a politically powerful entrepreneur-capitalist partner, Matthew Boulton, from the date of Watt's first idea to the construction of a commercially viable model. During most of this interval Watt was unable to produce a full-sized engine that was marketable, in good part because it was not known how to bore a cylinder with the requisite accuracy. He was forced to turn to rudimentary expedients: "... the cylinder of his first engine was made of tin and hammered to shape against a hardwood block; the gaps between the piston and cylinder were sealed as far as possible with felt, paper, oiled rags, and the like" (K. R. Gilbert, quoted in Rosenberg, p. 305). The problem was only solved by an entrepreneur who happened to be located nearby, cannon maker John Wilkinson, who needed accurate boring methods for his own purposes. Still, when the first practical Watt-Boulton steam engine emerged in 1776, it required another quarter century of improvement and dissemination effort before it was able to make more "than a limited impact ... on the broad range of British industries" (Rosenberg, p. 326; for an illuminating but brief account of the development of Watt's steam engine, see Scherer [1986]).

Not everyone uses Schumpeter's interpretation of the term *entrepreneur*, which we will follow here, albeit in modified and broadened form. Of course, there is nothing inherently objectionable about alternative usages. Still, they seem less well adapted to the central purpose of this book, which is to explore the role of economic leadership in the determination of an economy's growth and to examine some of the policy options pertinent to stimulation of that growth through encouragement of the entrepreneur's productive exercise of inventiveness and his propensity to depart from currently standard practices. To avoid misunderstanding, it is worth reviewing briefly some of the alternative ways in which the term has been employed.

A. Business Founding and Management. Sometimes the entrepreneur is defined simply as either the organizer or the effective director of a business firm (see, for example, much of the discussion of Casson [1982]). But since the establishment of new firms may entail little that is innovative, and the company's operations may in some cases be almost entirely routine, it follows that at least some such persons are not entrepreneurs in the sense that is employed in this book. In addition, we want to consider economic activity that takes place outside private business firms, and even outside what anyone would be willing to describe as a firm of any sort. Consequently, it is not convenient to base the analysis on this first alternative connotation of our focal term.

B. Innovative Entrepreneurship. Others, following Schumpeter, take the entrepreneur to be anyone who engages in innovative activity, here defining *innovation*, in contradistinction to *invention*, as the process whereby the latter is put into practice, transforming a disembodied idea into a workable and economically viable operation. Innovations, in the sense used here, follow Schumpeter in encompassing not only novel productive techniques within the realm of engineering, but also new products, new input sources, new marketing methods, and new forms of business organization. This interpretation is not in conflict with that which will be used in this book; but for our purposes it will be convenient to broaden the concept still further. In particular, it will be important for our purpose to distinguish the following subcategories, which we will also take to constitute entrepreneurship, even if at least a narrow interpretation of the Schumpeterian line of argument might not.

C. Imitative Entrepreneurship. The term *imitative entrepreneur* will be used to refer to a person who is occupied in the transfer of technology or of other innovative ideas or procedures from one firm or one geographic location to another. The activity can have all of the hallmarks of that of the Schumpeterian innovator, except that the main novel element of the activity is the selection of a new location for, say, a process that may have become well accepted and routine elsewhere.[2] In Schumpeter, as we have just noted, the imitator's role is entirely secondary, serving primarily to put an end to the innovator's domination of the market by virtue of novel and superior products or processes. The competition of the imitators robs the innovator of this temporary source of monopoly power, and forces that entrepreneur to embark once more upon the quest for profitable novelty, in order to prevent the innovative firm's profits from being reduced thereafter to no more than the normal level permitted by competitive forces during strictly routine operations. But, as will be seen, in our analysis the imitator plays a far more central, hardly secondary role.

In addition to this subcategory, our discussion will also concern itself with:

D. Unproductive Entrepreneurship. A key part of our story is the contention that the entrepreneur's activity can be, and in fact sometimes is, innovative, yet nevertheless make no contribution to the real output of the economy. Indeed, the activity can sometimes even serve to reduce output or restrain its growth. This abstract notion can be made clear by turning to our last category, itself a subgroup of the set of unproductive entrepreneurs.

E. Rent-Seeking Entrepreneurship. Rent seeking, a concept contributed by Gordon Tullock, refers to any activity whose objective is the acquisition of some of the monopoly profit or the economic rents currently generated or potentially available in the economy. For example, consider a regulated industry that is a bilateral monopoly. Suppose one of the monopolists is able to persuade the regulatory agency to readjust prices in a way that causes a larger share of the industry's total monopoly profits to flow into the coffers of that enterprise. Then it will have engaged in a successful act of rent seeking. Such an activity can clearly be innovative. A novel legal principle may, for example, be thought of and invoked by the rent seeker in persuading the regulatory agency to intervene in its favor. But the activity need not contribute anything to economic production or productivity. Indeed, as will later be discussed in somewhat greater detail, it can constitute an effective impediment to both of these, through misallocation of valuable resources into pursuits that from the viewpoint of the economy are useless, and by forcing the targeted firm to redirect its activities into unproductive directions for the sake of self-defense.

It is clear that entrepreneurship should not be taken as a synonym for virtuousness. Not everything that is entrepreneurial is necessarily desirable. That is, it cannot always be relied upon to promote the interests of society. Indeed, it is the contention of this book that one of the keys to rational policy relating to entrepreneurship is to be found here—in the pursuit of means to discourage or prevent entrepreneurial talent from devoting itself to unproductive courses.

While one cannot rely upon entrepreneurs to contribute to production, there is one thing for which one can depend upon them. Ultimately, the entrepreneur's role is that of disturber of the economy; it prevents the economy from falling into a rut and precludes those who constitute the economy from falling into lethargy. Schumpeter quite rightly stressed the entrepreneur's propensity to destroy anything that resembles a stationary equilibrium, for, ultimately, that is what a successful innovation must do. It precludes the economy's actors from surviving tomorrow through mere replication of activities that are entirely viable today. However, as Israel Kirzner has effectively called to our attention (1973), the entrepreneur is equally the enemy of *dis*equilibria. For by definition, any disequilibrium must entail some unrealized profit opportunity, and entrepreneurial alertness will restore equilibrium by taking advantage of the opportunity to a degree sufficient to draw off all of the profits it initially offered. That, for example, is the essence of what constitutes true arbitrage among currency-exchange rates that happen to be in disequilibrium.

In sum, the entrepreneur is, by occupation, incapable of leaving matters where they are. If they start off in equilibrium, that state of affairs will be undermined by the entrepreneur's innovative acts; but equally, if the initial state entails disequilibrium, the entrepreneur's alertness will not long permit it to endure.

1.5   A Note on the Origins of the Term

According to Fernand Braudel (1986, vol. 2, p. 329), the term *entrepreneur* had entered the French language by the beginning of the eighteenth century, but its use was still quite rare. It was not adopted by English-speaking writers until at least the middle of the nineteenth century (though the Oxford English Dictionary cites two fifteenth-century examples of its use in a manner close to its current connotation). Earlier in the nineteenth century it was employed in English to refer to a "director or organizer of musical entertainment" (!).

Richard Cantillon is generally credited as the first to use the term *entre-preneur* in a work on economics (1755, ch. 13). Cantillon uses the term to refer to merchant wholesalers who bear the risk of reselling agricultural and manufactured produce. Henry Higgs (see Cantillon [1755]) translates the term as *undertaker*, presumably following Malachy Postlethwayt's *Disserta-tion* of 1749, which reproduces extensive portions of the missing original English version of Cantillon's *Essai*. Probably J. B. Say (1803, 1829) is responsible for popularizing the term. He uses it to denote any organizer of a firm, who is carefully distinguished from the capitalist, that is, the supplier of funds. But Say also places considerable emphasis upon the entrepreneur as a intermediary between the work of the scientist and an industry's workers (e.g., 6th ed., book 1, ch. 6).

Before the word entered the English language, writers would sometimes instead employ the term *undertaker*, which is, of course, a direct translation of the French term and of its German equivalent—*unternehmer*—one who undertakes. But the more common, and probably far older, English term is *adventurer*, as in the fifteenth-century society of overseas merchants in London, the Merchant Adventurers. The term itself can plausibly be inter-preted to derive from the comings and goings of the merchants, for as the dictionary suggests, it derives from the Latin or Italian, *ad*, meaning *to*, as in to and fro, and *venire*, to come. One may suspect that the modern interpretation of the term *adventurer* alludes to the risks and encounters that befell medieval merchants more often than they might have wished. Still, and that is the point of this brief discussion, the word *adventurer* perhaps continues to capture the subject of this book more effectively than the more humdrum term *entrepreneur*. It is, indeed, the individual willing to embark on adventure in pursuit of economic goals who will be the prime focus of our discussion.

1.6   The Entrepreneur in Formal Models

Contrast all this with the entrepreneur's place in formal theory. If one looks for him in the indexes of recent writings on value theory, in neoclassical[3] or activity analysis models of the firm, the references are scanty or, more often, totally absent. Virtually all theoretical firms are entrepreneurless— the prince of Denmark has been expunged from the discussion of *Hamlet*.[4]

It is not difficult to explain the absence. Consider the nature of the generic model of the firm. In its simplest form (and in this respect we shall see that the more complex and more sophisticated models are no better), the theoretical firm must choose among alternative values for a small num-

ber of rather well-defined variables: price, output, perhaps advertising outlay, and, occasionally, a few others. In making this choice, management is ·
taken to consider the costs and revenues associated with each candidate set
of values, as described by the relevant functional relationships, equations,
and inequalities. Explicitly or implicitly, the firm is then taken to perform
a mathematical calculation which yields optimal (i.e., profit-maximizing)
values for all of its decision variables, and it is these values that the theory
assumes to be chosen and that are declared to constitute the company's
vector of decisions. There matters rest, forever or until exogenous forces
lead to an autonomous change in the environment. Until there is such a
shift in one of the relationships that define the problem, the firm is taken to
replicate precisely its previous decisions, day after day, year after year.

Clearly, the entrepreneur has been read out of the model. There is no
room for enterprise or initiative. The management group becomes a passive calculator that reacts mechanically to changes imposed on it by fortuitous external developments over which it does not exert, and may not
even attempt to exert, any influence. One hears of no clever ruses, ingenious schemes, valuable innovations, or any of the other stuff of which
outstanding entrepreneurship is made; one does not hear of them because
there is no way in which they can fit into the formal optimization model.[5]

What has just been said constitutes no criticism, not even an attempt to
reprove mildly the neoclassical model of the firm. That model does what it
was designed to do and does it well. Like any respectable analysis, one
hopes that it will be modified, amended, and improved with time, but *not*
because it is incapable of handling an issue for which it was not designed.
The model is essentially an instrument of optimality analysis of well-
defined problems, and it is precisely such (very real and important) problems that need no entrepreneur for their solution.

Some readers may suspect that what are subtly being put forward as
more appropriate candidates are alternative models of the firm with which
the present author has to some degree been associated. But this is certainly
not so, because these modified models are no better for the purpose than
the most hidebound of conventional constructs. For example, consider
what Oliver Williamson has described as the "managerial discretion models," in which the businessperson is taken to maximize the number of individuals employed, or sales, or still another objective distinct from profits.
True, this business director has (somewhere outside the confines of the
model) made a choice that was no mere matter of routine arithmetic calculation. She has decided, in at least some sense, to assign priority to some
goal other than profit. But having made this choice she becomes, no less

than the profit maximizer, a calculating robot, a programmed mechanical component in the automatic system that constitutes the theoretical model of the firm. Her only role is to make and enforce the maximizing decision, and in this the choice of maximand makes no difference.

Nor can the "practical pertinence" of the decision variables make the difference in carving out a place for the entrepreneur. Maximization models have been constructed in which, instead of prices and outputs, the decision variables are the firm's real investment program, its financial mix (the proportion of equity and debt in its funding), or the attributes of a new product to be launched by the company. These decisions seem to smell more of the ingredients of entrepreneurship. But though the models may be powerful and serve their objective well, they take us not a whit further in the analysis of entrepreneurship, for their calculations are again mechanistic and automatic and call for no display of entrepreneurial imagination or initiative.

Finally, it must be made clear that the timeless nature of these models has nothing to do with the problem. G. C. Evans (1924) long ago constructed a model in which the firm considered the consequence of its decisions for the time path of prices, and the calculus of variations served as his instrument of analysis. In other models the firm has been taken to choose not a stationary, once-and-for-all output level, but to select instead an optimal growth rate. None of these alternatives helps matters. In all these models, automaton maximizers the business people are and automaton maximizers they remain.

All this suggests why the body of economic theory, as it has developed, offers no promise of being able to deal effectively with the description and analysis of the entrepreneurial function. For maximization and minimization have constituted the foundation of the theory, and as a result of this very fact the theory cannot provide an analysis of entrepreneurship. The terminology of game theory has been extremely suggestive; the willingness of the behaviorists to break away from traditional formulations has been encouraging; but, at least until recently, there was little sign of breakthroughs in this area. At most, one encountered brilliant observations and descriptive insights such as those provided by Schumpeter and more recently by Harvey Leibenstein, but there was little progress toward a more formal, manipulable engine of calculation and analysis.[6]

One of the main task this book undertakes is to see where formal models related to the entrepreneur's activities are applicable and how they can be constructed. This goal will be pursued with the aid of illustrations. Such models make their appearance throughout the book. Some seem quite defensible and illuminating, while others may appear to be rather far fetched. But even the latter may be justified as suggesting directions for others to follow.

1.7 Is It Possible to Describe (or to Teach) What Entrepreneurs Do?

Since, as interpreted here, an entrepreneurial act must always be at least somewhat different from anything that has been done before, description of such activities going beyond the sort of generalities that have already been offered here may be all but impossible. One can, indeed, describe what entrepreneurs *used to do*, but simply by virtue of having been reported in detail such an act is transformed into one that is no longer entrepreneurial. I have once suggested that there is a sort of Heisenberg principle that holds for entrepreneurial acts. The very process of describing them can transmute pioneering entrepreneurial undertakings into routine managerial activities. The same problem, of course, besets the schools of business, which would like to be able to train at least some of their students in the ways of the entrepreneur, but which usually succeed in imparting only the skills of the manager. That is accomplishment enough, and certainly calls for no apology; for these schools, like any other entity, find it difficult to achieve the impossible.

It follows from all this that anyone who writes about entrepreneurship has two choices—either to deal with the past, or to discuss something other than the activities that today constitute entrepreneurship. This book employs both these options. Much of its evidence is drawn from historical sources. But the data found there are not used primarily to discuss the activities that constitute entrepreneurship. Rather, the book centers attention upon the nature of the institutional arrangements that encourage the exercise of entrepreneurship and that provide incentives for it to take productive directions. A bit more will be said on this later in the chapter.

1.8 On the Supply of Entrepreneurship

There is yet another reason why a marriage between theory and policy is not easily arranged in this area. In its discussions of inputs, formal economic analysis deals, by and large, with the way in which these inputs are used, and tells us relatively little about where they come from. In our growth models, for example, the behavior of the labor supply exerts a critical influence on the economy's expansion path. But the determination of the growth of the labor force itself is generally taken to be an exogenous matter. Similarly, in a neoclassical or a programming analysis of production one investigates how inputs should be used in the production process, but one assumes that their supply or their supply function is somehow determined outside the system. Thus, even if we were to design a model that was successful in advancing the theory of entrepreneurship to the level of sophistication of our treatment of other inputs, we would have defined the entrepreneurial role more effectively, but we would have added relatively little to our understanding of the determinants of the level of output of entrepreneurship.

From the point of view of policy, however, the priorities would seem to be reversed. The first order of business for an economy that exhibits very little business drive is presumably to induce the appearance of increased supplies of entrepreneurial skills, which would then be let loose upon the country's economic activity. The policymaker thus is interested primarily in what determines the supply of productive entrepreneurship and in the means that can be used to expand it. But there is reason to suppose that these issues are to a very considerable extent matters of social psychology, social arrangements, cultural developments, and the like. And perhaps this is why many of the recent discussions of the theory of entrepreneurship have been contributed by sociologists and psychologists.[7] This may, then, be no fortuitous development. The very nature of the more pressing issues relating to entrepreneurship may invite more directly the attention of the practitioners of disciplines other than theoretical economics.

1.9   A Place for Theory on Entrepreneurship

Despite these difficulties besetting any attempt to construct a pertinent economic theory in the area, one can still think of theoretical approaches to entrepreneurship which are not without promise. We may not be able to analyze in detail the supply of entrepreneurial ability, the entrepreneur's strategy choices, attitudes to risk, or sources of ideas. But one can hope to examine fruitfully what can be done to encourage productive entrepreneurial activity. Here, an analogy is illuminating. The analysis in Keynes's *General Theory* seems deliberately to devote little attention to the role of expectations, even though Keynes seems to have believed them to lie at the heart of investment decisions. He apparently downplays the expectations of businesspeople because they elude the influence of systematic government policy. Instead, Keynes's analysis seeks to come to grips with means that *can* be used by policymakers to stimulate investment; it does so by focusing more directly on the role of interest rates, whose magnitudes may, in some sense, influence investment far less than expectations do, but which are far more dependably amenable to government direction. In the same way, one can undertake to grapple, assisted by theoretical instruments, with policies that evade the highly relevant and very difficult sociological and psychological issues, but that nevertheless hold some promise of being able to encourage the *productive* exercise of entrepreneurship.

One way in which this can be attempted is to downplay the means that the entrepreneur employs or the process whereby he arrives at his decisions and by emphasizing instead the determinants of the *payoff* to his activity.[8] Such theoretical analyses can be of considerable significance for policy. For a growth-conscious world, encouragement (in the form of appropriate rewards) of the productive entrepreneur may well prove a key to enhancement of productivity and output. The view that this must await the slow and undependable process of change in the social and psychological climate is a counsel of despair for which there is little justification. Such a conclusion is analogous to an argument that all we can do to reduce spending in an inflationary period is to hope for a revival of the Protestant ethic and the attendant acceptance by the general public of the virtues of thrift. Surely, we have learned to do better than that, by increasing the reward for saving, that is, by producing a movement along the relevant functional paths rather than undertaking the more heroic task involved in shifting the relationships. This is precisely what one can hope to obtain from more careful study of the rewards of entrepreneurship. Without awaiting a change in the strength and prevalence of the entrepreneurial drive exhibited in our society, we can try to learn how one can modify the current system of rewards to stimulate the volume and intensity of entrepreneurial activity and to move it into more productive directions, thus making the most of what is permitted by current mores and attitudes. In following this path, then, we pursue the classical lines of economic analysis, with their emphasis upon the prices (remuneration rates) of inputs as one of the determinants of their allocation and usage.

This book will, in fact, explore a number of hypotheses that can, perhaps charitably, be interpreted as steps toward an expanded theory of the economic role of the entrepreneur, and of the variables that influence her performance. For example, substantial space is devoted to consideration of the part played by the entrepreneur in technology transfer, that is, in the international dissemination of invention, in the term's most general sense. It will be shown that in intercountry transfers of the pertinent skills and knowledge, the source country is itself often also a substantial supplier of the requisite entrepreneurial initiative. That is, the countries that provide the inventions supply not only the ideas and know-how, but often also the free-enterprising exporters of those invaluable properties. The implication for the recipient countries is that, while the availability of indigenous entrepreneurial talent may indeed be highly valuable, it may not be quite as indispensable for the process of getting the recipient, or imitator, country a share of the benefits of the world's advancing technology as has sometimes been thought to be true. In this connection, the book will also explore the hypothesis that such imitation (of an innovation originally produced in another country) plays a critical role in economic growth, that is, in growth in productivity and in output per capita, not only for less developed countries, but even for the world's industrial leaders. It will even be suggested that for a "typical" industrial country the contribution made by technology transfer is likely to be greater in the long run than is that derived from domestic innovation.

Perhaps even more than these, the book will emphasize the hypothesis that readily describable changes in an economy's set of "rules of the game" (which determine the relative returns, in terms of wealth, power, and prestige, that are offered by different lines of activity) can serve to redirect the flow of entrepreneurial effort. Consequently, a change in the economic ground rules can make a difference in whether entrepreneurial efforts take forms that are productive or rent-seeking or are (as can sometimes happen) even directly destructive to the economy. It will be suggested, then, that while encouragement of the *supply* of entrepreneurs is a suitable goal for policy, the design of measures that channel it into productive directions may merit still higher priority. Such observations, then, with evidence drawn heavily from economic history, will be used to derive inferences both for the design of policy and for the construction of theory.

Though entrepreneurship does not lend itself to garden-variety neoclassical analysis relying on formal maximization calculations, for reasons already emphasized, the divorce between the analysis of entrepreneurial behavior and standard theory is by no means final. If resource allocation theory is as applicable to entrepreneurial inputs as is suggested here, and if the relative rewards offered to this input in the different activities available to it are a critical determinant of its allocation, then much of the standard theoretical apparatus remains pertinent. It is also widely agreed that the entrepreneur's central domain is the growth of the economy. But if the allocation of entrepreneurial effort is a critical component of this process, then the neoclassical allocative mechanism itself breaks out of purely static analysis to a crucial role in the economy's development. The result may be increased unification of the analyses of the static and intertemporal performances of the economy.

In any event, there clearly exists a well-developed body of allocation theory and an armory of analytical weapons available for use in the theory of entrepreneurship. These ways of thinking are implicit in many of the chapters that follow.

1.10   The Entrepreneur as Resource Allocator and as Allocated Resource

The entrepreneur has a two-way relationship with the allocation process. One side of the matter is the entrepreneur's role as allocator of resources. The other side is that entrepreneurial effort itself must be considered an input in the production process, one that may (or may not, as we will see in the next chapter) contribute to the size of the economy's overall output or to its growth. As an input, entrepreneurship, like any other input, can be reallocated from one task to another by a change in the relative profit prospects offered by the available alternative uses to which entrepreneurship can be put. The entrepreneur influences resource allocation when he recognizes disequilibria as opportunities for profitable arbitrage. The neo-Austrians, particularly Israel Kirzner, have recognized this side of the entrepreneur, as the individual who is constantly alert for lacunae in the workings of the market process, which constitute opportunities to earn economic profits through improvements in the allocation of resources.

In turn, the efforts of entrepreneurs are reallocated by shifts in the sectors of the economy and the lines of activity where profit seems most easily to be earned. Perhaps not for all entrepreneurs, but surely for many of them, the identity of the line of endeavor that offers the most promising prospect of profits is no matter of great moment. In describing the logic of his (avowedly) tautological labor theory of value, Marx makes much of the way in which, in a capitalist economy, produced objects lose their concrete character as particular embodiments of use value. [T]he exchange of commodities is evidently an act characterized by total abstraction from use-value ... we see in [a product] no longer a table, a house, yarn, or any other useful thing.... When looked at as crystals of this social substance, common to them all, they are—values (*Capital*, vol. 1, ch. 1, sec. 1). Thus, in the profit-making production process a chair and a table lose their distinctive attributes as an item upon which one sits and an object upon which food is placed for eating. Rather, both are transformed into abstract embodiments of exchange value—into prospective sources of financial gain

—and are in that sense homogenized. The same is true of the alternative occupations available for the efforts of the entrepreneur. All become homogenized into abstract opportunities for the acquisition of wealth, power, or prestige, and the pricing arrangements that determine prospective profitability therefore can have a profound influence on the pattern of allocation of the economy's entrepreneurial resources.[9] We may perhaps say, then, that while the entrepreneurs (help to) run the market mechanism and its pricing process, that market mechanism and its pricing, in turn, (help to) run the entrepreneurs.

Some types of reallocation of entrepreneurial effort are of the sort one is likely to expect, and those require no comment here. When the development of an industry reaches a stage at which the opportunities for further innovation seem, perhaps temporarily, to be exhausted, it is not surprising to find entrepreneurial effort flowing out of that field and into others where the opportunities for the profitable introduction of change seem brighter. That, after all, is the market mechanism's counterpart to the planning activities of government agencies, such as Japan's Ministry of International Trade and Industry (MITI), which are intended to encourage the reallocation of capital and entrepreneurship into those arenas that offer the most encouraging prospects for growth. The propensity of entrepreneurs to redirect their efforts in this way has long been recognized and its contribution to the dynamism of the economy accepted.

However, sometimes such a relocation is a more questionable step. For example, in a less developed country, a change in the laws that greatly increases the hazards faced by entrepreneurs in directly productive lines of activity may induce them to turn their efforts to activities such as accumulation of land and advance in the government bureaucracy. And that may not just change the directions of the economy's productive efforts, but can reduce its output and impede its growth. This sort of reallocation of entrepreneurial effort, too, can be induced by changes affecting the relative returns to more productive and less productive exercises of entrepreneurship. Such changes are the subject of Chapter 2.

1.11   Some Qualifications on the Schumpeterian Model

It is easy to admire the Schumpeterian model, but that does not obligate us to accept it without modification. It will prove important for the discussion that follows to take note of Nathan Rosenberg's criticisms of the Schumpeterian tradition (which are clearly not intended to detract from that author's respect for Schumpeter's contribution). It is necessary here to note concurrence with those criticisms because several of the lines of discussion in this book grow out of them. Though there is much more to Rosenberg's analysis of the subject, for our purposes it can be summed up in three points: first, that Schumpeter's distinction between the roles of the inventor and the innovator is excessively sharp; second, that the same is true of his distinction between innovators and imitators, especially since an entrepreneur often performs all three roles; third, as is emphasized by Rosenberg, innovation is almost always a near-continuous process, proceeding in small steps, each of which contributes to the evolution of a new product or process. The evolutionary process not only gets under way, typically, well before the introduction of the novel item into the market, but usually continues as long as that item remains in use.

There is no question that the innovator and the inventor are often one and the same person; one need only mention Eli Whitney, Thomas Edison, and Edwin Land to provide some of the many available examples. Even where they have not been the same person, they have typically worked together, with the innovator suggesting modifications necessary for the invention in order for it to be viable commercially. Thus, one is misled by the suggestion that the innovator's common procedure is to seek out finished inventions that she can, so to speak, put into her inventory of novel items, to be withdrawn from the warehouse and introduced into the economy at the moment judged to be propitious.

Similarly, imitation is usually not mere reproduction but is, rather, a creative and innovative process so that, as Rosenberg emphasizes, there is often no clear dividing line between acts of imitation and innovation (a point that will also prove important for us in later chapters). This obviously must be so where the predecessor product is protected effectively by patent or secrecy, so that mere copying simply is not a practical option. Aside from that, because the object of even the Schumpeterian imitator is to get back into the race as an effective competitor, that person must seek to provide a product or process that is not merely just as good as the one that appeared earlier; rather, what must be aimed for is something newer and at least a bit more attractive—having novel features, or costing less, or in some other way differing from the predecessor item. Moreover, where the innovator seeks entree by concentrating upon a group of consumers not previously served, an application not previously recognized, or a geographic market not previously entered, the product will almost certainly require adaptation to the preferences of the new group of consumers, the requirements of the novel application, or the special climatic and other conditions that characterize the new geographic market. All of these adaptations are surely innovative steps, which often improve the product sufficiently to elicit some responsive redesign of the predecessor product.

Finally, Rosenberg takes exception to the view characterizing invention as an instantaneous breakthrough (presumably accompanied by a cry of "Eureka!") constituting a sharp break with anything that was known before. The continuity of the innovation process is equally clear from the evidence. Though particular inventions may undoubtedly entail one or more flashes of inspiration in the course of their development, the actual process of going from underlying idea to saleable product is almost always a time-consuming process, typically entailing a series of small innovative steps before the product can evolve into an item that is commercially viable. Moreover, this process of continual improvement does not normally come to an end when the item arrives on the market. Each invention and innovation is usually just an improvement over some predecessor model, and it is usually succeeded by a series of improved substitutes. Rosenberg provides a profusion of illuminating historical examples (see, e.g., 1976, pp. 66–75, and 1982, pp. 6–8, 62–70).[10]

There is another way to demonstrate the point. If inventions and innovations typically constituted discrete quantum leaps, then patent infringement suits would not be as complex as they are. The patented item would be sufficiently different from any other product to leave no doubt as to whether or not the item against which the complaint has been lodged is essentially the same and is not derived from a common ancestor of both the items in question. In practice, such a hearing is, on the contrary, apt to be incredibly complicated. One defense frequently invoked by the accused party is that the feature of the patented item that is the subject of infringement allegations is an obvious extension of some publicly available "prior art" or that the allegedly infringing product itself was based on such prior art. Under U.S. law, if there was an earlier product or process with a feature sufficiently similar either to the item claimed to be infringing or the one claimed to have been the subject of infringement, then the patent protection that has been invoked by the plaintiff will not hold up. Prior-art disputes in patent infringement cases are difficult to deal with precisely because of the continuity of the invention and innovation processes, which means that there generally do exist earlier items sufficiently similar in their specifications to the product at issue in the lawsuit to require the most painstaking scrutiny entailing laborious reexamination of highly technical details. (For a striking illustration, see the decision of the district court in Polaroid Corporation v. Eastman Kodak Co., October 11, 1985, USPQ, pp. 305–46.[11]) A reading of the pertinent portions of the record in such a case illustrates the fine line that may separate irrelevant prior art from prior art that is sufficiently close to the items at issue to invalidate the claim of infringement.

Rosenberg also suggests that the Schumpeterian discussion tends to attract attention away from the critical role of complementarity among inventions. Here he cites many examples, such as Watt's justly famed improvement of the earlier Newcomen steam engine. As noted, the former became commercially viable only when a process capable of boring a cylinder with sufficient accuracy emerged fortuitously from the mill owned by cannon maker John Wilkinson. Rosenberg also reminds us that while "many household appliances—the vacuum cleaner, clothes-washing machine, dishwashing machine—had made their appearances as early as the 1850s and 1860s ...," these inventions had to be shelved until the arrival of the small electric motor made them widely usable (Rosenberg, citing Siegfried Giedion [1982, p. 79 n. 34]).

1.12   On Methodological Orientation: Monism and the Search for Causation

The reader will find this book to be eclectic in the methods it employs. Some chapters rely primarily on the work of economic historians as their factual foundation. Others use rather simple-minded statistical approaches, and still others use the methods of formal theory, though not of a very esoteric or sophisticated variety. However, throughout the book I will adhere undeviatingly to two general principles: first, while this book is required by its very choice of subject to emphasize the role of the entrepreneur in influencing the rate of growth and state of prosperity of an economy, at no time will it be implied that this is the only important determinant, or that it is even necessarily *primus inter pares*; second, at no time will any attempt be made to determine "the causes" of any particular phenomenon.

The book should certainly not be taken to be monistic in its orientation simply because it is devoted to a study of the role of the entrepreneur. Nothing here is meant to deny the importance of other influences upon, say, an economy's rate of productivity growth. Natural resource availability, the education of the population, demographic developments, cultural influences, and other variables all undoubtedly have been of crucial importance. There is no way one can hope to rank their influence relative to that of entrepreneurship, particularly in light of the probable interdependence of entrepreneurial activity and the state of those other variables. There is good reason to believe that entrepreneurship *does* matter, and sometimes, for brevity, it will be convenient to speak as though it were the *only* thing that matters. But no such view will ever be intended.

In seeking to offer some broad conclusions, sometimes on the basis of a wide-ranging set of historical observations, this book attempts something in common with the work of a number of distinguished predecessors (e.g., Rostow [1960], Hicks [1969], North and Thomas [1973], and Olson [1982]). In particular, this volume owes a heavy debt to North and Thomas, and its point of view is not markedly dissimilar from theirs. However, there is one basic difference between the methodological approach of those books and this one. Their objective is to determine causes and explanations for historical events and developments. As North and Thomas put it, "The affluence of western man is a new and unique phenomenon.... This book explains that unique historical achievement.... This book focuses upon what causes economic growth" (pp. 1–2, order of statements changed). My goal here, in contrast, is far more limited. The discussion is concerned, so to speak, only with partial derivatives—with the outcome of pseudocontrolled experiments, in which the value of only one variable is permitted to change at one time. This variable, moreover, even if it is really subject to endogenous influences, is generally treated as though it were exogenously determined and imposed upon the economy by an unidentified outside force. Thus, for example, in Chapter 2 great emphasis is placed upon changes in the economic rules of the game that determine at some particular time and place which of the possible activities of the entrepreneur offers the highest rewards. Those ground rules, clearly, are in fact heavily affected by economic circumstances. But the *ceteris paribus* approach adopted here requires such alterations in the rules to be treated as exogenous.

This book adopts such an orientation because of doubts about the prospects of success for any attempt to determine *the* causes of any complex economic phenomena, such as the Great Depression of the 1930s or the prosperity of Europe during the High Middle Ages. Such developments are too complicated, the influences upon them too many, and the historical evidence too sketchy to offer much hope for anything approximating the bulk of the explanation. Physicists and biologists conduct controlled experiments, not because these scientists are averse to explaining all the interdependent relationships simultaneously, but because they usually judge that to be too difficult an undertaking to have much hope of success. How much more difficult must one judge such an undertaking to be for a complex phenomenon in economic history?

2 Entrepreneurship: Productive, Unproductive, and Destructive

It is often assumed that an economy of private enterprise has an automatic bias towards innovation, but this is not so. It has a bias only towards profit.

Hobsbawm (1969, p. 40)

When conjectures are offered to explain historic slowdowns or great leaps in economic growth, the entrepreneur is one of usual suspects that are regularly rounded up. Where growth has slowed, it is implied that a decline in entrepreneurship was partly to blame (perhaps because the culture's "need for achievement" has atrophied). At another time and place, it is said, the flowering of entrepreneurship accounts for unprecedented expansion.

As was asserted in the previous chapter, this book proposes a rather different set of hypotheses, holding that the entrepreneur is always with us and always playing some substantial role. There are a variety of roles among which the entrepreneur's efforts can be reallocated. And some of those roles do not follow the constructive and innovative script conventionally attributed to that person. Indeed, at times the entrepreneur may even lead a parasitical existence that is actually damaging to the economy.[1] How the entrepreneur acts at a given time and place depends heavily on the "rules of the game"—that is, the prevailing reward structure in the economy. Thus, the central hypothesis here is that it is this set of rules, and not the supply of entrepreneurs, that undergoes significant changes from one period to another, and helps to dictate the ultimate effect on the economy via the *allocation* of entrepreneurial resources.

This proposition, if sustained by the evidence, has an important implication for growth policy. The notion that our productivity problems reside in the "spirit of entrepreneurship," which waxes and wanes for unexplained reasons, is a counsel of despair, for it gives no guidance on how to reawaken that spirit once it has lagged. If that is the task assigned to policymakers, they are destitute—they have no means of knowing how to carry it out. But if what is required is the adjustment of the economic rules of the game to induce a more felicitous allocation of entrepreneurial resources, then the policymaker's task is less formidable, and it is certainly not hopeless. The prevailing rules that affect the allocation of entrepreneurial activity can be observed, described, and, with luck, modified and improved.

2.1   On the Historical Character of the Evidence

Given the inescapable problems for empirical as well as theoretical study of entrepreneurship described in Chapter 1, what sort of evidence can one hope to provide? Since the rules of the game usually change very slowly, a case study approach to investigation of our hypotheses drives us unavoidably to examples spanning considerable periods of history, and encompassing widely different cultures and geographic locations. Here we will proceed on the basis of historical illustrations, encompassing all of the main economic periods and places (ancient Rome, medieval China, Dark-Age Europe, the later Middle Ages, and so on) that economic historians almost universally single out for the light they shed on the process of innovation and its diffusion. These illustrations will be used to show that the relative rewards to different types of entrepreneurial activity have in fact varied dramatically from one time and place to another, and that this seems to have had profound effects on patterns of entrepreneurial behavior. Finally, evidence will be offered suggesting that such reallocations can have a considerable influence on the prosperity and growth of an economy, though other variables undoubtedly also play substantial roles.

None of this can, of course, be considered conclusive. Yet it is surely a standard tenet of scientific method that tentative confirmation of a hypothesis is provided by observation of phenomena that the hypothesis helps to explain, and that could not easily be accounted for if that hypothesis were invalid. It is upon this sort of reasoning that I hope to rest my case. Historians have long been puzzled, for example, by the failure of the society of ancient Rome to disseminate and put into widespread practical use some of the sophisticated technological developments that we know to have been in its possession, while in the High Middle Ages, a period in which progress and change were hardly popular notions, inventions that languished in Rome seem to have spread like wildfire. It will be argued that the hypothesis about the allocability of entrepreneurial effort between productive and unproductive activity helps considerably to account for this phenomenon, though it certainly will not be claimed that this is all there was to the matter.

Before getting to the substance of the discussion, it is important to emphasize that nothing that follows in this chapter makes any pretense at consitituting a contribution to economic history. The analysis relies entirely on secondary sources, and all of the historical developments described are well known to historians, as the citations will indicate. Whatever contribution may be offered by the following pages, then, is confined to enhanced understanding and extension of the theory of entrepreneurship in general, and not to an improved analysis of the historical events cited.

2.2   The Schumpeterian Model Extended: Allocation of Entrepreneurship

The analysis in this chapter rests on what seems to be the one theoretical model that effectively encompasses the role of the entrepreneur and that really "works," in the sense that it constitutes the basis for a number of substantive inferences.[2] This is, of course, the well-known Schumpeterian analysis, whose main shortcoming, for our purposes (aside from the criticisms referred to in the preceding chapter), is the paucity of insights on policy that emerge from it. It will be suggested here that only a minor extension of that model to give greater emphasis to the allocation of entrepreneurship is required to enhance its power substantially in this direction.

Schumpeter tells us that innovations (he calls them "the carrying out of new combinations") take various forms besides mere improvements in technology:

This concept covers the following five cases: (1) The introduction of a new good —that is one with which consumers are not yet familiar—or of a new quality of a good. (2) The introduction of a new method of production, that is one not yet tested by experience in the branch of manufacture concerned, which need by no means be founded upon a discovery scientifically new, and can also exist in a new way of handling a commodity commercially. (3) The opening of a new market, that is a market into which the particular branch of manufacture of the country in question has not previously entered, whether or not this market has existed before. (4) The conquest of a new source of supply of raw materials or half-manufactured goods, again irrespective of whether this source already exists or whether it has first to be created. (5) The carrying out of the new organization of any industry, like the creation of a monopoly position (for example through trustification) or the breaking up of a monopoly position.   (p. 66)

The obvious fact that entrepreneurs carry out such a variety of tasks suggests that theory can usefully undertake to consider what determines the allocation of entrepreneurial inputs among them. Just as the literature traditionally studies the allocation of other inputs—for example, capital resources—among the various industries that compete for them, it seems natural to ask what influences the flow of entrepreneurial talent among the various activities on Schumpeter's list.

Presumably the reason no such line of inquiry was pursued by Schumpeter or his successors is that any analysis of the allocation of entrepreneurial resources among the five items in the preceding list of entrepreneurial activities (with the exception of the last—the creation or destruction of a monopoly) does not promise to yield any profound conclusions. There is no obvious reason to make much of a shift of entrepreneurial activity away from, say, improvement in the production process and toward the introduction of new products. The general implications, if any, for the public welfare, for productivity growth, and for other related matters are hardly obvious.

To derive more substantive results from an analysis of the allocation of entrepreneurial resources it is necessary to expand Schumpeter's list, whose main deficiency seems to be that it does not go far enough. For example, it does not explicitly encompass innovative acts of technology transfer which take advantage of opportunities to introduce already available technology (usually with some modification to adapt it to local conditions) to geographic locales whose suitability for the purpose had previously gone unrecognized or at least unused.[3] Innovative technology transfer, the contribution of which can perhaps be compared to the utility contributed by transportation of an ordinary finished product to a new geographic market, will be the subject of chapters 8–11.

Most important for the discussion here, Schumpeter's list of entrepreneurial activities can usefully be expanded to include such items as innovations in rent-seeking procedures[4], for example, discovery of a previously unused legal gambit that is effective in diverting rents to those who are first in exploiting it. It may seem strange at first blush to propose inclusion of activities of such questionable value to society (we will call them acts of "unproductive entrepreneurship") in the list of Schumpeterian innovations (though the creation of a monopoly, which Schumpeter does include as one of his major types of innovation,[5] is, surely, as questionable), but, as will soon be seen, this is a crucial step for the analysis that follows. If entrepreneurs are defined, simply, as persons who are ingenious and creative in finding ways to add to their wealth, power, and prestige, then it is to be expected that not all of them will be overly concerned with whether an activity that achieves these goals adds much or little to the social product or, for that matter, even whether it is an actual impediment to production. Suppose that it turns out, in addition, that at any time and place the magnitude of the benefit the economy derives from its entrepreneurial talents depends substantially, among other variables, on the allocation of this resource between productive and unproductive entrepreneurial activities of the sorts just described. Then the reasons for including acts of the latter type in the list of entrepreneurial activities become clear.

Here, no exhaustive analysis of the process of allocation of entrepreneurial activity among the set of available options will be attempted. Rather, it will only be argued that at least *one* of the prime determinants of entrepreneurial behavior at any particular time and place is the prevailing rules of the game that govern the payoff of one entrepreneurial activity relative to another. If the rules are such as to impede the earning of much wealth via activity A, or are such as to impose social disgrace upon those who engage in that activity, then, other things being equal, entrepreneurs' efforts will tend to be channeled to other activities, which we can call B. But if B contributes less to production or welfare than A, the consequences for society may be considerable.

As a last preliminary note, it should be emphasized that the set of active entrepreneurs may itself be subject to change. If the rules of the game begin to favor B over A, some individuals may not switch activities from entrepreneurship of type A to that of type B. Rather, some persons with talents suited for A may simply drop out of the picture, and individuals with abilities adapted to B may for the first time become entrepreneurs. Thus, the allocation of entrepreneurs among activities is perhaps best described in the way Joan Robinson (following G. F. Shove's suggestion) analyzed the allocation of heterogeneous land resources (1933, ch. 8)—as the solution of a jigsaw puzzle in which the pieces are each fitted into the places selected for them by the concatenation of pertinent circumstances.

2.3 Productive and Unproductive Entrepreneurship: The Rules *Do* Change

Let us now turn to the central hypothesis of this chapter—that the exercise of entrepreneurship can sometimes be unproductive or even destructive, and that whether it takes such a direction or one that is more benign depends heavily on the structure of payoffs in the economy—the rules of the game.

Here, the term *productive activity* refers, simply, to any activity that contributes directly or indirectly to net output of the economy or to the capacity to produce additional output. In this sense, for example, financial activity which facilitates the work of the manufacturing sector is clearly productive, and so, arguably, is anything that contributes to the output of any good or service desired by consumers, even if that product is not approved of by society. This concept, then, has little resemblance to the terms *productive labor* and *unproductive labor* as used by classical or Marxian economists. To be considered "productive," in the sense used here, an activity does not have to be devoted to agriculture or yield tangible products rather than disembodied services, or be carried out for profit. All that is necessary is that the activity yield a positive marginal product, however indirect the route that the activity employs in achieving this.[6]

The rather dramatic illustrations provided by world history seem to confirm quite emphatically what can be described as:

PROPOSITION 2.1   The rules of the game that determine the relative payoffs of different entrepreneurial activities *do* change dramatically from one time and place to another.

These examples also suggest strongly (but hardly "prove"):

PROPOSITION 2.2   Entrepreneurial behavior changes direction from one economy to another in a manner that corresponds to the variations in the rules of the game.

Ancient Rome

The avenues open to Romans who sought power, prestige, and wealth are instructive. First, it may be noted that they had no reservations about the desirability of wealth, or about its pursuit (see, e.g., M. I. Finley [1985, pp. 53–57]). *So long as it did not involve participation in industry or commerce,* there was nothing degrading about the wealth acquisition process. Persons of honorable status had three primary and acceptable sources of income: landholding (not infrequently as absentee landlords), usury, and what may be described as "political payments." Finley writes:

The opportunity for 'political moneymaking' can hardly be over-estimated. Money poured in from booty, indemnities, provincial taxes, loans and miscellaneous exactions in quantities without precedent in Graeco-Roman history, and at an accelerating rate. The public treasury benefited, but probably more remained in private hands, among the nobles in the first instance; then, in appropriately decreasing proportions, among the *equites*, the soldiers and even the plebs of the city of Rome . . .

Nevertheless, the whole phenomenon is misunderstood when it is classified under the headings of 'corruption' and 'malpractice,' as historians still persist in doing. Cicero was an honest governor of Cilicia in 51 and 50 B.C., so that at the end of his term he had earned only the legitimate profits of office. They amounted to 2,200,000 sesterces, more than treble the figure of 600,000 he himself once mentioned (*Stoic Paradoxes* 49) to illustrate an annual income that could permit a life of luxury. We are faced with something structural in the society.   (p. 55)

Who, then, operated commerce and industry? According to Veyne (1961), it was an occupation heavily undertaken by freedmen—former slaves who, incidentally, bore a social stigma for life. Indeed, according to this writer, slavery may have represented the one avenue for advancement for someone from the lower classes. A clever (and handsome) slave might be fortunate in having a wealthy and powerful master. With luck, skill, and drive he could grow close to his owner, perhaps managing his financial affairs (and sometimes participating in his master's homosexual activity). The master then gained cachet, after a suitable period, by granting freedom to the slave, setting him up with a fortune of his own. The freedmen, apparently not atypically, invested their financial stakes in commerce, hoping to profit sufficiently to enable them to retire in style to the countryside. Thereafter, they characteristically shunned demeaning productive activity (outside of agriculture) and invested largely in land and loans in imitation of the upper classes.

Finally, regarding the Romans' attitudes about the promotion of technology and productivity, Finley makes much of the "clear, almost total divorce between science and practice" (1965, p. 32). He goes on to cite Vitruvius's monumental work on architecture and technology in whose ten books he finds only a single and trivial reference to means of saving effort and increasing productivity. Finley then reports:

There is a story, repeated by a number of Roman writers, that a man—characteristically unnamed—invented unbreakable glass and demonstrated it to Tiberius in anticipation of a great reward. The emperor asked the inventor whether anyone shared his secret and was assured that there was no one else; whereupon his head was promptly removed, lest, said Tiberius, gold be reduced to the value of mud. I have no opinion about the truth of this story, and it is only a story. But is it not interesting that neither the elder Pliny nor Petronius nor the historian Dio Cassius was troubled by the point that the inventor turned to the emperor for a reward, instead of turning to an investor for capital with which to put his invention into production?[7] ... We must remind ourselves time and again that the European experience since the late Middle Ages in technology, in the economy, and in the value systems that accompanied them, was unique in human history until the recent export trend commenced. Technical progress, economic growth, productivity, even efficiency have not been significant goals since the beginning of time. So long as an acceptable life-style could be maintained, however that was defined, other values held the stage.   (1985, p. 147)

The bottom line, for our purposes, is that the Roman reward system, although it offered wealth to those who engaged in commerce and industry, offset this gain through the attendant loss in prestige. Economic effort "was neither the way to wealth nor its purpose. Cato's gods showed him a number of ways to get more; but they were all political and parasitical, the ways of conquest and booty and usury; labour was not one of them, not even the labour of the entrepreneur" (Finley [1965, p. 30]).

Medieval China

In China, as in many kingdoms of Europe before the guarantees of the Magna Carta and the revival of towns and their acquisition of privileges, the monarch commonly claimed possession of all property in his territories. As a result, particularly in China, when the sovereign was in financial straits, confiscation of the property of wealthy subjects was entirely in order. It has been claimed that this led those who had resources to avoid investing them in any sort of visible capital stocks, and that this, in turn, was a substantial impediment to economic expansion (see Balasz [1964, p. 53]; Landes [1969, pp. 46–47]; Rosenberg and Birdzell [1986, pp. 119–20]; and Jones [1987, ch. 5]).

In addition, imperial China reserved its most substantial rewards in wealth and prestige to those who climbed the ladder of imperial examinations, which were heavily devoted to such subjects as Confucian philosophy and caligraphy. Successful candidates were often awarded high rank in the bureaucracy, a high social standing denied to anyone engaged in commerce or industry—even those who gained great wealth in the process (and who often used their resources to prepare their descendants to contend via the examinations for a position in the bureaucracy of scholars). In other words, the prevailing rules of the game seem to have been heavily biased against the acquisition of wealth *and position* through Schumpeterian behavior. The avenue to success lay elsewhere.

Because of the difficulty of the examinations, the Mandarins (scholar-officials) rarely succeeded in keeping such positions in their own families for more than two or three generations (see Marsh [1961, p. 159] and Ping-Ti Ho [1962, ch. 4 and appendix]). The scholar families devoted enormous effort and considerable resources to preparing their children through years of laborious study for the imperial examinations which, during the Sung dynasty, were held every three years, and only several hundred persons in all of China succeeded in passing them each time (E. A. Kracke, Jr., in Liu and Golas [1969, p. 14]). Yet regularly, some persons not from Mandarin families also attained success through this avenue (see, e.g., Marsh [1961] and Ping-Ti Ho [1962] for evidence on social mobility in imperial China).

Wealth was in prospect for those who passed the examination and were subsequently appointed to government positions. But the sources of their earnings had something in common with those of the Romans.

Corruption, which is widespread in all impoverished and backward countries (or, more exactly, throughout the pre-industrial world), was endemic in a country where the servants of the state often had nothing to live on but their very meager salaries. The required attitude of obedience to superiors made it impossible for officials to demand higher salaries, and in the absence of any control over their activities from below it was inevitable that they should purloin from society what the state failed to provide. According to the usual pattern, a Chinese official entered upon his duties only after spending long years in study and passing many examinations; he then established relations with protectors, incurred debts to get himself appointed, and then proceeded to extract the amount he had spent on preparing himself for his career from the people he administered—and extracted both principal and interest. The degree of his rapacity would be dictated not only by the length of time he had had to wait for his appointment and the number of relations he had to support and of kin to satisfy or repay, but also by the precariousness of his position.   (Balazs, p. 10)

Enterprise, on the other hand, was not only frowned upon, but may have been subjected to impediments deliberately imposed by the officials, at least after the fourteenth century A.D.; some historians claim it was true much earlier. Balazs tells us of:

... the state's tendency to clamp down immediately on any form of private enterprise (and this in the long run kills not only initiative but even the slightest attempts at innovation), or, if it did not succeed in putting a stop to it in time, to take over and nationalize it. Did it not frequently happen during the course of Chinese history that the scholar-officials, although hostile to all inventions, nevertheless gathered in the fruits of other people's ingenuity? I need mention only three examples of inventions that met this fate: paper, invented by a eunuch; printing, used by the Buddhists as a medium for religious propaganda; and the bill of exchange, an expedient of private businessmen.   (p. 18)

As a result of recurrent intervention by the state to curtail the liberty of the merchant class and take over any accumulated advantages it had managed to gain for itself through enterprise, "The merchant's ambition turned to becoming a scholar-official and investing his profits in land" (Balazs, p 32).

The Earlier Middle Ages

Before the rise of the cities and before monarchs were able to subdue the bellicose activities of the nobility, wealth and power were pursued primarily through military activity. Since land and castles were the medieval forms of wealth most highly valued and most avidly sought after, it seems reasonable to interpret the warring of the barons in large part as the pursuit of an economic objective. For example, during the reign of William the Conqueror (see, e.g., Douglas [1964]), there were frequent attempts by the barons in Normandy and neighboring portions of France to take over one another's lands and castles. A prime incentive for William's supporters in his conquest of England was their obvious aspiration for lands.[8] More than that, violent means also served to provide more liquid forms of income (captured treasure) which the nobility used to support both private consumption and investment in military plant and equipment, where such items could not easily be produced on their own lands and therefore had to be purchased from others. In England, with its institution of primogeniture (the exclusive right of the eldest son to inherit his father's estate), younger sons who chose not to enter the clergy often had no socially acceptable choice other than warfare as a means to make their fortunes, and in some cases they succeeded spectacularly. Thus, note the case of William Marshal, fourth son of a minor noble, who rose through his military accomplishments to be one of the most powerful and trusted officials under Henry II and Richard I, and became one of the wealthiest men in England (see Painter [1933]).

Of course, the medieval nobles were not purely economic men. Many of the turbulent barons undoubtedly enjoyed fighting for its own sake, and success in combat was an important avenue to prestige in their society. But no modern capitalist is a purely economic man either. What I am saying here is that warfare, which was of course pursued for a variety of reasons, was also undertaken as a primary source of economic gain. This is clearly all the more true of the mercenary armies that were the scourge of fourteenth century France and Italy. Such violent economic activity, moreover, inspired frequent and profound innovation. The introduction of the stirrup was a requisite for effective cavalry tactics. Castle-building evolved from wooden to stone structures and from rectangular to round towers (which could not be made to collapse by undermining their corners). Armor and weaponry became much more sophisticated with the introduction of the crossbow, the longbow and, ultimately, artillery based on gunpowder. Military tactics and strategy also grew in sophistication. These innovations can be interpreted as contributions of military entrepreneurs undertaken at least partly in pursuit of private economic gains.

This type of entrepreneurial undertaking obviously differs vastly from the introduction of a cost-saving industrial process or a valuable new consumer product. An individual who pursues wealth through the forcible appropriation of the possessions of others surely does not add to the national product. Its net effect may not merely be a transfer but a net reduction in social income and wealth.[9]

The Later Middle Ages

By the end of the eleventh century, the rules of the game had changed from those of the Dark Ages. The revival of the towns was well underway. Towns had acquired a number of privileges, among them protection from arbitrary taxation and confiscation and the creation of a labor force (from the granting of freedom to runaway serfs after a relatively brief residence —a year and a day—in a town). The free-enterprise turbulence of the barons had at least been impeded by the church's pacification efforts—the Peace and (later) the Truce of God in France, Spain, and elsewhere. Similar changes were taking place in England (see, e.g., Cowdrey [1970]), but Jones suggests that some free-enterprise military activity by the barons continued in England through the reigns of the earlier Tudors in the sixteenth century (1987, p. 94). All this subsequently "gave way to more developed efforts to enforce peace by the more organized governments of the twelfth century" (Brooke [1964, p. 350; also p. 127]). A number of activities that were neither agricultural nor military began to yield handsome returns. For example, the small group of architect-engineers who were in charge of the building of cathedrals, palaces, bridges, and fortresses could live in great luxury in the service of their kings.

But, apparently, a far more common source of earnings was the water-driven mills which were strikingly common in France and southern England by the eleventh century—a technological innovation about which more will be said. An incentive for such technical advances may have been the monopoly they conferred on their owners rather than any resulting improvement in efficiency. Such monopoly rights were sought and enforced by private parties (Bloch [1935, pp. 554–57], Brooke [1964, p. 84]) and by religious organizations.

The economic role of the monks in this is somewhat puzzling—the least clear-cut part of our story.[10] The Cistercian abbeys are generally assigned a critical role in the promotion of such technological advances. In some cases they simply took over mills that had been constructed by others (Berman [1986, p. 89]). But the Cistercians improved the mills, built many others, and vastly expanded their use, and at least some writers (e.g.,

Gimpel [1976, pp. 3–6]) seem to suggest that the Cistercians were the spearhead of technological advance.

Historians tell us that they have no ready explanation for the entrepreneurial propensities of this monastic order (see, e.g., Brooke [1964, p. 69], and also a personal communication from Constance Berman to the author; but see Ovitt [1987, especially pp. 142–47], who suggests that this may have been part of the twelfth-century monastic drive to reduce or eliminate manual labor in order to maximize the time available for the less onerous religious labors—a conclusion with which Bloch [p. 553] concurs).[11] But the evidence suggests strongly that avid entrepreneurs they were. They accumulated vast tracts of land; their domesticated animal flocks were enormous by the standards of the time; their investment rates were remarkable; they sought to exercise monopoly power—being known, after the erection of a water mill, to seek legal intervention to prevent nearby residents from continuing to use their animal-powered facilities (Gimpel, pp. 15–16); they were fierce in their rivalrous behavior and drive for expansion, in the process not sparing other religious bodies—not even other Cistercian houses. There is "a record of pastoral expansionism and monopolies over access established by the wealthiest Cistercian houses . . . at the expense of smaller abbeys and convents . . . effectively pushing out all other religious houses as competitors" (Berman, p. 112).

As with early capitalists, the asceticism of the monks, by keeping down the proportion of the monastery's output that was consumed, helped to provide the resources for levels of investment extraordinary for the period (Berman, pp. 40, 83). The rules of the game appear to have offered substantial economic rewards to the exercise of Cistercian entrepreneurship. The order obtained relatively few large gifts, but instead frequently received support from the laity and from the church establishment in the form of exemptions from road and river tolls and from payment of the tithe. This obviously increased the *marginal* yield of investment, innovation, and expenditure of effort, and the evidence suggests the diligence of the order in pursuing the resulting opportunities. Their mills, their extensive lands, and their large flocks are reported to have brought scale economies and extraordinary financial returns (Berman, ch. 4). Puritanical, at least in earlier years, in their self-proclaimed adherence to simplicity in personal lifestyle while engaged in dedicated pursuit of wealth, they may perhaps represent an early manifestation of elements of the Protestant ethic. Whatever their motive, the reported Cistercian record of promotion of technological progress is in diametric contrast to that of the Roman Empire.

Fourteenth Century

The fourteenth century brought a considerable increase in military activity, notably the Hundred Years' War between France and England. Payoffs, surely, must have tilted to favor more than before inventions designed for military purposes. Cannon appeared as siege devices and armor was made heavier. More imaginative war devices were proposed—a windmill-propelled war wagon, a multibarreled machine gun, a diving suit to permit underwater attacks on ships. A pervasive business enterprise of this unhappy century of war was the company of mercenary troops—the *condottiere*—who roamed Europe, supported the side that could offer the most attractive terms, and in lulls between fighting, when unemployment threatened, roamed Europe thinking up military enterprises of their own, at the expense of the general public. Clearly, the rules of the game—the system of entrepreneurial rewards—had changed, to the disadvantage of productive entrepreneurship. Of course, that was not the only influence undergoing change. Opportunities for the entrepreneur were being altered at the same time by political, demographic, and other developments. Still, it is hard to believe that the changes in the rules of the game themselves made little difference.

Early Rent Seeking

Unproductive entrepreneurship can also take less violent forms, usually involving various types of rent seeking, the type of unproductive entrepreneurship that seems most relevant today. Enterprising use of the legal system for rent-seeking purposes has a long history. There are, for example, records of the use of litigation in the twelfth century in which the proprietor of a water-driven mill sought and won a prohibition of use in the vicinity of mills driven by animal or human power (Gimpel, pp. 25–26). In another case, the operators of two dams, one upstream of the other, sued one another repeatedly at least from the second half of the thirteenth century until the beginning of the fifteenth, when the downstream dam finally succeeded in driving the other out of business as the latter ran out of money to pay the court fees (Gimpel, pp. 17–20).

In the upper strata of society, rent seeking also gradually replaced military activity as a prime source of wealth and power. This transition can perhaps be ascribed to the triumph of the monarchies and the consequent imposition of law and order. Rent-seeking entrepreneurship then took a variety of forms, notably the quest for grants of land and patents of monopoly from the monarch.

Military forms of entrepreneurship may have experienced a renaissance in England in the seventeenth century with the revolt against King Charles I. How that may have changed the structure of rewards to entrepreneurial activity is suggested by Eric Hobsbawm (1969), who claims that at the end of the seventeenth century the most affluent merchants earned perhaps three times as much as the richest "master manufacturers."[12] But, he reports, the wealthiest noble families probably had incomes more than ten times as large as those of the rich merchants. The point in this is that those noble families, according to Hobsbawm, were no holdovers from an ancient feudal aristocracy—they were, rather, the heirs of the Roundheads (the supporters of the parliamentary, or Puritan, party) in the then recent civil war (Hobsbawm, pp. 30–32). On this view, once again, military activity would seem to have become the entrepreneur's most promising recourse.

But other historians take a rather different view of the matter. Studies reported in Thirsk (1954) indicate that ultimately there was little redistribution of property as the result of the civil war and the Restoration. Rather (see Stone [1985, p. 45]), it is noted that in this period the "patrician elites depended for their political power and economic prosperity on royal charters and monopolies rather than on talent and entrepreneurial initiative." On this interpretation of the matter, it was rent seeking, not military activity, that remained the prime source of wealth under the Restoration.

By the time the eighteenth-century Industrial Revolution (*the* Industrial Revolution) arrived, matters had changed once again. According to Ashton (1948, pp. 9–10), grants of monopoly were in good part "swept away" by the Monopolies Act of 1624, and, we are told by Adam Smith, by the end of the eighteenth century they were rarer in England than in any other country. Though industrial activity continued to be considered somewhat degrading in places where industry flourished, notably in England during the Industrial Revolution, there was probably a difference in degree. Thus, Lefebvre (1947) reports, "At its upper level the [French] nobility ... were envious of the English lords who enriched themselves in bourgeois ways ..." (p. 14), while in France, "The noble 'derogated' or fell into the common mass if [like Mirabeau] he followed a business or profession" (p. 11). (See, however, Schama [1989], who tells us that, "Even a cursory examination of the eighteenth-century French economy ... reveals the nobility deeply involved in finance, business and industry—certainly as much as their British counterparts.... In 1765 a royal edict officially removed the last formal obstacles to their participation in trade and insustry" [p. 118].) In England, primogeniture, by forcing younger sons of noble families to resort to commerce and industry, apparently imparted respectability to these activities to a degree which, while rather limited, may have rarely occurred before.

The central point of the preceding discussion seems clear—perhaps, in retrospect, even self-evident. If entrepreneurship is the imaginative pursuit of position, with limited concern about the means used to achieve the purpose, then we can expect changes in the structure of rewards to modify the nature of the entrepreneur's activities, sometimes drastically. The rules of the game can then be a critical influence helping to determine whether entrepreneurship will be allocated predominantly to activities that are productive or unproductive, and even destructive.

Rent Seeking in the Modern World

Today, unproductive entrepreneurship takes many forms. Rent seeking, often via activities such as litigation, takeovers, and tax evasion and avoidance efforts, seems now to constitute the prime threat to productive entrepreneurship. The spectacular fortunes amassed by the so-called arbitrageurs revealed by the financial scandals of the mid-1980s were surely the reward of acts that were partially unproductive and sometimes illegal, but nevertheless entrepreneurial. Today's corporate executives devote much of their time and energy to legal suit and countersuit, and litigation is used to blunt or prevent excessive rigor in competition by rivals. Huge awards by the courts, sometimes amounting to billions of dollars, can bring prosperity to the victor and threaten the loser with insolvency. When this happens it must become tempting to the entrepreneur to select his closest advisers from among lawyers rather than engineers. Such prospective financial gain can induce the entrepreneur to spend literally hundreds of millions of dollars for a single legal battle. It can tempt him to be the first to sue others before those others can sue him. (For an illuminating quantification of some of the social costs of one widely publicized legal battle between two business firms, see Summers and Cutler [1988].) More will be said on these matters in later chapters, and it will also be emphasized that few activities among those just listed make absolutely *no* contribution to production, so that the line between productive and unproductive entrepreneurship is often difficult to draw. Indeed, some of the activities mentioned have, in the opinion of a number of knowledgable observers, made substantial contributions to productivity; yet this does not mean that they are free of rent-seeking components.

Taxes are another influence that can serve to move entrepreneurial effort in less productive directions. As Assar Lindbeck observed, "The problem with high-tax societies is not that it is impossible to become rich there, but that it is difficult to do so by way of productive effort in the ordinary production system" (1987, p. 15). He cites as examples of the resulting reallocation of entrepreneurship, "'smart' speculative financial transactions without much (if any) contribution to the productive capacity of the economy" (p. 15), as well as "illegal 'business areas' such as drug dealing" (p. 25).

2.4 Does the Allocation between Productive and Unproductive Entrepreneurship Matter Much?

We come now to the third proposition of this chapter.

PROPOSITION 2.3 The allocation of entrepreneurship between productive and unproductive activities, though by no means the only pertinent influence, can have a profound effect on the innovativeness of the economy and the degree of dissemination of its technological discoveries.

It is hard to believe that a system of payoffs that moves entrepreneurship in unproductive directions is not a substantial impediment to industrial innovation and growth in productivity. Still, history permits no test of this proposition through anything resembling controlled experiments, since other influences *did*, undoubtedly, also play important roles, as the proposition recognizes. One can only note what appears to be a remarkable correlation between the degree to which past economies rewarded productive entrepreneurship and the vigor shown in those economies' innovation records.

Historians tell us of several industrial "near revolutions," that occurred before the Industrial Revolution of the eighteenth century, which are highly suggestive for our purposes (Braudel [1986, vol. 3, pp. 542–56]; and, for a more skeptical view, see Coleman [1956]). We are told that two of the incipient revolutions never went anywhere, while two of them were rather successful in their fashion. I will report conclusions of some leading historians on these episodes, but it should be recognized by the reader that many of the views summarized here have been disputed in the historical literature, at least to some degree.

Rome and Hellenistic Egypt
Our earlier discussion cited ancient Rome and its empire as a case in which the rules did not favor productive entrepreneurship. Let us compare this with the evidence on the vigor of innovative activity in that society. The museum at Alexandria was the center of technological invention in the

Roman Empire. By the first century B.C. that city knew of virtually every form of machine gearing that is used today, and had a working steam engine. But these seem to have been used only to make what amounted to elaborate toys. The steam engine was used only to open and close the doors of a temple.

The Romans also had the water mill. This may well have been the most critical pre–eighteenth century industrial invention, because it provided the first significant source of power other than human and animal labor: "It was able to produce an amount of concentrated energy beyond any other resource of antiquity" (Forbes [1955, vol. 2, p. 90]). Like steam in more recent centuries, it offered the prospect of providing the basis for a leap in productivity in the Roman economy, as apparently it actually did during the eleventh, twelfth, and thirteenth centuries in Europe. Yet, according to Reynolds (1983, p. 17), the knowledgable Vitruvius, writing in about 25 B.C., listed water mills in a section of his great work devoted to "rarely-used machinery." And Finley (1965, pp. 35–36), citing White, reports that "though it was invented in the first century B.C., it was not until the third century A.D. that we find evidence of much use and not until the fifth and sixth of general use. It is also a fact that we have no evidence at all of its application to other industries (i.e., other than grinding of grain) until the very end of the fourth century, and then no more than one solitary and possibly suspect reference to a marble-slicing machine near Trier."

Unfortunately, evidence of Roman technical stagnation is only spotty and, further, some historians suggest that the historical reports give inadequate weight to the Roman preoccupation with agricultural improvement relative to improvement in commerce or manufacture. Still, the following quotation seems to summarize the weight of opinion: "Historians have long been puzzled as to why the landlords of the Middle Ages proved so much more enterprising than the landlords of the Roman Empire, although the latter, by and large, were much better educated, and had much better opportunities for making technical and scientific discoveries if they had wished to do so" (Brooke [1964, pp. 88–89]). It seems at least plausible that some part of the explanation is to be found in the ancient world's rules of the game, which encouraged the pursuit of wealth, but severely discouraged its pursuit through the exercise of productive entrepreneurship.[13]

Medieval China

The astonishing set of inventions produced in ancient China, mostly in the T'ang (618–906 A.D.) and Sung (960–1126 A.D.) dynasties, constituted one of the earliest prospective revolutions in industry. Among the many Chinese technological contributions, one can list paper, movable type, (per-haps) the compass, water wheels, sophisticated water clocks, and, of course, gunpowder. But those are only the beginning of the list. Mokyr adds the spinning wheel which "appeared about the same time in China and the West—the thirteenth century (possibly somewhat earlier in China)—but advanced much faster and further in China ... a small multispindle spinning wheel, not unlike Hargreave's spinning jenny ..." (1990, p. 212), a mechan-ical cotton gin(!), hydraulic trip hammers (eighth century), ship construction techniques that permitted the production of vessels "much larger and more seaworthy than the best European ships," the sternpost rudder, superior sail designs permitting far greater maneuverability than Western ships could muster before the fifteenth century, porcelain, the umbrella, matches, the toothbrush, playing cards, and many, many others.[14]

There was, perhaps partly as a result of this inventive activity, consider-able prosperity, particularly during the Sung period. The wonders reported by Marco Polo were seen by him during the succeeding Khan dynasty, that of the barbarian Mongols. By then, it is arguable, the rate of growth had begun to slow (most notably in the arts, where dramatic changes in style that had been striking in previous centuries all but disappeared). By the end of the Ming period, the Chinese economy seems to have been in retreat, both relative to the West, and even absolutely. Its spectacular voyages of exploration had come to an end, its metallurgical superiority had eroded, and the land had become "a culture of bamboo and wood" (Needham [1964(b)], p. 19]). It had forgotten the remarkable eleventh-century clock that is still cited as one of the most remarkable horological accomplish-ments in the history of timekeeping, and only learned about methods of keeping time from Western visitors. There is no point in citing further examples.

However, the most interesting issue, it seems to me, is not the puzzling slowdown and eventual halt in Chinese inventiveness. After all, the fact that the period of creativity lasted more than a thousand years is dramatic enough, and it is not so surprising that it eventually came to an end. It is equally difficult to be surprised at the multiplicity of hypotheses that have been offered as explanations for the decline (Mokyr, 1990, pp. 223–38). It was, obviously, a complex phenomenon, and it is not to be expected that it can be fully accounted for by any one or even a few explanatory elements.

Rather, to me, the much more striking manifestation was the apparent failure of the mass of inventions to serve as the basis for the growth and spread of *industry*[15] throughout the economy, even during the times of the country's greatest prosperity (see, e.g., Liu and Golas [1969]). Commerce did flourish, but there seems to have been little upheaval in the production of nonagricultural goods, taking them from the artisan's shop and into the factory. It would, no doubt, be unreasonable to expect to find the satanic mills of Birmingham and Manchester in medieval China, but the remarkable number and variety of water mills that crowded the banks of the Seine and dotted the landscape of southern England seem also to have been missing. It is noteworthy, then, that, as in Rome, the technical know-how was available in impressive abundance, but it seems never to have led to any commensurate innovation in the willingness of industry to make use of that knowledge.

Here, again, it is highly implausible that there is any single explanation, or that the phenomenon will ever be understood fully. But there is reason to believe that the sort of influence upon which this chapter focuses also played a substantial role here. In China too, as we have seen, the rules did not favor productive entrepreneurship. Balazs concludes that

... what was chiefly lacking in China for the further development of capitalism was not mechanical skill or scientific aptitude, nor a sufficient accumulation of wealth, but scope for individual enterprise. There was no individual freedom and no security for private enterprise, no legal foundation for rights other than those of the state, no alternative investment other than landed property, no guarantee against being penalized by arbitrary exactions from officials or against intervention by the state. But perhaps the supreme inhibiting factor was the overwhelming prestige of the state bureaucracy, which maimed from the start any attempt of the bourgeoisie to be different, to become aware of themselves as a class and fight for an autonomous position in society. Free enterprise, ready and proud to take risks, is therefore quite exceptional and abnormal in Chinese economic history.   (p. 58)

It is not difficult to cite evidence to the same effect from other authorities. In sum, it seems clear that one of the handicaps besetting the growth of industry in medieval China, despite all the inventions that seemed to be ripe for exploitation, was the fact that *prestigious* wealth was not to be found here, and had, rather, to be pursued along less productive avenues.

Slow Growth in the Dark Ages

In Europe, an era noted for its slow growth occurred between the death of Charlemagne in 814 A.D. and the end of the tenth century. Even this period was not without its economic advances, though they did proceed slowly, including the beginnings of the agricultural improvements that attended the introduction of the horseshoe, harness and stirrup, the heavy plow, and the substitution of horsepower for that of oxen, which may have played a role in enabling peasants to move to more populous villages farther from their fields (see White [1962, p. 39 ff]). But, still, it was probably a period of significantly slower growth than the industrial revolution of the eleventh to thirteenth centuries (Gimpel [1976]), about which more will be said. We have already seen that, in this time, military violence was a prime outlet for entrepreneurial activity. While this can hardly be *the* explanation of the relative stagnation of the era, it is hard to believe that it was totally unimportant.

The High Middle Ages

A good deal has already been said about the successful industrial revolution (and the accompanying commercial revolution sparked by inventions such as double-entry bookkeeping and bills of exchange; see de Roover [1953]) of the late Middle Ages, whose two-century duration makes it as long-lived as our own (see Gimpel [1976], White [1962], and Carus-Wilson [1941]). Perhaps the hallmark of this industrial revolution was that remarkable source of productive power, the water mills, which covered the countryside in the south of England and crowded the banks of the Seine in Paris (see, e.g., Gimpel, pp. 3–6, and Berman [1986, pp. 81–89]). The mills were not only simple grain-grinding devices, but they accomplished an astonishing variety of tasks and involved an impressive variety of mechanical devices and sophisticated gear arrangements. They crushed olives, ground mash for beer production, pressed cloth for papermaking, sawed lumber, hammered metal and woolens (as part of the "fulling" process—the cleansing, scouring, and pressing of woven woolen goods to make them stronger and bring the threads closer together), milled coins, polished armor, and operated the bellows of blast furnaces; for a more complete and systematic list of the remarkable variety of applications of the water wheel, see Reynolds (1983, pp. 77, 94). Their mechanisms entailed many forms of ingenuity. Gears were used to translate the vertical circular motion of the efficient form of the water wheel into the horizontal circular motion of the millstone. The cam (a piece of wood, metal, or some other solid protruding at right angles from a rotating shaft such as the axle of the water wheel) served to lift a hammer that was pivoted like a seesaw, then let it drop of its own weight, repeatedly and automatically (the can was apparently known in antiquity, but may not have been used then with water wheels). A crank handle extending from the end of the axle transformed the circular motion of the wheel into the back-and-forth (reciprocating) motion required for sawing or the operation of bellows.

The most sophisticated product of all of this mechanical skill and knowledge was the mechanical clock which appeared toward the end of the thirteenth century. As White sums up the matter, "The four centuries following Leonardo, that is, until electrical energy demanded a supplementary set of devices, were less technically engaged in discovering basic principles than in elaborating and refining those established during the four centuries before Leonardo" (1962, p. 129).[16]

In a period when agriculture probably occupied some 90 percent of the population, the expansion of industry in the twelfth and thirteenth century could not by itself have created a major upheaval in living standards.[17] Moreover, it has been deduced from what little we know of European gross domestic product per capita at the beginning of the eighteenth century that its average growth in the preceding six or seven centuries must have been very modest, since if the poverty of that later time had represented substantial growth from eleventh-century living standards, much of the earlier population would surely have been condemned to starvation. Still, the industrial activity of the twelfth and thirteenth centuries was very substantial. By the beginning of the fourteenth century, according to Gimpel, sixty-eight mills were in operation on less than one mile of the banks of the Seine in Paris, and these were supplemented by floating mills anchored to the Grand Pont. The activity in metallurgy was also considerable—sufficient to denude much of Europe of its forests and to produce a rise in the price of wood that forced recourse to coal (other historians assert that this did not occur to any substantial degree until the fifteenth or sixteenth centuries, with some question even about those dates; see, e.g., Coleman [1975, pp. 42−43]). In sum, the industrial revolution of the twelfth and thirteenth centuries was a surprisingly robust affair, and it is implausible that improved rewards to industrial activity had little to do with its vigor.

The Fourteenth-Century Retreat

The end of this period of buoyant activity in the fourteenth century (on this, see the classic revisionist piece by Lopez [1969] as well as Gimpel, ch. 9) has a variety of explanations, many of them having no connection with entrepreneurship. For one thing, it has been deduced from study of the glaciers that average temperatures dropped, possibly reducing the yield of crops (though recent studies indicate that the historical relation between climatic changes and crop yields is at best ambiguous) and creating other hardships. The bubonic plague returned and decimated much of the population. In addition to these disasters of nature there were at least two pertinent developments of human origin. First, the church clamped down on new ideas and other manifestations of freedom. Roger Bacon himself was put under constraint.[18] The period during which new ways of thinking brought rewards and status was apparently ended. Second, the fourteenth century included the first half of the devastating Hundred Years' War. It is unlikely that the associated renewal of rewards to military enterprise played no part in the economic slowdown.

The Eighteenth-Century Industrial Revolution

It need hardly be added, in conclusion, that *the* Industrial Revolution that began in the eighteenth century and continues today has brought to the industrialist, and the businessperson generally, a degree of wealth and respect probably unprecedented in human history. The fact that this period has yielded an explosion of output at least equally unprecedented is un-doubtedly attributable to a myriad of causes which can probably never be discovered fully and whose roles can never be disentangled. Yet the con-tinued association of output growth with high financial and respectability rewards to productive entrepreneurship is surely suggestive, even if it can hardly be taken to be conclusive evidence for our Proposition 2.3, which asserts that the allocation of entrepreneurship *does* really matter for the vigor and innovativeness of an economy.

There is, of course, a good deal more to be said about the subject; however, enough material has been presented here to indicate that a minor expansion of Schumpeter's theoretical model to encompass the determinants of the allocation of entrepreneurship among its competing uses can enrich the model considerably, and that the hypotheses that have been associated with the model's extension here are not without substance, even if none of the material approaches anything that constitutes a formal test of hypothe-sis, much less rigorous "proof." It is also easy to confirm that each of the hypotheses that has been discussed so far, like those on allocation of entre-preneurial effort between innovation and dissemination that will occupy a later chapter, yields some policy implications.

Thus, clear guidance for policy is provided by the main hypothesis (Propositions 2.1−2.3), that the rules of the game that specify the relative payoffs to different entrepreneurial activities play a key role in determining whether entrepreneurship will be allocated in productive or unproductive directions, and that this can significantly affect the vigor of the economy's productivity growth. After all, the prevailing laws and legal procedures of an economy are prime determinants of the profitability of activities such as rent seeking via the litigative process. Steps such as deregulation of the airlines or more rational antitrust rules can do a good deal here.

A dramatic example can make the point. The fact that Japan has far fewer lawyers relative to population and far fewer lawsuits on economic issues is often cited as a distinct advantage of the Japanese economy, as it reduces at least in part the quantity of resources devoted to rent seeking. The difference is often ascribed to a Japanese national character that is said to have a cultural aversion to litigiousness. This may all be very true. But closer inspection reveals that there are also other influences. While in the United States legal institutions such as the award of triple damages provide a rich incentive for one firm to sue another on the claim that the latter violated the antitrust laws, in Japan the arrangements are very different. In that country any firm undertaking to sue another on antitrust grounds must first apply for permission from the Japan Fair Trade Commission. But such permission is rarely given, and once denied, there is no legal avenue for appeal.[19]

The overall moral, then, is that we do not have to wait patiently for slow cultural change in order to find measures to redirect the flow of entrepreneurial activity toward more productive goals. Like the Japanese in the illustration just cited, it may be possible to change our economic rules in ways that help to offset undesired institutional influences or that supplement other influences taken to work in beneficial directions. Such policy issues will be discussed more extensively in the final chapter of this book.

3   Enterprising Rent Seeking: The Case of Corporate Takeovers

It only makes sense to view the cost of litigation as bargaining leverage to force a settlement on terms favorable to the party that can litigate the matter to death without worrying about the cash flow.

Philip Sperber, then vice president of Refrac, a firm that has been described as "a litigation factory" (*New York Times*, Business Section, January 14, 1990, p. 5)

Interviewer: "Mr. Sutton, tell me, why did you rob banks?"
Willie Sutton: "Because that's where the money is."

It was suggested in the previous chapter that rent seeking is the proto-typical variant of *respectable*, but unproductive, entrepreneurship in the twentieth century. Mafia godfathers may, of course, also be highly enter-prising, but they are hardly respectable. This chapter begins with a discus-sion of rent seeking, starting with the connotation of the term. Then, partly because of its pertinence for the analysis of a later chapter, some comments will be offered on the controversy over Richard A. Posner's suggestion that where there is perfect freedom of entry into a rent-seeking activity its net economic profit yield can, for the usual reasons, be expected to approxi-mate zero, so that the value of the resources of society wasted on such an activity must approximate the expected financial yield of the activity to those who carry it out successfully. Despite the cogent criticisms of such able analysts as Franklin M. Fisher, Hal Varian, and Gordon Tullock (the father of the concept), I will conclude that the Posner contention remains suggestive and of some value, particularly since no alternative and gener-ally valid approximation seem to have been offered. Finally, the chapter will turn for an illustration to a much-publicized activity—leveraged cor-porate buyouts—which, it will be contended, can at least sometimes serve very productive purposes, and yet at the same time, constitute a vehicle for spectacularly lucrative rent seeking.

3.1   Rent Seeking: Toward Definition

Professor Tullock has told us that he is dissatisfied both with the term *rent seeking* and with the connotation it has received in the literature. In the first sentence of a recent book of his (1989), he refers to "the topic which is, rather unfortunately, named *rent seeking*." He devotes Chapter 5 of the book to the "problem of definition," making it clear that, in his view, the concept has not been satisfactorily defined, with the consequence that some of the discussions have been unnecessarily obscure and complicated. To avoid these difficulties, he tells us, "My suggestion is that we use the term 'rent seeking' ... solely for cases in which whatever is proposed has a negative social impact" (p. 55).

Of course, one cannot legitimately argue that a definition is "incorrect." Yet I will propose an alternative definition, pointing out that the Tullock solution is, for our purposes, not really helpful, because it is in one respect too restrictive and in another too broadly inclusive. It is too restrictive for our needs because it excludes entirely any activity that is on balance productive, even if some individuals who play a substantial role in that activity derive wealth from it, add to its cost, but contribute little to its output. The Tullock definition could, for example, as mere tautology and without further inquiry, exonerate corporate takeover activity from any taint of rent seeking, provided it were agreed that, on balance, the effect of such acquisitions has been a net addition to output. On the other hand, the Tullock definition would appear to be inconveniently broad in that it seems to encompass *all* socially detrimental activities, whether or not they were even remotely connected to a productive process, and whether they involve what most observers would consider customary and generally accepted modes of behavior or, instead, automatically make the actor an outcast from society. Indeed, on this definition, one might well label all unproductive entrepreneurship "rent seeking" simply by virtue of the fact that it is unproductive, thereby erasing any distinction between the economic role of a robber baron or a drug lord and that of an attorney who seeks to preserve the exclusive license of a public utility in a perfectly accepted and legal manner.

It seems to me more useful here to build upon the concept of *economic rent* in order to provide a more flexible and illuminating distinction between rent seeking and other types of unproductive activity. For this purpose, one usually starts from the common concept of land rent, taking account of the observation that the available quantity of land is approximately fixed and unexpandable. This implies that any increase in the levels of payment to landowners will elicit no increase in the supply of land in return. That is, as far as the remainder of society is concerned, it receives no return on any increment in its expenditure on land use, unlike an input such as lumber, whose supply will presumably be increased by a rise in the price of wood.

By analogy, this concept has been generalized by economists, who define economic rent as that portion of the payment to an input which elicits no increase in output, that is, whose marginal product yield to the economy is zero. For example, if wages have reached a level at which further increases, rather than expanding the labor supply, simply make it possible for workers to enjoy more leisure, then any rise in wages above that transition point are classified as economic rent to the worker. Many inputs, then, are recipients of economic rents that constitute part of their total compensation. However, these rents accrue to them incidentally and automatically, without any special effort on the part of their suppliers to obtain income of that sort rather than income of another variety.

Rent seeking can then be defined as the expenditure of resources in (deliberate) pursuit of economic rents by means that do not (automatically) contravene the accepted rules of society. Since rents are defined in relation to the production process, this definition excludes transfers obtained by means of inherently nonproductive activities such as blackmail or the operation of a private army in a war-torn area. It also excludes activities such as the production or sale of illegal narcotics, which is arguably productive, supplying a commodity for which there is considerable demand, even though its consumption is widely deplored. However, to avoid ruling out those activities that are most frequently cited as examples of rent seeking, we must include in our concept of undertakings related to production all cases of governmental intervention in the productive process—regulation, the granting of exclusive licenses, or the enactment of laws by which the productive process is affected directly or through litigation.

It is rent seeking, as thus defined, that I conjecture constitutes the prime occupation of unproductive entrepreneurs in contemporary society.

3.2   The Controversy over the Cost of Competitive Rent Seeking

Concern about the phenomenon of rent seeking should immediately lead one to inquire into the magnitude of its cost to the economy. That cost is pertinent for our purposes because it can be interpreted as the damage caused directly and indirectly by the exercise of enterprising entrepreneurship. It is clear that estimation of this figure is extremely difficult, and

I know of only one attempt to provide a statistical figure (Laband and Sophocleus [1990]), in which a census is undertaken of activities that are devoted to rent seeking and rent preservation, where rent seeking is defined broadly as any attempt to transfer wealth to the persons who undertake it, without an offsetting contribution to production on their part. Thus, for example, the production of locks is interpreted as a waste necessitated by the efforts of prospective victims to protect themselves from burglary, a purely redistributive activity that can be interpreted as a form of rent seeking. Reasoning by analogy, the authors take defense expenditure largely to constitute exactly that sort of waste—as an outlay a nation undertakes to protect itself from larcenous activities by unscrupulous foreign states (assuming the country in question is not itself a "rent-seeking" aggressor). Adopting a classification in this spirit, with suitable reservations and caveats, the authors arrive at an estimate, indicating that in the United States in 1985 some $448 billion, more than 10 percent of GNP (gross national product) was devoted to such nonproductive activities. Whether one is prepared to accept their classification (as a result of which more than half their total is constituted by military expenditures), two conclusions seem to emerge clearly from their work. First, the magnitude of the activities at issue is at least not negligible. Second, and more important for our purposes, their survey demonstrates unequivocally that the social cost of enterprising rent seeking far exceeds just the opportunity cost entailed in the efforts of these entrepreneurs themselves. Like the enterprising activities of the robber barons of the nineteenth century, the resulting transfers can impose enormous wastes far exceeding that opportunity cost alone.

While the limitations of the Laband-Sophocleus study (which are stressed by the authors themselves) indicate how difficult it is to evaluate the costs of rent seeking, theoretical analysis of the subject has provided some pertinent qualitative propositions that seem generally to be agreed upon. Most notably, the economic literature generally accepts the proposition that the economic costs of monopoly were considerably underestimated in some writings predating the rent-seeking literature—in cases where large quantities of resources have to be expended in acquiring the monopoly, or where there is competition over the possession of the monopoly and resources are used up in the contest over its retention or acquisition (as when the license for a public utility is scheduled for renewal, and the licensing authority throws the process open for bidding). Specifically, in a number of earlier publications it was asserted that the economic burden imposed by a monopoly corresponds to the "deadweight loss" resulting from its adoption of the profit-maximizing prices of its products, and the reduction in the quantities of those products purchased by consumers when the prices exceed their competitive levels. That deadweight loss is, of course, measured by the associated reduction in consumers' surplus minus the increase in producer's surplus (the monopoly profit), and is attributable to the fact that the monopolist's method of transferring income from consumers to itself incidentally but unavoidably entails a misallocation of resources. It is now agreed that this figure is generally an underestimate of the economic damage because it leaves out of the account the valuable resources wasted in the process of obtaining the monopoly or of holding on to it against the attempts of others to take it over.

But how large is that underestimate? It would appear to be a magnitude capable of enormous variation, or at least it seemed so before an ingenious suggestion by Posner (1975) appeared to provide a handle with which one could generate an orderly and simple analysis of the matter. Posner suggested that even where the object was the acquisition of a monopoly, in a substantial number of cases many agents were apt to engage in the attempt and barriers to entry into the fray were negligible. The process of monopoly acquisition might, as a somewhat ironic consequence, itself be highly competitive. But where an activity approximates perfect competition (or perfect contestability), it is generally taken for granted that the expected profits will be zero, that is, in Posner's words, "at the margin, the cost of obtaining a monopoly is exactly equal to the expected profit of being a monopolist" (p. 809).

Where the requisite premises are valid, this, then, provides a remarkable simplification of the issues. It tells us that where there is free entry into the competition for a license that offers an expected payoff of, say, $35 million, one can expect market forces to induce the same amount, $35 million, to be expended in pursuit of this innovation. But that conclusion immediately raises three questions. First, how commonly is entry into a rent-seeking activity absolutely free, or very nearly so? Second, if the amount spent on such a rent-seeking project is correctly evaluated by Posner's observation, does the entire expenditure constitute social waste? Third, even if the Posner assumptions are satisfied, does it necessarily follow that the expected costs of the struggle for the rent-yielding asset will approximately equal the rent that it promises? Critics have argued that all three questions must be answered in the negative.

Thus Fisher (1985) has argued persuasively that the profits of pursuit of monopoly cannot normally be expected to be zero, because entry into the rent-seeking contest is usually subject to substantial entry barriers. In addition, Tullock notes that a considerable share of the outlay in rent seeking is likely to be sunk and irretrievable, meaning that exit is also not free. Consequently, the activity will in general approximate neither perfect competition nor perfect contestability, and so the zero-profit theorem is simply not applicable. Besides, Fisher and Varian (1989) argue, quite correctly, not all of the private cost the firm incurs in the process of rent seeking will necessarily constitute a social cost; indeed, much of the cost of the inputs used may well itself turn out to be rent, whose loss to the individual input supplier constitutes no cost to society. Thus, in many cases the true social cost of rent seeking may turn out to be lower than the Posner proposition claims, though it is possible for matters to turn out the other way.

Let us examine the arguments in somewhat more detail. The notion that pursuit of monopoly can be a perfectly competitive process is an intriguing one. One can imagine a local government that has decided to "privatize" its electricity supply by granting a license to a single private firm to take over the profitable activity previously conducted by the municipality. Smelling profits, prospective suppliers may emerge from everywhere, and descend upon the license-granting authority with the aid of specialized professional representatives (lobbyists), each of whom provides persuasive arguments on behalf of his or her client, perhaps along with costly lunches, gifts, or even naked bribes. Entry into this process may well be unrestricted, with the participants on an equal footing before the unprejudiced licenser, who does not care from whom the emoluments are derived. In that case, so long as the process promises positive economic profits of any substantial magnitude, entry can be expected to continue until the total expenditure on lobbying activities rises sufficiently to wipe out all incentives for further entry. As Fisher (1985) puts the matter, "The picture of resources expended on lobbying for a monopoly license until the eventually successful applicant has spent all the rents to be earned is one of some plausibility" (p. 414).

But, Fisher argues, this case is probably the exception. Thus when the rent-seeking battle is over a monopoly that has not been created by government, the pursuit of its possession is unlikely to meet the requirements of competitive equilibrium. "Competition involves free entry, and monopolies are typically characterized by barriers to entry with incumbents enjoying advantages over potential entrants" (p. 112). This is likely to be so even when the monopoly is granted by the public sector, since "[once the license has been granted] ... regulatory authorities may be reluctant to transfer it [so that] rents may exceed even the value of the resources expended to obtain the original monopoly license ... [and certainly] it is unlikely that the resources expended will equal the rents to be earned" (pp. 414–15). Tullock notes, in this connection, that rent-seeking outlays are very likely to be sunk, meaning that entry entails a commensurate risk cost which can itself constitute a formidable barrier to entry. "Suppose, for example, that we organize a lobby in Washington for the purpose of raising the price of milk and are unsuccessful. We cannot simply transfer our collection of contacts, influences, past bribes, and so forth to the steel manufacturers' lobby. In general, our investments are too specialized, and in many cases, they are matters of very particular and detailed good will to a specific organization.... Our investment has not been paid, but there is nothing left to transfer" (Tullock [1980, p. 98]).

Fisher goes on to point out that, even if the process were competitive, an attempt to explain how entry into rent seeking reduces profits to zero is not quite straightforward. He notes that, "in an ordinary competitive activity ... when profits are being earned, new entrants come in and existing firms expand. The consequent expansion of supply bids prices down, reducing revenues.... [But] what is the 'supply' of monopolies generally the expansion of which will bring down price?" (p. 412). Tullock uses an observation of this sort as the basis for the construction of a counterexample showing that, at least in theory, unlimited entry may be unable to reduce the earnings of competitive rent seeking to zero. In Chapter 7, this example will be reported and discussed in some detail because of its implications for the returns to competitive research and development activities. Here, it is rather more to the point to end the discussion by describing the last set of objections that has been raised against the Posner argument.

Both Fisher and Varian, the latter in considerably more detail, emphasize that even where the zero profit theorem of perfect competition is applicable, the costs that equal the rent returns are the private costs incurred by the rent seekers, and those need not all be social costs. In particular, if there are diminishing returns to rent seeking, part of the cost incurred in buying the inputs used in the process will itself be rent, and hence, not a social cost at all. That is to say, the opportunity cost of the corresponding portion of the inputs used up in rent seeking must be zero because, by definition, the allocation of those inputs to the pursuit of rent will entail no loss in output. More generally, any allocation to that task of inputs that otherwise would not have been contributing to output elsewhere in the economy entails a zero social cost, even if the prices (private costs) of those inputs are exceedingly high.

A second reason, cited by Varian, why the social cost of rent seeking may fall short of its private cost is that the rent-seeking process itself may create utility for a number of persons so that those expenditures cannot be considered to constitute pure waste, even if we are not enamored of the beneficiaries. If the lobbying process consists of the enthusiastic consumption of elegant and costly meals by legislators and lobbyists, the expenditure cannot be considered any more wasteful that the expenditure of a similar amount for travel or opera attendance or any other purpose desired by any consumer. The resources used up create utility and so can hardly have been wasted, even though, from the point of view of the person paying for the lobbying effort, the outlay is pure cost.

Varian lists several other reasons why the social costs of rent seeking may fall short of the private costs. The inputs used in pursuit of the rents can provide a producer's surplus to the input supplier (for example, the restaurateur who sells lunch to the lobbyist and his target), and this surplus must be deducted from the private cost because it does not constitute a waste. Second, the rent-seeking activity may in fact use up no resources but simply constitute a transfer, as when a lobbyist gives a cash bribe to a legislator. Third, if the situation would have violated the requirements of optimality in the absence of rent seeking, then this activity may conceivably rectify matters (see, e.g., Bhagwati [1982]). An example of this is when more than an optimal amount of a polluting output would have been produced in the absence of rent seeking, but the latter, by using up resources that would otherwise have gone into the commodity, forces its output to be cut. Finally, rent seekers may spend less than the Posner argument suggests when they act as free riders upon the efforts of other rent seekers, as when one textile producer benefits from import restrictions attained through the lobbying efforts of another but the former contributes nothing toward covering the lobbying expense.

These points, clearly, are all well taken. They suggest that the Posner valuation of the social costs of rent seeking is apt to constitute an overestimate, though as Fisher and Bhagwati point out, matters can conceivably go the other way, making the social costs exceed the private costs (as when the rent-seeking activity uses an input whose production generates pollution). All in all, we are then left with a very vague conclusion—that rent seeking normally uses *some* valuable resources in pursuit of its goal, that this use of resources can sometimes be extremely costly, constituting a high opportunity cost for society, but that, if used with care, and only in suitable circumstances, Posner's argument nevertheless offers a suggestive approximation indicating the possible order of magnitude of those costs.

3.3   Illustration: Corporate Takeover Activity as a Lure for Entrepreneurial Talent[1]

In this and the following chapter I will discuss several phenomena that are widely suspected of having attracted a good deal of entrepreneurial talent into unproductive activities. These examples will be offered primarily for two purposes: first, to offer some further evidence for the hypothesis that entrepreneurship can be reallocated between productive and rent-seeking activities by the relative returns offered in the two fields and, second, to illustrate one of the difficulties the policy designer faces in dealing rationally with the resulting problems. These difficulties stem from the fact that many activities of the sort that concern us here are a very mixed bag, containing some influences that stimulate production and others that impede it.

A case in point is the illustration discussed in this chapter—the boom in corporate mergers and acquisitions in the 1980s. It will be argued presently that the boom in corporate takeover activity that had its origin in the 1960s and reached its crescendo two decades later has both productive components and elements that attracted a swarm of rent seekers. The contention that takeover activity has its two sides from the point of view of the general welfare will be argued in some detail because it constitutes a serious complication besetting the formulation of public policy toward rent seeking generally, an issue that will occupy us in the last chapter of this book. That is, activities tainted by rent seeking are often not entirely unproductive. Indeed, sometimes, as many capable students of the subject have concluded about the acquisition-merger boom of the 1980s, the activity in question, taken as a whole, may contribute materially to the economy's production. Yet its rent-seeking components remain unproductive and constitute a deduction from the overall achievement. This mixed character of many economic activities exacerbates the complexities with which rational policy must deal.

In any event, it is clear that takeover attempts are primarily financial activities that do not directly entail the enterprising introduction of technical changes in the physical process of production of tangible commodities. Economists have, of course, long rejected the notion that the supply of valuable outputs that are intangible is "unproductive," but still, it is in the sectors of the economy that provide agricultural and manufactured outputs that we are habituated to look for technical innovations that contribute materially to productivity growth, so that entrepreneurship that moves out of those arenas may well be entering fields in which the opportunities for productive innovation are relatively restricted. It may then be that such a reallocation of entrepreneurship will slow productivity growth in the same way as a government subsidy that attracts managerial talent away from expanding industries to industries that are in decline. Of course, if it is true, as some observers believe, that the acquisition-merger boom contributed nothing to output or growth, then the reallocation of entrepreneurs in that direction is an even more serious matter. It is at least suggestive to contrast the attractions to exercise of entrepreneurship offered in "normal" industrial activities with the rewards that were provided by takeover activity.

Lee Iacocca, who, as chairman of the board of Chrysler Corporation, was widely credited with saving his firm from collapse, is surely among the most celebrated contributors to the viability of a productive enterprise in recent decades. The compensation he received for his success in rescuing the firm that he headed was widely considered to be generous. Indeed, considerable attention and not a little comment were attracted during the 1980s, the period when takeover activity was at its peak, when the press reported that Iacocca had received compensation totaling $37.5 million over a three-year period, that is, $12.5 million per year. However, during this same period, Michael R. Milken, then head of the high-yield "junk-bond" division of Drexel Burnham Lambert Inc., the division dedicated to supplying the financing for takeover acquisitions, received compensation of some $500 million per year, and others engaged in related activities, including Ivan F. Boesky and T. Boone Pickens, were reported to have earned comparable amounts. It is not difficult to surmise, from the contrast between the two figures, which field would tempt a prospective entrepreneur dedicated to the pursuit of wealth.[2]

3.4   The (Hostile) Corporate Takeover Process: A Brief Review

There is, of course, nothing new about the acquisition of one firm by another. There have been earlier takeover booms. For example, as *The Economist* magazine reminded us (April 27, 1991, pp. 10–12), mergers and acquisitions played a central role in the accumulation of the fortunes of the Vanderbilts, the Morgans, the Rockefellers, and other business giants of the latter decades of the nineteenth century. What is specially noteworthy about the takeover upsurge in the two decades spanning 1970 to 1990, aside from the sheer volume of the activity, was, perhaps above all, the fact that a substantial proportion of the acquisitions involved the purchase of firms reluctant to be bought, so that the takeover attempts could appropriately be referred to as "hostile." This fact, in turn, spawned a number of innovations in corporate governance and financing procedures, representing the enterprising inventiveness of the group intent on making an acquisition (the "raiders") and the equally innovative countermoves introduced by the management of the reluctant target firms.[3] The innovative character of the evolving process is dramatized by the colorful vocabulary that it elicited: risk arbitrage, put into play, junk bonds, greenmail, poison pills, scorched-earth tactics, crown-jewel lockup, golden parachutes, white knights, and shark repellents are only some of the more common terms that entered the financial-market vocabulary.

This innovative type of economic enterprise elicited rather divergent evaluations from observers in the economic and legal communities. Some judged it to constitute a very valuable contribution to the effectiveness with which the market mechanism promotes economic efficiency (see, e.g., Marris [1963], Council of Economic Advisers [1985], Manne [1965], Easterbrook and Fischel [1982], and Jensen and Murphy [1988]). Others have suggested that the economic contribution of takeovers has, at best, been exaggerated (see, e.g., Scherer [1988]), while still others take a relatively strong view deploring the phenomenon and its consequences (e.g., Lowenstein [1988]). Here a rather more eclectic view will be taken, suggesting that takeovers can and often do make productive contributions, but that they also have invited a considerable amount of rent seeking and that it is hard to believe that this has not imposed considerable costs upon society. To justify this conclusion, it is necessary to review some elements of the takeover process, at some points taking a rather heterodox view of the matter.

For the takeover process to entail rational behavior on the part of the raiders, it must either be true that they expect to derive some ancillary earnings from the process, as we will see they sometimes do, or the target firm taken as an undivided entity must have a prospective market value higher than the price of the shares needed to acquire control of the enterprise. Lowenstein puts the matter well, suggesting that there may be two distinct markets in which the stocks of a firm can be traded: "First, a day-to-day trading market for shares, with the payoff in future share prices, and, second, a market with a different class of buyers who are seeking whole companies and are able to price on the basis of cash flows, asset values, tax savings, and other rewards that do not depend on share prices. The bidder on a tender offer, therefore, may be simply arbitraging across markets for reasons having little to do with good industrial policy" (Lowenstein [1988, p. 127; see also pp. 139–41]). In the discussion that follows, much will be made of this two-market interpretation, though one of the conclusions will be that the consequent arbitraging activity can contribute a good deal to the economy's production. The damaging side of takeover activity lies elsewhere, in the tactics of the raiders and the counterstrategies of embattled managements.

The steps in the takeover process are easy to outline. The prospective raider begins by acquiring as much stock of the target company as it can without drawing attention to its purchases, both in order to be able to buy the securities at as low a price as possible, and in order to avoid alerting the management of the target firm so that it can take early countermeasures. However, once the raider acquires 5 percent of the target's stock, the law requires it to make this fact and its intentions public. It then normally makes a *tender offer* for additional shares of the company's stock, commonly financed by *junk bonds*, that is, high-risk, high-yield bonds, thus seeking to carry out a *leveraged buyout* financed, it is often noted, with "other people's money."[4] The tender offer will propose to purchase shares at a price usually considerably above the level that recently prevailed on the market. The offer often will hold for only a brief period of time and only for a fraction of the shares of the target sufficient to give control to the raider.

Such restrictions on the tender offer are said to make the offer *coercive*, meaning that even those stockholders who are opposed to the takeover will nevertheless be coerced into offering their shares because they fear that if they do not do so other stockholders will, and that after the transaction is completed the stock price will drop back to its former low level. (Lowenstein describes such an offer as one under which the stockholder is faced with the prisoners' dilemma: can one of the arrested criminals risk refusal to confess when he fears that his partner in crime, also arrested, cannot be trusted to remain silent?) Some raiders, however, have chosen to make *noncoercive* offers, proposing to purchase any and all stock offered to them (and most raiders offer to pay for it entirely in cash, and not in junk bonds). A primary purpose of such noncoercive offers is to strengthen the position of the raider before the courts in the litigation that is very likely to follow.[5]

The management of an unwilling target company will often have planned ahead and have adopted rules designed to impede a takeover. Such a *shark repellent* measure may, for example, be a rule in the company's bylaws that no more than one-third of the board of directors can be replaced in any one year, so that even a successful raider will find achievement of effective control to be a discouragingly slow process. Such staggered terms may serve as a disincentive to the prospective raider, but they seem rarely, if ever, to have prevented a bid from being made or kept a successful bidder at bay for very long. The target company's managers may also have arranged generous compensation (*golden parachutes*) for themselves in the event that they are fired after a takeover, thus simultaneously protecting themselves and imposing a cost (albeit one that is usually relatively minor) upon the prospective purchaser of control of the firm, which may make the company somewhat less attractive. For the latter purpose management may also sell off some of the company's most profitable assets (the *crown jewels*) and it will often seek a *white knight*—an alternative purchaser with whom the old management feels it can make a viable arrangement. Sometimes management may seek to buy the raider off by offering to buy back any shares the raider has acquired at a very high price (thereby paying *greenmail* to the raider). However, perhaps the most effective defense, where the courts will permit it, is the *poison pill*, one form of which provides inactive stock certificates (*warrants*) to the company's stockholders as of a certain date. Those warrants contain a provision that transforms them into active stocks when it is revealed that anyone has acquired, say, 5 percent of the company's stock. Thus, if one poison pill share has been issued for every normal share of the company's stock, the raider that has paid for 5 percent of the stock will find that it has actually acquired only 2.5 percent of those shares. This can be enough to delay the takeover process or even to bring it to a halt. More often, the effect is to move the process into the courts, with the raider or a group of current stockholders suing to force withdrawal of the pill on the grounds that it is depriving stockholders of their right to sell their stock to someone who is making a very attractive offer.

3.5   The Social Contribution of Takeover Activity[6]

Those who believe that takeover activity contributes to the effective working of the economy most often cite its role in getting rid of poor managements and in providing the incentive for a capable management to work as effectively as it can to promote the interests of the stockholders. Any dispassionate assessment of the behavior of the management and the directors of a firm in relation to a takeover offer must recognize that what is good for management is not necessarily good for the stockholders. The compensation of managements is generally not structured in a way that creates a near perfect incentive for promotion of the interest of the stockholders. Thus, one study by Jensen and Murphy (1986) estimates that for every \$1,000 increase in the value of a large firm's securities its chief executive officer, on the average, obtains an increase in *lifetime* wealth of only $1.40. Though this study, like most studies on the general subject, has drawn some criticism, its qualitative implication surely has much validity. Moreover, the members of a management group, quite understandably, have more than a little interest in retaining their jobs. They are generally well remunerated, and enjoy power, prestige, and a number of attendant perquisites. No one likes to be dismissed from his or her occupation, even one that is rewarded far more modestly. Even the most golden of parachutes is apt only to cushion the fall entailed in dismissal. Thus one can well empathize with the characteristic distaste of managements for tender offers and the accompanying threat to their job security.

However, the welfare of management is, clearly, not the pertinent issue. And in takeovers there is invariably a wedge between the interests of the principals—the stockholders—and their agents—the directors and the management personnel. Most obviously, where management is ineffective or incompetent the welfare of stockholders calls for the elimination of impediments to their replacement via the takeover process. But even where management is competent, stockholders' interests require that management not be accorded artificial protection from purchase of the firm, for that would free it from the discipline of the market. To borrow from Dr. Johnson, the perpetual presence of such a threat (like the threat of hanging) "focuses the mind wonderfully," spurring management on to still greater effort on the stockholders' behalf. The market mechanism is a stern disciplinarian, and Adam Smith long ago warned us that those who are subject to its sway can be expected to use any means they can to undermine it.

While the natural instincts of management tend to impel it to resist any tender offer, and to engage in the erection of defenses against a tender offer's success, such defenses can prove extremely costly, and not only in the direct pecuniary sense. They can prove damaging to stockholders, and can be harmful to the public interest generally. Where such defensive steps work to impede the market mechanism and to subvert its disciplinary effects, this threat is apt to be most enduring and most serious. While the stockholders are the legal proprietors of the corporation, in a large corporate enterprise those stockholders are effectively deprived of virtually any control over the operation of the enterprise. The possibility of a takeover is one of the few forces that preserves the influence of the stockholder. Since most stockholders own only a negligible proportion of the outstanding shares of the firm, their power as individuals to influence management's course of action is ordinarily minimal. Only the most egregious misbehavior by management can unify the stockholders in their purpose sufficiently to achieve a change in directors or top managers. A takeover can be far more effective and more expeditious in achieving such a change, and sometimes it may be the only way of doing so.

Thus, hostile takeovers and the threat of their occurrence can contribute to production and productive efficiency, first, by facilitating replacement of inefficient managements and, second, by providing an incentive for competent managements to work harder on behalf of the interests of their stockholders.

Third, though it is often overlooked in discussions in the economic literature, a major contribution to productive efficiency by the takeover mechanism may well be its crucial role in ensuring that the value of the company's stocks will approximate the true value of the enterprise as measured by the present value of its expected stream of current and future earnings. Suppose, for example, that the current market value of the company's stocks should happen to undervalue the enterprise significantly relative to its prospective earnings.[7] Then there may be nothing any small group of stockholders or potential stockholders can do about it. It may seem that they can be counted upon to rush in to buy up the low-priced stocks, thereby driving the price upward; but such a move is irrational if it is feared that the undervaluation may grow even greater in the future. As Martin Shubik once put the matter, "A bargain which is expected to become a greater bargain is no bargain." Once such expectations take hold, only an outright purchase of the firm, elicited by the low value of its shares, may be able to rectify the price of those shares. The takeover may then be the only instrument capable of preserving the correspondence of share prices to the earnings prospects of the enterprise. This is, of course, the arbitrage process so eloquently described by Lowenstein, with its important role of bringing more closely together the prices of the company's shares in the two markets that he describes:[8] the market for small claims on the firm's future earnings by holders of small stock quantities, and the market for firms purchased, in effect, in their entirety.[9]

The cost to current stockholders of a shortfall of stock price below earnings prospects is clear, because it prevents them from realizing the appropriate value of their share of the company. But society, too, has a good deal at stake, for undervaluation of a company's stocks means that it is correspondingly expensive for the enterprise to raise capital, at least through the use of equity as the capital-raising instrument. Indeed, when the price of company stocks is low, the terms on which funds are available from other sources are likely to be affected adversely. As a result, the company is apt to find itself forced to undertake less than the socially optimal amount of investment in its plant, equipment, and general operations. Thus, the economy, and with it the public interest, may suffer a substantial resource misallocation and a corresponding loss in productive efficiency if impenetrable barriers are erected preventing acquisition of the firm from bringing stock prices into correspondence with the prospective earnings of the firm.

An illuminating way of looking at the contribution of takeovers to the efficient flow of capital to the firm rests on the relationship between the magnitude of takeover activity and the value of the measure known as "Tobin's Q." Q was defined by James Tobin as the ratio between the market value of the firm, as measured by the price of its securities, and the replacement cost of its assets. The evidence seems to indicate clearly that the magnitude of takeover activity has had its upsurges in periods when the value of Q has been low, and for many firms it has been less than unity. This means, of course, that such a firm could hypothetically be acquired for an amount less than the value of its assets, and it should not be surprising that a rise in takeover attempts should have resulted when Q was so depressed.

Various hypotheses have been offered to account for this phenomenon. For example, it has been suggested that the high real interest rates that persisted in the early part of the 1980s and the accompanying macro-economic policies depressed the stock market and led to undervaluation of firms. It has also been suggested that managerial policies such as pursuit of high sales volume rather than maximum profit could also have served to depress the value of the firm, for example, by leading management to resist selling off unprofitable portions of the firm. But neither of these conjectures makes sense except on the assumption that the normal group of small stockholders is powerless to force management to pursue profits undeviatingly and to use the firm's assets to bring in all the profits that they are capable of yielding, taking macroeconomic policies as a fixed datum. For otherwise, it is not easy to see how the market value of the firm could fall short of the value of its assets.

This view of the matter, then, lends support to Lowenstein's view that there are two markets in which firm ownership is sold, and indicates that, left to itself, the price of stocks in the market for ownership of small portions of the firm may well fall considerably below the level called for by the company's potential maximum earnings. In such circumstances there is room for the raider to perform the part of arbitrageur, but such arbitrage can be of great value to society. For it, and perhaps it alone, can ensure that prices in both of the firm-ownership markets approximate the appropriate levels, and in that way, it can make it possible for capital flows to approximate an efficient pattern.

3.6   Studies of the Data

The empirical evidence seems to suggest that all of these benefits are in fact, at least sometimes, offered by takeovers, though any particular take-over may perhaps rarely provide more than one of these types of contributions to economic efficiency. Some of the empirical investigations of the consequences of takeovers have devoted the bulk of their attention to the effects upon stockholders in the target companies and those in the acquiring firms. This is not our main concern here unless one is willing to accept uncritically the premise that stock prices and financial returns are an accurate mirror of the firm's productive performance, so that information about the one automatically also is pertinent to the other. However, that is something one cannot legitimately assume so long as some qualified observers continue to attribute much of takeover activity to undervaluation of a firm's shares.

Still, it is of some interest to learn from a recent survey of post-1980 empirical studies (Jarrell, Brickley, and Netter [1988]) that the evidence reported until the time of writing of that book "indicates substantial gains to target shareholders ..." with premiums in stock prices over pretakeover prices (after adjustment for changes in the general performance of the stock market) ranging from some 20 to 35 percent, depending upon the decade studied (pp. 51–52). The authors go on to report that, "The evidence further suggests that the premiums in takeovers represent real wealth gains and not simply redistributions" (p. 66). In sharp contrast, "Acquirers, however, receive at best modest increases in their stock price, and the winners of bidding contests suffer stock price declines as often as they do gains" (p. 66).

The authors of some empirical studies conclude that poor management performance is indeed a characteristic incentive for takeover attempts: "that targets of hostile bids have many characteristics indicative of the need for external discipline" (Shleifer and Vishny [1988, p. 11]). These authors report elsewhere that, "*Fortune 500* targets of hostile takeovers indeed are very poorly performing companies: the ratios of their market values to the replacement cost of their physical assets are roughly 38 percent below those of all publicly traded *Fortune 500* companies" (Mørck, Shleifer and Vishny [1989, p. 10]).

Another study (Lichtenberg and Siegel [1987]) showed that most of the firms whose ownership changed were performing poorly in terms of (multi-factor) productivity. The productivity of these firms was "at least 4 percent lower" than that of other plants in the same industries. It is, of course, difficult to get conclusive evidence on this subject, since there is no obvious way to measure managerial performance in distinction from other influences affecting the productivity and profitability of the firm.

Still, there is some evidence that poor performance of the firm or its management is not all that goes into the choice of takeover target. A study by Lowenstein and Edward S. Herman reported in Lowenstein (1988, pp. 131–34) examined fifty-six hostile takeovers begun during the period 1975–1983 and concluded that, "In each of the five years before the announcement of the bid, the target companies were as least as profitable as the bidders who eventually acquired them.... What is significant is that on average the targets performed *no less well* than comparable companies in their respective industries" (p. 133). In particular, targets during the years 1981–1983 "were performing about as well as any group of companies in America, as well as [the companies in the comparison control group], and much better than the bidders" (pp. 135–36). The same book reports that, "In a survey of more than two hundred corporate directors, 84 percent said that excellent management was a major plus in assessing potential targets, and 91 percent said that poor management was either no attraction [69 percent] or a minor one [22 percent]" (pp. 129–30).

This implies that if takeovers do make a productive contribution it will, at least sometimes, *not* operate through improved management. That, in turn, suggests that facilitation of access to the capital market through an increase in the market valuation of the firm may well play a part in that productive contribution. Scherer (1988) notes that this is not really ruled out by looser variants of the efficient market hypothesis. He observes that under Fischer Black's criterion of market efficiency, (90 percent of the time) the price of each firm's stock "is more than half of value and less than twice value." Consequently, "[I]f Black's estimate represents the 90 percent confidence bounds about a log normal distribution, for example, then 16 percent of corporate stocks would be undervalued by 34 percent or more at any time. Such a distribution of actual prices creates enormous incentives for would-be acquirers who believe that their estimate of true value is more accurate, or based on insider information, than the stock market's" (pp. 72–73). Scherer also provides material indicating why control of an entire firm may sometimes be more valuable than the sum of the shares owned by small stockholders. He reminds us of the fact that a number of acquirers proceeded to sell off portions of the target after obtaining control, thus leading to the conclusion that the parts of the target firm were more valuable than the whole. Reporting a study by Ravenscraft and himself, Scherer observes that this phenomenon followed a wave of acquisitions in the 1960s and 1970s that were intended to reduce risk for the acquiring firm by increasing its diversification. According to Scherer, these diversifications "were much less than a resounding success" (p. 76). Where organizational complexity resulting from the diversification interfered with the radical surgery that the situation called for, a profitable opportunity was provided for a takeover that enabled those newly in control to sell off selected assets. This certainly illustrates one way in which control of the entire firm may become more valuable than the sum of the values of the smaller stock holdings, though it does not seem plausible that it is the only way the phenomenon can arise.

Whatever the means, it is generally agreed that acquisition does have some effects on profits and productivity, though there is considerable disagreement about the direction of those effects. It would appear to have varied by the decade in which the acquisitions occurred. Earlier studies, reported by Lowenstein and by Scherer, indicate that at least for a time, the acquisitions were disappointing and either served to reduce the profits of the acquiring firms or did not change them significantly. Lowenstein recounts:

The bidders in the early years, 1975−78, found targets with lower rates of return than their own.... They achieved for the combined operations of the two companies' profitability rates that quickly exceeded even their own good results in the years before the bid. For example, their returns on equity rose from a very acceptable 13.9 percent in the year immediately before the announcement of the bid to an even better 14.8 percent in the first year after completion of the takeover, and a remarkably good 15.3 percent in the second full year. No such good marks were earned by the 1981−1983 transactions, which were on average much larger in size. Returns on equity for the bidders dropped from 14.1 percent in the year before the bid to less than 9 percent in the first three years after the takeover. (1988, pp. 136−37)

Lowenstein goes on to point out that this last report is somewhat misleading because the recession of 1982−1983 depressed profitability rates of many firms. Correcting for this by using the Standard & Poor's 400 Industrials Index as a control group, "The overall conclusions remained unaffected, [but] the comparisons with the control group did mute somewhat the otherwise sharp contrast between the successful early bids and the much less successful later ones" (p. 137).

Scherer's report of the 1987 Ravenscraft-Scherer study indicates that U.S. Federal Trade Commission data for 1950−1976 permitted an analysis of the profitability of the acquired lines of business (in contradistinction to the firm as a whole, the focus of most other studies) for the three years

1975–1977, "which on average followed the takeover by nine years. Lines subject to tender offer induced acquisition were 23 percent less profitable on average than otherwise comparable lines not involved in tender offers." To allow for the possibility that this poor performance was attributable largely to payment of excessive prices for the acquisitions, the ratio of cash flow to sales was substituted for the rate of profit on the amount paid for the acquired assets. "The estimated tender offer effect was still negative but smaller and statistically insignificant, showing average tender offer line performance 11 percent less than that of otherwise comparable non-tender lines" (Scherer [1988, p. 75]).

Some more recent studies (notably Lichtenberg and Siegel [1987, 1989] and Lichtenberg [1992]) report that takeovers produce clear improvements in productivity, on the average. Using U.S. Census Bureau data pertaining to several thousand companies involved in buyouts during the period studied (1981–1986 in the more recent study), the authors found that, "following ownership change, [acquired manufacturing] plants tend to experience above-average improvements in productivity" (p. 1). This was even more true of plants taken over in leveraged buyouts (that is, buyouts financed in good part by borrowed funds): "Plants involved in LBOs during 1981–1986 had significantly (about 14 percent) higher rates of productivity growth over that five-year span than other plants in the same industry.... Among MBOs—the subset of LBOs in which the acquirer includes the managers of the acquired unit—the productivity growth differential was even larger—about 20 percent" (p. 32). Presumably such managerial buyouts perform particularly well because, with management on the side of the new owners, principal-agent problems and the conflict of interest that they entail are at a minimum.

No doubt, these results, like virtually every other statistical result in the area, will be the subject of some controversy. Nevertheless, the methods of the study are sufficiently sophisticated and its results seem sufficiently strong to make it difficult to conclude that takeover activity generates no productive benefits, just as the studies discussed earlier make it difficult to accept the view that they are unambiguously and invariably beneficial.

3.7   Rent-Seeking Elements in Takeover Activity

Even if it were universally agreed that, on balance, takeover activity generally stimulates production and productivity, one could not rule out the possibility that it encompasses some elements that impede production. As a matter of fact, it is easy to show that such enterprises provide an abundance of rent-seeking or rent-preserving opportunities both to the prospective raider and to the management of the target.

Let us begin with the raider. Perhaps the clearest example of such a class of opportunities is provided by the phenomenon of greenmail. In starkest terms, one can imagine a raider who has no intention of acquiring control over the target, but hopes instead to obtain enough of the target's stock to make the threat credible, and to make enough of a nuisance, actual or prospective, of himself to make it attractive to management to attempt to buy him out. Such a deal can entail repurchase of the raider's shares at a price sufficiently attractive to him to make it worth his while, in exchange, to go away and promise not to resume his attack upon the target.

Such a greenmail payment is, obviously, a transfer, with the raider providing absolutely no return in terms of production in exchange for the payment. The pursuit of greenmail constitutes rent seeking by our definition because an increase in the amount of money paid out to the raider contributes no increment to the production of the target firm or of the economy. The money's source is the target's stockholders or its employees or some other victim. But unlike a theoretical transfer, it is hardly costless to society, having taken the time, effort, and thought of many expensive lawyers, financiers, and others specializing in such work; having effectively distracted the target's management from its productive responsibilities; and most pertinent to our analysis, having engaged the probably powerful entrepreneurial talents of the organizer of the raid, who, had the rules of the game been different, might have found enterprising contributions to output to be the more promising avenue to financial gain. This is not an invented scenario. Observers reported that during the 1980s greenmail had become easier to extract and was paid out with increasing frequency. It is also reported (to cite a much-publicized case) that, "While [T. Boone Pickens] has made many a hostile bid, however, he has never completed one, settling time and again for greenmail" (Lowenstein [1988, pp. 171, 178]).

Another example of the pursuit of rent by raiders (or their untrustworthy allies) is provided by the insider trading which has led to the conviction and imprisonment of a number of the leading takeover entrepreneurs.[10] Information provided by the prospective raider indicating that some firm was about to be put into play has been used by insider traders to purchase shares of the target company at bargain prices for later resale to the raider. The trader thereby employs the inside information to arrange a transfer from the unsuspecting shareholders who sell him their stock at current low prices, not knowing that the price is virtually certain to take an upward leap. The insider is also likely to benefit at the expense of his fellow raiders who usually have to pay a higher price for the stock when they buy it from the insider trader than they would have paid had they bought the shares directly from the earlier stockholders, before the price had risen much.[11]

Once more, the collection of such rents is not costless to society, and while those costs may or may not be as high as the Posner hypothesis suggests, they are likely to be very substantial. Anyone who has ever participated in any part of the takeover process, as this author once did, can hardly fail to have been impressed with the fact that transaction cost was a very minor consideration in such an undertaking, in which money is frequently tossed about with little concern for the amounts entailed. Such payments, as we know, correspond imperfectly with the true social costs, but the magnitude of the one is surely a reasonable rough indicator of the size of the other.

There are many other rent-seeking elements in raiders' activities. Not the least of these are the lawsuits and countersuits they launch in an effort to modify the legal rules governing the takeover process in a way that circumscribes the target's management and facilitates the task of the raiders. A court victory is generally worth a very substantial sum, but also represents yet another form of transfer obtained at substantial resources cost to society.

Let us now turn from the raider to the target's management, which is more plausibly taken to be defending its rents when its firm is put into play, rather than pursuing new ones. But the social costs are similar. Golden parachutes, scorched-earth tactics, poison pills, and managerially launched litigation all have more or less substantial rent-preservation components.

On first consideration, it may well seem that a golden parachute—a compensation package guaranteed by the firm to the current management if its members are dismissed—is a *pure* transfer from current or future stockholders to management, so that the effort devoted to adoption of such an arrangement would appear to constitute unmitigated rent seeking. However, Williamson (1985, pp. 314–16) has taught us to look at the matter differently. Acquisition of specialized skills and knowledge by a company's management to some degree constitutes a *sunk* investment because much of the knowledge and facility entailed is useful for that firm alone, and is useless to other enterprises. A rational member of management will therefore avoid such an investment if management is in danger of dismissal at some unforeseeable date with no compensation for any pains it has taken to arm itself with the abilities the company's interests require. Thus, if the golden parachute does elicit an amount of entrepreneurial investment in the management's own human capital that is closer to the optimum, the consequences will be productive. Or looking at the other side of the matter, if management cannot escape investing heavily in sunk human capital when it enters the firm, then if it is not protected by a golden parachute of some sort, management can be expected to demand specially high compensation levels to make up for that lack. But under such an arrangement management will have an even greater reason to fight off any takeover attempt, even if that takeover would serve the interests of its stockholders. The golden parachute, then, serves as a means to reduce substantially the divergence between the interests of the firm's owners and its management, the principal-agent problem. In evaluating this matter, it is probably easy to go too far in one direction or the other. It seems plausible that when management arranges a lavish cushion to protect itself from the possibility of a fall, both productive consequences and rent will be entailed, in proportions that vary from case to case. It is also probably true that the act of arranging for such a golden parachute is rather modest in its use of resources, so that its social cost may not be very high.

Matters are likely to be very different where scorched-earth defenses or crown-jewel lockups are employed to protect management's comfortable position against takeover threats. Both of these are designed to drive a raider away by reducing the attractiveness of the target firm. The former entails the acquisition by the firm of assets deliberately calculated to reduce its liquidity or its profitability, while the latter entails the sale by the firm of some of the assets management believes to be most attractive to the raider. It should be obvious that either step is apt to be detrimental to stockholders and an impediment to the profitability and productivity of the enterprise. While the transaction cost of either of these defenses may not be enormous, it would seem that the social cost of these means by which a well-compensated management may seek to protect its perquisites can be high.

Poison pills used by management to protect its jobs may well do so at the expense of stockholders who are thereby denied the opportunity to accept the high share prices offered by the raider. One cost to economic efficiency is that it can reduce the attractiveness of investment in stocks, thereby artificially impeding the flow of capital to the firm. In addition, there is the required outlay of time and effort by capable people that might otherwise have contributed directly to production. That social cost is likely to be increased materially when, predictably, some stockholder group or the raider brings a lawsuit to force management to retract the poison pill.[12]

Legal action when a firm is put into play is as likely to be initiated by management as by the raider, but the rent-seeking (or preserving) objectives and the high transaction costs are similar. The army of lawyers, their legions of witnesses, the sizable staffs, the judges, and the staffs of the courts all constitute an opportunity cost in the form of talent that could have been employed for more productive purposes. And among them there are likely to be persons of imagination, initiative, and daring—precisely the sorts of individuals who in other circumstances might have become productive entrepreneurs.

There have been other social costs of corporate takeovers, or at least so some observers believe. For example, it is widely held that the takeover boom, because of its emphasis on leverage, left many firms saddled with debt, which in turn increased considerably their vulnerability to an unfavorable turn in business conditions. Thus it is said, firms that otherwise could have weathered the recession of 1990–1991 without difficulty were forced to retrench severely, and some of them were consequently driven out of business altogether. In addition, many have argued in congressional testimony and elsewhere that hostile takeovers have cut into the nation's research expenditure. Firms under attack have reduced outlays on research and development to enhance the funds available to management for the immediate battle. Firms that emerged deep in debt were driven to avoid the additional risks that innovation entails. Predictably, this conclusion, too, has been disputed on the basis of empirical evidence (see Bronwyn Hall [1988]).

Rent seeking is not an invention of the twentieth century, but if it is carried out in an enterprising manner its forms can be expected to undergo change. It is as susceptible to innovation as the manufacture of computers, but it escapes the workings of the invisible hand whose act of magic is the transformation of the pursuit of self-interest into the promotion of the general welfare. What is good for the rent-seeking entrepreneur is not generally good for society and is sometimes very costly.

The primary purpose of the discussion of the merger-and-acquisition boom in the 1980s was to illustrate how entrepreneurial talent can be reallocated from uses that appear clearly to be productive, to other uses, whose return to society may be rather more mixed. Thus one of the costs of rent seeking is the opportunity cost entailed in the diversion of entrepreneurial talent from productive pursuits. The hypothesis that an apparently observed reduction in the number of productive entrepreneurs is to be attributed in considerable part to such a reallocation is surely more plausible than the more common view that a mysterious disappearance of the economy's supply of entrepreneurs has occurred, attributable, presumably, to a mutation which destroyed the population's entrepreneurial genes.

4   Enterprising Litigation and Entrepreneurs Enmeshed in the Law

The strategic use of regulation is pervasive. There is a lot of wealth at stake there, and managers would be remiss in their fiduciary responsibilities if they ignored profits available through (legal) manipulation of governmental processes. The decision to invest resources lobbying to prevent the entry of rivals, to form a regulatory cartel, or to impose costs on existing rivals does not differ materially from all the other decisions that managers make on a daily basis.

McCormick (1984, pp. 26–27)

(The innovation stage in the process of technical advance is) . . . a struggle against stupidity and envy, . . . secret opposition and open conflict of interests. . . .

Rudolph Diesel, inventor of the diesel engine, as quoted in Mokyr (1990, p. 155n)

The legal system is another arena in which one finds a delicate balance between what is generally agreed to be invaluable protection of the legitimate interests of society and the rights of the individual, as against the provision of a flourishing haven for rent-seeking activity. It is not easy to divorce the two. Every measure that strengthens the power of the law to play what is conceded to be its appropriate role seems unavoidably to broaden the license offered to those who turn to litigation as a means to accumulate wealth without in return contributing correspondingly to economic production.

This avenue seems to have been particularly attractive to firms whose rent earnings were threatened by a competitor's successful innovations. If the imperiled rent earner can get the courts or the regulatory agency to believe that the innovation in some sense constitutes "destructive" or "predatory" competition, which should be prohibited or impeded by the law, then the rents may be preserved with the aid of the legal system. The opposition to innovation by workers of the Luddite school, who were, reputedly, prepared to use virtually any means to sabotage the introduction of new productive techniques and new products is well known. But somehow, the equally predictable sabotage attempts by competitors, notably by recourse to the legal system, seem to have attracted far less attention.

Antitrust activity is a prime example, one on which this chapter will focus. The orthodox view of this institution is that of a defender of competition against the inroads of the forces of monopoly. But as will be shown presently, rent-earning firms threatened with disquietingly effective competition by more innovative or more efficient rivals have frequently sought to preserve their rents from such perils by hauling their rivals into court, claiming that the success of those rivals was attributable to "destructive competition" that constituted a program of "monopolization" forbidden under the antitrust laws. In initiating their lawsuits or in attempting to induce the antitrust agencies to do so on their behalf, these runner-up enterprises apparently have hoped to erect a protective wall around their rent-yielding markets, by preventing the entry of competitors, or handicapping them sufficiently to weaken their ability to cut down the rents earned by the plaintiff firm. Yet antitrust suits, either by public agencies or private firms, are hardly all illegitimate, and any measures that inhibit recourse to the antitrust laws by those seeking to use them to prevent competition are also likely to obstruct the legitimate use of those laws to oppose assaults upon competition.

This chapter will describe the ways in which regulation and antitrust have been used as rent-creating or rent-preserving instruments. It will also describe the experience with the legal system that has been the characteristic fate of innovators—suggesting that anyone who innovates is apt as a result to be entangled in protracted litigation that is surely both a direct impediment and a disincentive to further innovative activity. This seems to constitute evidence for the view of the United States as a society tied up, perhaps more than any other industrial nation, in massive litigation constituting a self-inflicted handicap upon economic competitiveness. Whether that is so or not is difficult to say, given the paucity of the available evidence. But the evidence will suggest that the extent to which societies such as Japan's are better off in this respect is not entirely a matter of cultural differences, but is attributable in good part to differences in institutional arrangements that provide incentives for the allocation of entrepreneurial talent into other, more productive directions.

4.1 The Use of the Antitrust Laws to Impede Competition: General Observations

Antitrust law certainly has its legitimate purposes and, despite some expressions of skepticism in the literature, it seems clear that these laws have prevented or at least impeded a number of serious abuses. The ability of private entities, notably business firms, to institute lawsuits on antitrust grounds also can be valuable to society, because the vigilance of those who are damaged by anticompetitive behavior, and the determination with which they act, may well exceed those of a watchdog government agency. Still, a law intended to prevent damage to competition can easily be distorted into a rule for the protection of incompetent enterprises against the all-too-effective competition of rivals. "Faced with a loss of sales to a new or established rival, the firm can respond by cutting price, by improving product quality ... or by taking any of a number of other actions that characterize the normal workings of a competitive market economy. Alternatively, the firm can appeal to the government for protection. It can lobby for favorable legislation, attempt to influence a bureaucratic ruling, or instigate an antitrust suit either on its own or by supplying information about possible violations to the public antitrust enforcers" (Shughart [1990, p. 58]).

Of course, private antitrust suits can be very legitimate in their purposes and socially beneficial in their effects. But they can also be used for purposes that are the antithesis of their presumed goals; that is, they can be used to deter or even to destroy effective competition, and to preserve the entrenched market power of the plaintiff whose comfortable market niche is threatened by the effective rivalry of a more efficient firm. Thus the very fact that the antitrust laws permit certain types of behavior to be punished and prohibited can be used directly as an effective means to subvert the competitive process.

This can be true even when the probability of victory by the complaining party is low. Indeed, that appears to be the case. Well-grounded estimates indicate that in private antitrust cases that are allowed to proceed until a final decision is reached, the plaintiffs win only somewhere between 15 and 30 percent of the time. One may well ask why, then, are there so many private antitrust suits, when the probability of victory is so small? Part of the answer is that there are indirect ways of winning, without a favorable court decision. The cost of an antitrust suit can be very high to the defendant, which in the U.S. normally bears all its legal costs, even if it wins, and, in addition, must pay the legal costs of the plaintiff if it loses. The author has participated in several private legal suits in which the costs of trial preparation and the trial itself added up to several hundred million dollars for just one of the parties. Add to this the fact that the defendant must often pay three times the amount the court estimates the damages caused by the illegal acts to have been, and we can understand why even the threat of such a suit may be able to stop an effective competitor in its tracks, or at least induce it to decrease the vigor of its competitive activities substantially.

We can see also that the prospect of being paid triple damages, to which any plaintiff with standing to sue is entitled under section 4 of the clayton Act, is an added incentive for the initiation of private lawsuits as an attempt to use the courts to extract wealth from rivals while at the same time blunting their competition. Indeed, the process often smells of blackmail, with the suit undertaken in the hope of a riskless out-of-court settlement, in which a defendant, unwilling to face the uncertainties of court litigation (particularly if it involves a jury), "pays off" the plaintiff in order to free itself from the latter's threats. Thus, even if the plaintiff does not win in the courts, it may hope to score an economic victory by forcing the defendant to compromise in an out-of-court settlement, sometimes in the process even driving the defendant into financial difficulties. According to Professor William Baxter of the Stanford Law School, out-of-court settlements were arrived at in 82 percent of a sample of 671 private antitrust lawsuits in the period between 1964 and 1970 examined by him (Baxter, 1979).

Moreover, even a small chance of victory can become an attractive proposition when (some) law firms are willing to take the case on a contingency basis, that is, they do not require the plaintiff to pay any fee unless the case is won. Because of this, and the fact that the plaintiff is not generally required to compensate a victorious defendant for the latter's outlays on the case, such rent-seeking undertakings need not entail any great risk for the firm that engages in enterprising litigation.

In any event, there are often grounds for such an enterprise to believe that it can win. Vigorous competition *does* generally make life difficult for the rival whose efficiency or product quality is second best, and it is, consequently, commonly not too hard to make an activity that merely constitutes effective competition appear to be a program of "predation" whose purpose is to destroy one's rivals. And courts are, at least sometimes, reluctant to refuse to extend protection to a firm that appears to be the object of a predatory attack, at least so long as the possibility cannot be rejected beyond reasonable doubt. While the doctrine now generally accepted by the courts is that their task is to defend *competition*, but not to provide protection to *competitors*, at least some government agencies have displayed a more protectionist predisposition, as is shown by the history of economic regulation in the United States, to which we will turn briefly in a later section.

As has already been said, private antitrust suits are by no means all discreditable. But the fact that in a substantial proportion of such cases the lawsuits are initiated by a plaintiff who is a competitor of the accused enterprise certainly strengthens the suspicion that many such cases are undertaken as a means to undermine competition rather than to promote it. "One of the most troubling aspects of private antitrust enforcement is the frequency with which firms bring suits against their competitors. Of course, it is possible that specialized business knowledge puts competitors in the best position to spot unlawful activities. But another possibility is that firms employ the antitrust laws as a weapon to handicap their successful rivals; firms attempt to win in the courts what they are unable to win in the open marketplace" (Shughart, p. 55). Sallop and White (1986) have estimated that in more than 36 percent of private antitrust suits the plaintiff is a competitor of the defendant. The concern raised by this fact is increased by the sharp rise in the number of private antitrust suits, which is reported to have increased from some 225 cases in 1960 to well over 1,000 in every year from 1971 to 1984, the last year for which figures seem to be available (Shughart, p. 54).

To the extent that one can believe that the profit motive is the prime guide of the parties, a curious rule of thumb emerges when a competitor sues to prevent a prospective merger on antitrust grounds. Roughly speaking, when two firms undertake to merge, they are very likely to have one of two objectives in mind. Either they may hope that the merger can contribute to efficiency, by reducing duplication in research, purchasing, and other activities; by gaining from the power of combined knowledge and experience; and in a variety of other ways. Alternatively, the merger may be undertaken in the hope that it will yield market power and permit monopolistic exploitation of consumers and others. Obviously, mergers that promise to achieve the first of these two goals are socially beneficial and merit encouragement, while the latter type clearly threatens to damage the general welfare by undermining competition. The paradoxical rule of thumb is this: if the competitors of the prospectively merging firms protest against the merger and attempt to prevent it in the courts, then there is good reason to believe that the merger is of type I, promising to provide efficiencies that will make life more difficult for the protesting rivals. But if the proposed merger is greeted with silence or approbation by competitors and no antitrust action is undertaken by them to prevent it, then there is good reason to suspect that the merger is of socially undesirable type II, and so is likely to reduce competition, raise industry prices, and so on. Such a merger will elicit no objections from competitors, because reduced competition, enhanced prices, and other exercises of market power by the merged enterprises will all make life more secure and comfortable for its rivals.

4.2   The Use of Antitrust to Impede Competition: Some Examples[1]

Let us now examine a few examples to illustrate the form taken by attempts to use the antitrust laws to subvert competition, and to demonstrate by illustration that the phenomenon is real. Recourse to the law by individuals or firms seeking to protect their rent-generating havens is hardly a twentieth-century innovation. Its venerable history has been traced back at least to the thirteenth century, and it undoubtedly has antecedents that extend back as far as the first laws designed to regulate commerce. While one can take the view that before the passage of the Sherman Act in 1890 there was no formal antitrust legislation that could be co-opted for the purpose, the common law and specific acts such as the English Statute of Monopolies of 1624 dealt with similar issues[2] and offered scope for enterprising efforts to devise ingenious means using the law to protect rents from the inroads of competition. The two early examples and the more recent illustrations that follow are only a selection of many such cases. Their purpose is to demonstrate that the phenomenon exists and to suggest that it continues to occupy the energies of enterprising business executives and attorneys, allocating their entrepreneurial talents into unproductive channels. It is, of course, difficult to determine how extensive the resulting diversion of talent actually is or, indeed, how often such rent-seeking litigation actually occurs in practice.[3] The following illustrative cases are clearly not intended as the basis for such an estimate.

Example 1. The London Fuller's Case (1298). Chapter 2 has already described the important role of the water mill during the late Middle Ages, as the first major source of inanimate productive power. The discussion also described the many uses to which water mills were put, in cloth making, metallurgy, paper production, and so forth. It was noted that a very important application of the water wheel was in the laborious process of fulling, whose purpose was to clean and strengthen wool before it was made into cloth. Fulling had previously been done by human hand (or foot) and a good deal of the activity had been carried out in London. However, the absence of swift streams in the city put urban fullers at a competitive disadvantage to the mill-using fullers in the countryside. In 1298 (in the reign of Edward I) the London fullers consequently undertook a lawsuit seeking protection from the king, claiming that if the country mills were permitted to continue their activity there would be "grave damage" to the men employed in the city. The king rejected their request but offered some concessions to ease their difficulties (Carus-Wilson [1941, pp. 55, 58]).

The records provide a profusion of rent-seeking cases related to water mills (see, e.g., Gimpel [1976, ch. 1])—cases in which the mill owner sought to enforce a monopoly by securing a prohibition of the use of human-powered mills by rivals and even by consumers, or cases in which upstream and downstream users fought for the water's power via a battle over the location of the dam sites and the height of the dams. One case is reported to have dragged on for more than a century, and was only settled, finally, by bankruptcy of one of the parties, thus illustrating one of the strategic approaches still used by litigating rent seekers: by imposing sufficient financial pressure upon the other party (or threatening to do so) one can destroy the opponent or force surrender, regardless of any decision by the court.

Example 2. The Schoolmaster Case (1410). Our second example occurred a bit more than a century after the first, when two Gloucester schoolmasters sued a third who had opened a competing school. The defendant was charged with trespass, and the plaintiffs cited the fact that he had reduced the fee per pupil by about 70 percent. The judges rejected the argument, one of them declaring, "Though another equally competent with the plaintiffs comes to teach the children, this is a virtuous and charitable thing, and an ease to the people, for which he cannot be punished by our law" (Court of Common Pleas, 1410, reign of Henry IV).

Example 3. Kobe v. Dempsey Pump (1952). Our first modern example involves the manufacture of hydraulic oil well pumps by the Kobe firm, which had gathered every available patent to ensure itself of a monopoly. Dempsey nevertheless entered the field and put out a competing pump. Kobe sued, claiming patent infringement, conspiracy to lure away a Kobe employee, and "unfair business practices." As often happens in such cases, Dempsey launched a countersuit, claiming abuse of patent monopoly and violation of the Sherman Act.

The courts upheld Dempsey, dismissed the Kobe claims, and awarded substantial damage payments from it to Dempsey. The decision commented:

This suit was no more than a part of the original [monopolistic purpose] and was designed to nip competition in the bud.... [We] must not permit the courts to be a vehicle for maintaining and carrying out an unlawful monopoly which has for its purpose the elimination and prevention of competition....

To hold that there was no liability for damages caused by this conduct, though lawful in itself, would permit a monopolizer to smother every potential competitor with litigation. (U.S. Court of Appeals, 10th Circuit, 1952, pp. 423–25 [198 F.2d 416])

Here, it should be noted that the court took an explicit stand against the use of litigation with the purpose of prevention of entry, and even imposed a penalty for use of this tactic.

Example 4. Belfiore v. the New York Times (1987).[4] A number of independent newspaper-delivery firms had enjoyed territorial monopolies the newspapers had conceded to them. Steadily declining sales of the *New York Times* by these deliverers led the publishers of that newspaper to conclude that the service was overpriced and otherwise rendered in a manner unattractive to local readers. The *Times* consequently established competing delivery routes which it operated itself, charging fees substantially lower than those of the independent deliverers. The latter sued the newspaper, claiming that the paper was exercising monopoly power deriving from the absence of competition in the "upscale daily newspaper market" and that it was employing predatory pricing practices to drive competitors from delivery service. Both the lower court and the Court of Appeals rejected these claims, granting summary judgment (that is, dismissal of the case without full hearing) in favor of the newspaper. The appeals court's decision stated, "Plaintiffs' real complaint is that competition from the Times is pressuring them to lower their prices. Such competition is precisely the conduct the antitrust laws were designed to foster, not suppress" (U.S. Court of Appeals, 2nd Circuit, 1987, p. 181 [826 F.2d 177]).

Example 5. Allen-Myland Inc. v. International Business Machines (1988). Allen-Myland Inc. (AMI) is a small firm specializing in the upgrading of computers. For many years the firm prospered in this line of work, during a period when the upgrading of a computer's capacity entailed a slow and laborious installation process. Then technological innovations came along that had the effect of reducing major computer upgrades to the simple act of installation of a small and highly reliable part, a process that took just a few minutes of essentially unskilled labor to carry out. Thus the cost of upgrading was drastically reduced, and many of the services of the upgrading firm were rendered obsolete. AMI sued, seeking to persuade the court to impose pricing restrictions on IBM that would have established an artificial and expensive market niche for upgrading services, with AMI permanently protected from the competitive pressures stemming from innovation. The court's decision upheld IBM's position completely (693 F.Supp. 262 [E.D.Pa. 1988]), but this decision has been appealed (U.S. District Court, Eastern District of Pennsylvania, July 21, 1988 [693 F.Supp. 262]).

Example 6. Sewell Plastics Inc. v. the Coca-Cola Company, Southeastern Container, et al. (1989). The Sewell Plastics Company had a preponderant share of the manufacture of plastic soft-drink bottles in the United States. At one time it sold two-liter bottles at a price somewhat above thirty cents per bottle. A group of Coca-Cola bottlers in the Southeast (none of them horizontal competitors), feeling the price was too high, agreed to form a cooperative firm dedicated to the manufacture of plastic bottles for themselves. Each sponsoring firm signed a five-year contract agreeing to purchase 80 percent of its bottle requirements from the cooperative, which had been named Southeastern Container. Within five years of its launching, Southeastern had reduced its cost to less than fourteen cents per bottle, and real retail prices of soft drinks also fell, both absolutely and relative to other soft-drink prices. Sewell also reduced its prices but, with its manufacturing costs higher than Southeastern's, its price still remained above the latter's. Despite rising national sales and profits, Sewell decided to sue Southeastern, explicitly admitting that it was seeking to persuade the court to force a sale of Southeastern to Sewell or, as a possible alternative, to force Southeastern's customers to sign exclusive purchasing contracts with Sewell. Sewell charged the defendants with price-fixing (on the ground that the cooperative's members all paid the same price for their bottles) as well as boycott and conspiracy. After extensive pretrial activity, the judge granted a motion of summary judgment in the spring of 1989 and dismissed Sewell's claims (U.S. District Court, Western District, North Carolina, Civil Action C-C-86-363-M [April, 1989]). Sewell appealed the decision, while Southeastern filed a countersuit against Sewell, in effect claiming that the latter had deliberately used its lawsuit to harass and intimidate Southeastern's customers (U.S. District Court for the Western District of North Carolina, March 28, 1989).[5] An out-of-court settlement of these two suits, reportedly very favorable to Southwestern, was finally agreed to by the parties.

As these examples show, victory in rent-seeking litigation is by no means guaranteed. The courts may and sometimes do go so far as to impose a substantial penalty upon a plaintiff that in their view has attempted to subvert the judicial system into an instrument for the prevention of competition. There is, as a matter of fact, a set of explicit precedents making a firm liable to punishment if it engages in litigation whose primary purpose is harassment or weakening of a rival, though the Supreme Court has recently moved in the opposite direction (see Chapter 12, note 5).

Yet we must not forget that the plaintiff's accusations against the defendants are *sometimes* fully justified. This is, indeed, the heart of the difficulty that inevitably besets any attempt to draw a bright line distinguishing instances in which the antitrust laws have been invoked legitimately and those in which they entail "sham litigation"[6] by a rent seeker. One must not be misled by the illustrative cases reported here, because they unavoidably constitute a very biased sample heavily overvaluing the probability that the rent-seeking plaintiff will lose. The bias occurs because the examples were selected by a computer search requesting antitrust cases in which the court had found sham litigation to have been entailed, since we could think of no better criterion on which to carry out our search (and since, in any event, our purpose was not to provide an estimate of the proportion of rent seeking in private antitrust suits, but only to show that such attempts at misuse of the antitrust mechanism do occur with some frequency). This method of selection means that every case in our sample was bound to have been one in which victory went to the defendant.

4.3   Regulatory Promotion of Rent-Preserving Arrangements

In the United States, for more than a century, it has been customary to regulate the prices and other decisions of public utilities, transportation modes, and other enterprises considered vital for the public interest—those that were either granted a monopoly position by law or were suspected of possessing substantial monopoly power. Some very knowledgeable observers have concluded that over the years, at least until the period of deregulation launched by the Carter and Reagan administrations, the governmental agencies charged with this regulatory task had become "captives" of the firms that they were required to regulate, in effect doing the bidding of those firms or at least serving their interests in regulatory decisions, though some veneer of concern for the public interest served to camouflage this relationship. My own conclusion, based on thirty years of observation and participation in the regulatory process, was rather different. Though no single and comprehensive characterization of all regulatory actions is possible, a reasonably good approximation of the facts is, in my view, that regulators consistently sought to avoid difficulties for themselves by attempting to preserve a viable existence for all firms that fell under their jurisdiction, whether those firms were run competently or incompetently, whether or not those enterprises were positioned by location or other characteristics to serve the market efficiently, and whether or not those companies had a record of sustained innovation. At the same time, these regulatory agencies, in my view, undertook to ensure that no firm under their jurisdiction could enjoy such a degree of success that it would attract unfavorable public or political attention, doing so in particular by placing ceilings on profits that denied any regulated firm the possibility of unusually high earnings, even through the achievement of a record of extraordinary productivity growth and product or process innovation.

It is easy to supply highly suggestive evidence that the regulatory agencies had not become mere servants of the firms they were regulating (as is suggested by the model of regulation just mentioned, whose basic premise is that the regulatory agencies are the captives of the firms they regulate). Certainly this is indicated by the decades in which American railroads were driven to the brink of bankruptcy and beyond by regulatory restrictions. Further support comes from the years during the 1970s in which the earnings of firms in every field of regulated enterprise were kept well below the current cost of capital (so that economic profits were kept negative) by regulatory unwillingness and delay in adjusting permitted prices to costs increased by the economy's unprecedented rate of inflation. Similarly the regulators' persistent fostering of competition in telecommunications during the 1960s and 1970s, despite the bitter opposition of the one firm previously permitted to serve as the prime interstate carrier, seems to indicate conclusively that the welfare of the regulated firms was not the exclusive or even the primary objective of the regulatory agencies. Rather, as I have suggested, their main objective seemed to be the erection of a protective structure that would prevent harm to any of the enterprises under its jurisdiction, not excluding those firms that happened to be so inefficient that their demise would have occurred in short order in an unregulated competitive market, and whose survival in a regulated arena could only be achieved (in the absence of substantial subsidies) through the imposition of prices far higher than consumers would have had to pay in the absence of regulation.

This protectionist predisposition of the regulatory agencies was an open secret. The Interstate Commerce Commission (ICC), whose primary task was (and continues to be) the regulation of interstate transportation of freight, once went so far as to describe its role as that of "a giant handicapper," making certain that none of the firms it regulated achieved such efficiency or other advantages over other enterprises as to constitute a danger to its competitors. In another of its decisions, the ICC expressed its dim view of a system of pricing that adjusted the price charged "over each facility to accord with their respective costs of operation." The objectionable feature of such an arrangement, in the ICC's view, was that "this latter alternative would be certain to divert tonnage from the facilities with the high costs and charges to the facilities with low costs and charges, thus because of the decreased volume of business further increasing the charges at the former facilities and further lowering the charges at the latter facilities. The cumulative effect of such a policy would lead to the handling of most of the traffic by the facility or facilities which happened to be able to maintain the lowest cost and therefore the lowest charge, a result which plainly would be undesirable to the carriers" (ICC Reports, no. 27266, Lake Coal Demurrage, decided July 10, 1939, pp. 773–74).

Before the 1970s such protectionist propensities of the ICC were abetted by the law. The Reed-Bulwinkle Act of 1948, for example, explicitly legalized the "rate bureaus," collusive rate-setting organizations whose members were the regulated railroads or trucking firms. The act exempted these bureaus from the antitrust laws, which they so plainly violated. And while the laws guaranteed a railroad the right of "independent action" in setting prices for itself, without the approval of any rate bureau, the ICC adopted procedures that made a step of this kind all but impossible, for example, by requiring such a maverick railroad to give advance and public notice of any planned rate reduction, and permitting the members of the rate bureau to take retaliatory action in the form of responsive rate reductions of their own, in a classic pattern of cartel behavior. The important feature of the rate-setting procedure of the rate bureaus, for our purposes here, is that every member of the bureau was virtually granted veto power over any price proposed by a competitor, so that no firm was permitted to charge a price so low as to threaten the rents of any of its rivals.

However, there was no such automatic protection against rate competition among *different* freight transport modes—the railroads, barges, and trucks. The result was that over the decades of the postwar period before the great inflation of the 1970s eliminated attempts by firms to cut their prices, price-setting cases before the ICC rarely involved complaints of overcharging, as common sense might lead one to expect for an agency charged with regulation in the public interest of firms believed to possess monopoly power. Rather, in the vast preponderance of such cases the regulated firm found itself accused of charging prices that were too low! These complaints were invariably made by rival firms providing another transport mode, or the charges were brought at their behest, in what can only be interpreted as blatant acts of rent seeking. This situation was replicated before virtually every regulatory agency during this period, and all of these agencies adopted rules that effectively handicapped price reductions. Firms were not permitted to base their rates on marginal or incremental costs[7] as economist observers advocated, but were required to set prices sufficiently high to cover an admittedly arbitrary accounting cost figure that was deemed to be "compensatory." The ICC went even further, requiring the railroads to base their prices not on their own costs but, unbelievable as it may seem, on the accounting costs of the rival water carriers, in order (in the words of the ICC) "to preserve the inherent advantages" of the latter.

Rent seekers were able to have their way not only in pricing, but in imposing crippling delays upon innovations. During the period in question a number of such innovative steps were proposed. "Big John" aluminum hopper cars had twice the capacity and half the weight of conventional boxcars and were easier to load and unload. Unit trains were long trains, typically composed of one hundred cars, that carried a single commodity from a single source to a single destination, with obvious savings entailed (Hoogenboom [1976, pp. 167–68]). "Piggyback" operations entailed the loading of entire truck trailers onto a railroad car instead of unloading the commodity from the truck and reloading it into a railroad car. This permitted a variety of economies, some not immediately obvious, and offered the railroad a competitive advantage by roughly cutting the cost of shipment approximately in half (for a fuller discussion, see Friedlaender [1969, pp. 38–40]). Yet all of these innovations were delayed because of complaints to the ICC by competitors, who opposed the reductions in prices that the resulting efficiencies would have permitted, and thereby effectively denied the innovator any competitive advantage as a reward for making the required outlays and undertaking the accompanying risks. In each case the introduction was, in this way, delayed for years, and in one case at least (the Big John cars) apparently for more than a decade.

The implication of all this is that rent-seeking litigation can, indeed, sometimes pay. So much so that for much of the postwar period many regulated firms came to act, apparently, in the belief that this was the only remunerative activity open to them. During that period, in conversation, it was often remarked to me that the attorneys employed by such firms were a cut above their managements in intellectual capacity and enterprising initiative. If such casual observation is to be believed, then entrepreneurship had to a considerable extent been reallocated from productive innovation to innovative litigation.

All of this changed radically in 1980 with the passage of the Staggers Act and deregulatory acts in other arenas. The rate bureaus were abolished and the railroads were resubjected to the antitrust rules against collusive price setting. Firms were widely permitted to cut rates quickly, substantially, and confidentially (in contracts between the regulated firms and their customers), at least so long as the adopted prices covered the incremental costs incurred in the transactions at issue. The payoff structure had changed.

4.4   The Litigative Destiny of the Enterprising Inventor

So far, this chapter has illustrated the phenomenon of enterprising litigation, a rent-seeking activity that is hardly uncommon, and which appears
to occupy the talents of a number of able people, many of whom, it seems
plausible, would be capable of productive entrepreneurship were they not
otherwise engaged. Suggestive evidence has also been provided (and more
will be offered presently) to indicate that changes in the rules of the game
are capable of inducing or forcing these able people to reallocate their efforts out of the rent-seeking activities in which they are currently occupied.

Now, however, we turn from those who have undertaken litigation
to others who have had it thrust upon them. Our subjects are the
most renowned of productive entrepreneurs—Robert Fulton, Eli Whitney,
Thomas Edison, Henry Ford, and others of their breed—those from whose
careers the nonfictional tales of legendary American entrepreneurship are
derived. Hollywood depictions of these giants show them slaving day and
night with wires, pistons, and chemical retorts, almost never leaving the
laboratory or workshop, to the distress of wives and sweethearts. But the
truth is somewhat different, because almost all of them did, in fact, spend
endless days and hours outside their workshops—in courtrooms, fighting
charges of monopolization, battling against challenges to their patent
claims, and embroiled in ancillary types of litigation to defend themselves
not only from rival inventors, but also from enterprising free riders or
runner-up rivals who hoped to siphon off some of the returns deriving
from the inventions of the fabled innovators. Careful perusal of a substantial sample of their biographies has yielded few exceptions. Virtually all
found that their choices of career as enterprising innovators had enmeshed
them, apparently inescapably, in a seemingly endless ancillary career of
litigation. Before turning to a few examples to suggest the flavor of their
litigative activities, it should be emphasized that the point here is straightforward. My basic contention is that the rules of the game that attract
capable entrepreneurs into rent-seeking litigation handicap productivity
growth not only by allocating their talents into other channels, but also by
prompting them to impede the work of those who are in the vanguard of
productive enterprise.

Example 1. Robert Fulton (1765–1815). Fulton's inventive activity included the design of a rope-making machine, equipment for the sawing and
polishing of marble, an entertainment device referred to as his "panorama,"
various projects for improvements in the construction of canals, the building of a submarine capable of firing torpedoes, and, of course, the steam-

boat. His steam warship was credited with keeping the British away from New York during the War of 1812. Fulton was hardly the first to have experimented with the construction of a steam-driven ship, and he conceded that none of the components of his vessel was of his own devising. But he maintained quite persuasively, as the basis of his patent, that no one before him had been able to put the parts of the ship together in a way that made it workable. He and his partner, Robert Livingston, were the entrepreneurs who constructed the successful steamboats and ran them, very profitably, between New York and Albany.

However, Fulton and Livingston found much of their time taken up in negotiation over patents, in lobbying at the legislatures of New York and New Jersey, and in a series of time-consuming lawsuits, entailing battles, among others, with Livingston's brother-in-law, a former partner, and the clerk of the U.S. Patent Office, who was prepared to issue steamboat patents to *himself* when that seemed advisable (and after he had, apparently, seen Fulton's patent application). While Fulton eventually won most of his cases, the effort is reported to have exhausted him. Indeed, his death came within three weeks of a close and harrowing victory in the New Jersey legislature upholding the Fulton-Livingston rights in the steamboat. But even after his death the litigative struggles continued. The monopolies that state legislatures had granted to the partnership were set aside in a decision by John Marshall, the chief justice of the U.S. Supreme Court, while "an earlier attempt to extend [Fulton's patent] for the benefit of Fulton's widow and children dismally failed" (Philip [1985, p. 348]).

Example 2. Eli Whitney (1765–1825). Unlike Fulton's steamboat, the invention of the cotton gin by Eli Whitney seems to have been as close to a one-man contribution as technological history provides. According to the *Dictionary of American Biography,* "There is probably no other instance in the history of invention of the letting loose of such tremendous industrial forces so suddenly as occurred with the invention of the cotton gin" (vol. 20, p. 159). In 1792, two years before Whitney patented the invention, U.S. exports of cotton amounted to about 140 thousand pounds. Within eight years this figure had grown more than one-hundredfold, to some 18 million pounds. Yet Whitney earned virtually no return from his invention. His 1794 patent was almost immediately inundated by infringements. In 1797 his first infringement suit was tried and lost. Many other suits followed, but Whitney did not obtain a favorable verdict until 1807. "Whitney's boon to the cotton industry almost became his Armageddon, patent infringements forced him to bring scores of lawsuits, which drained him emotionally and financially. Even when he prevailed in a suit and collected damages, legal fees chewed up the award and more. Disgusted with the fight to make the ginning business profitable, Whitney looked to other endeavors ..." (*The Inventive Yankee*, 1989, p. 9).

Example 3. Samuel F. B. Morse (1791–1872). Though several inventors had produced a telegraph before him, Morse transformed it into an exceedingly practical device, by inventing the Morse code, which permitted the transmission of worded messages by signal. For the first time complex information could be moved at great speed. Within fifteen years after 1844, when the famous message "What hath God wrought?" was sent over the congressionally funded line from Washington to Baltimore, some eighteen thousand kilometers of cable had been laid, including a transatlantic cable between England and the United States. "The telegraph had an enormous impact on nineteenth-century society—possibly as great as that of the railroads. Its military and political value was vast, as was its effect in coordinating international financial and commodity markets. Unlike the railroad, it had no close substitutes.... Information had never before travelled faster than people" (Mokyr [1990, p. 124]).[8]

However, after 1844, Morse "could not escape ... from the harassments of almost continuous litigation and detraction. Of all his enemies, Francis Ormond Jonathan Smith, who had championed Morse in Congress and become one of his partners, proved the most unscrupulous and implacable, pursuing the inventor even to his death-bed. Morse's rights were upheld in the courts ... [but this did, not shield him from the] many controversies" (*Dictionary of American Biography*, vol. 13. p. 250).

Example 4. Cyrus H. McCormick (1809–1884). After producing his first reaper in 1831, McCormick apparently had to wait more than a decade before an extensive market for the device emerged, and before it had been improved sufficiently to make it attractive commercially. However, by 1850 he had built up a national business and the machine had swept American agriculture.

He, too, found himself constantly in court defending his patents.

In an effort to obtain the benefit of his unexpired patents, McCormick's rivals employed skillful patent lawyers to combat reissues [of those patents], to find fault in the loose wording of specifications, and thus to secure advantages to which they were not entitled. Political influence was brought to bear upon the Patent Office and Congress. The press was resorted to in an effort to prejudice public opinion. When all else failed, patents were frequently infringed. McCormick battled to the last in defense of his rights and for this reason was constantly in litigation. Eminent lawyers, such as William H. Seward, Abraham Lincoln, Reverdy Johnson, Judah P. Benjamin, and Roscoe Conkling were engaged as counsel for or against him. (*Dictionary of American Biography*, vol. 11, p. 608).

"When he wasn't suing them for infringement, they were suing him.... Opposing sides pelted each other to stupefaction with claims and counter-claims, attachments and counterattachments, writs and restraints ... [and] endless litigation" (*Innovation and Achievement*, pp. 75, 77).

Example 5. Alexander Graham Bell (1847–1922). There is no point in recapitulating the oft-told tale of Bell and the telephone, except to recall that Bell literally beat a rival to the Patent Office by a matter of hours. We need merely note that "Patent litigation to establish the true authorship of the telephone dragged on for 18 years" (*Innovation and Achievement*, p. 140). "After the most prolonged and important litigation in the history of American patent law, including about 600 cases, the U.S. Supreme Court upheld all of Bell's claims" (*Dictionary of American Biography*, vol. 2, pp. 150–51).

Example 6. Henry Ford (1863–1947). Ford, of course, did not invent the automobile. But he was the pioneer of the inexpensive vehicle and of the use of mass-production methods in its production. His capture of the auto-motive mass market, and the enormous wealth that it enabled him to accumulate, are well known. Less widely known, perhaps, is the patent struggle in which he was embroiled during the early years of his success. The Ford-Selden patent battle had its beginnings in 1879 when George Selden, a patent attorney, filed for a patent to produce "a safe, simple, and cheap road locomotive, light in weight, easy to control, possessed of suffi-cient power to overcome ordinary inclination" (Graves [1934, p. 43]. Although Selden was finally awarded the patent in 1895, in the sixteen-year interval he had done nothing to put his idea into practice. Mean-while, several inventors, including Ford, *had* developed motor vehicles. The legal battle commenced in 1903, the year the Ford Motor Company was founded and started to sell cars. When Ford failed to comply with the terms of the Detroit auto manufacturers who were involved in this monopoly of the industry, they sued his company. It was only after eight years of litigation that the issue was finally settled in 1911, in Ford's favor. William Greenleaf (1961) writes: "The economic stakes involved in the Selden patent war were enormous. Few industries in the United States equalled the strides made by automobile manufacture during the years of litigation. In 1904 there were 121 motor car factories. Five years later, the number stood at 265, and the amount of capital invested had increased by more than 550 percent. Had every [automobile] builder in the country been licensed, the aggregate of royalties would easily have amounted to $10,000,000.... [The suit] became of more financial importance than any other patent cause that had ever been tried in the United States" (p. 239).

Example 7. Thomas A. Edison (1847–1931). Edison, the quintessential inventor-entrepreneur, is undoubtedly *primus inter pares* in our group, by virtue of his fame, as well as the broad span and economic significance of his inventions, including the stock ticker, the phonograph, the incandescent lamp, motion pictures, and the electrification of an entire urban area. But above all, he is our prime example because of his explicit decision to embark on invention as a business, turning items out on demand, as it were, from his "invention factory." However, he, too, spent enormous amounts of time in the courtroom, and litigation is said to have covered years of his career. Matthew Josephson, in his definitive biography of Edison, eloquently describes the numerous and lengthy legal battles endured by the inventor. A particularly long and bitter patent war was fought over his "quadruplex" telegraph (during which Edison was caught between the rival barons, Gould and Vanderbilt). The patent struggle over his incandescent lamp was dubbed the "Seven Years' War"; Edison and his company prevailed finally, when the judge in the case ruled that the priority of Edison's carbon filament lamp patent over others was complete. But Josephson writes, "This great legal victory, as it turned out, was virtually barren. It had been won at a cost of about two million dollars [this was in 1891] to the company; Westinghouse [the loser in the case] was said to have been made almost insolvent. And by the time the court's decision could be enforced, only about two years remained before the life of the lamp patent expired. Moreover, Edison no longer owned the Edison General Electric. Well he could say, 'My electric light inventions have brought me no profits, only forty years of litigation'" (p. 358). Ten years of patent litigation also marked his motion picture inventions (which included the path-breaking Kinetoscope), though his patents were again upheld in the end.

Clearly this is a selected sample, but it includes most of the glamorous figures in the history of American inventive entrepreneurship. Other cases offering a similar moral can readily be provided. No doubt, exceptional cases must exist, and it is not my contention that the fates condemn *every* inventor to be driven over an identical path. These illustrations, in fact, suffice to prove my point here, that a very substantial portion of inventors have found themselves harassed by litigation or by the need to embark on litigation against others whom they have reason to believe are embarked on a parasitic course of rent grabbing.[9] Moreover, the litigative activity which the inventor should expect *ex ante* to be his likely fate is apt to be no minor annoyance; rather, it is likely to devour enormous amounts of that person's time and nervous energy. It may well have driven some talented but unaggressive individuals from the field or discouraged them from entering altogether. This is exacerbated by the fact that the litigative process is always, to some degree, a gamble whose outcome may hinge on a technicality and defy commonsense notions of obvious justice.

4.5   The Legal Process and the Cost of Rent Seeking

The preceding discussion has dealt with only a few of the ways in which legal activities can serve as a vehicle of rent seeking. Much has been written about the explosion in personal-injury and product-liability litigation, with huge awards provided by some juries, the enormous costs it has imposed on the practice of medicine, and the inhibitions it has posed for the introduction of new drugs and other promising products.

The role of changes in the pertinent guidelines—of changes in the rules of the game—and incentives for enhanced activity in the arena have been stressed. "Before the 1960s, damages could generally be collected only under a number of fixed conditions—if the defendant was actually at fault, if the plaintiff had not contributed to the accident, if the plaintiff had not voluntarily assumed obvious risk, and so on.... But gradually, judges undermined these conditions" (Brimelow and Spencer [1989, p. 198]). As the grounds on which a manufacturer of a product, an insurer, a doctor, and others could be sued were successively broadened, the number of lawsuits predictably rose dramatically, and more talented lawyers became specialists in the liability arena.

The plaintiff lawyers in such liability cases, stimulated by the prospect of earnings that have been estimated to range up to $40 million per year (putting them on a par only with the financial wizards of the 1980s and superstar entertainers), have proved themselves to be strikingly entrepreneurial and even inventive in finding ways to encourage lawsuits and in discovering novel grounds for the grant of generous compensation to their clients. The newspapers have gleefully reported some of the more bizarre examples. Divorce, inheritance, and other arenas of litigation have also been the subject of the entrepreneurship of lawyers, and much of this activity seems legitimately to be classifiable as rent seeking. Many other examples are easily cited.

The association of the activities of lawyers with rent seeking underlies two interesting attempts to provide estimates of the social cost of rent seeking. Murphy, Shleifer, and Vishny (1990) carried out a number of regressions using the Summers-Heston (1988) data on real per capita gross domestic product for ninety-one countries, or rather its growth rate, as their dependent variable. In addition to a number of independent variables previously used by Barro (among them, real government consumption and primary school enrollment), Murphy et al. include as variables data on a country's "college enrollment in law as a measure of talent allocated to rent seeking, and on college enrollment in engineering as a measure of talent allocated to [productive] entrepreneurship" (p. 25). The results of one of their regressions is sufficient to indicate the flavor of their statistical conclusions: "In the regression for all countries, we find a positive and significant effect of engineers on growth, and a negative and basically insignificant ... effect of lawyers on growth. The signs of the coefficients are consistent with the theory that rent-seeking reduces growth while entrepreneurship and innovation raise it. If an extra 10 percent of enrollment was in engineering, which corresponds roughly to doubling the average engineering enrollments, their growth rate would rise .5 percent per year. If an extra 10 percent were in law, which also corresponds to doubling enrollments, growth would fall .3 percent per year" (p. 26).

The figures are suggestive, though one may suspect that they are somewhat distorted by a two-way relationship. A rapidly growing economy presumably provides a good market for engineers and so attracts more students to the field, thus contributing to the correlation between growth and number of engineering students. The reverse scenario may, arguably apply, to lawyers.[10] Yet the results make sense, and give us some feeling for the orders of magnitude that may be in question.

The second study, by Laband and Sophocleus (1988), calculated two regressions, one with real gross national product for the United States as the dependent variable, and numbers of members of the bar association and bank employees as independent variables, all for the years 1947–1983. A closely related cross-sectional regression was carried out for the separate states of the United States. Both of these interpreted the number of lawyers as a proxy for "legal/political rent-seeking" activity, and their results were consistent with their hypothesis: an increase in the number of lawyers had a significant inverse association with the level of income, both over time and in different states of the United States.

4.6   The Rules of the Game vs. Cultural Predisposition to Litigation

It seems to be believed rather widely that the problem of enterprising litigation is especially severe in the United States, and that the source of our difficulty is the dominant position of the legal profession in our society and, perhaps, some special cultural propensity of Americans to seek recourse in the courts. One study (Galanter [1983]) examines data for fifteen countries and concludes that the situation is rather mixed: "The United States has many more lawyers than any other country—more than twice as many per capita as its closest rival. In contrast, the number of judges is relatively small." In addition, "The United States rate of per capita use of the regular civil courts in 1975 ... [was] in the same range as England, Ontario, Australia, Denmark, New Zealand, somewhat higher than Germany or Sweden, and far higher than Japan, Spain or Italy" (p. 55). Galanter then turns to anecdotal evidence suggesting that there are a number of societies (for example, at the time, Yugoslavia) that are, by virtue of their cultures, far more litigative than we.

But far more important for our purposes is his (also partly anecdotal) evidence indicating the importance of institutional incentives, that is, the rules of the game, in influencing the magnitude of such litigative activity:

One comparison with a less litigious society merits closer examination because it is often made as part of the diagnosis of American hyperlexis. The American situation is juxtaposed with that of Japan, which appears in contrast as a peaceful garden that has remained uncorrupted by the worm of litigation. The Japanese have few lawyers, few judges and a low rate of litigation. It strikes many outsiders as a society that is free of the appetite to transform grievances into adversary contests. Social harmony promotes, and is reinforced by, the resolution of disputes through conciliatory means. In this view the small number of lawyers and judges in Japan reflects the low level of demand for their services, which in turn reflects an inbred cultural preference for harmonious reconciliation and disapproval of the assertiveness and contentiousness that are associated with litigation....

However, Professor John Haley provides a reading of the Japanese scene that argues the inadequacy of the classic view of Japan as anti-litigious. Haley contends that the much-cited preference for conciliation in Japan reflects the deliberate constriction of adjudicative alternatives by successive Japanese regimes.[11] Summarizing Henderson's research, Haley recounts that:

Tokugawa officialdom had constructed a formidable system of procedural barriers to obtaining final judgment in the Shogunate's courts. The litigant was forced each step of the way to exhaust all possibilities of conciliation and compromise and to proceed only at the sufferance of his superiors.... Conciliation was coerced ... not voluntary. Yet ... litigation still increased.[12]

Modern statutes providing for formal conciliation were not "the product of popular demand for an alternative to litigation more in keeping with Japanese sensitivities."[13] Rather "they reflected a conservative reaction to the rising tide of lawsuits in the 1920's and early 1930's and a concern on the part of the governing elite that litigation was destructive to a hierarchical social order based upon personal relationships."[14] Mandatory conciliation brought about not a decrease in litigation, but an even greater increase in the number of cases channeled in the formal process, now enlarged to include additional remedial tracks.

The real check on Japanese litigation is the deliberate limitation of institutional capacity: the number of courts and lawyers is kept small. Haley asserts that maintenance of a small judicial plant in Japan reflects a government policy of restricting access to judicial remedies.

> [T]he number of judges in Japan has grown but little for the entire period from 1890 to the present. Thus as the population has grown the ratio of judges to the population has declined from one judge to 21,926 persons in 1890 to ... one judge to 56,391 persons in 1969.[15]

> Of course many jobs done by lawyers in the United States are done by non-lawyers in Japan[16]—and practically everywhere else. The small number of lawyers in Japan, however, reflects not an aversion to law, but a severe constriction of opportunities to enter the profession. There is a single institute from which graduates may enter bench, bar or prosecution. Places are limited to about 500 per year.[17] Haley notes that "the number *per capita* of Japanese taking the judicial examination in 1975 was slightly higher than that of Americans taking a bar examination, ... in the United States, 74% passed, compared to 1.7% in Japan."[18] In sum, the low rate of litigation in Japan evidences not the preferences of the population, but deliberate policy choices by political elites.   (Galanter, [1983] pp. 57–59, some footnotes omitted)

The moral of all this is, of course, one of the central themes of this book: the allocation of entrepreneurship between productive and unproductive activities is not something decreed by the fates and beyond modification. Rather, it can be changed by amendment of the rules of the game which induce or force the entrepreneur to change the activities to which that person's efforts would otherwise preponderantly be devoted.

This ends the protracted discussion of some of the forms that unproductive entrepreneurship has taken in our contemporary economy. There is, then, reason to believe the issue is a real one. There is also some reason to believe that it is substantial and growing. According to one report:

As [lawyers'] fees and incomes have headed for the stratosphere, so have their numbers. In 1960 America had 260,000 lawyers. Ten years later the number had risen by a third, to 355,000. Then the real fun began. By 1980 541,000 lawyers were in practice; this year [1990] the number has swelled to 756,000—more, it is said, than in the rest of the world put together. In the 30 years from 1960, the number of lawyers per 100,000 Americans has gone up from 145 to 301. Much of this swollen industry is created not by clients but by other members of the industry, as if doctors went round injecting diseases for other doctors to cure. Is this really a boost to living standards?

Lawyers are not alone. In 1960, the United States Senate had 365 paid lobbyists on its register. In July 1990 it had 33,704, 337 for each senator.... There are countless other examples.   (*The Economist*, November 10, 1990, p. 22)[19]

This chapter has deliberately focused on just two avenues of rent seeking—enterprising litigation and takeover activities—because they have attracted a good deal of attention, because I believe they constitute significant problems, and because they both exhibit the same fundamental difficulty besetting any simple solutions. This is the fact that there are very legitimate and socially valuable reasons both for litigation and for the acquisition of firms by outsiders, and that there exist no simple criteria permitting unambiguous separation of the socially desirable cases from those that are detrimental to the public interest. The problem, as already noted, is that any simple change in the rules of the game that makes it more difficult to undertake an undesired form of one of these activities is, at the same time, likely to impede their legitimate exercise. This is a matter to which I will return in the last chapter, where some ways of grappling with the dilemma will be suggested.

5   Innovative Effort and Enterprising Sabotage

The strategy of business—the line of least resistance and greatest present gain runs in the main by way of a vigilant sabotage on production.

Thorstein Veblen (1923, p. 217)

The central point of Chapter 4 was that the less successful rivals of successful innovators do not, generally, just sit by, watching the markets for their products evaporate, as customers leave them for the superior or cheaper products that have emerged from the innovation process. Rather, the runners-up can be expected to use their entrepreneurial capabilities to launch countermeasures, possibly innovative ones, turning to the law or to whatever other means come to hand, to neutralize or destroy the innovator's competitive advantage. In other words, to borrow Veblen's felicitous phrase, those who would otherwise come off second best often turn to "systematic sabotage" of the innovation process.[1] This is, surely, one of the standard components of the economy's rent-seeking or, rather, rent-preserving, activity.

In this chapter we will carry that observation a step further, using it to illustrate one approach to construction of a model of the entrepreneur's activities. For this purpose, we will view the process of innovation and sabotage as an extended game, or as a feedback process, in which one step leads to another, and which generates an intertemporal trajectory whose qualitative properties can be examined with the aid of the standard tools of economic dynamics. We will see that this feedback process can entail systematic oscillatory behavior, in which periods of substantial innovative activity are interspersed with slowdowns in the innovation process. A formal illustrative model will be used to demonstrate that such an oscillatory time path can indeed emerge, and to indicate how it can occur. Probably, it is mainly a curiosity that, as the model shows, chaotic behavior can, at least in theory, emerge.

The outlines of the feedback process underlying the dynamic model are easily described. Sabotage of innovation is hardly a costless process, as the hundreds of millions of dollars it can take to run a private antitrust case show dramatically. Thus, a program designed to sabotage innovation will not, in general, be undertaken lightly. Moreover, an efficient profit maximizer will decide on the budget to be devoted to the purpose on the usual principles. In particular, the magnitude of the threat posed by innovation, which itself is apt to be a function of the budget devoted to the purpose by the successful innovator, will affect the size of its rival's expected outlay on the sabotage campaign. We thereby emerge with a functional relationship in which the size of the sabotage budget of the runner-up is influenced by the size of the innovation expenditure of its innovative rival. But there is, clearly, likely to be a second relationship that goes the other way. That is, the innovator is all too likely to be discouraged from spending a good deal on innovation, if all that is expected to result is warfare mounted by its laggard competitors. Thus, the innovation budget is likely to be affected by the amount of competitors' expenditures on sabotage, just as the magnitude of the resources devoted to sabotage will be affected by the magnitude of innovation expenditure.[2]

This, then, is the two-way relationship that underlies the feedback process examined in this chapter. Such a process, if it is to any degree approximated by business behavior in reality, obviously can have significant implications for the productivity growth performance of an economy.

5.1   The Counterinnovation Response Function

The objective of this section is to describe the first of our reaction functions, which relates the magnitude of the economy's outlays devoted to the erection of impediments to innovation (the counterinnovation budget, c_t) to the size of expenditure on innovation, v_{t-k}, in an earlier period, $t - k$. That is, we will seek to find a plausible shape for the *counterinnovation response function*,

$$c_t = f(v_{t-k}) \quad 0 < k < t, \tag{5.1}$$

where k is the lag in firm B's response to A's innovation.

There is undoubtedly much truth to the observation that while almost everyone feels impelled to speak of the virtues of competition in the abstract, few really like being subjected to it themselves. By forcing one to strive harder or to run faster merely to be able to stand still, competition systematically serves to make life uncomfortable for the competitors. Competition's ability to restrain earnings, for which it is so much admired in the economic literature, is hardly calculated to increase its popularity among the competitors themselves. Moreover, for any one of them, the process is more likely to be disliked the greater the efficiency, vigor, and inventiveness of its rivals. All of this suggests, as has already been implied, that the greater the expenditure by rivals of some firm, X, on invention and innovation, the more it will pay X to expend on countermeasures, as will presently be confirmed by a very elementary comparative-statics argument.

However, that is to be expected only after the severity of competition reaches a point that is sufficiently substantial. When it is below this level, countermeasures may simply not be worth the trouble and expense, particularly if they entail some considerable element of fixed cost. More than that, there exists substantial evidence that, characteristically, *some* degree of competition can be better than none. The entry of a second department store into a shopping center can be expected to attract to the center a considerably larger number of customers than before, thereby benefiting not only the newcomer store but also the one that had preceded it. The same sort of phenomenon has been encountered in the sale of unfamiliar products where the presence of additional sellers who bring with them a considerable advertising budget can make consumers more conscious of the product's availability, as well as its virtues. Thus, in patent infringement cases one can expect a defendant who has been found guilty to introduce as part of its damage argument evidence that its entry into the prohibited arena expanded the total volume of sales, thereby providing some offsetting benefits to the patent holder. While such arguments, mustered in the course of legal battle, can hardly be considered disinterested, the evidence does seem to lend some support to them.

In innovation there are particular reasons to expect such a relationship to arise. The literature on invention and innovation emphasizes the severity of the free-rider problem that characterizes this arena. Firm A's innovation expenditure is likely to confer some benefits on other enterprises, particularly if the latter operate in related fields, so that the innovation is likely to be applicable to their activities. Even if the innovation does contribute temporarily to the competitive strength of the firm that introduces it, there is evidence that in the longer run it often yields even greater benefits to the firm that comes in a bit later, perhaps with a close substitute innovation that builds on the market and engineering experiences of its predecessor. (This is one element in the "waiting game" interpretation of the innovation process, a topic that will be considered later in this book.)

A's innovations help firm B not only by teaching the latter about the novel product or process, but also by contributing to the efficacy and efficiency of B's own innovating activities.

Thus A's innovations may be helpful to B's innovation processes. But they will also stimulate the latter by increasing the urgency of some response on B's part. Whatever A's innovations contribute to its own competitive prowess enhances the necessity of a countermove by B. And so long as A's moves are not so revolutionary as to make the prospects for an innovative response by B unpromising, this course of action may well be more attractive to B than a program of counterinnovative sabotage. But precisely in the same way that a modest level of innovative activity by A can serve as a stimulus to that of B, B's modest competing innovations can, as it were, return the favor, reducing A's cost of further innovation, and increasing A's incentive for that activity.

What is being suggested, then, is that low levels of innovation outlay by A can elicit what may be considered to be *negative* counterinnovative effort on the part of B—steps by B that encourage A's innovative outlays, rather than impeding them. The same argument applies to the aggregation of such outlays in the economy. *Up to a point* innovation stimulates further innovation, without eliciting any noticeable amount of outlay on competitive sabotage of the innovation process.[3]

This can be expected to hold *only* up to a point, however. As innovative activity grows in magnitude, it is certain to become threatening to the well-being and even to the survival of enterprises that are not particularly good at it, and when this occurs, some of them can be relied upon to turn to defenses that are more direct. Beyond that point, it can be assumed that the higher the level of overall business expenditure on innovation, the greater will be the equilibrium outlays by runners-up on systematic sabotage of innovation.

The conditions for this to be the rational response of a profit-maximizing runner-up are straightforward enough, as a very elementary argument readily confirms. For this purpose, let us take $\pi(v, c)$ to be the profit function of the runner-up firm (B), using v, as before, to represent the innovative outlays of its rivals and c to represent B's own counterinnovative expenditures. Using subscripts in the usual manner to denote partial derivatives, since c is B's only decision variable, its first-order condition for a maximum is, of course,

$$\pi_c = 0. \tag{5.2}$$

Thus B's equilibrium response to an exogenous change in the value of v must satisfy

$$d\pi_c = \pi_{cv}\, dv + \pi_{cc}\, dc = 0, \tag{5.3}$$

that is,

$$dc/dv = -\pi_{cv}/\pi_{cc}. \tag{5.4}$$

Now since the second-order condition requires $\pi_{cc} < 0$, (5.4) will be positive iff $\pi_{cv} > 0$, that is, if an increase in counterinnovative expenditure reduces the marginal reduction in B's profits that results from a rise in other firms' innovative outlay, v.

The upshot of all this is that we can expect the counterinnovation response function (5.1) to assume the general shape represented in figure 5.1 by curve CC', with c obviously equal to zero when there is no innovative activity to be opposed, then declining to negative values as v rises; then, ultimately, beyond some value of v, counterinnovative expenditure begins to increase so that c eventually becomes positive and continues to rise monotonically thereafter.

As an illustrative explicit relationship to be used later in a formal dynamic analysis, we adopt as our counterinnovative response function the quadratic[4]

$$c_t = -av_{t-k} + bv_{t-k}^2, \quad a, b > 0. \tag{5.5}$$

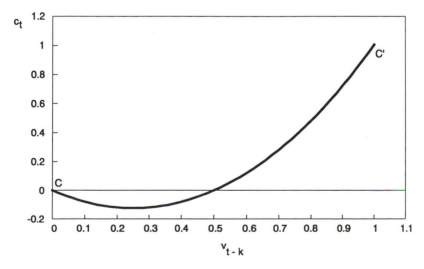

Figure 5.1
Counterinnovation response function

5.2   The Innovators' Reaction Function

The nature of our second functional relationship,

$$v_{t+1} = g(c_t), \tag{5.6}$$

which will be called the *innovators' reaction function*, is considerably more straightforward than that of the counterinnovation response function described in the previous section. It is assumed that in any place and historical period there is a "natural" upper limit upon the economy's level of expenditure on innovation, which will not be exceeded no matter how large a negative value c assumes. That ceiling may depend on the level of the economy's output and accumulated wealth, which circumscribe the resources that society can afford to devote to the purpose, and the rate of creation of new inventive ideas, which limits the quantity of resources that it pays to channel in that direction. Thus, as in figure 5.2, in which curve VV' is the graph of our innovators' reaction function, we see that near its leftward end, where the value of c is large and negative, the curve flattens out as one moves further toward the left.

However, as the value of c increases, the incentive for expenditure on innovation is eroded, so that the curve declines monotonically toward the

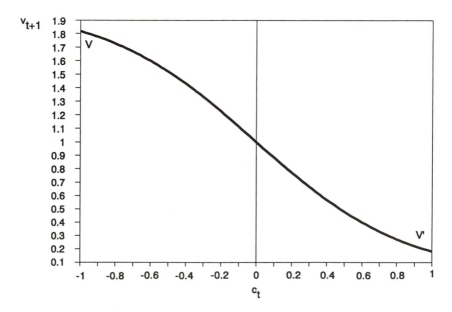

Figure 5.2
Innovator's response function

right, finally approaching a positive asymptote, as the field is left to entrepreneurs who disregard the reality of the sabotage measures that will be
undertaken in response to success in their innovative activities. The illustrative functional relationship selected here for the purpose, and the one that
underlies figure 5.2, is

$$v_{t+1} = w/(r + s^{c_t}). \tag{5.7}$$

5.3   The Innovation-Sabotage Feedback Model

It is now a straightforward matter to combine the two underlying relationships to obtain the basic equation of our feedback model. By substituting
(5.1) into (5.6), or rather, for concreteness, substituting (5.5) into (5.7), we
obtain the first-order nonlinear difference equation

$$v_{t+1} = h(v_{t-k}) = w/(r + s^{-av_{t-k}+bv_{t-k}^2}). \tag{5.8}$$

Note that $(t - k)$ and $(t + 1)$ are two consecutive decision points in time for
firm A. Therefore, in formal terms (5.8) is equivalent to

$$v_{t+1} = w/(r + s^{-av_t+bv_t^2}). \tag{5.8a}$$

This is the basic equation governing our dynamic system. Its graph is
depicted as the *phase curve HH'* in figure 5.3, which is the *phase diagram*
determining the trajectory (time path) of the innovation-budget variable, v_t.
It will be noted that HH' is hill-shaped, with the height of the hill and the
slopes of its sides *tunable*, that is, subject to adjustment by variation of the
magnitudes of the parameters in (5.8). We also see from the figure that it is
possible for HH' to cross the 45-degree ray at a point, E, at which the slope
of the former is negative. Here E is the equilibrium point of the system, that
is, the point at which, clearly, $v_{t+1} = v_t$. Indeed, it seems, *a priori*, probable
that at that point the slope will be negative, since by (5.1), (5.6), and (5.8),

$$h' = f'g', \tag{5.9}$$

where f' is positive throughout most of the relevant range, and g' is negative everywhere.

The negative slope of HH' at E is pertinent because, as is well known, a
phase curve of this form generates an oscillatory time path, giving cobweblike cycles that surround point E (trajectory MNPQ . . . emanating from
initial point v_0). In the case shown, equilibrium point E is obviously unstable, with the cobweb path moving away from that point. The path is
unstable because the parameter values have been chosen so as to make
$h' < -1$.

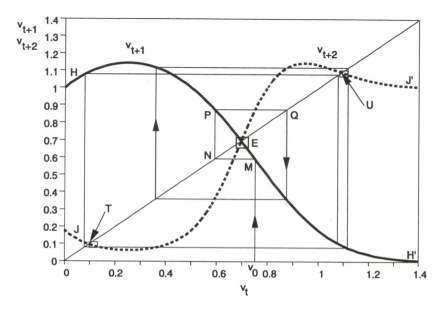

Figure 5.3
Simulated innovation-sabotage feedback with stable two-period limit cycle

However, this illustrative case was designed to yield a time path that converges to a stable two-period limit cycle. That is, as the diagram suggests, the time path converges to a square (not shown), two of whose corners are points T and U, both lying on the 45-degree ray. This rectangle is a time path which, once entered, repeats itself forever, with v_t alternating between two values, call them v^* and v^{**}, to yield the time path v^*, v^{**}, v^*, v^{**}, v^*....

The location of this limit cycle is revealed to us by the second curve, JJ', in figure 5.3. This curve, constructed from our basic difference equation (5.8), describes the relationship between successive values of our variable, not in two successive periods, as in (5.8), but in every other period, *with one intermediate value of the variable omitted*. That is, instead of relating v_t to v_{t+1}, as before, curve JJ' relates v_t to v_{t+2}. The point is that equilibrium in a two-period limit cycle is defined, obviously, by $v_t = v_{t+2}$ (rather than by $v_t = v_{t+1}$, as in a stationary equilibrium), and our objective in seeking the precise location of the limit cycle is to determine at what values of v this cyclical equilibrium condition will be satisfied. To determine the equation of JJ', which we write as $v_{t+2} = j(v_t)$, we use (5.8) and substitute $v_{t+1} = h(v_t)$ into $v_{t+2} = h(v_{t+1})$, obtaining

$$v_{t+2} = h[h(v_t)] = j(v_t).$$
(5.10)

The explicit form of $h(\cdot)$ in (5.8) now, in turn, yields an explicit expression for $j(\cdot)$. This permits us to draw the graph of JJ' that corresponds to the HH' curve shown in the figure, where it will be recalled that HH' is the graph of $h(\cdot)$.

Now we see that JJ' crosses the 45-degree ray twice, at points T and U. These, then, must be the equilibrium points of the two-period limit cycle, that is, the points at which $v_{t+2} = v_t$. For the moment that completes our discussion of the analytics of the time path of our innovation-outlay variable, but we will return to the subject presently.

5.4 Stable Noncyclical Equilibria: Economic Interpretation

Before dealing further with the limit cycle phenomenon, it is appropriate to consider an alternative possibility—the case in which the stationary equilibrium point E is stable. This, as we know, will be so if the slope of the phase curve HH' is less than unity at E, where it crosses the 45-degree ray. In that case the time path may or may not exhibit oscillations, but even if they occur, oscillations whose amplitude exceeds any preassigned magnitude, however small, must constitute a transitory phenomenon, so that the time path must ultimately settle into a neighborhood very close to E. This is what one might perhaps have expected to occur in the circumstances under discussion if the matter were not given some considerable thought.

This equilibrium point exhibits some of the main qualitative attributes that may be expected of it *a priori*. Specifically, we will see next that the equilibrium level of innovative effort will be smaller the greater the value of f for each v over the relevant range, that is, the greater the sabotage outlay elicited by each given level of expenditure on innovation. This is, of course, what one would assume in advance to be the main moral of the systematic sabotage hypothesis: that society's rate of innovation, besides being held down by free-rider problems and other difficulties usually cited in the literature, is effectively reduced by the propensity of runners-up in the innovation process to undertake steps to sabotage the activities of the successful innovators. We will confirm now that this apparently obvious conclusion is valid so long as the stationary equilibrium is stable. However, later it will be seen that in the case where it is unstable—a case that is not inherently pathological—matters can be more complex.

To prove our comparative-statics result, we insert a shift parameter, z, into our counterinnovation response function, (5.1), rewriting it as $f(v_t, z)$, where we define z so that $f_z > 0$ for $v_t > 0$, that is, so that the partial derivative of f with respect to z is positive, except where $v = $ zero. The stationary equilibrium point, E, is, of course, defined by $v_{t+1} = v_t = v$, where we now use v to represent the equilibrium value of our focal variable, and the objective of the exercise is to prove:

PROPOSITION 5.1   For the range of values of v_t where $f_v > 0$ and $v > 0$, we must have $dv/dz < 0$; that is, a rise in the propensity to spend on counter-innovation will reduce the equilibrium level of innovation, v.

Proof: By (5.1) and (5.6), the equilibrium requirement $v_{t+1} = v_t$ is

$$g[f(v, z)] - v = 0. \tag{5.11}$$

To find the equilibrating response in the value of v to an exogenous change in the shift parameter, z, we differentiate (5.11) totally, obtaining

$(g'f_v - 1)\, dv + g'f_z\, dz = 0$, that is,

$dv/dz = g'f_z/(1 - g'f_v) < 0$, since $g' < 0$ and $f_v > 0$.

That completes the formal argument. An intuitive view of the matter is readily obtained with the aid of figures 5.1–5.3. We know from the first of these that an upward shift in the CC' curve, which is what a rise in z is defined to produce, will increase the value of c, the counterinnovation outlay, corresponding to any given level of innovation expenditure, v_t. But the rise in c, in turn, will reduce v_{t+1}, as is shown by figure 5.2. That is, the increase in sabotage outlay will hold back innovation outlay in the next period. Thus, for every value of $v_t > 0$, the corresponding value of v_{t+1} will be reduced. In sum, the rise in z will cause a downward shift in HH' in figure 5.3, thus forcing the equilibrium point to move downward along the 45-degree ray.

This confirms the innovation-stultification effect of counterinnovative efforts in the case where the stationary equilibrium point, E, is stable. As already remarked, that is hardly to be considered surprising. What is more apt to be unanticipated is the nature of the increased complexity of the relationship where E is unstable, as in figure 5.3. We will return to this matter after exploring somewhat further the possible types of time path that open up where E is unstable.

As with all of the family of cobweb models, the explanation of the oscillatory behavior generated where E is unstable, and occurring initially, even where E is stable, is not difficult to account for heuristically. The point is that any burst of innovation serves to induce a commensurate increase in sabotage activity. That, in its turn, dampens innovation in the succeeding period, which brings with it a decline in the intensity of innovation-blocking outlays. Finally, the reduced impediment to innovation once again elicits an expansion in the resources devoted to innovation. In this way, any change in the intensity of innovative effort, whatever its direction, sows the seeds of rapid reversal.

There still remains the question of whether, in fact, these oscillations must *necessarily* approach a stable limit cycle that is two periods in length and, if so, why they should be expected to do so. The answer, as we will see, is that there is no reason that they must generally do so, and that considerably more complicated time paths may indeed be possible.

5.5   Cycles with Longer Periods, and the Possibility of Chaos

The *existence* of an equilibrium in the form of a two-period limit cycle is, indeed, established by our geometric analysis, at least for functional forms of the sort selected for our illustrative purposes. The presence in figure 5.3 of two intersection points of JJ' with the 45-degree ray assures us that this must be so. On the other hand, it offers us no assurance of the *stability* of that limit cycle. Indeed, there is no reason to believe that this cycle will, in general, be stable.

Just as instability of equilibrium point E follows from the fact that the slope of HH' at point E in figure 5.3 happens to exceed unity in absolute value, we would have instability of the limit cycle if the two intersection points, T and U, of JJ' with the 45-degree ray were points at which the slope of JJ' exceeds unity in absolute value. As drawn in the graph these slopes are smaller than this, and so the cycle is stable. However, the slopes at points T and U of JJ' are by no means preordained. As has already been noted, the hill, HH', is tunable, meaning that its height and the steepness of its sides can be varied by changing the values of the variables of our functions.

Specifically, we see from (5.10) that at any particular value of v, write it as $v\#$, $j'(v\#) = h'(v\#)h'(v\#\#)$, where $v\#\# = h(v\#)$. But by (5.9), for any particular value of v, $h' = f'g'$, where f' and g' are the slopes of our two basic reaction functions. Thus, if the response of counterinnovative budgets to a rise in innovation outlays, as well as the response going the other way, are both large, the slope of JJ' will be correspondingly great. By varying the values of the parameters of $f(\cdot)$ and $g(\cdot)$ suitably, then, one can expect to raise the critical slopes at T and U above unity in absolute value. This, of course, makes the two-period limit cycle unstable, for reasons familiar from cobweb theory or from elementary analysis of difference equations.

What is likely to happen then is straightforward. The time path can be expected to move away from the two-period cycle, and toward a stable cycle four periods in length. The reasons are precisely analogous to the departure in figure 5.3 of the time path away from the unstable stationary equilibrium point, E, and toward the two-period cycle, which in that graph is stable. But the four-period cycle itself will be stable only if f' and g' are not too large. That is, they must be sufficiently large to destabilize the two-period cycle, without doing so to the four-period cycle. When the magnitudes of f' and g' exceed the threshold at which the four-period cycle is deprived of its stability, the time path will move away from that limit cycle, and toward a limit cycle eight periods in length, which may now be stable. (For details on this and the material of the next few paragraphs, see Baumol and Benhabib [1989].)

The upshot of this discussion is that the time path generated by our model need not be of the simple two-period variety corresponding to figure 5.3. As the length of the limit cycle increases from 2 to 4 to 8 to 16 ..., the time path traversed before returning to the "initial point" of the cycle can become exceedingly complex. Indeed, if the hill, HH', becomes sufficiently steep, the complexity of the cyclical pattern can reach a sort of limiting qualitative state—the state referred to in the mathematical literature as "chaos." One may well be skeptical about the applicability of this currently fashionable concept to our subject. Still, since we cannot rule out the possibility of chaotic behavior here, a few words on the topic seem appropriate.

5.6   The Implications of the Possibility of Chaos for Our Analysis

The term *chaos* does not seem to have been assigned any agreed-upon formal definition. However, its general attributes will indicate what is entailed. Pure chaotic behavior refers to a time path generated by a perfectly *deterministic* model in which the aggregation of a number of cycles, the length of some of them exceeding any preassigned finite bound, yields a trajectory that appears to undergo (frequent) random disturbances. Indeed, none of the standard tests of randomness seems to be capable of distinguishing between behavior that is subject to truly random shocks and behavior that is perfectly deterministic but chaotic. Moreover, a truly chaotic time path will ultimately depart from any time path characterized by cycles that are finite in length, never returning to it.

Two other phenomena that are particularly disturbing are encountered in chaotic regimes: (1) *abrupt qualitative changes in time path*, meaning that the time path generated by a simple chaotic model can display a fairly simple and relatively repetitious pattern for a very considerable number of periods, and then suddenly and completely without warning switch to a pattern that is entirely different, and, after some periods, it may switch again, equally unexpectedly; and (2) *extreme sensitivity to changes in parameter values and initial conditions*, meaning that a tiny change in, say, the fifth decimal place of one of the parameters of the model or in the initial value of one of its variables can produce so great a qualitative change in the time path as to transform it unrecognizably from the time path generated before the change.

These last two properties are important for economics because they suggest that in a chaotic regime forecasting may be all but impossible. The first of the preceding attributes, the propensity to abrupt qualitative change, effectively precludes extrapolation, which relies for whatever validity it may have on the premise that the future, in some respects, will be a mere continuation of the past. Similarly, in a chaotic regime the second of the two preceding properties effectively undermines the alternative analytic approach to forecasting: the use of structural models of the underlying relationships and econometric estimates of their parameter values. For if an error in the fifth decimal place can yield a time-path projection that bears no resemblance to the one that is really sought, then the inherent inaccuracy of economic observations may well force us to give up that avenue to forecasting altogether, wherever the presence of chaos is suspected.

This, however, is peripheral to the main concern of this chapter—analysis of the consequences of the counterinnovative activities of runners-up upon the level of innovation that one can expect to be achieved by the economy. We now return to this subject.

5.7 Counterinnovative Effort and Innovative Outlay Where Stationary Equilibrium Is Unstable

We have seen in an earlier section of this chapter that where the stationary equilibrium point is stable the comparative-statics properties of the relation between intensity of counterinnovation response and the level of innovative outlays are precisely of the sort that should be expected. A rise in the propensity to sabotage, that is, an upward shift in the counterinnovation response function, will reduce the equilibrium level of the economy's outlay on innovation. However, where that equilibrium is unstable and some form of limit cycle (of greater or lesser complexity), or even a chaotic regime, prevails, matters need not be so straightforward.

Intuition may suggest the hypothesis that when a limit cycle in our model surrounds the stationary equilibrium point, E, in the phase diagram, a rise in the sabotage propensity, as it shifts E toward the origin, will tend to move the pertinent limit cycle in the same direction. A glance at figure 5.3 immediately suggests two reasons why that need not be so. First, E is, clearly, not at the center point of the two corner points, T and U, of the limit cycle rectangular trajectory. Since E is not located in the center of that rectangle, it may well move further toward, say, corner T, while T remains stationary or even moves away from the origin. Second, while there is "plenty of room" for E to move toward the origin, T is already "fairly close" to it, and may not be able to go much farther in that direction. What this means, clearly, is that the limit cycle solution itself may be approaching a corner and that, at such a corner, increases in the propensity to sabotage may be incapable of shifting the limit cycle path toward a level of innovation outlays that is lower, say, in terms of the average value of v.

A corner solution of the sort just mentioned is illustrated in figure 5.4 which, while only representing a particular case, can permit some degree of generalization without great difficulty. We see here that the time path has ended up in a two-period limit cycle, JABH, where point J lies at the origin of the phase diagram. Incidentally, the parameter values in figure 5.4 are

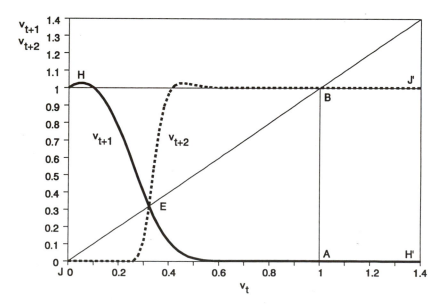

Figure 5.4
Simulated innovation-sabotage feedback with corner solution

identical with those of 5.3, except that the value of b in the counterinnovation response function (5.5) has been multiplied fivefold. A moment's glance at (5.5) confirms that b can be treated as the shift parameter, z, of Proposition 5.1, a rise in the value of b shifting $f(\cdot)$ upward.

Now we see that the lefthand corner of the limit cycle rectangle has moved downward and to the left just as far as it can go, since v must obviously be nonnegative. What about the upper righthand corner, B? This, too, cannot be moved downward any further by any additional rise in the value of b, since the height of B is equal to that of H, the leftmost point on the phase curve, corresponding to $v_t = 0$. We know that this height cannot be changed by a modification of the value of b in our illustrative functions, since by (5.8a) the height of HH' just above the origin (where $v_t = 0$) is equal to $w/(r + 1)$, where neither w nor r is a function of b. From this we conclude:

PROPOSITION 5.2 Where the time path is characterized by a stable two-period limit cycle, and the lower of the two values assumed by v in this cycle is zero, an upward shift in the counterinnovation response function need not produce any change in the time path of innovation outlay, v, and so it will then not reduce the mean value of innovation outlay. In particular, this will be true if the upward shift in the response function does not affect the value of the vertical intercept of the phase curve, HH'. (It should be clear that a similar proposition must hold for a phase curve that yields a stable limit cycle of *any* duration.)

From this discussion we cannot conclude that there is no general tendency for an upward shift in the counterinnovation response function to depress average innovation outlays. We can only say that there exists a set of cases encompassing nonzero ranges of the values of the pertinent parameters in which no such depressing effect will manifest itself.

However, the innovation-impediment problem for society may conceivably reassert itself in another form. That is, the effects of sabotage efforts may still depress the stream of innovation *benefits* enjoyed by society, even if it does not reduce the total *expenditure* over time that is devoted to innovation. For, once cyclical behavior enters the matter, these expenditures will necessarily vary from year to year, and the degree of variability of the outlays must, obviously, vary with the amplitude of the oscillations. It is more than plausible that a stop-go pattern of injection of resources into the innovative process will entail sufficient disruption to reduce the innovative yield of a given outlay of resources below what could have been achieved had the influx of resources been steady and reliable. In other words, we may take the stream of innovation flow to be a function $i(v, \sigma)$ of both the magnitude of the expenditures for the purpose and the variability (here represented by their standard deviation, σ) of their magnitude. In that case, even if an enhanced sabotage propensity does not decrease the size of the *funds* devoted to innovation, it may nevertheless succeed in reducing what society gets for this money. This possibility may be particularly pertinent in a chaotic regime, where fluctuations can be large, and are certainly bound to be unpredictable, thereby undermining the reliability of any planning efforts.

In a general way, the more formal investigation of this chapter emerges with results consistent with the obvious *a priori* notion that efforts to sabotage innovation, which appear to be a not insignificant component of contemporary rent-seeking (rent-preserving) activity, can be an impediment to innovation that is, perhaps, of substantial proportions. Still the analysis has suggested that there can be exceptional cases, whose degree of prevalence can only be gauged by empirical investigation. But the model used in the chapter has also raised other disturbing possibilities that are rather less obvious. The introduction of another source of fluctuation into the workings of the economy, and even the remote possibility of chaos, are hardly virtues of this form of rent-seeking entrepreneurship.

6 Innovation as Routine Process and Its Depressing Effect on Profit

[The entrepreneur's innovative] function is already losing importance and is bound to lose it at an accelerating rate.... For ... innovation itself is being reduced to routine. Techno-logical progress is increasingly becoming the work of trained specialists who turn out what is required to make it work in predictable ways.

Schumpeter (1942, p. 132)

Invention was once ... simply a nonroutine *economic activity, though an economic activity nonetheless. Increasingly, it has become a full-time, continuing activity of business enterprise, with a routine of its own.*

Schmookler (1966, p. 208)

The preceding chapters have concerned themselves with circumstances in which entrepreneurial talent can be lured away from productive innova-tion, when prospects elsewhere become more attractive. That is, we have considered the possibility that entrepreneurs will, at particular times and in particular social and political circumstances, be attracted away from devot-ing themselves to technical innovation, as the *supply* of entrepreneurs is drawn in other directions. This chapter and the next consider *demand*-side forces that may affect the allocation of entrepreneurial talent in similar directions. We will examine the partial transformation of the innovation process which has changed the affected portions of the activity from an entrepreneurial to a managerial affair. Specifically, we will suggest that the demand for entrepreneurial talent as an instrument of technical change may have declined as firms have increasingly taken over the process of technical change, making it an internal affair governed by the bureaucratic and mana-gerial procedures that also control many of the other activities of the large corporation.

Among the consequences of this development is a marked change in the profits to be expected from innovation. Indeed, it will be suggested that there is a two-way relationship here—the nature of the profit-earning mechanism has driven firms toward routinization of the innovation process, and routinization, in turn, has tended to limit the resulting profits. We have seen that the engine of growth in Schumpeter's early model is the extraordinary profit that innovation promises to the lone entrepreneur. But in one of the many industries composed of a multiplicity of rival and actively innovating firms, a stream of viable innovations can be insufficient to ensure positive economic profits to a particular enterprise. Rather, as will be argued in this chapter, it is often necessary for that firm's innovative performance to exceed that of its competitors. Consequently, in a number of industries in which rapid innovation has become the norm, many managements have come to feel that they cannot afford to leave their innovations to chance—to the fortuitous appearance of new ideas often contributed in unpredictable fashion by sources outside the firm, and as likely to be offered to other enterprises as to itself. Rather, such firms have come to treat the generation of new techniques and, even more, of new products as a *routine*, albeit critical, element of their operations, one that is built into the company's organization and budgeted like any of its other activities. Specialized persons are assigned full-time to this task, and elaborate facilities are put at their disposal. Although this may not remove the uncertainty from any one of the innovation-development projects, it increases the likelihood that *some* innovations will emerge from the effort in reasonably regular intervals.

At least two consequences follow from this routinization phenomenon. The first is an implication relevant primarily to the parochial concerns of the economic theorist, for it may restore something of the pertinence of the optimality calculations which, I have argued earlier, can hardly cast much light on the untidy decision processes of the true entrepreneur, but which *can* offer very substantial insights into the more regularly structured activities of the R&D (research and development) manager.

Routinization has a second consequence with far more general significance. This relates to the profitability of outlays on technical change. Because of the sometimes heavy costs of the innovation process it follows that the most innovative firm will not necessarily be the one that is most profitable, since the high costs of its extraordinary innovation efforts may well offset much, if not all, of the resulting gain. This conclusion, clearly, differs considerably from that which may be suggested by a superficial reading of Schumpeter.

Moreover, if entry is absolutely free, then, *ex ante*, the representative firm can expect *no* economic profit from its routine inventive-innovative activity, no matter how rapid the rate of technological progress it is able to achieve. In a world that is perfectly competitive or perfectly contestable, every enterprise will be forced, in order to survive, to undertake the optimal amount of innovation expenditure. But the competition of other innovating firms means that, unless it has some extraordinary talent or other superior inputs at its disposal, it cannot expect to receive any economic profits for its pains. Routinized innovation cannot, in such circumstances, promise any more profit than similarly routinized outlays on machinery or marketing, and even any unusual and continued innovative success attributable to superior personnel or other superior inputs will go to the suppliers of those inputs in the form of rents, rather than yielding economic profits. Though it will be suggested that the innovation process itself may require some modification of this conclusion because it can impede entry and exit to some degree, reality seems to offer more than a few examples consistent with the picture that associates no more than normal profits with innovative outlays, a picture clearly very different from that painted by the Schumpeterian model.

Before proceeding with the substance of the discussion, one terminological point must be made. In this chapter it will generally be convenient to use the term *innovation* in an inclusive, portmanteau sense, to encompass *all* the pertinent terms—the processes of *invention*, of successive *improvement* before introduction, as well as of *introduction* itself, which is what the term usually connotes in the literature.

6.1   Competitive Pressures and the Routinization of Innovation

Observation appears to confirm that in reality the innovation process has veered toward becoming yet another humdrum activity of the firm, with corporate R&D taking over a substantial portion of the field and transforming it into a preprogrammed activity. This is not to say that it has altogether preempted the work of the innovating entrepreneur, which may still account for the most spectacular and revolutionary of the economy's innovations. But from the evidence offered by so many observers that much productivity growth is attributable to the accumulation of small improvements and minor technical modifications of preexisting products and processes, it becomes clear that the routinized portion of the innovation flow is likely to be of substantial significance (see, e.g., Rosenberg [1982, pp. 62–70]).

Quite a few observers, following Schumpeter's recognition of the phenomenon (1947, ch. 12), have remarked on the growing share of the economy's innovations that flow in a routine manner from ongoing operations of the corporation. The innovation process is typically carried out by a division of the firm that has been assigned the task of producing the flow of inventions among which management can pick and choose, deciding when and how they should be introduced (see, e.g., Scherer [1980, pp. 408–10]). Routinization is, perhaps, illustrated most unambiguously in the automobile industry, where the annual introduction of new models, obviously not all of them equally novel, has long been standard operating procedure. The securities market often is highly responsive to the firm's performance in the introduction of novel processes and products. The price of the firm's stock is apt to suffer if anticipations are disappointed either because a new product does not match up to expectations or fails to appear on schedule. The financial pages of newspapers are full of stories of this sort, particularly stories pertaining to computer hardware, with new models anticipated well before their actual emergence.

Even as early as 1953, according to Schmookler (1957), some 60 percent of the patents granted derived from business firms, with the remaining approximately 40 percent contributed by independent inventors. Of the business-derived patents, some two-thirds were contributed by firms' R&D personnel, and the bulk of the remaining third by supervisors, engineers, and scientists in the operating end of industry (for more recent evidence, see Griliches [1989, pp. 291–330]).

The logic of the Schumpeterian analysis suggests that this phenomenon is hardly fortuitous. The very nature of the pursuit of profit presses firms in this direction. To see why this is so it is necessary to modify the standard Schumpeterian scenario in which a single entrepreneur shares the field with no one but a host of prospective imitators. Let us posit instead, rather more in tune with reality, that the market contains a number of innovating firms, all of which are introducing product and process changes, perhaps regularly, perhaps intermittently, with varying degrees of success.

In a technologically progressive industry in which product and process change is a way of life, every firm will be forced to participate and, in the absence of collusive arrangements, to strive constantly to outperform at least most of the others. Even the firm that does introduce new products and/or cost-cutting processes can find itself at a serious competitive disadvantage if its rivals succeed in bringing out new products that are even more attractive to buyers and process innovations that cut costs at a rate even more rapid. The consequence is that no firm in such an industry is apt to risk leaving its technical changes to chance. Rather, firms will be driven to organize their product and process development into an orderly and ongoing activity which offers reasonable assurance of a flow of viable novelties. Innovation will then, so far as possible, be transformed into a routine and predictable process, one that lends itself to the humdrum talents of capable managers and relies less than the unorganized innovation process on the boldness and imagination of the entrepreneur.[1]

There can be little question that all this is standard in a wide variety of firms in reality, most notably in telecommunications, computer manufacturing, and pharmaceuticals. But it is also true in many other industries, all of which devote a substantial staff and substantial facilities largely or exclusively to the creation of new products and processes. The control of such facilities is normally in the hands of persons who are clearly managers rather than entrepreneurs, and many of these undertakings are subjected to complex bureaucratic controls that discourage free-swinging and heterodox approaches to the task. This is not the realm of the unexpected—of the unrestricted exercise of imagination and initiative that is the stuff of entrepreneurship. It is, rather, the domain of memoranda, rigid cost controls, and standardized procedures that are the hallmark of trained management.[2] And as we have seen, there is reason to believe that such routine processes account for the preponderant part of private outlays on research and innovation in today's industrial economies. There seems to be little reason to expect the role of routinized innovation to narrow.

6.2   Routinized Innovation, Sunk Costs, and Optimal R&D Expenditure Flow

It has already been noted here that when innovation becomes routine one must be prepared to modify sharply the notion that it is usually a source of economic profits. We will see now that, even if its products prove to be exceedingly viable and their usage enduring, there is no ground on which to expect the profits of the innovator to be positive in general. There are two reasons for this. First, the economic status of the pertinent costs can change drastically when one transfers to a scenario in which innovation is routine from one in which it is sporadic and heavily dependent on happenstance. Second, where processes are routine, current competition together with freedom of entry may be able to reduce expected economic profits toward zero.

We begin with the first of these matters—the difference between the roles of innovation costs under routine and nonroutine innovation. When innovation is an irregular process with inventions apparently (though probably not really) becoming available by happenstance at fortuitous intervals, so far as the firm is concerned, much of its cost constitutes a sunk outlay of the past, a cost whose future counterpart cannot now be planned and which, therefore, should be ignored in "rational" current decisions. This is even more clearly so for the outlays of the single-invention producer—the entrepreneur or the group that devotes, perhaps, even a lifetime of effort to one innovation. The investment in the project is clearly a sunk outlay whose magnitude should, in a rational decision process, affect neither prices nor marketing decisions on the day the innovation is made available to users.

Matters become radically different when the firm regularly adopts a budget that lays out the funds to be used for the purchase of equipment and the hiring of personnel devoted primarily to invention and innovation. Such continuing outlays must be planned, and the firm that innovates most may not be the most profitable if its innovation costs are disproportionately high. There is then apt to be an intermediate level of innovative outlay for the firm that is optimal in terms of its objectives.

The role of sunk costs will be critical in the discussion of this and the following sections for a number of reasons. At this point it is important because there are circumstances in which the magnitudes of the sunk costs *should* affect the outcome of the decision process, and other circumstances in which they should not. The standard conclusion in the economic literature that rational decision makers should ignore sunk costs because bygones are bygones and are not subject to retrospective modification by current acts is quite right if interpreted with care. But sunk costs *do* matter *before they are incurred*; in fact, they can make an enormous difference. They can even restore a role to costs sunk in the past if the decision maker can learn something about the future from the history of costs sunk earlier. For example, a country that expropriates foreign investments, believing that foreigners can no longer do anything about them, is very likely to find those foreigners much more reluctant to sink capital in that country thereafter. The dependence of current and future cost-sinking decisions on the experience of the past is particularly important in a continuing process in which such outlays are required at regular intervals. There, sunk costs and the returns to them clearly *do* matter for current and future decisions, and cannot be left out of account in a rational decision process.

For our discussion, the distinction between sunk costs that are irrelevant and those that are directly pertinent corresponds, at least roughly, to the difference between invention produced more or less by happenstance and invention derived from a routine and continuing process. Where an act of invention is a unique event, even if, as is so often true, it has required substantial outlay of effort and capital to bring its product to a usable state, those past outlays become irrelevant bits of ancient history once the product reaches the market. All that matters is the revenue that it can generate on the market, whether or not past outlays are covered by them. If the returns are insufficient to cover the debts incurred through the sunk outlays of the past, it will matter to the proprietors of the innovating firm who may face bankruptcy (though "unsinking" those costs will be impossible). However, this still may not matter to society, since the firm's failure may merely transfer the assets to other hands.

A critical implication of this argument for such nonroutinely produced innovations is that the greater the change in revenues or future production costs they contribute, the more successful they are apt to be, regardless of the cost incurred in the processes of invention, development, and innovation. If innovation A cuts production costs 10 percent more than B, it will be the more successful on the competitive marketplace, regardless of the relative sunk costs incurred by the two innovations, all other things being equal. The same will be true of the new product that elicits the greater shift in demand. This is obvious if both innovating firms have gone bankrupt and their successors escape any share in their sunk costs; but it can be equally true if no such transfer has taken place. For once-and-for-all innovation processes, the sunk innovation costs can indeed be irrelevant ancient history.

Matters are patently different if the innovation process and the cost sinking it entails are continuous. Here tomorrow's sunk costs are still entirely variable today, and they must affect any rational decision on the magnitude of the flow of resources to be devoted to innovation. This, in turn, will presumably determine the expected frequency of the innovations that emerge as well as what we may call the "magnitude" of the typical innovation, as measured by the percentage cost reduction or the percentage outward shift in demand that it makes possible. It will no longer be true that what we may think of as the innovation assembly line that yields the most revolutionary innovations will be the most successful privately, or make the greatest contribution socially, if the sunk costs of the assembly line that produces the innovations of greatest magnitude are disproportionately larger than those that yield more modest changes in products or productive techniques.

6.3   Competition and Expected Profits under Routine Innovation

Where the firm's R&D activities become as routine as its warehousing or its marketing, one would expect from standard analysis that the presence of anything resembling absolute freedom of entry (perfect contestability) would drive the firm's *expected* economic profits toward zero, no matter how effectively it operated its warehouses, ran its marketing, or conducted its routine innovation. There would seem to be nothing special about use of innovation as a garden-variety instrument of competition that would endow it with a capacity greater than that of any other routine activity of the firm to generate economic profits. Market pressures should force every firm to select the optimal level of investment in innovation, and entry should reduce prices or raise input costs sufficiently to squeeze out any profits. While some firms will be better at the game than others, the superior inputs that are the source of this superiority in performance will capture any remaining surplus in the form of higher compensation—differential rent. We will see that there is reason to believe that this story is not quite right, and that, because of its very nature, innovation automatically erects a barrier to entry sufficient to permit some positive profit. Still, there is sufficient truth in the tale to lead to a reevaluation of the Schumpeterian profit analysis, if applied to routine innovation. Consequently we will begin with a brief inquiry into the effect of competition among innovators upon the profits to be expected from the process.

To impart concreteness to the argument let us assume that none of the innovations taking place changes any of the industry's product specifications, but that they all serve to reduce production costs to a greater or smaller degree. Let us assume also that the industry is rather contestable, that is, that entry barriers other than the costs sunk in the innovation process are fairly minor. In that case, a firm that succeeds in attaining regular reductions in its costs, but nevertheless lags behind most of the others in this process, will find the innovation race to be no advantage to itself. It will clearly find itself at exactly the same sort of disadvantage vis-à-vis its rivals as it would have suffered in the standard Schumpeterian scenario in which it has one successfully innovating competitor, but has no innovation of its own. It is true that, when the rivals of the laggard firm take advantage of their more rapid productivity growth and cut their prices correspondingly, the losses to which that firm is thereby exposed will be smaller the more rapid its own mediocre productivity growth performance turns out to be relative to that of the others. Nevertheless, it can expect losses of some magnitude in these circumstances, and certainly it can hardly hope that its own comparatively lackluster innovations will bring it positive economic profits. It is even possible that this problem will confront every firm in the industry other than the leader in productivity growth, which may find it advantageous to cut prices sufficiently to drive all competitors from the field. The rapid decline in the leader's cost should protect it from the antitrust authorities, even when the firm's prices are set sufficiently low to destroy its rivals.

Still, the productivity leader may elect not to adopt such drastic price cuts. If entry is sufficiently cheap and easy, price cutting can eliminate all rewards, even of what can be mischaracterized as "a pattern of intertemporal predation." That is, temporary adoption of prices sufficiently low to drive rivals from the field may never yield the rewards of monopoly pricing if competitors can reenter quickly and cheaply. Where there is little hope that rivals can be *kept* out of the market, even if they are driven out temporarily, the innovation leader is likely to find it better to adopt higher and more profitable prices—prices that, incidentally, permit at least the closest of the runners-up to operate profitably.

Though the preceding paragraphs have dealt, for expository simplicity, only with cost-reducing process innovation, it is not difficult to show that similar arguments apply to rivalry in product innovation as well. But all of the discussion must assume that there is *some* impediment to entry. Otherwise, the standard theory of perfect competition or perfect contestability assures us, the expected economic profits of the most innovative firm must be driven to zero, and losses must be the fate of all runners-up. For positive profits will constitute an irresistible lure to entrants, whose arrival in the field will force down product prices, raise the prices of inputs, and produce other similar consequences that preclude all expected profits and impose losses upon all the inferior performers.

This argument is so standard that it would require no elaboration had not Tullock (1980) produced an analysis that appears to undermine the conclusion. It will be argued here that the Tullock analysis, while it seems to be valid for rent-seeking activities (to which he applies it), does not legitimately extend to the domain of innovation, where it may at first also seem pertinent. To understand the issue, we must recall the widely accepted view (see Posner [1975] and Chapter 3) that freedom of entry into rent-seeking activity will inevitably result in complete dissipation of the rents through socially wasteful outlays devoted to acquisition of those rents. A utility license expected to yield $10 million in profits to the firm that obtains it will, on this view, tend to elicit a total outlay of $10 million on lawyers, witnesses, supporting staff, and so on by all the firms engaged in pursuit of that license. The same free-entry argument as that of the preceding paragraph underlay this conclusion about the social cost of rent seeking. However, Tullock undermined this easy argument with the aid of a simple game-theoretic model which showed:

PROPOSITION 6.1   Even in the limit, as the number of entrants into a rent-seeking endeavor approaches infinity, aggregate outlays can fall considerably short of the available stock of rent, thus yielding a positive profit; or, instead, those expenditures can exceed the rents, and can do so by a large margin.

It is appropriate to review the model briefly, partly to explain why I differ somewhat with Tullock about the reason for his result. More important, the review will enable us to see why the analogous result must be modified, but not altogether discarded, for the returns to routine innovation. Tullock posits the availability of a *fixed* quantity of rent, R, for which n rent seekers bid competitively, the ith rent seeker bidding x_i dollars, which are not refundable (even the unsuccessful license applicants cannot get back their legal fees). The probability, p_i, that i will win the R-dollar prize is assumed to be

$$p_i = x_i^r / \sum x_j^r \ (j = 1, \ldots, n), \tag{6.1}$$

where the exponent r is some given and presumably nonnegative constant. Then Tullock adopts two assumptions: (a) that each rent seeker will select the outlay that maximizes her expected net yield on the assumption that each other player's bid is given, and (b) that the given bid of each other player will in fact turn out to be that same expected-value maximizing outlay.

We can now proceed to the Tullock argument that yields Proposition 6.1. The expected yield of player i is, of course,

$$E_i = p_i R - x_i = R[x_i^r / \sum x_j^r] - x_i. \tag{6.2}$$

We can then set equal to zero the derivative of E_i with respect to x_i to obtain the optimal value, x_i^*, of the rent-seeking outlay of player i, and since every other player is assumed to adopt the same optimal outlay, in the first-order condition $dE_i/dx_i = 0$ we substitute x_i^* for each of the x_j (so that $\sum x_j = nx_i^*$). After some manipulation this yields

$$x_i^* = Rr(n - 1)/n^2 \text{ and } nx_i^* = Rr(n - 1)/n = \text{total rent-seeking expenditure.} \tag{6.3}$$

Consequently, in the limit, as n, the number of rent seekers, approaches infinity,

$$nx_i^* = Rr. \tag{6.4}$$

Thus for any $r < 1$ the total outlay of the (infinite) group of rent seekers will clearly be less than R, and their expected profit will clearly be positive, while the reverse will be true for $r > 1$.

Despite the straightforward character of the counterexample, the result is puzzling. Why is exit not capable of eliminating the negative expected profits when r is large? And why is entry not capable of eliminating the positive expected profits when r is small, as we are led to believe by our intuitive understanding of competitive equilibrium analysis? Tullock offers several explanations, among them an absence of scale economies in rent seeking, whose pertinence to the matter is not entirely clear. He also cites the sunk costs entailed in participation in the process: "Suppose, for example, that we organize a lobby in Washington for the purpose of raising the price of milk and are unsuccessful. We cannot simply transfer our collection of contacts, influences, past bribes, and so forth to the steel manufacturers' lobby" (1980, p. 98). We will return to this sunk cost argument presently since, it will be suggested, this really does make a crucial difference for the profitability of routine innovation activities.

Further consideration of the Tullock model shows that this discussion has not yet brought out the key special feature that gives him his result—the feature that, in my view, precludes the analysis from being directly relevant for the innovation issue. For what makes the Tullock model work as it does is the premise that the total revenue to be derived from the rent-seeking opportunity in question is *fixed*, and does not vary in response to a change in the number of rent seekers. Consequently, if each act of entry leads every incumbent rent seeker to react by reducing her outlay sufficiently, the total investment can easily converge to a number less than R, the fixed rent-seeking return. That is precisely what happens in the scenarios that entail positive profits in Tullock's analysis.

This story may be plausible for some rent-seeking situations. For example, the profits (ignoring the rent-seeking costs) promised by an exclusive utility license may not be affected by the number of rivals pursuing that license. However, the story contrasts sharply with what one can expect to occur in response to entry in competitive product markets. There, in the classic scenario, entry depresses prices and can always do so sufficiently to cut total revenue down to cost. After all, even if the pertinent costs are very close to zero, competitive entry can also cut price toward zero. That is why in product markets unrestricted entry *can* always eliminate all profit, while in the Tullock model it need not be able to do so. In the former there simply can exist no equivalent to the fixed pool of available total revenue that is entirely plausible for the latter.

What about routine innovation, our main subject here? It seems clear that this arena, too, provides no fixed revenue pools. After all, innovators must always, ultimately, obtain their revenues through sales, and competitive pressures can always reduce the available profits by proliferation of either rival cost-reducing process innovations or competing improvements in products. Thus in a regime of perfect competition or contestability, routine innovation should not exhibit the Tullock phenomenon—positive profits to an activity that is open to all comers. In such an industry, positive profits, whether from investment in innovation or in marketing or in any other activity, should be an irresistible lure to entry, and there would seem to be nothing to inhibit the ability of entry to reduce prices to a point that cuts expected profits to zero. This conclusion is clearly at variance with the Schumpeterian tradition, in which episodic innovation in a perfectly competitive industry offers temporary market power and a stream of temporary economic profits without any offsetting losses, and whose discounted present value is therefore positive.

However, that is not quite the end of the story, since the very nature of the innovation process may preclude perfect competition or contestability in an industry in which the outlays necessary for success in routine innovation activity are substantial. For such outlays, like the activities of the lobbyist in the Tullock parable, are surely preponderantly *sunk*. That is, expenditures on R&D, or on the actual introduction of a new product, may leave very little that is of value or that is transferable to other endeavors if the innovative act that requires those outlays proves to be abortive. Such costs, then, are clearly sunk—they are recoverable only if the project is a success and, even then, they are likely to be recoverable fully only after a considerable period of time has passed.

But as has been argued in the literature on contestable markets, the need to sink costs constitutes the purest form of barrier to exit and entry. Sunk costs are all but synonymous with costliness of exit, for they mean that the firm that incurs them cannot simply walk away with its financial investment intact. And costliness of exit is, in turn, equivalent to riskiness of entry. Where exit is difficult, entry must incur a commensurate risk cost, and entrants will not be attracted unless expected profits are sufficient to cover that cost. More than that, the need to incur sunk costs makes the entrant vulnerable to strategic countermeasures by the incumbents, in the manner described by game theory, and that possibility must clearly exacerbate the risks of entry.

Any economic profits that accrue to the incumbents in the industry will, then, be protected from erosion through the entry process so long as they do not exceed the minimum amount needed to attract new firms into the field, given the risks entailed in any required sunk investment. For this reason, while the conclusion of the previous paragraphs remains formally valid, it is considerably weakened. It remains true that if an industry that engages in substantial routine innovative activity could approximate perfect contestability, the expected economic profits of that activity would be near zero. However, one may well question whether the activity is very often compatible with anything approximating perfect contestability. And, if not, the zero-expected-profit scenario is likely to require significant amendment.

Still, casual observation suggests that there is *something* to the story. The most extreme cases of routine and predictable innovation—the annual introduction of automobile models or spring fashions—do not seem to promise vast economic profits to the participants. This seems even more true of the continuing innovation wars that characterize the computer industry. True, some firms come away from such a competitive engagement with spectacular gains, but those gains may well be offset by the losses incurred by those who come off second and third best. At the very least, such impressionistic evidence serves as a warning against easy acceptance of the standard theoretical view which treats innovation as a reliable source of economic profits.

6.4   Digression: Does Competition Tend to Accelerate Routine Innovation?

The preceding discussion suggests a few casual remarks about another conjecture related to routine innovation: the possibility that rivalry in this activity will force the participants, as it were, to raise the ante repeatedly with the passage of time, thereby making for acceleration in the flow of innovations.

Superficial review of the number of rather common products that were unavailable only a few decades ago is likely to leave the strong impression that the pace of innovation is, indeed, increasing. This seems to be reflected in the public's attitude. In my childhood, my playmates and I would stop in midgame to stare at a passing airplane. One has the impression that no such widespread wonderment is elicited by any new product today. Rather, the jaded public seems to accept product change as an attribute of everyday living that hardly merits special notice. Such impressions naturally give rise to the sense that there must be some feature of the market mechanism speeding up the process of change.

It need hardly be noted that this issue would not have been worth raising before the advent of the Industrial Revolution. The Middle Ages surely did bring with them a number of important inventions, as we have seen in Chapter 2. Still, as I have noted elsewhere, a wealthy Roman magically transported into an eighteenth-century stately home in England would have found few unfamiliar products whose technology was puzzling —clocks, window panes, printed books and newspapers, smoking implements, the musket over the fireplace, and little else. As late as 1870 the innovative products in common home use provided few additions to that list, though production, transportation, and agriculture had obviously undergone major changes. But since then, at least from the viewpoint of the consumer, the pace of change has quickened to the point that the availability of new products has almost become a humdrum affair.

There are, indeed, forces making for acceleration of innovation and for increases in the optimal amount to be budgeted for the purpose. Schmookler (1966) offers extensive evidence indicating that the amount of innovation is indeed limited by the size of the market. That is, the flow of patented invention appears to be closely parallel to the volume of sales of a product both over the business cycle and in terms of longer-run trends. It follows that growing population and expanding GNP can both be expected to speed up the pace of innovation. And technical progress can help to reduce the cost of the innovation process itself, as has surely been done by the computer, for example. For the usual reasons, such a continuing reduction in (marginal) cost will tend to produce a continuing increase in the optimal scale of the activity. Cost reduction must also have been contributed by the externalities generated in the course of the innovation process, A's successful innovation contributing to the efficiency with which B can carry on its own innovation activity.

Still, there are countervailing forces (which will be emphasized in the analysis provided in a companion volume). In particular, there is the problem of the "cost disease" of the technologically stagnant personal services, which besets research in the same way that it affects education, legal activity, the performing arts, and a number of other services. This is the persistent rise in real cost that plagues those services whose productivity is not easily increased year after year, so that there is no productivity offset to rising wages as in other economic sectors. The act of thinking continues to be a crucial component of the research process, but there seems to be little reason to believe that we have become more proficient at this than were Leonardo da Vinci or Isaac Newton or even their contemporary investigators of somewhat less stellar eminence. With the productivity of labor having risen at an annual rate of some 2 percent compounded, the real product of an hour of labor increased about sixteenfold over a span of about 140 years. This means that the opportunity cost of an hour devoted to the technologically stagnant process of thinking must have risen by about 1,500 percent! If we treat R&D as just another input in the production process, then we recognize that such a rise in its relative price can hardly fail to elicit some response in its derived demand—inducing some substitution away from this input and toward other inputs that benefit more readily from technical change. The cost disease of the stagnant component of research, then, may well prove to be a major impediment to acceleration in the pace of innovation.

We would appear to emerge with no clear conclusion, nor even with an unambiguous presumption about the balance of forces determining whether innovative activity can be expected to accelerate or decelerate. However, we have not yet considered the role of competition in this process. Earlier in the chapter the dangers threatening the laggard in the innovation process were stressed. Even if a firm is engaged steadily in the innovation process, it may find its position in the market threatened if its rivals outpace its performance. Note that this can be true even if those rivals invest more than the profit-maximizing amount in innovation, indeed, even if some of them go bankrupt as a result, but successors take over their marked down assets and continue to operate as before.

One consequence is that the current rate of innovation in an industry may operate as though controlled by an automatic ratchet. Once the typical firm begins to spend x percent of its revenues on the innovation process, retreat from this standard by any major firm in the industry may become all but impossible. No enterprise will feel itself in a position to invest less than this, and no entrant may dare to open for business with lower R&D outlays. Then there will surely be those who are tempted to beat the game by investing more than x percent, in order to jump ahead of their rivals. If so, each such foray will raise the average standard above its previous x percent level. Such a process way well be cumulative, and while it is probably not typical of modern industry, it seems a fair description of what goes on in a number of those that are on the frontier of technical advance.

6.5   Applicability of Optimality Analysis to Routine Innovation

There is a clear place in this discussion for use of the standard sorts of optimality calculations to determine the most profitable size for the firm's routine innovation expenditure. The point is that when innovation begins to entail repetitive and routine decisions the economist's standard analytic tools regain their pertinence to the process, to which they are largely irrelevant when the process is directed by the more imaginative and fundamentally heterogeneous decision patterns of the entrepreneur.

It also becomes possible in a regime of routine innovation to employ an optimality approach more broadly to analyze a considerable variety of the decisions that determine the character of the innovation activities. For example, one can use such an approach to analyze the much debated relationship between firm size and level of innovative activity. A number of writers have argued on various grounds that large firms have an advantage over small ones in the innovation process and have suggested that level of innovative activity can be expected to increase with size of firm. The empirical evidence is not altogether consistent with this view. The evidence does suggest that R&D outlays increase, both absolutely and relatively, with size up to a point, but that beyond that point the ratio of outlay to whatever measure of size is employed begins to level off or even to fall (for a review of these matters see, e.g., Scherer [1980, pp. 413–15 and 418–22]). Those who question the advantages of bigness for innovation have argued that where competitiveness declines as firm size increases, the market pressures for innovation tend to fall concomitantly. On the other side, it has been maintained that bigness gives the firm the considerable financial resources needed for significant innovation activities, and that larger size permits the firm to benefit more from the public-good character of knowledge production, whose costs are largely unaffected by an increase in the magnitude of the outputs or in the number of different products to which its results are applied. Consequently, it is suggested, a firm that turns out a larger variety of products or turns them out in larger quantities will find it profitable to devote disproportionately larger amounts of resources to the innovation process.

One can use a (clearly oversimplified) model of the process merely to illustrate how the matter can be approached analytically. We will employ such a model to derive:

PROPOSITION 6.2   In a routine process that generates revenue-enhancing (or cost-reducing) innovations, one can expect the profit-maximizing rate of innovation expenditure to be an increasing function of the output of the firm.

We will assume, for simplicity, that the firm produces only a single product. Since output level as well as the level of expenditure on innovation are both endogenous variables in the firm's decision processes, we cannot simply impose an increase in output, dy, on the profit-maximizing firm and examine the effect on innovation activity. Instead, we must assume that the superior size of the larger firm is a consequence of some difference in the cost or demand functions that face it. We will proceed by letting marginal cost shift exogenously, and study its effect on both the profit-maximizing output and innovation flow.

We use the following notation:

y = the quantity of output produced by the firm;

$C^*(y) + c^*y$ = the firm's net operating cost at time $t = 0$, i.e., its total cost other than the cost of the innovation process at that date, with c^* a shift variable;

$R^*(y)$ = total revenue;

w = the rate of increase of $R^*(y)$, where the magnitude of w is determined by the size of the firm's outlays on (product) innovation;

$G^*(w)$ = the innovation cost outlay per unit of time;

r = the interest (discount) rate; and

π = the present value of the firm's expected profits.

Then, the firm is taken to maximize

$$\pi = \int_0^\infty e^{-(r-w)t} R^*(y)\, dt - \int_0^\infty e^{-rt}[G^*(w) + C^*(y) + c^*y]\, dt. \qquad (6.5)$$

Here we assume $r < w$ so that $\pi < \infty$, that all the functions are twice differentiable, and that $C^*(y)$, c^*, dC^*/dy, dG^*/dw, and d^2G^*/dw^2 are all positive, for obvious reasons. Integrating (6.5) we obtain

$$\pi = R^*(y)/(r - w) - [G^*(w) + C^*(y) + c^*y]/r. \qquad (6.6)$$

This can be generalized slightly and the notation simplified by recognizing that r is fixed exogenously and rewriting (6.6) as

$$\pi = f(w)R(y) - G(w) - C(y) - cy, \quad df/dw > 0, \; d^2f/dw^2 < 0 \qquad (6.7)$$

(diminishing returns to innovation activity); and so, writing π_w for the partial of π with respect to w, and so on, our first-order maximum conditions become

$$\pi_w = f_w R(y) - G_w = 0 \quad \text{and} \qquad (6.8)$$

$$\pi_y = f(w)R_y - C_y - c = 0. \qquad (6.9)$$

Differentiating totally to obtain the equilibrating response in w and y to a change in c we obtain

$$d\pi_w = \pi_{ww}dw + f_wR_ydy = 0 \quad \text{and} \tag{6.10}$$

$$d\pi_y = f_wR_ydw + \pi_{yy}dy - dc = 0. \tag{6.11}$$

This is a pair of simultaneous linear equations in dw and dy, for which one can solve in terms of dc, using Cramer's rule. We obtain directly

$$dw/dc = -f_wR_y/D, \quad dy/dc = [f_{ww}R(y) - G_{ww}]/D = \pi_{ww}/D, \tag{6.12}$$

where D is the determinant of the system, and is positive by the second-order maximum conditions. Since f_w is positive by (6.7), R_y is positive by (6.9), f_{ww} is negative, and G_{ww} is positive by our diminishing returns assumptions, both expressions in (6.12) must be negative. Thus a downward shift in the marginal cost curve, which will elicit a rise in the value of y, will also increase w, as was to be shown. That is, an increase in the profit-maximizing output of the firm that occurs in response to a fall in its marginal cost will, indeed, be accompanied by a rise in the absolute size of its optimal expenditure on innovation.

All of this is merely meant to illustrate the restored pertinence of optimization calculations to a firm in which innovation has become routine, and to make clear the critical role of the costs of the innovation process in any analysis of the subject.[3] But the result clearly does not begin to grapple with the true issue of the firm size/innovation expenditure debate, which is not whether larger firm size tends to be accompanied by larger R&D expenditure, but whether that expenditure increases *more than proportionately* with size.

6.6   An Inventory-Theoretic Model of Optimal Decision Making in Routine Innovation

We can make a bit more of the observation that in some industries innovation has become so routine that its products are introduced on a known and regular schedule, as in the launching of new automobile models. In practice, the timing is undoubtedly decided primarily by considerations related to the calendar and regularities in consumer demand patterns (say, once a year for cars, four times per year for new clothing designs, and so on).[4] However, one can still use the timing decision to provide yet another illustration suggesting ways in which optimization analysis may offer insights related to routine innovation. Here one can make use of an analogy with standard inventory decisions. In rudimentary inventory theory the process is pictured as one that entails a steady stream of consumer purchases from the retailer's inventory of the product in question. As the stock of the product is depleted, there comes a point when it becomes economical for the retailer to replenish the inventory by reordering from the producer. Excessive frequency of reordering leads to high transactions costs—the effort of making the arrangements, record keeping, billing, and the like. However, insufficient frequency of reordering also imposes unnecessary costs because it means that the retailer must order large quantities of stocks at each replenishment date and incur the interest cost of the large amounts of money that this ties up until the goods are sold. There is, consequently, an intermediate frequency of reordering that balances these two costs and so minimizes the total cost of keeping customers supplied. This yields the optimal timing of inventory replenishment. In practice, of course, there normally are uncertainties in the process, and inventory theory takes them and other complications into account (for more information, see, e.g., Whitin [1953]); however for our purpose—illustration of the approach—there is no need to deal with such issues.

For us, the analogue of depletion of a commodity inventory is the erosion of the competitive edge made possible by the launching of an innovation. It is generally held that an innovation tends to undergo a life cycle, and that its competitive benefit tends to erode fairly rapidly as rival innovations make their appearance, or the market becomes saturated with the new product, or the item loses its appeal to consumers. One can then picture an intertemporal pattern of expected revenues, whose rate of flow jumps discontinuously upward on the date of introduction of an innovation, and then declines more or less steadily until the next innovation makes its appearance. The graph of revenue flows then assumes the sawtooth appearance made familiar in the inventory and the cash-demand literature. If there are no exogenous changes in purchases or costs, and timing is under the control of management, it will clearly be optimal to plan to introduce innovations at regular and equal time intervals. This will obviously be so *ex ante*, though in any particular case special developments may, of course, call for deviations in timing in one direction or another.

Letting T represent the length of the "interinnovation" period, it is clear that too low a value of T will reduce the flow of net profits by raising the cost of the R&D process itself ("crash programs" are notoriously expensive), multiply the cost of introduction (for example, the total outlay on the advertising needed to draw attention to each of the large number of innovations), and increase disproportionately the other transaction costs. But too large a value of T will also reduce profits because of the long portion of the interinnovation period during which the demand for the previous innovation will have been eroded significantly. The objective, then, is to find the intermediate value of T that balances off these two sources of profit diminution—the value of T consistent with maximization of the profits of the enterprise. In determining this value we will derive:

PROPOSITION 6.3   A rise in the marginal revenue yield, R_T, of a lengthening of T can lead to a rise in the optimal value of T which increases *more than proportionately* with R_T. That is, at least in a simple model, $\partial T/\partial R_T$ and $\partial^2 T/\partial R_T^2$ must both be positive.

We use the following notation:

$R^*(T, t) = R(T) - kt =$ revenue flow at time t with an interinnovation period of duration T;

$R_{avg} =$ the mean value of $R(T, t)$ over the time period T;

$G =$ the cost incurred during the introduction of an innovation;

$C =$ the flow of other costs per unit of time (one year); and

$\pi =$ profit per year.

We have, then, assumed that the value of R^* declines linearly at rate k over the time period T. We assume also that the period at issue is sufficiently brief that omission of discounting does not produce an unacceptable approximation. Then because of the linearity of the depletion process, R_{avg} will simply be the mean of the initial and the terminal value of R^*, that is,

$$R_{avg} = (R + R - kT)/2 = R - kT/2. \tag{6.13}$$

Over a unit period (one year) this, then, will also equal total revenue for the firm. Similarly, C will equal total (nonintroduction) cost per period. The expression for introduction cost is obtained by noting that, since the time between innovations is T, the number of introductions per period must be $1/T$, so that the total introduction cost must be G/T. Bringing these three elements together, we obtain

$$\pi = R - kT/2 - G/T - C \tag{6.14}$$

so that, differentiating with respect to T we obtain the first-order maximization condition

$$\pi_T = R_T - k/2 + G/T^2 = 0, \tag{6.15}$$

that is,

$$T(\text{optimal}) = [G/(-R_T + k/2)]^{1/2}. \tag{6.16}$$

This result, aside from one surprising feature, is entirely consistent with what intuition suggests. The optimal length of the interinnovation period varies directly with the marginal revenue yield of lengthened value of T (presumably corresponding to the superior quality of the innovation permitted by increased R&D time). It also varies directly with G, the introduction cost, since the higher that cost the less frequently it will pay to introduce innovations. Finally, the optimal value of T, for obvious reasons, varies inversely with k, the speed of depletion of the revenue flow during the times when no innovations are being introduced. The only curious feature of the result, one to which economists have become habituated by the literature on the inventory model of the transaction demand for cash, is the square root form of solution. This shows that changes in the parameter values do not affect the optimal value of T proportionately, but that, rather, an element of diminishing (increasing) returns is entailed in the process. In particular, the relationship between the optimal value of T and dR/dT is easily shown from (6.16) to exhibit increasing returns, as Proposition 6.3 requires.[5]

As has already been suggested, the oversimplification of our model argues against devotion of a great deal of attention here to details of our results, such as the presence of the square root in (6.16). The purpose of the calculation has merely been to illustrate once more one of the central points of the chapter: the restored pertinence of optimality calculations that routine innovation makes possible. We will see more of this in the chapters that follow.

Before closing the chapter one remark is required as a matter of balance in our discussion. It must be emphasized that despite the substantial role of routinization in the modern innovation process, the entrepreneur is not condemned to obsolescence, much less to total disappearance from the arena of technical change. There are some innovations that simply do not recommend themselves to a bureaucratic management, because they are too risky or too revolutionary, or because they threaten to disturb the calm and comfortable existence of the managerial hierarchy. Scherer (1980, p. 438; see also pp. 416–17) lists some of the "really revolutionary new industrial products and processes" of the past century and points out that a "disproportionately high share" was (and perhaps continues to be) introduced new entrants, firms that were at the time quite small and not widely known. Finally, some innovations are cheap to carry out and so tend to be beneath the notice of the larger corporation, but not that of the independent little entrepreneur whom we find contributing new food products and new toys and games, for example. Contrary to Schumpeter's view of the matter (1942, p. 132), there seems to be little evidence that the innovating entrepreneur is a vanishing breed and that the opportunities for her to practice her occupation are evaporating. The innovation that constitutes a quantum leap will probably never become the predictable product of routine innovative activity, but will, perhaps, always have to derive from the offbeat efforts of the unpredictable, imaginative entrepreneur, independent and unorthodox—in short, the entrepreneur of legend.

Yet if it is true, as knowledgeable observers report, that the social benefits attributable to the initial innovations are typically smaller than those provided by the accumulation of subsequent incremental improvements, many of them not particularly exciting individually, then it may follow that the public's greatest debt in this domain is to the dogged manager of R&D activities, rather than to the inspired entrepreneur.

7　　Models of Optimal Timing of Innovation and Imitation

[Because of] improvements in the methods of reproducing [their] fixed capital ... enterprises frequently do not flourish until they pass into other hands, i.e., after their first proprietors have been bankrupted [and] their successors [can] buy them cheaply....

Marx (1897, vol. 3, p. 112)

Once routinization of the process of invention, innovation and imitation becomes significant, the timing of the steps that make up the sequence becomes yet another decision that lends itself to analysis with the aid of the standard tools of optimization. The timing of a major innovative step illustrates the issue most clearly. There is an obvious trade-off between haste and deliberate delay. By rushing the introduction of the novel item in question, one speeds the date at which its stream of benefits begin to flow. Two years of delay can mean that two years of benefits will be forgone. In addition, if speed contributes competitive strength (heading off rivals who threaten to get there first, or undermining the opportunities for profitable imitation by others seeking to invade the innovator's market), then there is a second cost of delay which is apt to be considerable. In an industry where constant product change is a way of competitive life, delay until 1994 of a product that could have been brought out in 1993 may mean that in 1994, while competitors are offering customers a product whose technology was conceived, say, in 1991, our company will find itself forced to supply a now obsolete model of engineering vintage 1990.

The other side of the matter is that delay in the date of introduction is likely to permit further improvement of the new item or reduction in its cost and, in particular, avoidance of the high costs of a "crash" development program. Thus, there is the usual trade-off that means that some dates can be too early from the point of view of maximization of the profits gained from introduction of the new item, while other dates will entail excessive delay. Optimality, of course, refers to the intermediate introduction date that yields maximal profits to the innovator.

A similar timing issue affects the decisions of the imitator, who, as we shall see in Chapter 9, is often also necessarily something of an innovator, so that the resemblance of the character of the considerations facing the two should not be altogether surprising. But in addition, the matter is complicated by the race/waiting-game character of the innovation process, which recent writings have stressed. Tautologically, it is the timing decisions that determine whether the introduction of a particular novelty will take on the character of a waiting game, in which each enterprise hopes another will assume the risk of moving first, or that of a race, in which each strives to arrive before the others. Timing also determines which of the participants in the process will turn out to be *the* innovator, and which will assume the role of imitator.

This chapter will provide several simple models describing the analytics of the pertinent optimization process. In addition to offering the formal conditions for optimality and their economic interpretation, it will provide a bit of comparative-statics analysis, showing how changes in some of the parameters, such as speeding up of improvement of the process or product, or the rate of reduction of costs, affect the optimal timing decision. The main moral that will emerge is that the timing consequences of such exogenous changes are complex, sometimes delaying the optimal introduction date, sometimes hastening it. This conclusion, however, will not be left as amorphous as it sounds, for it will be possible to describe the circumstances that produce one result and those that lead to the other.

The logic of the matter can be brought out with the aid of an analogous and very familiar issue. The reader will know all too well that when a consumer product's technology evolves very rapidly, the timing of the purchase poses an unnerving dilemma for the buyer. Too great a delay means deprivation of the product's benefits for an excessive period of time, while too much haste subjects the buyer to the risk of early obsolescence. What purchaser of a personal computer, for example, has not wrestled with this dilemma?

This analogy also indicates the reason for the ambiguity besetting some of the comparative-statics results of this chapter. Imagine a research breakthrough that increases the speed with which the product is improved, year after year. Obviously, this will exacerbate the dilemma. The one side of the matter is the likelihood that the product will have improved to a degree that raises materially the opportunity cost of delay in its purchase. On the other side, acceleration of improvement means that the rate of obsolescence of the purchase will also be increased. Let us begin to see where these countervailing consequences of acceleration of the improvement process are apt to leave the timing decision. For the rather surprising answers, we must turn to some formal models.

7.1   On the Timing of Purchase of a Rapidly Improving Consumer Good

The formal analysis that follows is, then, readily interpretable in either of two ways: first, as the choice of the optimal date, T, for the introduction of an innovation that is undergoing a process of continuing improvement until date T, or alternatively, as the process of determination of the optimal date, T, for the purchase of a product like a computer that is undergoing continuous improvement. The discussion that follows is expressed initially in terms of the latter interpretation, leaving the translation to the selection of the optimal time of introduction of an innovation for the next section. The case that is simplest to describe, that with which we begin, is the one in which the only effect of progress is to reduce cost and, hence, purchase price. This restriction permits direct quantification of the rate of technical progress and it is, therefore, a device that will repeatedly prove convenient here and in later chapters.[1] The sole purpose of the product in question is assumed to be the (constant) stream of revenues (benefits) that it yields to the purchaser.

We use the following notation:

R = the flow of revenues per unit of time, before the purchase;

S = the flow of revenues per unit of time, after the purchase date (where $S > R$);

Ce^{-wT} = the purchase price of the improved product at time T;

r = the (continuously compounded) rate of interest (discount);

w = the rate of cost reduction through technical progress, $0 < w < 1$;

T = the purchase date; and

$B(T)$ = the present value of the net benefits obtained by the purchaser, as a function of the date of purchase.

Then, the consumer's objective is to maximize

$$B(T) = \int_{t=0}^{T} Re^{-rt}\,dt - Ce^{-(r+w)T} + \int_{t=T}^{\infty} Se^{-rt}dt, \qquad (7.1)$$

that is (by straightforward integration), to maximize

$$B(T) = R/r + (S/r - R/r)e^{-rT} - Ce^{-(r+w)T}. \tag{7.2}$$

Thus the first-order condition for maximization becomes

$$B_T = (R - S)e^{-rT} + (r + w)Ce^{-(r+w)T} = 0, \tag{7.3}$$

where we write B_T for the partial derivative of B with respect to T. As is to be expected, equation (7.3) simply tells us that equilibrium requires the marginal opportunity cost of delay, in the form of forgone gain per unit of time, $S - R$, to equal the associated marginal cost-reduction yield achieved through continuing improvement in technology, as well as through postponement of expenditure.

Let us turn, next, to the critical issue: does a speeding up of the rate of technical progress lead to a hastening or to a postponement of the optimal purchase date?

PROPOSITION 7.1   An increase in the rate of technical progress, w, will generally change the optimal date for purchase of a rapidly improving product (the optimal date for introduction of a product or a process innovation). There will be a critical date, I, such that if the initially optimal date, T, was less than I, then $dT/dw > 0$, while if T was greater than I, then $dT/dw < 0$.

We will first prove this for the case of cost-reducing process improvement, and then turn to the case of product improvement. To deal with the former, we must find the response of T, the optimal purchase date, to a change in w. This requires us, in accord with the usual procedure of comparative statics, to calculate the total differential of (7.3), obtaining from the requirement that equilibrium condition (7.3) must be satisfied both before and after the change in w,

$$dB_T = B_{TT}\, dT + B_{Tw}\, dw = 0 \quad \text{or}$$

$$dT/dw = -B_{Tw}/B_{TT}, \tag{7.4}$$

where we know $B_{TT} < 0$ by the second-order condition. Consequently, the sign of the derivative in (7.4) will be the same as the cross-partial derivative of B with respect to T and w, that is, the numerator of (7.4). Direct differentiation of (7.3) tells us that this equals

$$B_{Tw} = Ce^{-(r+w)T}[1 - T(r + w)], \tag{7.5}$$

which will take the sign of the expression in square brackets. That is, dT/dw will be positive if T (the [initially] optimal purchase date) is sufficiently small to yield $1 - T(r + w) > 0$, and it will be negative if T is sufficiently large to reverse that sign, as Proposition 7.1 asserts.

Thus, (7.5) tells us that the rise in w calls for postponement of the optimal purchase date of the product if that date is relatively early in a regime of slower technical progress, and for a hastening of that purchase date if the date was relatively late under such a regime. Let us try to find an intuitive explanation for this apparently curious result.

Here, the geometry of the matter is of some help. Figure 7.1 is a graph of B (7.1), the *total* benefit the consumer derives from a purchase of the novel item, as a function of the date the purchase is made. The graph only suggests the asymptotic approach of the benefits curve to the horizontal axis as one moves toward the right—asymptotic behavior as the cost of the product approaches zero with the compounding of cost reduction over time that is crucial for the explanation we seek. In the case shown, the selected rise in the value of the improvement rate, w, leads to a slight rightward move in the highest point of the curve and, hence, to an increase in the optimal value of T.

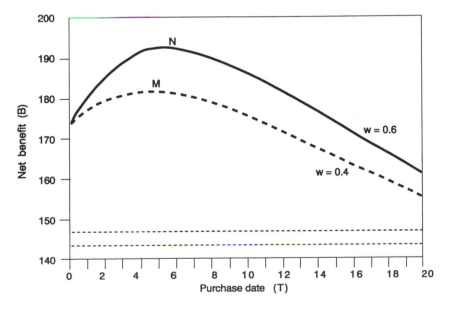

Figure 7.1
Net purchase benefits as function of purchase date

However, insight into the matter is offered only in figure 7.2, which plots (7.3), the curve of *marginal* benefits of waiting, taken as a function of T, that is, it shows the behavior of B_T, the partial derivative of B with respect to T. It also shows the effect on that marginal benefit curve of a change in the value of w. We see that a rise in w has two consequences.

First, it raises the vertical intercept of the B_T curve; that is, it adds to the initial benefits of delay—the marginal benefit of a unit addition to the elapse of time before buying—by offering the consumer a less costly product as a reward for waiting, with the product's marginal reduction in price greater than that corresponding to a more modest value of w. Second, the rise in w must ultimately *reduce* the height of the marginal benefits curve, B_T, by ensuring that the cost of the product, having approached zero sooner, must begin to level off at a lower value of T, meaning that there remains relatively little more to be gained through further postponement of the purchase date. The initial heightening and later lowering amounts to a rotation of the curve.

The net effect of the initial raising and later lowering of the benefits curve when there is a rise in w is that the curve corresponding to the higher value of w must at some point, I, intersect the marginal benefits curve for

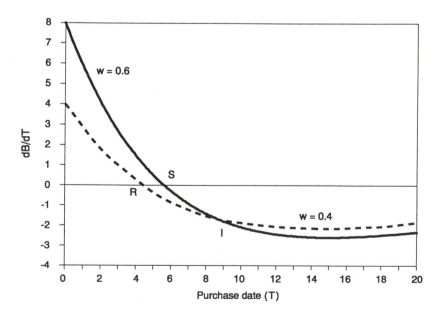

Figure 7.2
Derivative of net benefits with respect to purchase date

the lower w. That means that if the optimal value of T, corresponding to the first-order requirement $B_T = 0$ (point R or S), lies to the left of I, as in figure 7.2, then the rise in w will increase the reward of additional waiting before buying. Thus, the optimal point, corresponding to the intersection of the B_T curve with the horizontal axis, will move to the right (the move from R to S). However, if the optimal point had been to the right of I, then the effect of the rise in the value of w would have been the reverse, because for high values of T the marginal reward of additional waiting is thereby reduced. It remains only to suggest what determines whether the optimal value of T will be relatively low or relatively high. This can be studied directly from (7.3), which tells us that when this equilibrium condition is satisfied we must have

$$e^{wT} = C(r + w)/(S - R).$$

In other words, a rise in purchase cost, C, relative to the net benefits, $S - R$, of the novel product, or a rise in the rate of reduction, $r + w$, of the present value of that cost, must raise the optimal value of T because it shifts the B_T curve upward, that is, because it raises the marginal benefit of delay to some degree, for every value of T. The intuitive reason should be self-evident.

The preceding geometric discussion should suggest that our results about the consequences of a change in the rate of technological progress, as represented here by the value of w, do not depend on the particular functional forms we have selected for illustrative purposes, so it is plausible that our conclusions have some degree of robustness. A rise in the (percentage) rate of cost reduction will, surely, shift the cost curve downward, and initially cause it to fall more rapidly in the general case; but it will also cause that curve to level off earlier than before in order to avoid crossing the horizontal axis. After all, technological progress rarely if ever succeeds in reducing a commodity's production cost to a negative level. But these two qualitative attributes of the effect of a change of w on the time derivative of cost—the initial stimulation and the later depression of the absolute rate of decline of product cost—are all that is needed for our results.

We can easily modify the preceding model to encompass the case where delay in purchasing gives the consumer an improved product, and does not merely make it cheaper, as assumed so far. That is, the model will now be extended to cover product innovation in addition to cost-reducing process improvement. Then, letting v be the rate of improvement per unit of time of the new product, we need merely replace S by Se^{vT} in (7.1), so that the last term in the expression for B becomes

$$Se^{vT} \int_{T}^{\infty} e^{-rt} dt.$$

Thus (7.2) changes to

$$B = R/r - (R/r)e^{-rT} - Ce^{-(r+w)T} + (S/r)e^{(v-r)T}, \quad \text{so that} \tag{7.6}$$

$$B_T = Re^{-rT} + (r+w)Ce^{-(r+w)T} + S[(v-r)/r]e^{(v-r)T} = O. \tag{7.7}$$

Consequently,

$$B_{Tv} = (S/r)e^{(v-r)T}[T(v-r) + 1]. \tag{7.8}$$

It now follows immediately from a relationship analogous to (7.4) that dT/dv will have the same sign as B_{Tv}, which, in turn, will take the sign of the bracketed term in (7.8). In particular, it is clear that if $v - r$ is positive then dT/dv must always be positive, because then the rate of progress will increase the stream of revenues more rapidly than the discount rate erodes its present value. Consequently, a rise in v will then always make it worthwhile to wait longer before purchasing. However, as is easily verified from (7.7), in this case, because $v - r > 0$, every term in the expression for B_T must be positive, and we are left with the absurd conclusion that it pays to wait forever before buying because the rate of product improvement constantly swamps the cost in terms of present value of further delay in purchasing. In the less paradoxical case where $v - r$ is negative we immediately obtain a comparative-statics relationship identical to that found in Proposition 7.1 for changes in the value of w. That is, we can see now that, if the optimal value of T is relatively small, dT/dv will be positive so that it will pay to wait longer before making the purchase of the rapidly improving product, while if the initially optimal value of T is sufficiently large, that derivative will be negative, and the rise in the value of v will lead to an optimal purchase date earlier than it would have been otherwise. Intuitively, the explanation is only slightly different from that of the cost-reduction case that was considered earlier in this section, though it is now rather more convoluted.[2] This completes our discussion of the consumer's optimal timing of the purchase of a rapidly improving product, and leads us directly to our models of the timing of innovation.

7.2   Digression: On Optimal Length of Product-Safety Testing Period

The preceding argument has an interesting and simple application to another issue in the field of product innovation—testing for product safety, for example, in new medicines. This application will be described briefly before turning to systematic analysis of our main issue—the optimal timing of innovation.

In his classic 1973 article Sam Peltzman demonstrated the damage to the welfare of the public that can result from the adoption by government of excessively strict testing requirements for new drugs. For the uninformed observer it undoubtedly strained credulity to think that the severe testing requirements adopted by the United States in 1962 might not only fail to protect his interests, but that they could in fact prove unambiguously deleterious to the health of the general population, both by postponing the date at which valuable medications were released for general use, and by reducing the flow of new medicines. If we use average length of testing period as a simplifying index representing the severity of testing requirements, it is now clear to every thoughtful observer that this period of time can well be set so as to be excessive from the point of view of the public welfare. But it should be equally clear that too weak a testing requirement can also be detrimental, not only to the interests of consumers of health care, but also to the longer-term well-being of the drug manufacturers. In the absence of a governmental testing requirement it is more than conceivable that competitive pressures and, in particular, the entry of unscrupulous producers, could drag even the most conscientious of manufacturers into a race to cut costs by shaving of testing time and effort. This would surely harm those firms in the long run, not only by subjecting them to legitimate lawsuits, but it might very well reduce sales by undermining the confidence of doctors and their patients in the quality and safety of medical products. Thus there must be some *optimal* intermediate length of the required testing period, a period that lies between levels that are clearly inadequate and those that are patently excessive. We can readily construct a model for determination of the optimal length of testing period. Moreover, formulating the model in extremely general terms, we can obtain comparative-statics results about the effects of an improvement in testing techniques that are completely analogous to those of the previous section, as will now be shown.

For this purpose, let

T = the length of time a new medical product must be tested;

$N(T)$ = the number of new pharmaceuticals introduced per year;

$W(uT)$ = the mean social benefit (loss) from the testing of one drug;

u = a technical progress parameter; and

$G(T)$ = the net social gain from the entire testing process, where we take N, W, and G to be twice continuously differentiable.

Here, for reasons already suggested, we expect W to increase with T initially, but eventually to reach a maximum and begin to decline. We also expect N to be a decreasing function of T, since a lengthening of the (required) testing period increases the cost of new product introduction. The optimal T, then, will be the magnitude that maximizes gains per new product times number of new products, that is,

$$G(T) = N(T)W(uT). \tag{7.9}$$

This, of course, requires writing $G_T = \partial G/\partial T$, and so on, and for brevity, W' and W'' for the first and second derivatives of W with respect to uT,

$$G_T = N_T W + uNW' = 0. \tag{7.10}$$

We have, by assumption, and by the second-order conditions

$$N_T < 0, \quad W'' < 0 \quad \text{and} \quad G_{TT} < 0. \tag{7.11}$$

From (7.10) and (7.11) we obtain directly

$$W' = -N_T W/uN > 0. \tag{7.12}$$

Intuitively, this tells us that since an increase in T always reduces the number of new medicines undergoing development, optimality requires that T never be set so high that $W' < 0$, that is, that the opportunity cost of delay in availability of new medicines swamps the benefits of any associated reduction in risk.

First-order condition (7.10) can now be used in an ordinary comparative-statics calculation to determine the effect of a rise in the value of u on the optimal value of T. Thus, setting the total differential of (7.10), dG_T, equal to zero we obtain

$$dG_T = G_{TT}\,dT + G_{Tu}\,du = 0, \quad \text{or,} \tag{7.13}$$

$$dT/du = -G_{Tu}/G_{TT}, \text{ where, by (7.10),} \tag{7.14}$$

$$G_{Tu} = TN_T W' + NW' + uTNW'', \quad \text{or,}$$

$$G_{Tu} = T(N_T W' + uNW'') + NW'. \tag{7.15}$$

Our objective is to determine the sign of dT/du, as given by (7.14). Now, by the second-order maximum condition, G_{TT}, the denominator of (7.14), must be negative. Hence the sign of (7.14) must be identical with the sign of (7.15). But by (7.11) and (7.12) the coefficient of T in (7.15) is clearly negative, while the last term in (7.15) is positive at the equilibrium. Hence, for T less than $K = NW'/(N_T W' + uNW'')$, dT/du will be positive, while for $T > K$ that derivative must be negative in the neighborhood of T^*. Gathering all this information together, we obtain essentially the same solution as that of the previous section:

A technical improvement in the testing process, $du > 0$, will increase the optimal length of the testing period, T, if the optimal value of T had been relatively low ($T < K$) before the technical change. On the other hand, $du > 0$ will lead to a reduction in the optimal length of testing period if the initial value of T had been relatively high.

7.3   Models on the Optimal Date for Launching an Innovation

We will proceed in our discussion of the innovation timing decision in three stages. The first will consider this decision in isolation, abstracting from the role of rivalry in the process. For that simple case we will find that the preceding models of the timing of purchase take us most of the way, at least so far as the formal characterization of the optimal choice is concerned. Second, we will consider the case in which there is a rival of our protagonist who may introduce the novel product either before or after our decision maker does so. We will continue to abstract from anything resembling oligopolistic interaction, taking the rival's introduction date to be fixed and immutable, and leaving our firm to decide between a date of entry earlier or later than the rival's, thereby choosing between the role of original innovator and that of imitator. In the third and final stage of our discussion, a bit of elementary game-theoretic manipulation (following the work of Partha Dasgupta) will be used to introduce the interactions of the two competitors in the innovation process.

   We begin, then, with the case of the innovator whose decision process is immune to considerations of rivalry. Here, we will combine the cases of product innovation and cost-reducing process innovation. For our decision maker, the choice between an earlier and a later date of introduction can entail at least five considerations. The choice of the later date can do the following:

1. Postpone the date of commencement of any increase in the flow of revenues that the innovation will entail

2. Reduce the length of the period of time during which the enhanced revenues accrue

3. Extend the period during which outlays required by the invention-innovation process continue

4. Enhance the magnitude of the postinnovation flow of net revenue per unit of time because the delay permits an improvement in the quality or a reduction in the cost of the item introduced by the innovation

5. Reduce the costs that have to be incurred by the act of introduction of this item

Obviously, not all of these consequences need result from postponement in every case, and other consequences are conceivable. Still, this seems at least to be a representative list, and it is easy to see that the following profit function encompasses all of the entries in that list. For simplicity it will be assumed that there is a fixed terminal date, h, for the flow of enhanced net revenues generated by the innovation, say, because a better product sure to render the new item obsolete is scheduled to make its appearance at date h. This artificial premise is easily modified, say, by changing that terminal date to $T + h$, where T is the date selected for the introduction of the new item on which we focus our attention. However, the fixed-horizon case has the advantage of representing the possibility that delay of the innovation date may actually shorten the total lifetime of the new item as an economically viable product. Indeed, it may be considered to constitute a polar case of such a consequence.

We now use π to represent the total profit yielded by the innovation, as a function of its date of introduction, with the other symbols corresponding closely enough to those used in the model of the purchase timing decision to require no explicit definition. The objective of the innovator is, then, taken to be maximization of

$$\pi = R \int_{t=0}^{T} e^{-rt}\, dt - Ce^{-(r+w)T} + Se^{vT} \int_{t=T}^{h} e^{-rt}\, dt. \tag{7.16}$$

It is not difficult to show that (7.16) encompasses all five of the consequences of delay in the innovation date, T, that have just been listed. Postponement obviously means that the flow of the higher postinnovation revenues, S, will be delayed by precisely the amount of time given by the rise in the value of T. The reduction of the length of time during which the enhanced revenues are enjoyed corresponds to the decrease in the period from T to h that is covered by the last integral in the equation. Since preinnovation revenue, R, is taken to be net of cost, including outlays on the innovation process, the lengthened period of innovation outlays is represented in the first term of (7.16). The enhancement of the postinnovation rate of net revenue flow is shown by the e^{vT} by which S is multiplied in the last term in (7.16). Finally, the reduction in introduction cost, C, permitted by delay is clearly represented by the middle term in the equation. Of course, other expressions can be used to represent similar relationships, but (7.16) is at least one reasonably simple expression that contains them all.

The last thing to be noticed here is the clear formal similarity between this profit equation, and those describing the benefits to a consumer from the purchase of an innovative product in section 7.1 (equation [7.1] and the maximand corresponding to (7.6)]. It follows that there is little or nothing to be gained by formal manipulation of (7.16) along the lines carried out in the purchase decision discussion. The results will be essentially unchanged, both in formal and in intuitive terms. In particular, we see that Proposition 7.1 applies, unmodified, to the optimal date of introduction of both process and product innovations, provided only that the process yields a finite optimal introduction date (as will not be true if, v, the rate of technical progress [the rate of intertemporal revenue growth elicited by the product improvement] exceeds the interest [discount] rate, r).

7.4 The Case of the Unresponsive Rival: Deciding between the Roles of Innovator and Imitator

We are now in a position to take a first step toward analysis of the preference of the firm's management between the position of "true innovator" and that of imitator. In this discussion we will also begin to approach the management's choice to act in a way that invites a rival to turn the competition between the two into a race to innovate, or instead, to transform it into a waiting game. For example, if our firm's management takes aggressive steps to enhance its market share with the aid of the projected innovation, that may well invite a response that inaugurates a race between the two to be the first to introduce the new item in question. On the other hand, if our management elects to act as imitator, seeking to come into the arena in second place, this may tempt a rival also to put off the launching date of the new product, thereby setting a waiting game into play.

However, this section will not deal with competitors' interactions. On the contrary, to simplify the analysis, the rival's launching time will be taken as a datum exogenously given, and the selected date will not be permitted to move in response to our firm's choice of the launching date of its own product. The assumption is similar to the premise implicit in the study of one firm's decision, given that the other has already announced its commitment to enter at some point of time, θ (the announcement effect). The device is clearly artificial, yet it probably is not entirely unrealistic. Perusal of the history of a considerable number of inventions and their public inauguration suggests that quite frequently the introduction date seems to be determined largely by the rate of progress in the item's design and production process, the condition of the market, and other considerations (besides the state of competition). However, this claim must not be pressed too far, since the evidence for it is at best impressionistic. In any event, the following analysis seems to offer some illumination, even if it were true that every innovator and every imitator were predisposed to the most active forms of rivalrous response and interaction.

It is natural to conduct the analysis by studying the behavior of our firm's total profit, $\pi = \pi(T|h)$, expressed as a function of its own launching date, T, conditional upon the competitor's hypothetically fixed launching date, h. We can call this the innovating firm's *conditional introduction-date profit function*. From this calculation two main results will emerge:

PROPOSITION 7.2   The graph of the conditional introduction-date profit function will, in general, not be a single-peaked hill. Rather, it may well be characterized by *two* substantially separated peaks.

PROPOSITION 7.3   In contrast to behavior in the Hotelling location model, where a second entrant finds it advantageous to position itself as closely as possible to its predecessor(s), the most profitable date, T, for the firm to launch an innovation is apt to be substantially separated from the corresponding date, h, of its rival.[3]

We will provide evidence for the two propositions with the aid of an example, a procedure that is legitimate since neither proposition claims to provide a result of universal validity. For this purpose it will be convenient to focus our attention upon a period of limited duration, H, and assume that the rival has selected a launch date $h < H$, one which is known to our firm's management (in the illustrative graphs we take $h = 10$, $H = 22$). In light of this information, management then settles upon its own introduction date, T, choosing the value of T that maximizes the present value of the firm's prospective profit flow, π. If it transpires that $T < h$, then management will have chosen to seek the role of initial innovator. On the other hand, if we obtain $T > h$, then it will have elected the position of imitator.

Next, we formulate the pertinent profit function. Its form will be completely familiar from that of profit function (7.16) of the preceding section. Only two new complications affect the formulation here. First, it is necessary to take account of the effect of the entry of the rival's product on date h. In all cases, this is taken to reduce our firm's rate of profit flow, at least temporarily. Second, it is necessary to formulate a profit function for the case in which our firm acts as an imitator, which can differ from that for this firm when it serves as the innovator, though the two functions will turn out to be similar in form. Using notation like that of (7.16), but with K representing the reduced rate of profit flow after the rival's entry date, we have as the profit function of our firm (if its management elects the role of innovator by setting introduction date $T = T^* < h$),

$$\pi_{in} = R \int_{t=0}^{T} e^{-rt}\, dt - Ce^{-(r+w)T} + Se^{vT} \int_{t=T}^{h} e^{-rt}\, dt + K \int_{t=h}^{\infty} e^{-rt}\, dt.$$

$$(7.17)$$

Figure 7.3 shows the time path of the undiscounted values of these profit flows as the solid curve. For example, it takes the value R for the interval $0 \leqslant t < T$. At time T^* (in the graph we arbitrarily set $T^* = 5$) the height of the graph is equal to $R - Ce^{-wT^*}$, thus yielding the downward spike at T^*. Then in the interval between T^* and h the height of the graph equals Se^{vT^*}, and so on.

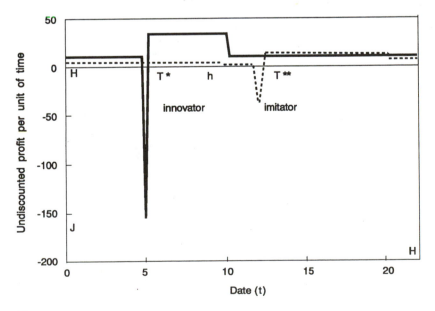

Figure 7.3
Undiscounted profit flows, innovator vs. imitator

Correspondingly, we have, for the later introduction date $T = T^{**} > h$, the imitator's profit function

$$
\pi_{im} = A \int_{t=0}^{h} e^{-rt} \, dt + B \int_{t=h}^{T} e^{-rt} \, dt - De^{-(r+w)T}
$$

$$
+ Ee^{bT} \int_{t=T}^{H} e^{-rt} \, dt + A \int_{t=H}^{\infty} e^{-rt} \, dt. \tag{7.18}
$$

This is so similar to (7.18) that explanation is redundant. Figure 7.3 also illustrates the time path of the undiscounted profit flows corresponding to (7.17), the dashed curve showing these imitators' profit flows, with T arbitrarily placed at $T^{**} = 12$, merely for illustration.

If we carry out the integrations indicated in (7.17) and (7.18), we can calculate the discounted present value of total profit as a function of T, our entrepreneur's selected entry date. The calculation, precisely analogous to that of $B(T)$ in section 7.1 of this chapter, enables us to plot the graph of $\pi(T|h)$. This graph is shown in figure 7.4. It is, indeed, seen to be composed of two hills, as Proposition 7.2 asserts, with a discontinuity at $T = h$. A little experimentation with parameter values, always keeping them within plausible bounds, shows that it is easy to vary the curvatures and the

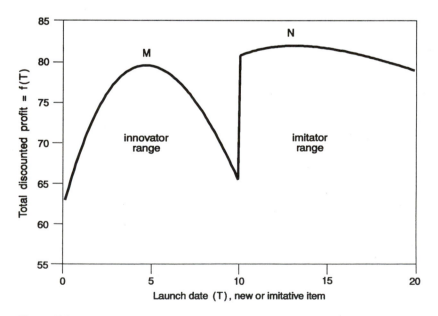

Figure 7.4
Total discounted profit, innovator vs. imitator (as function of T)

relative heights of the two hills. It is, of course, possible for the portion of the graph that lies to the left of h, or that which lies to its right, to have a positive or a negative slope throughout, thereby possibly yielding a corner solution at $T = 0$ (immediate launch) or $T = h$ (the Hotelling solution in which the second entrant crowds the incumbent as closely as possible).[4]

In the graph, the apex, M, of the innovator's profit hill, to the left of $T = h$, lies below N, the apex of the imitator's hill. Thus in this case, our firm will choose to be an imitator if its objective is to maximize its profit. Management will then, clearly, select launch date T_N.

It will also be noted that, in the case shown in the graph, T_M and T_N (respectively, the optimal launch dates of innovator and imitator) both lie relatively far from h within the range of pertinent dates. This confirms the assertion of Proposition 7.3 that, in the relation of innovator and imitator, it is at least theoretically possible to obtain an anti-Hotelling case in which the two firms, far from trying to select neighboring launch dates, seek rather to keep them a considerable interval apart. This is not merely a formal possibility. It is clear that the original innovator will seek a considerable difference between the date of launch of that firm's new product and the date at which the imitator enters and begins to erode those profits. A glance at (7.18) confirms that this is indeed built into the profit function, and can contribute considerably to its decline as T approaches h from the left.

But there can also be good reason for the imitator to keep its distance from the launch date of the innovator. Delay saves capital cost, for the usual reasons. It offers the imitator a longer period to carry out R&D, thereby coming out with a more marketable product. It permits additional free-riding upon the improvement efforts of the incumbent, thereby possibly avoiding the worst problems and risks of the earliest models. Finally, if there is a prospect that the original innovator will go bankrupt, as has so often happened, waiting may enable the imitator to acquire the innovator's assets at bargain prices. Not all of these considerations have been built overtly into (7.18), but enough of them make their appearance to help materially to account for the distance between T^{**} and h.

It remains only to consider in this section what determines the relative altitudes of M and N, that is, the relative profitability of "pure innovation" and imitation. Here, there seems to be little more to be said beyond mere listing of the major influences at work. This will not offer us much that can serve as a handle for formal analysis, but it will show why one cannot really generalize about the relative advantages of the positions of "original innovator" and imitator. Certainly, history provides examples showing that it was sometimes the one, sometimes the other, who turned out to have made the more profitable choice, and suggesting that fortuitous elements played a substantial role in this outcome.

The state of competition among the actors and prospective actors is one of the key considerations here. A proliferation of potential imitators will tend to favor the decision to pursue the position of innovator by precluding high returns to imitation, while the threat of early entry by imitators will cut down the relative and absolute returns to innovation. An equally clear role is played by the comparative costs of the R&D entailed in the two processes and, in particular, the extent to which patents add to the outlays that imitators are forced to make in order to avoid legal entanglements. The durability of the product in question can also be of some significance, for if the innovator succeeds in saturating the market with a product that is very long-lived, the imitator may find that only minor improvements will prove insufficient to attract customers until the distant date when the old, original item is ripe for replacement.

At least two other considerations are likely to be of importance. One is the magnitude of the risk that must be undertaken by the innovator firm, as influenced by the degree to which the area into which it has chosen to venture is terra incognita. The second influence affecting the relative profitability of the two positions is the magnitude of the spillover benefits that the innovator provides to imitators, in the form of risk reduction via both market and technical exploration, through improvements in the pertinent techniques of R&D, and in a variety of other ways. The next section, which reports a model provided by Dasgupta, will describe one way of taking these spillovers into account. For now, it would appear that the preceding list of pertinent influences is sufficient to show that there is no a priori reason to expect the advantage to go uniformly to the innovator or to the imitator, that is, for a process of vigorous competition among prospectively innovating firms either uniformly to constitute a race or, alternatively, always to become a waiting game.

One can, however, say something about the strategic interactions among the players that can arise in the two cases. Game theory is what is obviously called for, and for this purpose we cannot obviously do better that to describe the model mentioned in the preceding paragraph. As usual in such game-theoretic analyses, general conclusions are difficult to arrive at since small changes in the structure of the game can affect the solution substantially. As a result, the highly simplified model to which we turn now may be all that is called for here, since it is not clear that a model that is more complex or more sophisticated will elicit conclusions that are more robust or even more suggestive.

7.5   Simple Game-Theoretic Models of Innovator-Imitator Interactions

The Dasgupta model (1988) entails a game with very simple rules and circumstances. It involves $N + 1$ firms, all of which invest in R&D in order to play their roles as either innovators or imitators. The decision of each firm, i, consists in the choice of magnitude of $x_i \geq 0$, the amount it spends on R&D. The payoff rules are straightforward. If there is a single firm, j, whose $x_j > x_i$ for all $i \neq j$, then firm j's payoff is $Ax^\alpha - x_j$, and every other firm, i, receives $Bx^\alpha - x_i$, where $x = x_j = \max x_i$. On the other hand, if more than one firm bids (spends) $\max x_i$, then each of these tied high bidders, j, receives the lower of $Ax^\alpha - x_j$ and $Bx^\alpha - x_j$.

The game is presented in normal form. It is assumed that all bids (the x_i outlays) are forfeited, that is, R&D expenditure is a sunk outlay. Firms are taken to maximize their expected profits, and to play noncooperatively. The rules of the game are taken to be common knowledge to the players, each of whom seeks optimal strategies in response to the expected strategies of the other players. This makes for solutions that are Nash-Cournot equilibria, meaning that so long as player i expects no change in the strategy to be chosen by any other player in such a solution, then i will have no motivation to change its own strategy. As we will see, the solutions turn out to entail mixed strategies, which Dasgupta interprets as each player's probabilistic expectation about the choices of pure strategies that other players will make. That is, if j expects i to select either strategy x^* or x^{**} with respective probabilities p^* and $p^{**} = 1 - p^*$, then the mixed strategy that represents j's expectation about i's behavior has the Neumann-Morgenstern representation $p^* x^* + (1 - p^*) x^{**}$, taking the x's to be measured in terms of utilities.

Dasgupta interprets the case $A > B$ to constitute a race, in which each player is offered motivation to achieve the position of initial innovator. Similarly, if $B > A$, we have a waiting game, in which each player aspires to become an imitator, and hopes that someone else will be driven to assume the more poorly compensated role of innovator. Here, it is noteworthy that B constitutes a quantification of the spillover from innovator to imitator, with the gross payoff, Bx^α, to the latter depending on x, the R&D outlay of the innovator, rather than on x_i, the corresponding expenditure of the imitator.

Model 1: A Race
In his first model, that of a race, Dasgupta takes $A > B \geq 0$ and, for simplicity, assumes $\alpha = 0$, so that gross payoffs do not depend on the size of R&D outlays. Then he observes:

PROPOSITION 7.4   The game has no Nash-Cournot equilibrium in pure strategies.

Proof: First we note that no firm, i, will invest $x_i > A - B$, since otherwise its profit will be $A - x_i < B$, while if instead it bids $x_i = 0$, its profit must equal B.

Now suppose i bids $x_i = A - B$. Then each other firm's optimal bid becomes zero, so that it now becomes optimal for i to reduce its bid below $A - B$ to some small positive number. That is, $x_i = A - B$ is not consistent with Nash equilibrium.

Next consider any other pure strategy bid, $x_i < A - B$. Then it pays firm j to bid $x_i + \varepsilon < A - B$, where ε is a small positive number. But then i should, clearly, raise its bid to $x_i + \varepsilon + \delta < A - B$, where $\delta > 0$. Thus, since of the possible pure strategies, $x_i > A - B$, $x_i = A - B$, and $x_i < A - B$ are incompatible with Nash equilibrium, it follows that no such equilibrium in pure strategies exists.

PROPOSITION 7.5   The game does possess a Nash equilibrium in the mixed strategies made up of all of the pure strategies x_i (for firm i) with each x_i assigned a probability corresponding to the *cumulative* distribution $F(x_i) = [x_i/(A - B)]^{1/N}$, and where $0 \leqslant x_i \leqslant A - B$.

Proof: If there exists a mixed strategy equilibrium, then the representative firm, i, must be indifferent among all the pure strategy bids that may enter its mixed strategy, that is, all bids x_i in the interval $[0, A - B]$. But if i bids zero its expected profit is B, while if it bids $x^* > 0$, let $[F(x^*)]^N$ be the joint probability that every other firm will spend less than x^*, so that the representative firm's expected payoff if it spends x^* becomes

$$A[F(x^*)]^N + B\{1 - [F(x^*)]^N\} - x^*.$$

Thus, indifference between the bid x^* and the bid zero requires

$$B = A[F(x^*)]^N + B\{1 - [F(x^*)]^N\} - x^*. \qquad (7.19)$$

Consequently, in such an optimal mixed strategy we see from (7.19) that

$$x^* = (A - B)[F(x^*)]^N \quad \text{or} \quad F(x^*) = [x^*/(A - B)]^{1/N}. \quad \text{Q.E.D.}$$

PROPOSITION 7.6   Each firm, i, can be expected to invest $(A - B)/(N + 1)$ in R&D.

Proof: The expected value is

$$E(x_i) = \int_0^{A-B} x_i f(x_i)\, dx_i,$$

where the density function $f(x) = dF(x)/dx = x^{(1-N)/N}/N(A - B)^{1/N}$, so that

$$E(x_i) = [x_i^{(N+1)/N}/(N + 1)(A - B)^{1/N}]_0^{A-B} = (A - B)^{(N+1-1)/N}/(N + 1)$$

$$= (A - B)/(N + 1).$$

Dasgupta concludes that in this model R&D outlay per firm is a declining function of the number of competitors, $N + 1$, though this is not necessarily true of the total outlay of the industry. Indeed, he notes that in this case total expected industry expenditure is fixed at $A - B$, though he remarks that this is a pure artifact of the simplifying assumptions of the model. Next, he turns to:

Model 2: A Waiting Game
Dasgupta's second model differs from the first only in two respects. This time it is assumed that $B > A$, and that $1 > \alpha > 0$. Here it clearly is preferable to be an imitator, so it does indeed constitute a waiting game in which every firm hopes some other enterprise will act as the innovator. Now we have:

PROPOSITION 7.7   If $N = 0$ so that the industry is a monopoly, the firm's profit-maximizing investment is $x^* = (\alpha A)^{1/1-\alpha}$.

Proof: This follows directly by differentiation with respect to x of the profit function $\pi = Ax^\alpha - x$. That must be the monopolist's profit function, since with no one else in the industry this firm has no choice but to act as innovator, for otherwise its profits will be zero.

Finally, one obtains:

PROPOSITION 7.8   There exists a Nash equilibrium in mixed strategies in which each firm bids either $x = 0$ or $x = x^*$ (the profit-maximizing bid of the monopolist in Proposition 7.7) with the former bid assigned the probability $p(0) = \{[B - (1 - \alpha)A]/B\}^{1/N}$.

Proof: If any other firm makes a nonzero bid, x', and so becomes the innovator, it obviously maximizes firm i's profits to spend nothing on R&D, thereby obtaining the profit Bx'^α. On the other hand, if every other firm bids zero, and so firm i wishes to make a nonzero bid rather than ending up with no profits at all, then the profit-maximizing bid for i is obviously $x_i = x^*$. Thus an optimal mixed strategy will encompass only these two pure strategies. Moreover, as before, optimality requires that the firm's expected profit be the same whether it turns out *ex post* to have bid x^*, yielding expected profit $\pi(x^*)$, or it instead bids zero, with expected profit $\pi(0)$. Thus, we require

$$\pi(0) = p(0)^N 0 + [1 - p(0)^N]Bx^{*\alpha} = [1 - p(0)^N]Bx^{*\alpha}$$

to equal[5]

$$\pi(x^*) = p(0)^N(Ax^{*\alpha} - x^*) + [1 - p(0)^N](Ax^{*\alpha} - x^*) = Ax^{*\alpha} - x^*.$$

That is,

$$Ax^{*\alpha} - x^* = [1 - p(0)^N]Bx^{*\alpha} \quad \text{or}$$

$$[(A - x^*/x^{*\alpha})] = B - Bp(0)^N.$$

This immediately yields the value of $p(0)$ called for by Proposition 7.8, that is,

$$p(0) = \{[B - (1 - \alpha)A]/B\}^{1/N}.$$

Dasgupta concludes from all this that

For a given level of industrial concentration, $(N + I)$, the greater the imitation possibilities the less will each firm be expected to conduct R&D.... Furthermore, there is a positive chance that no innovation will occur, and it is $\{[B - (I - \alpha)A]/B\}^{(N+1)/N}$. And this chance increases with greater competition, growing to the limit of $[B - (I - \alpha)A]/B$ as the number of firms increases without limit. By the same token, there is a positive chance that an innovation *will* occur, and this decreases with increasing competition. There is thus a positive relationship between industrial concentration and the probability that an innovation will occur. Notice as well that each firm's *expected* R&D expenditure increases with the pure profitability of the innovation; that is, it increases with A. Thus, the larger the market, or the greater the innovation opportunities, the larger is the volume of R&D investment expected to be.

These results are congenial to intuition. Spillovers hold firms back from investing in R&D. But they do not hold them back completely, even when spillovers are so large as to make it positively beneficial to be an imitator. For if all hold back forever there will be no-one to imitate!   (1988, p. 78)

This chapter has described several analytic models which offer a variety of concrete results about the innovation and imitation processes, with particular emphasis on the timing issues involved. It is not easy to provide a convincing judgment of the robustness of the results, since the models can hardly pretend to achieve a high level of generality, and one can only surmise the degree to which changes in the model specifications will modify the conclusions offered here. It seems plausible that the earlier models in the chapter, which avoid the complex interactions that may arise among competing innovators, may prove the most robust, though that is by no means certain. One feature that does argue in the other direction is the fact that the game-theoretic models produce results that are so "congenial to intuition," to use Dasgupta's words. The very fact that our initial timing model produces results that are less obviously intuitive is at once its strength and its weakness, for this indicates that the insights provided by the model are relatively novel but that they are correspondingly suspect.

The reliance of the analysis of this chapter upon the standard tools of optimality calculation is, of course, explained by the managerial character of the decisions examined, in arenas in which the innovation process has become routine. Thus, while this chapter has focused on innovation and imitation, it, like Chapter 6, has *not* dealt with entrepreneurship, in the sense that the term is used here. As was emphasized in Chapter 6, it is the managerial character of routine innovation (imitation) processes that restores the pertinence of formal optimality calculation.

In saying this it must be made clear that our concern with imitation, as distinguished from "true innovation," is *not* a valid reason for leaving the entrepreneur out of the discussion. The next section of the book focuses upon technology transfer as a crucial product of imitation. The discussion will emphasize that imitation can be an extremely entrepreneurial act, particularly if it entails the opening of new markets for the innovative product and further adaptation of the product to the requirements of those markets. Thus the discussion will constitute a continuation of our central theme— the allocation of entrepreneurship. This time, however, it will deal with allocation of entrepreneurs between "initial innovation" and imitation, examining the influences that determine that allocation, and considering its consequences for the economy.

8 The Rich Mutual Gains from Technology Transfer: Dissemination and the Market Mechanism

Where an open communication is preserved among nations, it is impossible but the domestic industry of every one must receive an encrease from the improvements of the others.... Every improvement, which we have since made, has arisen from our imitation of foreigners.... Yet we continue still to repine, that our neighbors should possess any art, industry, and invention; forgetting that, had they not first instructed us, we should have been at present barbarians.

Hume (1758)

It may be seriously argued that, historically, European receptivity to new technologies ... whatever their origin, has been as important as inventiveness itself.

Rosenberg (1982, p. 245)

As was argued in the first chapter, technological progress is determined by two complementary elements: the rate of invention and innovation, and the speed with which new technology is disseminated and adopted in firms throughout the world. The entrepreneur plays a critical role in *both* of these activities. Her contribution to innovation is well recognized in the economic literature, but her part in enhancing speed of dissemination is virtually absent from the discussions.

In an imaginary world economy in which all commodities were traded and in which products were perfectly homogeneous, no firm might be able to survive as a producer of good X if it fell behind in production techniques and therefore had to cover higher costs than the innovation leader among its rivals, or if it lagged behind them in product quality. Consequently, in such an economy only the latest and the best technology might be viable, and there would be no need for dissemination in order for consumers to reap the full benefits of the latest ideas. However, the world is not like that. Many goods are produced and consumed in the same vicinity. More important, a large share of the world's products are heterogeneous, particularly in industries characterized by rapid technical change, where firm A may produce a variant of product X that is superior in one new feature, while firm B remains a viable producer of X because its product has a different valuable new feature. In these circumstances, it is possible for an invention either to be used exclusively by one of the firms, or to be shared by them both. It is obvious that if sharing can be arranged in a way that does not discourage investment in innovation, productivity will grow more rapidly, just as it will if the flow of innovations is increased. If firm A has quick access to B's new technology and vice versa, both can expect to benefit from speed of product improvement and cost reduction superior to what each could have achieved on its own.

As we will see, one of the growth contributions of the entrepreneur has been to carry out or facilitate the dissemination of technology. Thus, innovation is not her only role in the growth process. In this chapter and several that follow, the dissemination of technology, and the part played in the process by both the entrepreneur and the manager, will be explored.

This chapter offers three principal conclusions. One of them is already widely recognized by some who have studied the matter carefully (though not by the wider constituency), while the others seem relatively novel:

1. Technology transfer among nations makes an enormous contribution to growth of both the individual industrialized economy and to that of the world in general. Indeed, there is reason to believe that technology transferred from other countries may typically contribute considerably more to the productivity of an economy, even in a representative industrialized country, than do the innovations that are based on the work of native inventors.

2. While the acquisition of technical knowledge by one country from another clearly benefits the recipient, it is not a beggar-thy-neighbor policy. On the contrary, marked mutual gains in productivity and product quality are provided by the interchange of information among economies. Far from being a zero-sum game, the process is superadditive.

3. There is strong reason to believe that the performance of the market mechanism in this arena is far better than the economic literature would appear to imply.

Economic theory has always awarded the market mechanism very high marks on its consequences for static allocative efficiency. But in the long run it is surely its effect on the *growth* of efficiency that matters most, and here standard theoretical analysis is, at best, grudging in its praise. The literature suggests that in market economies the free-rider problem seriously inhibits the dissemination of technological advances. To deal with this problem, a business firm seeking to profit from its outlays on R&D and related expenditures will use patents, secrecy, or whatever other means it has available to prevent or at least impede the use by others of the product and process ideas and information the firm generates.[1] The result, one might expect, would be a relatively stately pace of technology *transmission*, perhaps far slower than the general welfare requires.

The second central conclusion of this chapter is that this view of the matter is not supported by the facts. Rather, the historical evidence depicts technology traveling from firm to firm and from country to country with astonishing speed. And since in the market economies governments have had either a minor role or virtually no role at all in the process, it would appear to follow that rapidity of transfer is the work of private enterprise. This must mean either that private firms are not very effective in their allegedly determined efforts to keep their innovations from others or that their opposition is not quite as unrelenting as has been supposed. In the chapters that follow we will examine some of the means by which the market appears to have stimulated the spread of technology. We will find that the entrepreneur has played a substantial part, this time in the role of creative imitator rather than that of innovator. But we will also see that even the results of routine innovation activity in large firms, rather than always being zealously guarded and kept from others, often will deliberately and systematically be offered to other enterprises, even to business rivals. We will even discover, in Chapter 10, circumstances that hardly seem uncommon in which failure to share proprietary technological information is apt to be penalized heavily and systematically by the market.

This is all of considerable importance for the general welfare if rapid dissemination of technology does contribute a great deal to growth in output and productivity. We therefore begin this chapter with an examination of this hypothesis, and of the stronger conjecture that nothing else, neither domestic innovation nor investment, makes as much of an incremental addition to long-run growth in the productivity of a "representative" *industrialized* economy as its speed in adopting technological innovations from other countries. In the next chapter we will return to the role of the entrepreneur in this task and to the allocation of entrepreneurial effort between "pure innovation" and technology transfer.

8.1 On the Undervalued Contribution of Imitation (Technology Transfer)

Imitation has usually served as a starting point for a country's development. Historically, Japan is certainly not the first country to base the early stages of its economic takeoff on imitation. The Flemish and, later, the Dutch, when they were about to become the world's economic leaders, borrowed their early commercial technology from the Italians (North and Thomas [1973, p. 138]). As the mantle of leadership passed to the English from the Dutch, the inhabitants of the United Kingdom, in turn, profited from the productive techniques in use in the Low Countries and elsewhere on the continent (Nef [1934], Coleman [1975], among others). The United States then learned many of its industrial techniques from the English and others.

Technology transfer is important not only to an economy that is in the process of overtaking another. It can contribute enormously to growth in any industrialized economy. The quantitative importance of borrowed technology is suggested by an illustrative comparison that follows a line of argument offered by Tullock (1986). Using numbers selected only for illustrative convenience, imagine a world economy containing exactly ten very similar industrialized economies, each of which introduces the same amount of innovative technology each year, each such invention having a useful life of ten years. Suppose, moreover, that two years after its initial introduction each new technique or a close substitute will have been acquired by the other nations in the group by license, reverse engineering, industrial espionage, or other means.[2] Then it follows directly from the arithmetic that, at any given time, nearly 90 percent of the techniques in a country will have been derived by imitation of others rather than from domestic innovation.

As we will see presently, the facts indicate that this numerical conclusion, though quite hypothetical, does not correspond too poorly to reality. But the basic point does not rely on the particular numbers. It is virtually obvious that where a considerable number of countries all contribute to the world's flow of innovations, and where all end up using the latest technology, each of them *must* end up deriving the bulk of its technological advances via some form of imitation from abroad.

To get some notion of the pertinent facts we turn to the Organization for Economic Cooperation and Development (OECD) and its twenty-four member countries,[3] which include most of the world's industrialized market economies. Table 8.1 reports the number of patents granted by each of them to its own residents in 1988. It also reports the ratio of this number to the population (in millions) of the corresponding country and, most important for our purposes, for each country the percentage of total 1988 OECD patents held by other countries. Number of patents issued clearly has many serious defects as an accurate measure of inventive activity (for

Table 8.1
Patents issued to residents, OECD countries, 1988

Country	Total patents	Patents/mil. population	% held in other OECD countries
Japan	47912	391	64.0
U.S.A.	40497	165	69.5
West Germany	15704	258	88.2
France	8822	158	93.4
U.K.	4447	78	96.7
Switzerland	2995	454	97.7
Italy	2787	49	97.9
Sweden	2424	289	98.2
Austria	1364	180	99.0
Canada	1184	45	99.1
Australia	988	61	99.3
Spain	909	23	99.3
Finland	776	157	99.4
Netherlands	720	49	99.5
Denmark	344	67	99.7
Norway	277	66	99.8
Belgium	245	25	99.8
New Zealand	240	72	99.8
Greece	177	18	99.9
Luxembourg	76	208	99.9
Turkey	54	1	100.0
Ireland	10	3	100.0
Portugal	10	1	100.0
Iceland	0	0	100.0

Source: World Intellectual Property Organization (1989).

an excellent discussion see Griliches [1990], but as a rough indicator, which is all we require here, it will do).

We note, first, that Japan led the list in number of patents it granted to its residents,[4] with the United States very close behind. Despite the imperfect correspondence between number of patents and number of inventions, and the very poor information the former provides on the *importance* of the inventions a given country provides, this evidence should serve to raise serious doubts about the contention that Japan's productivity performance rests largely on its propensity to imitate the technology of other economies.[5] Most pertinent here, we see that, even for the Japanese, 64 percent of the OECD patents were available only from residents of other OECD countries, and that for all but three countries (Japan, the United States, and West Germany) more than 90 percent of the OECD patents were held by residents of other countries. Mansfield (1990, p. 342) reports, "In 1978, the [Japanese] Ministry of International Trade and Industry carried out a survey of Japanese business leaders to determine the relative contributions made by domestic and foreign technologies to product quality and production processes. According to the results, purely indigenous technology accounted for only about 5% of the advances in product quality and about 17% of the advances in processes." Clearly, for most countries, if they are to keep from falling behind, they must be prepared to undertake a very considerable amount of importation of technology.

In any event, whatever the correct numbers for each individual country, it remains true, *tautologically*, that if all the countries in the group employ essentially the same technology, and the OECD group accounts for the bulk of innovation, then for the "average" economy in the twenty-four–nation group approximately twenty-three–twenty-fourths of current technology *must* derive from other members rather than having been contributed by its own inventors.

In contrast, a profusion of examples suggests that the role of first inventor offers little enduring advantage to a country. Britain and the Netherlands provided the key inventions for the accurate clock and watch, but by the middle of the nineteenth century the bulk of that industry had passed to Switzerland and the United States. In this century, when the Swiss invented the quartz watch the new technique was so well suited to Japanese production methods that Switzerland came perilously close to losing the industry altogether. The British, from the middle of the nineteenth century onward, saw one of their inventions after another taken over by foreign producers: German, American, and, more recently, Japanese. Mass-produced steel, railroad equipment, penicillin, and jet aircraft are only a few older and more recent examples. The Japanese have achieved preeminence in the productions of many items that they did not invent: television sets, cameras and color film, automobiles, and watches. The United States is reported to dominate the market for automatic teller machine systems in banking, a concept invented in Japan. Thus countries clearly have no reason to expect to retain leadership in the production of some item just because they happen to have invented it, and ambitious countries need not waste their efforts and resources in pursuing the role of primary inventor. Perhaps the most ironic example is provided by the British just before the First World War. By then they had lost their preeminence in most of the industries that had been launched through their invention. But in one industry they remained at the top—the construction of steamships—an invention of which the United States had produced the first workable examples (Robert Fulton's riverboats) and to whose development the United States had certainly contributed.

8.2 Alternative Interpretation of the Relative Contribution of Invention and Imitation

We turn, next, to another sense in which imitation can be taken to offer a superior contribution to an economy's output capacity. The slightly formal discussion that follows approaches the issue by examining explicitly in what sense society is called upon to allocate resources between the two activities—innovation and imitation. We will also see that the claimed advantage of imitation rests on an exceedingly simple-minded phenomenon. This is the fact that, in many circumstances, imitation may be able to achieve a given increase in productivity far more cheaply, in terms of real resources consumed in the process, than can be done by innovative effort. That is, given an invention that can increase the value of an imitator's output by x percent or reduce its cost by y percent, then society benefits more from such a transfer of the technology to the imitator than if the latter were, instead, to invest its funds in research toward development of a new invention that yields precisely the same results. This is so because the transfer generally uses up a quantity of society's resources smaller than those required to develop an invention "from scratch."

One can now extend this argument somewhat into a proposition dealing directly with the optimal allocation of a given quantity of resources between innovation and technology transfer, dealing with both product and process innovations:

PROPOSITION 8.1   Assuming that the gross benefit from each additional use of an invention by another firm is constant (that is, the same as the benefit from its use by any other firm) and that the (constant expected) cost per imitation is less than the (constant expected) cost per invention, then if resources are sufficient to finance more than one innovation and at least one imitation, a socially optimal allocation of these resources will entail at least one invention, with as many firms imitating the invention as are available to use it, and with a second invention provided only if there are resources left over after *every* firm that can do so has imitated the first invention.

Proof: Let

$N =$ the number of inventions;

$T =$ the number of firms to which each invention is transferred;

$B =$ the benefit of use of the invention by an additional firm;

$K =$ the quantity of productive resource available;

$C_N =$ the constant expected cost of an additional invention; and

$C_T =$ the constant expected cost of transfer to an additional firm.

Then the social goal is to maximize the total benefit of innovations and transfers

$$\pi = BN + BTN \tag{8.1}$$

subject to the resource availability constraint

$$C_N N + C_T TN = K. \tag{8.2}$$

As usual, this requires a comparison (using subscripts to represent partial derivatives) of the marginal return per additional dollar of innovation expenditure,

$$\pi_N / K_N = B(1 + T)/[C_N + C_T T] \text{ if } N \neq 0. \tag{8.3}$$

with the marginal return on an additional dollar spent on transfer,

$$\pi_T / K_T = BN/C_T N = B(1 + T)/C_T(1 + T). \tag{8.4}$$

Since by hypothesis, $C_N > C_T$, it follows at once that iff $N > 0$ then (8.4) must exceed (8.3), so that then the marginal yield of an additional dollar spent on T must be greater than the marginal yield of a dollar spent on N. However, if $N = 0$, then $\pi_T = BN = 0$, while $\pi_N = B(1 + T) > 0$.   Q.E.D.

Clearly, this argument is oversimple to the point of naïveté, and its downplaying of the relative contribution of innovation is a considerable exaggeration. Still, it would appear that the point, though now obvious, has not been widely recognized, and that it is not entirely without substance.

8.3   Empirical Evidence on the Contribution of Imitation

M. Ishaq Nadiri has provided an exemplary survey of the available empirical evidence on innovation and technological spillover (1991), including reports on his own fundamental contributions to the field. In the course of the discussion he reviews the evidence on the relative contributions of innovation and imitation and, in particular, on the international dissemination of technological information. Thus, he reports:

Regressing total factor productivity of the industry on its own R&D and borrowed R&D (both expressed as ratios of industry output) [Terleckyj (1974, 1980)] reported a 45% rate of return for borrowed R&D and about 28% for own R&D in the manufacturing sector. When R&D was decomposed into private and public R&D, the return to borrowed R&D was even higher ... (Nadiri [1980]). Other studies such as Postner and Wesa (1983) confirmed similar patterns, i.e., the rate of return on borrowed R&D was more than twice that of own R&D (see Mohnen [1990] for details) (Nadiri [1991, p. 26]).

Results reported by Mansfield (1984) for fifteen U.S. chemical and petroleum firms for the period 1960–76 suggests a substantial contribution of overseas R&D. In fact the influence of overseas R&D on productivity was several times larger than that of domestic R&D (p. 40).... Finally, the fragmentary econometric results that are available suggest a major effect of foreign R&D on domestic industries' total factor productivity, the rate of return on borrowed technology from abroad often exceeding that of the domestic R&D. (p. 42)

Nadiri also reports that, "In the past few years the pace of technology transfers has been increasing rapidly, particularly among the OECD countries. Statistics on international payments for patents, licenses and technical know-how among the OECD countries have been growing substantially. The statistics on technology balance payment ... among the OECD countries indicate a rapid increase in technology trade.... For Japan and the U.K. the total transaction between 1970 to 1988 increased by about 400%, France and the U.S. experienced an increase of about 550% while West Germany had a spectacular increase of over 1000% between 1979 and 1988." He adds that, "The U.S. and, to some extent, the U.K., still remain net exporters while France, Germany, and Japan remain net importers of technology ..." (p. 36). Aside from Switzerland, "All other OECD countries are net importers" (p. 39).

Clearly, the empirical data seem consistent with the position proposed here, that technology transfers in general, and transnational transfers in particular, are important and probably growing contributors to productivity growth. Moreover, it would appear that their contribution is probably at least comparable to that of domestic invention, and may well exceed the latter.

8.4   Convergence as Suggestive Evidence on the Importance of Imitation[6]

There is another historical phenomenon that can be taken to provide suggestive evidence on the relative importance of technology transfer. This is the sharp convergence in per capita output and productivity levels that has occurred at least among a limited group of nations. That is, per capita incomes and productivity levels in these countries have grown increasingly similar ever since the end of World War II, and probably since a considerably earlier date. There have also recently been many other studies in this area, which all seem to conclude that after adjustment for the role of the so-called ancillary variables, such as intercountry differences in educational expenditures, investment in equipment, political stability, and so on, the convergence phenomenon is far more widespread and far more persistent than even the earlier studies indicated.

However, the point to be made in this section—that convergence itself constitutes strong indirect evidence for the efficacy and pervasiveness of the process of technology transfer—is perhaps made most easily with the aid of one of the earliest statistical studies of the phenomenon (Baumol [1986]). In that study I reported on the convergence that seems to have occurred in the productivity levels and per capita incomes of a selected group of sixteen nations, in the 110 years to which the productivity data provided by Angus Maddison pertain (1982, p. 8). Maddison's data indicate that during that time there has occurred a dramatic narrowing of the range between the productivity of the highest and lowest of the countries

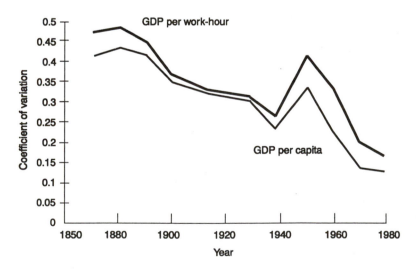

Figure 8.1
Coefficients of variation, gross domestic product (GDP) per work-hour and GDP per capita, sixteen Maddison countries, 1870–1979
Source: Maddison (1982, p. 212), as portrayed in Baumol, Blackman, and Wolff (1989, p. 93).

in the sample, from a ratio of 8:1 in 1870 to approximately 2:1 in 1979. Figure 8.1 shows the time path of the coefficients of variation (the ratio of the standard deviation to the mean) in *both* GDP per capita and GDP per work hour (labor productivity). The graph confirms that, except for a sharp but temporary reversal during World War II, this convergence for the limited group of countries involved was quite persistent throughout the 110-year period.[7]

It follows tautologically that if the less affluent members of the convergence group are catching up to the wealthier countries in, for example, per capita income, then per capita incomes in the former must be growing at a more rapid rate than those of the latter. That is, in order for convergence to have occurred, the poorer a country in Maddison's sample was in 1870, the more rapidly its per capita income *must* have grown ever since. Statistical study to determine whether the facts do exhibit such a relationship is, then, yet another way of testing the convergence hypothesis. And the data do indeed produce results consistent with it, as is confirmed for this (non-random) sample of sixteen countries, by the regression equation obtained from the Maddison data:

Growth Rate, GDP per cap., 1870—1979
$= 7.68 - 0.91 \ln(1870\ \text{GDP per cap.}),\ R^2 = 0.92.$
          [12.4]

(where the t ratio is shown in brackets under the coefficient). The closeness of fit is almost startling. Indeed, as will be seen presently, it is much too good.

The pertinence of convergence for us here is that an attempt to account for this phenomenon must also throw some light on the part that technology transfer plays in the interrelationships of a club of nations converging in their levels of productivity and prosperity. For in order for such convergence to occur, it must, surely, be possible for laggard nations to learn more from the leaders than the leaders can learn from the laggards (for an excellent discussion, see Abramovitz [1986]). That this must be so seems obvious enough, since their very position implies that the leaders must have accumulated a stock of pertinent knowledge involving both basic principles and techniques of execution which the laggards had not yet acquired. If both sets of countries possess a cadre of what may be called "imitating entrepreneurs," similar in capability and avidly engaged in the importation of proven innovations from wherever they can find them, it is only to be expected that in a given period the imitating entrepreneurs in the laggard countries are likely to gain more in the process. Such a scenario by itself can contribute materially to an explanation of the convergence phenomenon, but it can do so only if the acquisition of foreign techniques is not an activity of minor importance.

This suggestive evidence can be carried one step further. The apparent tightness of the regression relationship itself poses a puzzle which is pertinent because it seems to admit a sensible resolution only if the active acquisition of foreign techniques is as important as is suggested here. The high R-squared in the preceding estimates seems to suggest the rather absurd conclusion that a country's economic growth since 1870 depended *almost entirely* on its initial income level.[8] Nothing else would seem to have mattered much—not propensity to save, nor the openness of the economy, nor growth policies, nor cultural attributes. It is as though some poorer nations simply had been selected by fate to approach ever closer to the richer ones, regardless of what they or the others did about it. Moreover, exactly the same puzzling sort of tight regression relationship is obtained from the data on labor productivity.

The apparent implication that nothing besides a country's initial position mattered for subsequent growth of productivity or per capita income is, of course, quite implausible and, indeed, almost certainly false.[9] As we will see, even if it were not beset by statistical problems, it would nevertheless probably be incorrect. The role assigned here to technology transfer derives some added credibility from its ability to contribute to a simple explanation of this as well as the equally implausible implication of the regression equations, in *appearing* to show that 1979 levels of productivity and output per capita are (retrospectively) "predictable" from just the corresponding figures for 1870. While as we have just seen, this *seems* to imply that differences in policy among nations hardly made any difference for their relative 110-year growth records, there is an alternative explanation which is far more plausible.

Pervasive and effective imitation activity during the period would have enabled even a country with poorly designed productivity policy or institutions that impede productivity growth quickly to obtain benefits very similar to those enjoyed in a country in a better position in this arena. Thus, suppose country A (with much innovating activity stimulated by felicitous policy, culture, or institutions) invents an extraordinary number of revolutionary processes as a result. Within a few years imitative entrepreneurs or other agents of technology transfer operating in countries B, C, and D will enable their own industries to use those process themselves, or will offer them some close substitutes. The rapid international diffusion of a variety of inventions—the computer, the transistor, the commercial jet airplane, television, and many others—confirms that this must be so. Imitative activity clearly may be able to permit *all* industrialized countries to enjoy, rather quickly, the fruits of a successful growth policy in any one of their number.

It is at least plausible that this is why an effective growth policy made little difference for the *relative* growth of productivity and per capita income in these countries. The contagion of successful ideas tends to make them spread quickly to those economies that are susceptible. Imitative entrepreneurship or other transfer mechanisms make an international public good of any one nation's innovating activities, the fruits of its effective growth policies— from which it is almost impossible to exclude other industrialized nations in the longer run, even those with less promising growth policies.

8.5   On the Mutual Gains from Technology Transfer

It is clear that a recipient country is apt to benefit from technology transfer. But there is more to the story. *All* countries are borrowers and none to an inconsiderable degree. Beyond that, it is very likely that *all* countries grow far faster as a result of learning from others.

To understand why dissemination can contribute substantially to growth of all countries simultaneously, we must pause to note yet another way in which one can be misled by the standard theory. The mainstream writings on innovation, from those of Schumpeter to more recent pieces that treat R&D as a race or a waiting game, would have us think of competition in innovation as a process in which several rivals seek to design a *common* new product or process, for example, all working on high-definition television or a laptop computer with a color screen. Of course, cases of such similarity in the goals of innovating rivals do occur. But the evidence indicates that an alternative scenario is much more common. That is the case in which the innovations of competing firms and firms in different countries are not only different, but complementary. Each may reduce costs but the two firms' innovations together may cut costs far more than either does by itself. Or one computer manufacturer may come up with a battery that lasts longer before recharging, while another producer may find a way to cut the weight of the machine by 25 percent. A laptop computer that has both these new features will be more avidly desired by consumers than a machine that offers only one of them.

The fact that innovations frequently differ from firm to firm, and from country to country, and that they are often complements (not substitutes), is highly pertinent to our discussion. In a world where this is true the firm or the economy that innovates successfully normally need not, as a consequence, achieve even temporary dominance of the market. Rather, it is likely to continue to face very viable competitors, each of which has retained its position by introducing new products or processes of its own.

Then rapid dissemination of technology will surely benefit consumers, because each firm can offer products that incorporate *all* of the improvements. Or if the inventions in question are cost-reducing process changes, each of which cuts costs by, say, 1 percent, technology dissemination may permit a process that takes advantage of all the innovative efficiencies and reduces cost by a substantial multiple of that 1 percent that each improvement by itself makes possible. Put another way, in a world where no producer is put out of the pertinent line of business by its rival's inventions, quick and easy dissemination of every such invention among many enterprises serves to *multiply* its benefits by permitting many producers, rather than only one of them, to provide to consumers the cost or product advantages that the invention makes possible. By such multiplication, dissemination of technology can enhance the power of each invention manyfold and it thereby can contribute correspondingly to the productive powers of the world economy. And each economy that becomes proficient in the acquisition of technology from elsewhere (making itself welcome to do so by offering easy access to its own technology to others) will indeed end up doing well by doing good.

8.6   On Speed of Dissemination and the Market Mechanism

Let us, for the moment, leave our discussion of the first major topic of the chapter—the substantial contribution of imitation to an economy's productivity performance. We turn, next, to the surprising efficacy and speed with which the market mechanism appears to carry out the vital process of technology transfer, despite all the theoretical grounds that question its performance. The theoretical models focusing upon innovation as a competitive tool usually deal with one of two basic cases: models in the first group, beginning with Schumpeter's, examine the case of a lone innovator who has achieved a marked competitive advantage through its valuable new products or processes, an advantage that firm will retain until imitators are able to cut into that lead; models in the second group focus upon rival firms each seeking to come up with what is essentially the same invention, either running a race or treating the process as a waiting game. In either case, the innovating firm has much to gain by making it as difficult as possible for rivals to obtain access to its proprietary technology. In that view of the matter, this enterprise will do everything it can to sabotage or prevent the transfer of its technology to other enterprises. Having argued that such technology transfer can be highly beneficial to the economy, it would appear to follow from the theory that the performance of the market mechanism in this arena can be expected to fall far short of optimality. Add to this the widespread contention of the literature in innovation theory that spillovers can generally be expected to lead to underinvestment in R&D and innovation (that is, that firms are apt to invest less than the socially optimal amounts in technical progress, because so large a share of the benefits will go to others), and one is left with the impression that economic theory gives low grades to the market as an instrument of productivity growth, in contradistinction to the high marks it is awarded for its static efficiency in resource allocation. This judgment will probably come as a surprise to noneconomists who are more likely to be impressed by the remarkable growth records of the market economies than by their allocative efficiency.

The evidence, as will be argued next, seems to support this common wisdom against the Schumpeterian tradition, at least as far as the efficacy of technology transfer is concerned. It indicates that technology is, in fact, transferred from one economy to another with dramatic speed. In the two chapters that follow some analytical reasons will be offered to help explain why the technology transfer performance of the market economies seems to be so much better than the theory might lead one to expect. But, first, the available evidence on that performance will be recapitulated.

Some concrete evidence indicating how quickly techniques spread today will be presented. Perhaps more surprising is the speed with which they traveled in earlier times, when transportation was far slower and more dangerous, and information normally could move no faster than the person who carried it. For example, the first documented use of the post windmill (one that shifts direction with the direction of the wind) occurred in Yorkshire in 1185; within a decade it had been imitated throughout Europe to an extent sufficient to make it worthwhile for the Pope to impose a tithe upon them (Mokyr [1990, p. 45]). Mokyr tells us also that, "Like the windmill, the printing press spread with dazzling speed" (p. 49). Equally rapid was the spread throughout Europe of Newcomen's steam engine (which itself was hardly the first steam engine; see, e.g., Gomory [1983, p. 576]). It made its appearance in 1712—half a century before Watt's improved version. "Within a few years of its inception, it spread to France, Germany and Belgium and by 1730 it was operating in Spain, Hungary and

Sweden" (Mokyr [1990, p. 85]). However, far more remarkable was the speed of the transfer of the railroad steam locomotive. Though rail transport had been used in mines for some years, the first successful passenger locomotive was Stephenson's English Rocket in 1829. In that same year two British locomotives landed in the port of New York. *Within a year*, the first American-built locomotive, the Tom Thumb, designed by Peter Cooper with three times the traction power of the Rocket, had a successful run on the tracks of the Baltimore and Ohio Railroad (*Encyclopedia Britannica*, 14th ed., vol. 44, p. 279).

It is hardly surprising that speed of technology transfer has continued into more recent times. This is strikingly confirmed by several careful empirical investigations. A study of the early transfer of substantial semiconductor innovations (Tilton [1971]) found that none of them had required more than four years to be spread throughout the industrial world, and that the average transfer lag was about two and a half years. A study with a broader range was carried out by Mansfield and his colleagues (1981). They report, on the basis of data provided by one hundred American firms in a variety of manufacturing industries, that "information concerning development decisions is generally in the hands of rivals within about 12 to 18 months, on the average, and information containing the detailed nature and operation of a new product or process generally leaks out within about a year" (p. 217). Another impressive study, by Levin, Klevorick, Nelson, and Winter [1987], examined, among other things, the "cost and time required for imitation" and reached results that were "consistent with those of Mansfield, Schwartz and Wagner" (p. 811).

Perhaps these results should have been expected just from observation of the great similarity of the production techniques employed in the leading industrial countries, which implies that technology *must* travel quickly unless, as hardly seems likely, the bulk of these common techniques were invented simultaneously and coincidentally in all of the countries that use them. Those production methods are, indeed, strikingly similar in technologically sophisticated lines of industry. The equipment and production techniques used in a Swedish auto plant in 1993 are, clearly, far more similar to those of a French plant in 1993 than they are to those used in the same Swedish plant in 1973. But for this to be so the French engineers must have followed Swedish developments carefully, and the Swedes must have monitored French techniques to a comparable degree, while both must have watched developments elsewhere with vigilance and made determined efforts to acquire the use of those developments for themselves. And in both countries there could not have been great lags in the acquisition of new techniques from abroad, because that would inevitably have caused substantial differences in their current production methods.

Such observations as well as substantial anecdotal evidence only serve to supplement the careful empirical investigations of Mansfield and his colleagues, and those of Levin and his colleagues. There simply seems to be little reason to doubt the conclusion that technology travels through the industrial world with dramatic rapidity, with speed that seems to conflict with the depiction of firms and the competitive process itself as determined and effective enemies of technology transmission. Chapters 9 and 10 will offer a different view of the market mechanism, arguing that both entrepreneurs and the managers of routine innovation processes have substantial incentives for active promotion of technology transmission, and that in some circumstances the competitive process gives them little alternative to active participation in the process.

8.7   On Market Performance and Socially Optimal Investment in Innovation and Imitation

First, however, it will be useful to list some of the main impediments to optimal performance by the market in the allocation of resources to technology transfer activities. For it is to be emphasized that nothing in this book is meant to imply that the performance of the market in terms of investment in innovation or technology transfer necessarily even approximates achievement of any abstract requirements of social optimality in these arenas. None of the obstacles to optimality that will be listed next will occasion any particular surprise. They entail variations on the sources of market failure usually noted in the literature of welfare economics, and often noted in theoretical writings on the market mechanism and innovation (see, e.g., Katz [1986] and Katz and Ordover [1990]). It is only later when their place in the subsequent discussion becomes clear that some new insights on the subject may emerge. In particular, at one point or another, the discussion will focus on the following three possible sources of market imperfection in the process of technology transfer:

A. Eased Technology Transfer as Exacerbator of the Innovator's Free-Rider Problem. As has already been noted, the literature usually concludes that a free competitive market investment in innovation will tend to be less than the optimal amount because so large a proportion of the benefits of an innovation is likely to be enjoyed by others in the form of spillovers. The original innovator, who bears the cost of the innovation process alone, is therefore likely to obtain only a portion, and perhaps only a small portion, of its benefits. It would seem to follow that anything that facilitates dissemination of innovation, desirable though that may be in itself, threatens inherently to exacerbate the innovator's free-rider problem and any resulting inadequacy of investment in innovation. For whatever reduces the cost of imitation seems simultaneously to decrease the share of the profit of innovation that goes to the innovator. There would, then, appear to be an unavoidable trade-off between inadequacy of innovation activity and inadequacy of dissemination. We will see presently, however, that the market mechanism may offer means which, while they do not eliminate the trade-off altogether, may considerably decrease the magnitude of the sacrifices entailed when resources are reallocated between innovation and dissemination.

B. *The Public-Good Character of Information Gathering.* A second type of externality problem that seems to beset the dissemination process arises from the public-good attribute of the acquisition of information. In a domestic industry containing forty firms it will be far more costly if each firm seeks to monitor all foreign developments by itself. If an article reporting a technical breakthrough appears in Swedish in a journal, most if not all British firms in the field are apt to miss it when it first appears. Monitoring and translation by a British trade association or by a British government agency may be able to cut the cost and speed up the process dramatically. As we know, the public-good property of this information-gathering process is apt to impede the private sector's technology transfer activity, holding it below its socially optimal level. This, too, is a matter to which we will return later in our discussion of promising policy measures.

C. *Deliberate Erection of Impediments to Transfer.* When an innovator erects barriers that make it more difficult for an imitator to make use of the invention in question, that is tantamount to the insertion of a wedge between the private marginal cost of imitation and its marginal social cost. The imitator is forced to pay more to acquire the ability to use the innovation than the minimum cost at which such a transfer can be carried out. The excess cost can take the form of outlays on industrial espionage, reverse engineering, the design of variants of the item in question that avoid patent restrictions, and so on. Such deliberate inflation of the price of technology transfer above its (minimum) marginal social cost seems likely to restrict the amount of transfer activity below its socially optimal level.

We may describe the case in which imitation is handicapped by the deliberate imposition of such costs as that of a *hostile transfer* or a *hostile imitation.* When no such costs are imposed by the innovator we can speak of a *friendly transfer* or a *friendly imitation.* Such friendly transfers do occur in reality, as when an innovation in a German multinational corporation is transferred to its Mexican division, or when two firms decide to cross-license their patents to one another. The contrast between hostile and friendly transfer will play a role in the discussion in the two chapters that follow, and the next chapter will describe some empirical evidence indicating the magnitude of the difference of the costs incurred by the two types of transfer.

No doubt there are other externalities and sources of market failure generally that affect the market's allocation of resources to technology transfer. However, in this book only the three that have just been described will enter the discussion explicitly.

8.8   Imitative Skill: Key to Entry into the Convergence Process?

It is important to end this chapter by repeating an earlier disclaimer in more specific form. Nothing that has been said here is meant to imply that technology transfer is the only thing that matters for economic growth, or that it alone is sufficient to bring about the takeoff of an economy that wishes to begin a catch-up process. The role of imitation has been emphasized, and perhaps even exaggerated, here because it tends so often to be denigrated and is usually accorded, at most, a poor third position—after domestic invention and investment—in the list of activities that contribute to the expansion of productivity. Certainly, I do not believe that a less developed country (LDC) can expect to solve all of its growth problems simply by making itself efficient in imitating. Surely the problems are far more complex. It is probably true that, without some degree of efficiency in importing suitably sophisticated technology, no LDC can hope to achieve membership in the convergence club. But while such imitative activity and the help of the entrepreneurs who undertake it is probably indispensable, it is undoubtedly not enough.

Lack of natural resources, inadequate capital, and insufficient training of the labor force, for example, clearly can sometimes constitute crippling handicaps, and government policies that discourage or even exclude foreign enterprise can also act as critical impediments. But this is not the place to attempt anything resembling a systematic discussion of the full set of requisites for success in achieving an economic takeoff. There is a considerable body of literature addressed to this subject, and those who have contributed to it are by no means in agreement among themselves. Any brief discussion here is condemned in advance to naïveté. The point here, only, is to avoid the appearance of a desire to oversell the prospective accomplishment of imitative effort alone, or to suggest that if something *can* be done by policymakers on that score, then the growth problems of the LDCs will be easy to solve.

The Mechanisms of
Technology Transfer, I:
Enterprising Imitators

[By 1870] if local entrepreneurship was lacking, foreign initiative was available. It was an old tradition in Europe for migrants to bring and establish new skills and industries.
W. Arthur Lewis (1978, p. 159)

This chapter begins our exploration of the means by which the market mechanism is able to carry out the surprisingly rapid transfer of technology described in Chapter 8. It will be suggested here that so long as innovation, preponderantly, was not a routine process, the primary instrument of dissemination was a class of entrepreneur whose specialty is what can be described as "innovative imitation." With growing routinization of the innovation process other transfer mechanisms have developed. Among them are multinational firms, the manufacturers of production equipment (about which only a few words will be said here), and what will be referred to as "technology-sharing consortia," the subject of the next chapter.

The allocability of entrepreneurial effort, which is the central theme of this book, is important for society not only insofar as it relates to the choice between productive and unproductive lines of innovative activity. It is also important in the assignment of entrepreneurial efforts among alternative production options, some of which may not at first strike one as highly entrepreneurial. This chapter focuses upon one such activity—imitation, which, as has just been emphasized, characteristically contributes a good deal to production. More to the point, it will be argued that the ready mobility of entrepreneurs extends to the choice between innovation and dissemination, and also to the choice between dissemination to domestic or to foreign locations. The evidence indicates that the entrepreneur is willing to travel, either in person or via movement of colleagues, funds, and information, and to go wherever the rewards are high and conditions propitious. Even if one particular entrepreneur is unwilling to move to a promising geographic location that offers opportunities not yet fully exploited, a host of others are ready and anxious to take her place.

This is important for policy, particularly in developing nations, where it often seems to be held that the economic takeoff process cannot really get under way until a cadre of sophisticated and experienced native entrepreneurs has been formed. It may well be true that a supply of native entrepreneurs eventually becomes essential for continued prosperity of an emerging economy, and for many other reasons as well. But the moral of entrepreneurial mobility is that no nation need wait patiently for full fruition of the slow process of evolution of a body of homegrown entrepreneurs. It is at least arguable that a number of today's industrial leader nations were launched on their growth process by entrepreneurs who came from abroad, sometimes despite the best efforts of their home governments to prevent their migration. This suggests that, while a country with development ambitions may find it advisable to do what it can to stimulate the formation of a group of entrepreneurs from among its own inhabitants, high priority may also appropriately be assigned to measures that reduce impediments to entrepreneurs from other countries. It may not require much to attract them in abundance, and their presence may be able to contribute materially to economic growth in relatively short order.

It will also be argued here that the imitator typically finds it necessary to be highly innovative and entrepreneurial. By its very nature, the task usually entails some imagination and alertness in finding new *markets* for the products. But in addition, the process often forces her to undertake innovative adaptations of transferred products and techniques, some of them constituting genuine improvements for all users, whatever their location. This role is patently very different, and more directly productive, than that of the imitator in more traditional models of the innovation process.

9.1 The Schumpeterian Imitator

The imitator makes an appearance in the Schumpeterian model, and plays an important role in its scenario. But her task is essentially passive, and is of little interest in itself. She may be a runner-up, already inside the innovator's market, who is forced by the innovator's success to scramble to catch up, by means of some substitute for the new product or process, or even by outright duplication, in order to keep from being driven from the field. Alternatively, the imitator may be a parasite who waits passively for the innovator to bring off a successful coup and, then, having been shown the way, leaps in with a duplicative offering, hoping to secure some leavings from the profit opportunity provided by the original innovation.

Even this "parasitic" imitator serves a real social purpose, by acting as the spoiler who brings to an end the market power acquired by the innovator through the superiority of her products or her greater efficiency. Thus, the Schumpeterian imitator's task is to ensure that some of the stream of benefits flowing from the innovation are shared with the consuming public, by bringing to an end the abnormal profits that, before the appearance of the imitator, accrued exclusively to the innovator. If the imitator does not enter too early, thereby reducing the incentive for innovative activity below its optimal level, then the presence of the Schumpeterian imitator is entirely beneficial, though her role is certainly not heroic.

There are at least two respects in which reality demands modification of this portrait of the imitator. First, as Rosenberg has argued so cogently, it makes too sharp a distinction between the two occupations—the innovator's and the imitator's (see, e.g., [1976, pp. 75–77]). Second, it considerably underplays the imitator's role in ensuring widespread use of new technology—in guaranteeing that no suitable sector of the world's economy remains untouched by new ideas of economic significance.

9.2   The Unavoidable Inventiveness of Imitating Entrepreneurs

One of the many fundamental observations that emerge from Rosenberg's writings (see, e.g., [1976, pp. 75–77]) is the characterization of invention, innovation and dissemination as a continuing process, whose stages overlap and merge into one another, and which typically occupy considerable periods of time. Here our concern is with the work of the entrepreneur as disseminating imitator rather than as producer of inventions. A moment's consideration confirms that pure replication of the innovator's product by the imitator is a rare exception, if it ever occurs at all.[1]

There are many reasons why this should be so. First, exact imitation may be prevented by patent restrictions or success of the innovator's secrecy. Second, the imitator will often be locked in competitive combat with the initial innovator and, as Johnny-come-lately, will only have a chance of winning out if she can offer an improved or less expensive product. These are, probably, among the prime reasons why the imitator is driven to modify, and thereby to invent and improve upon the replicated item. And that, in turn, helps to explain why the evolution of new technology is almost always a continuing process without clearly separable stages, one without identifiable beginning and end points. And even if a particular event can be deemed *the* act of introduction of a particular invention, it is born, not infrequently, as a feeble and relatively useless thing (hence Benjamin Franklin's mot: "What is the use of a new-born babe?"). In many cases, it is only the subsequent work of the improving imitators that transforms such a novel item from mere curiosity into invaluable contribution to the workings of the economy (consider, for example, the uses of electricity in the eighteenth century). Rosenberg (1976) cites the case of the steamboat and concludes, "It is clear that the overall increase in total factor productivity associated with this major transportation innovation came in the years *following* its initial introduction" (p. 196). Thus the subsequent improvements after the earliest innovation are, characteristically, of critical importance, and it is often the imitator rather than the original inventor or innovator who is responsible for those improvements. A good illustration is George Westinghouse's introduction of alternating current as a means to compete with Thomas Edison, who was arguably the innovating entrepreneur in the communitywide provision of electric current from a central power station. It is, incidentally, worth recalling that Edison determinedly fought this modification of his direct-current installation, claiming that the rival AC product was extremely hazardous.

If the imitator is also a disseminator, that is, if he does not strive only for a place in the market already occupied by the earlier innovator, then by the very Schumpeterian interpretation of the concept he automatically becomes an innovator as well.[2] It will be recalled that Schumpeter's list of innovative activities includes the opening of new markets as one of its major categories. It is true that the disseminator focuses upon the discovery of new markets rather than technological improvements or new products, but there is surely no reason to regard one of these activities as less entrepreneurial than the other.

Where the imitation process entails technology transfer to another and very different region or economy, the forces making product innovation a requirement of success in imitation frequently become compelling. Success in the transfer process compels adaptation of the invention to local conditions in the new market. Differences in the availability of raw materials, sources of power, labor supply, topography, climate, income level, and culture all have been known to require substantial modifications in transferred products or techniques. It would be easy but otiose to provide for each of these influences some illustrations of major changes in technology they have elicited. Still, a few examples can underscore and lend credence to the point.

Example 1. Raw Material Supply. The abundance of lumber in the American colonies led to modifications in the techniques of housing construction and the design of sawmills, and even provided an incentive for widespread use of wooden wheels in clock machinery, as a substitute for the scarcer and more expensive metals used for the purpose in Europe (on much of this, see essay 2 in Rosenberg [1976]).

Example 2. Labor Cost. From an early date real wages in the United States seem to have been considerably higher than those in Europe. It is arguable that this helped to stimulate modifications in the technology of guns, watches, and other sophisticated products of European origin, and in particular, to the adoption of a system of standardized, interchangeable parts, an innovation in which Eli Whitney played some role. Before this development, each component of a watch, for example, was laboriously produced and required careful fitting to match the other parts. There was no such thing as replacement of a broken or worn piece by an identical component taken off the shelf. The Old World had to learn this improvement of the technology it had originally fathered, via reverse technology transfer from America to Europe.

Example 3. Income Levels and Historical Influences. No one can be sure precisely why the Europeans developed the smaller variants of that arguably American invention, the automobile. However, it is more than plausible that lower European incomes after World War II helped to lead them away from large U.S. cars, with their high cost, their gas-guzzling, and the difficulty of maneuvering them through twisting and narrow medieval streets. As we know, Americans are still at work mastering the techniques of economical small car construction, at which they are the imitators of the Europeans and the Japanese.

Example 4. Cultural Differences. Many products have had to be tailored to the cultural circumstances of their foreign adopters. Nineteenth-century Japanese clock producers had to invent a system of movable hour markers to adapt clocks to the method of measuring time in that country, which divided the daily period of darkness into twelve equal intervals and did the same for the period of light, in winter and summer alike. Similarly, the complexities of the written languages of the Far East have required special innovations in the keyboards of the typewriter and the computer. These modifications probably do not improve the product for other users, but there are other cases where that has happened. A noteworthy example is the invention of the mechanical clock, which has been attributed to the timing needs of Christian religious practice. The unreliability of water clocks in freezing weather and of sundials on cloudy days made these timing devices unacceptable for the purpose. In western Europe, where the mechanical clock presumably emerged, it was undoubtedly just an improvement on the more primitive timekeeping techniques which had been imported from elsewhere. Of course, the mechanical clock then went on to conquer the world, and to regiment the schedules of human activity as they had never been regimented before, probably even in the birthplaces of timekeeping devices, wherever they may have been.

The main conclusion from all this is that the term *imitative entrepreneur* entails no internal contradiction. The imitation process, particularly where it is successful and/or results in the transfer of technology, is unavoidably innovative and often inseparable from the continuing process of what may be called "innovation proper." Generally then, the imitator also turns out to be entrepreneur and innovator even if he is so *malgré lui*. The central fact is that Schumpeter's "mere imitators" are commonly far more than that. They are essential agents of improvement who are responsible for establishing the commercial viability of the original innovation, which usually could not have prospered in the marketplace without those improvements.

9.3 Mobility of Entrepreneurship and Technology Transfer

Having argued that imitation and diffusion are, inherently, activities calling for the talents of entrepreneurs, we turn now to the second main topic of the chapter, the allocation of entrepreneurial effort between innovation and imitation. It will be suggested that there has been and continues to be considerable mobility of entrepreneurs between what may more conventionally be regarded as innovative endeavors and the related activities of imitation, dissemination, or transfer of technology. The basic contention of this section is that if the rewards are suitable, a substantial group of entrepreneurs will allocate their efforts to activities that entail technology transfer. These imitating entrepreneurs will often be natives of the technology-exporting country in which the new techniques were first introduced. In the process, even they themselves will often be available for export, along with the transferred techniques.

On this subject, the historical evidence seems quite clear, and sufficient by itself to confirm the conclusion. Migrating entrepreneurs have long exported both their native technology and themselves. In the late Middle Ages the Netherlanders and the English learned banking and other financial techniques from invading Italian entrepreneurs (who in England were generally referred to as "Lombards"—hence Lombard Street, the place where they congregated in London). The English learned about cloth-making techniques from Flemish immigrants. North and Thomas (1973, p. 153) point out that grants of monopoly by the British government were used to attract such peripatetic foreign entrepreneurs, and served, like patents, to internalize the associated externalities—the fact that the financial rewards from new techniques, once introduced, are in danger of being garnered largely by free riders.

Early in the Industrial Revolution, English inventions were often carried abroad by Englishmen who recognized very promising opportunities for profit.

Time and again we find on the continent of Europe the first factories or machine-workshops started by some Englishman, the first native machines copied from some British design (illegally smuggled if before 1825, legally acquired thereafter). Europe was full of Thorntons (Austria and Russia), Evans and Thomas (Czechoslovakia), Cockerills (Belgium), Manbys and Wilsons (France) or Mulvanys (Germany), and the universal spread of football in the twentieth century is largely due to the work teams started by British owners, managers or skilled operatives in all parts of the continent. Inevitably we find the first railways—and often the bulk of railways—built by British contractors with British locomotives, rails, technical staff and capital.   (Hobsbawm, [1969, p. 137]; see also, e.g., Landes [1969, pp. 148–49] and Coleman [1975, pp. 14–15, 29–32])

In post-Revolutionary America the transfer of technology was often carried out by foreigners, including a number of well-known names such as the French-born industrialist, Eleuthère Irénée Dupont, and the English-born architect, Benjamin Henry Latrobe (Stapleton [1987]). The compliment was returned soon enough when Robert Fulton migrated to Europe (exporting the future inventor, though not yet any inventions). There he subsequently attempted to market his submarine, his torpedo, and still later, his steamboat, successively to Napoleon and to the British government, albeit with little success.

Thus, imitative entrepreneurship was not stopped by political boundaries then, and it is not now. Americans still systematically export technology, and the Japanese open plants throughout the industrial world, bringing their managerial techniques as well as their robots with them. The imitative entrepreneur literally "has invention, will travel." Indeed, it seems impossible to stop him by direct prohibition. Medieval laws failed in their repeated attempts to prevent the emigration of those in a position to transfer technology to others. The failure of British prohibitions before they were abandoned in 1825 is well documented (see, e.g., Jeremy [1977]).[3]

9.4 Impediments to Transfer Erected by Prospective Recipient Countries

It is ironic that while technology-exporting countries have usually failed when they attempted to prevent leakage of their information, the intervention of the governments of potential *recipient* countries—those which stand to gain the most from the transfer process—seems often to have proved effective in impeding the process of technology transfer from abroad. The disdain of imperial China at its apex and of ancient Rome for anything contributed by the "barbarians," including in this category most foreign technology, may well help to explain the disappointing technological performance of the economies of those two countries that has been described in Chapter 2. In contrast, the receptivity of the High Middle Ages in Europe to ideas from classical and Arabic sources may shed some light on the superior technological record of the West in terms of dissemination and utilization of new production methods.

Today, many of the LDCs (as well as some of the countries that were, until recently, centrally planned economies) continue, self-destructively, to erect effective barriers against the acquisition of technology through the efforts of imitating entrepreneurs from the prosperous market economies. Restrictive rules inhibiting the operation of private enterprise, high taxes (perhaps falling especially heavily upon foreigners and their business undertakings), political instability and uncertainty about the pertinent regulations and their future, bureaucratic impediments, unrealistic or highly volatile exchange rates, and the threat of expropriation or worse, have all served to reduce and even sometimes to destroy altogether the attractiveness of particular economies for foreign entrepreneurs. Once more, it seems to be true that the rules of the game play a critical role in determining the allocation of entrepreneurial effort, in this case among economies, and between dissemination and "pure" innovation. And the mobility of entrepreneurs is underscored by their repeated rush into previously hostile economies immediately after any marked change in government orientation that seems to make prospects more promising for the operation of private enterprise.

In contrast, governments and firms in other countries have worked very hard to acquire technology from abroad. That is, initiative in this arena sometimes originates not only in the technology-exporting country, but in the importing country as well. Some governments, notably those of Japan and the former Soviet Union (at least before its 1990–1991 upheavals), have agencies that specialize in the accumulation of information on foreign technology, the spread of that information among the economy's firms, and the encouragement of rapid adoption of promising new techniques by industry. However, reports to me by Russian economists indicate that in the USSR these activities usually failed in their purpose. Stimulative measures were entangled in bureaucracy and handicapped by shortage of foreign exchange with which to purchase any required equipment from abroad. Adoption of foreign innovations (or even of innovations from domestic sources) was also resisted by the managers of the firms to which these efforts were directed, because radical technical change would disrupt production and make it difficult for the factory to meet its output target in the year of transition. Since the managements' rewards were based on meeting production targets, and since successful innovation threatened factories with higher and more demanding targets for the future, one can understand why only limited enthusiasm greeted attempts to encourage the adoption of foreign (or even domestic) innovations in the Soviet economy.

In the industrialized free-market economies things have been quite different. In many firms, management has been anxious to learn about foreign developments and to put them rapidly to use. Often, the transfer has been carried out on a friendly basis, for example, through payment of a negotiated royalty for the licensing of a foreign-held patent. More will be said about voluntary transfers in the next chapter. And sometimes, as we know, the transfer can be said to be unfriendly, with information acquired through direct espionage in the plants of foreign rivals; or by recourse to "reverse engineering," entailing the dismantling of foreign products to find out what makes them tick, and to discovering ways to produce substitute products sufficiently different to avoid any patent violations. The next section describes some estimates suggesting the magnitude of the saving that the imitator can obtain by arranging for a transfer to be friendly, a saving that will prove important for our subsequent discussion.

9.5   The Relative Magnitudes of Imitation and Innovation Cost

As part of our discussion of the mechanisms of technology transfer it is appropriate to describe the available evidence on the costs of the process. These costs must be examined as part of any evaluation of the efficiency with which the market governs the allocation of resources to innovation and technology transfer.

It may at first appear that acquisition of technology is virtually a costless process, apart from any expenses entailed in dealing with patents or other barriers against imitation deliberately erected by the original innovator or others. This is a view encouraged by the theoretical model that treats information as a pure public good. However, the matter is not quite so simple. Transfer of technology entails a number of tasks, and some of them are, characteristically, expensive. For one thing, the pertinent information must somehow be conveyed from the original source to the new user, and sometimes this will be carried out most efficiently by costly physical transportation of expensive equipment that embodies the techniques, rather than by mere transmission of a set of abstract specifications and plans. The new user must also assemble and train a work force to master the techniques and use them with a sufficient degree of skill. In this, the original innovator may enjoy an advantage, starting off production with a work force that acquired the requisite skills via learning by doing, during the development of the item in question. The new user will often encounter "bugs" in the process, and have to spend whatever is required to get rid of these imperfections. Then, as already discussed, there is frequently the need to adapt the technique to local conditions—customary operating procedures, training of the labor force, climatic circumstances, patterns of customer preference, and so on. It is clear from just this partial list of the necessary elements in the imitation process that it is inherently far from costless.

Empirical evaluation of the magnitude of the cost of technology transfer is, however, a formidable task, since the costs themselves are not easily observable nor even clearly defined (particularly when an outlay constitutes a common cost, serving several purposes simultaneously, as when the purchase of the equipment embodying the technique provides both a piece of productive capital and some of the required design information about the new product or process). In addition, the financial information required for statistical evaluation of the cost of the transfer is itself also usually proprietary.

Thus, it should cause no surprise that empirical studies of these costs are rather scarce and that investigators differ somewhat both on the facts and on their implications (for a brief summary of the state of the discussion, see Teece [1977, pp. 242–43]). Nevertheless, there exist at least two careful empirical studies (Teece [1977] and Mansfield, Schwartz, and Wagner [1981]), and they agree that the costs entailed in technology transfer are substantial. According to Teece, even when the transfer is entirely within a single (multinational) firm, the costs are unlikely to be negligible. In twenty-six cases studied by him, the transfer costs, calculated as a percent of the "total project cost," ranged from a lower decile value of 6 percent to an upper decile value of 42 percent, with a median of 17 percent. Mansfield et al., who studied forty-eight recent product innovations ("chosen more or less at random") in the chemical, drug, electronics, and machinery industries, found that, "On the average, the ratio of imitation cost to the innovation cost was about 0.65, and the ratio of imitation time to the innovation time was about 0.70 ... [but] there is considerable variation about these averages. In about half the cases. the ratio of imitation cost to innovation cost was either less than 0.40 or more than 0.90. In about half the cases, the ratio of imitation time to innovation time was either less than 0.40 or more than 1.00" (pp. 909–10).

There is, clearly, a substantial difference between the Teece estimates and those of Mansfield and his colleagues. It is plausible that a major reason for this difference is the fact that the Teece study involved "friendly" technology transfers within different divisions of multinational corporations, while the acts of imitation observed by Mansfield et al. in the latter study were, apparently, usually unsanctioned by the innovator, so that outlays such as the cost of inventing one's way around a patent constituted a significant proportion of the imitation costs. This provides us with an indication of the order of magnitude of the advantage of "friendly" technology transfer. It offers the recipient firm low-cost access to the inventions of other firms (a cost amounting to some 17 percent of the cost of creation of the innovation), while "hostile" acquisition of the invention or a viable substitute is much more expensive (perhaps 65 percent of the cost of the initial innovation—and it probably entails a considerably greater delay).

In any case, it is clear that the imitator does not enjoy a fully free ride. The costs the imitation process entails are considerable. In addition, the imitator's benefits from the innovation itself may be significantly lower than the innovator's, a disadvantage that can be increased very substantially by the generally unavoidable lag between the innovator's introduction date and the date at which the imitator can have the item in full operation. On the other hand, that difference in benefit is sometimes reduced to a large degree to the extent the imitator can avoid the innovator's risks stemming from product unreliability, deficiencies of the early models, and the unpredictability of the reception of the product or process change by the market.

To summarize, the costs of imitation can be great, though they undoubtedly vary considerably. The magnitude of the expense warns us that imitation, and particularly unauthorized imitation, may often be considerably less attractive financially than the pure public-good depiction of information transfer may lead one to believe. More important for our purposes, the evidence suggests the rough order of magnitude of the relative cost of a "friendly" and a "hostile" transfer of technology, in comparison to that of the original invention. It indicates that the imitator who succeeds in arranging for the transaction to be friendly may save, on the average, an amount approximately equal to some 50 percent of the cost of the initial innovation. The fact that this saving can be so substantial will prove significant for the discussion of the following chapter.

9.6   Transfer Instruments for Routine Innovation Processes

Today enterprising imitators continue to play a part in the export of technology. But along with the previously discussed routinization of the innovation process, there have been similar changes in the way that technology is transferred. Large firms that engage heavily in both of these activities are not inclined to leave either their own innovations or their part in the dissemination process to the fortuitous appearance of entrepreneurs who may undertake to carry out the tasks. A variety of managerial transfer mechanisms have emerged, most of them widely recognized. I have little or nothing to add to the illuminating discussions of the most frequently noted of these arrangements that have appeared in the literature (see, e.g., Katz and Ordover [1990] and Mowery and Rosenberg [1989]), though the next chapter will offer some analysis of another managerial transfer device that may, perhaps, contribute a novel view of the role of the market in the dissemination of technology. Here I will only mention the most recognized of the transfer devices in order to emphasize some of the lacunae in the present discussion.

Three institutions come to mind at once as instruments of managerial technology transfer. The first is the research joint venture, in which several firms pool funds and other resources, to facilitate the design of new products or processes, and to reduce the cost borne by each sponsoring enterprise. Some, but by no means all, of these have proved very successful. But even when they succeed they suffer from some limitations, for example, generally offering the participating firms little opportunity for learning by doing.

Often, new or improved products or processes are introduced by the manufacturers of capital equipment, who use them to promote their own sales to the makers of final products. Because these equipment suppliers generally seek to obtain as large a market as they can for their product lines, they will, in the process, promote dissemination of their inventions.

This is often very effective in speeding the diffusion of technology but, perhaps even more than the joint venture, it is likely to deprive the user firms of the insights and experience that direct participation in the development process provides.

The multinational corporation is another instrument of technology transfer across national boundaries. Frequently, it has found itself a prime target of opprobrium among the citizens of less developed countries, who interpret acts of investment inside their boundaries by residents of industrialized countries as manifestations of imperialist exploitation. The irony is that, whatever the sins that have been committed by particular multinationals, they have also often provided the most direct conduit for the importation into the LDCs of the modern technology that these countries need so urgently. The transfer of technological information among subsidiaries of a business firm located in different countries is in this case, of course, entirely friendly, and is therefore likely to be relatively inexpensive and unimpeded by lack of cooperation, let alone any attempt at sabotage. In the process, employees native to the LDC in question are likely to be exposed to the techniques and to acquire the experience necessary to work with them effectively. There remains the question whether this is, in fact, what commonly occurs, or whether the new techniques are predominantly worked with by company personnel coming from outside the LDC. It also remains to be determined whether the presence of the multinational firm in the developing country facilitates the acquisition of new techniques by native companies—by enterprises owned and operated exclusively or predominantly by nationals of the LDC. That issue is largely beyond the scope of our discussion here, but it certainly merits further investigation.[4]

As in Chapter 2, the primary objective here was to suggest that a minor expansion of Schumpeter's theoretical model to encompass the determinants of the *allocation* of entrepreneurship among its competing uses can enrich the model and its implications considerably. It also seems clear that the extension yields policy implications going well beyond those previously offered by his model. For example, as has already been said here, the evidence indicating that there can be easy and rapid mobility of entrepreneurs from countries with novel technology and their propensity to disseminate it to other economies means that the first priority of an LDC should perhaps not be the slow process of stimulating the emergence of a cadre of its own native entrepreneurs, though that may become important later. Rather, it may be more urgent to change the rules so as to make it more attractive for foreign entrepreneurs to enter the economy, bringing the newest and most suitable technology with them. Such inducements for the appropriate reallocation of entrepreneurial efforts have previously helped other economies, now prosperous, to attain their current technological sophistication. A developing economy can, no doubt, facilitate the process by reducing restrictions on foreign enterprise, cutting political risks such as the threat of expropriation, and taking a variety of other obvious steps. The associated hypothesis of the preceding chapter that technology transfer is a major source of prosperity and growth even in advanced industrial economies also suggests that governmental encouragement of this activity in those countries, with some budget devoted to the accumulation and dissemination of knowledge about foreign economic advances (as is done by Japan's Ministry of International Trade and Industry [MITI]), may offer considerable promise, particularly where elements of the process are characterized by public-good properties that reduce their attractiveness to individual firms.

The summary conclusion is that here, too, entrepreneurship should be treated as a resource allocated by market forces, but one whose directions can be influenced by changes in the rules of the game. Here too, this view of the matter invites systematic consideration of the opportunities for policy to influence the uses to which entrepreneurial efforts are directed, and to influence them in a manner that is beneficial to society. These subjects will be explored in the final chapter.

10 The Mechanisms of Technology Transfer, II: Technology Consortia in Complementary Innovations[1]

The knowledge of the man of science, indispensable as it is to the development of industry, circulates with ease and rapidity from one nation to all the rest. And men of science have themselves an interest in its diffusion; for upon that diffusion they rest their hopes of fortune, and, what is more prized by them, of reputation too. For this reason, a nation, in which science is but little cultivated, may nevertheless carry its industry to a very great length, by taking advantage of the information derivable from abroad.

J. B. Say (1819, 1834, p. 82)

Managers approached apparently competing firms in other countries directly and were provided with surprisingly free access to their technology.

Allen, et al. (1983, p. 202)

Conventional business wisdom says: never let the competition know what you're doing. But at Novell, we believe the secret of success is to share your secrets. So we established the Novell Labs program to openly share our networking software technology with other companies.

Advertisement in *The Economist*, Sept. 21, 1991, by Novell Computer Company

The two preceding chapters commented on the remarkable similarity of the technology employed throughout the industrialized world and ascribed a substantial role in this homogenization of techniques to the imitating entrepreneurs who specialize in imaginative acts of dissemination and adaptation of innovations, and in perceptive recognition of profitable opportunities for such transfers. But we have so far paid little attention to the market's technology transfer process in today's more usual circumstances under which much of innovation has become routine. It will be suggested here that, just as innovation appears to be subject to competitive influences that cause it to be incorporated more and more into the province of the manager rather than that of the entrepreneur, there is a mechanism that tends to drive the adventitious elements from the technology transfer process and to incorporate it instead into the regular and predictable portion of the firm's *voluntary activities*. This is in direct contrast with a common view of firms as zealous guardians of the proprietary innovations in their possession, using patents, the courts, or secrecy to keep their technical knowledge from others for as long as possible, in order to prolong the period during which their technological information provides them with a differential advantage, and the stream of supercompetitive profits so effectively described by Schumpeter.

It will be shown here, on the contrary, that market forces frequently motivate enterprises to enter into a variety of information-exchange arrangements ranging from implicit contracts to carefully spelled out legal commitments. This chapter constructs a theoretical model describing the benefits offered to a firm by membership in what I call a "technology-sharing consortium." The model demonstrates that the market may impose severe penalties upon any firm that remains outside such a consortium and does not share technical information. It is shown, in addition, that the welfare consequences of these consortia tend to be beneficial, and that they may even serve to stimulate investment in innovation by helping to internalize its externalities. Next, reasons are given indicating that the consortia can be quite stable if the sharing game is repeated many times. The chapter also provides some (unsystematic) survey evidence implying that such consortia are fairly widespread in reality.

This is all of considerable importance for the general welfare because rapid dissemination of technology can contribute a great deal to growth in output and productivity. Indeed, as was suggested in Chapter 8, it is entirely plausible that nothing else, neither domestic innovation nor investment, may make as much of an incremental addition to long-run growth in the productivity of a "representative" industrialized economy as its speed in adopting technological innovations from other countries. If that is so, it may be essential, in evaluating the contribution of the market mechanism to the general welfare, to examine whether it impedes or facilitates the transfer of technology.

10.1   On Some Empirical Evidence: Preliminary

As we have seen in Chapter 8, a number of studies have found that innovation is disseminated far more quickly than one might be led to expect by the hypothesis that the firm, aided by the legal system, does everything in its power to prevent or delay dissemination. For example, that chapter reported a study by Mansfield and several colleagues (1981), indicating, on the basis of data provided by one hundred American firms in a variety of manufacturing industries, that "information concerning development decisions is generally in the hands of rivals within about 12 to 18 months, on the average, and information containing the detailed nature and operation of a new product or process generally leaks out within about a year" (p. 217). This and the other evidence of impressive speed of dissemination provided in Chapter 8 seem to imply that if the economic world is populated by private firms each striving determinedly to keep its innovations entirely or largely to itself, these enterprises are doing an uncharacteristically ineffective job of pursuing this goal.

As a matter of fact, there are studies that confirm that the behavior of firms does not always fit the common picture of the enterprise determined to keep its proprietary technological information from all others, and particularly from its horizontal competitors. In the nature of the subject, these rely heavily on samples and case studies. For one cannot expect to find systematic statistics on the extent of technological cooperation among otherwise independent business firms. The acts of cooperation are inherently heterogeneous, and can differ both in their importance and in their general character. The exchange can have an overt and formal structure, as when a trade association runs a research facility whose findings are available to all members of the association, and whose expenses are divided among them on some predetermined basis. The same is true when two or more firms organize a research joint venture. Or private and independent research organizations may offer the information they produce to all comers at a price.

In addition, firms can *and do* exchange information that is produced internally and that could, instead, have been treated as proprietary. This, too, can take a variety of forms. The information can deliberately be disseminated on the explicit initiative of company personnel, perhaps with the knowledge and consent of top management. Or instead, company A may simply be prepared to answer inquiries from company B and to come to B's assistance when it runs into technical difficulties, always with the understanding that such assistance is a two-way process. Firms may welcome highly revealing plant visits by engineers and technicians from other companies, even when those companies are direct competitors, foreign or domestic. One enterprise may even undertake to train the technical personnel from another firm in the use of an unfamiliar process or technique, expecting the favor to be reciprocated in the future.

There are also very formal arrangements for the exchange of technology, employing instruments such as carefully drawn contracts and cross-licensing of patents. Some evidence and further details will be described later in this chapter.

Throughout the chapter, the term *technology consortium* will be used generically to describe all of the technology-exchange arrangements that have just been mentioned. Recently, the economic literature has begun to argue that there are, in fact, a number of reasons why firms may want to share some of their proprietary technical information (for an excellent overview, see Katz and Ordover [1990]). The reason that is, perhaps, most frequently given (it is also frequently cited by businesspeople) is the high cost of the innovation process, which is more easily shouldered by a group of firms than by a single enterprise. This, and several other explanations that will be noted later, seem valid enough. However, this chapter will stress an entirely different market mechanism that may provide an incentive for technology sharing far more pervasive and powerful than those that have previously been noted.

10.2   Complements and Substitutes in Innovation[2]

Why do not all firms conform to the Schumpeterian model in which each battles fiercely for an overwhelming technical or product advantage over its rivals, and struggles to preserve any such advantage by determinedly trying to keep its technology out of the hands of others? The relatively ready acquiescence and, perhaps more often, enthusiasm of management for technology sharing, for which evidence will be provided later, seems to suggest that the firm has something to gain in the process. I will argue with the aid of the technology-consortium model that follows that this is indeed so, and that market pressures can even *force* firms to share their technology.

The basic feature that differentiates the model provided here from so many of the models of competition in innovation in the current literature is the distinction between innovations that are *substitutes* and hence, mutually competitive, and those that are *complementary*. When two firms are working toward innovations that are, at least to some degree, substitutes, as is implicitly assumed by most of the models of the innovation process, then their managements do, indeed, have a strong incentive to resist leakage of the knowledge they acquire. But the incentives provided by the market are reversed when, as seems so often to be true in practice of the fruits of the more routine R&D activities of large firms, the innovations in question are complementary, in a sense that will presently become clear.

Traditionally, economic models of innovation seem to have focused on the case of substitutes. Schumpeter's work of 1911 is, of course, the *locus classicus* of innovation models. There the successful innovator, firm, or entrepreneur, X, is threatened by a swarm of imitators, all striving to bring out a good substitute for what X has introduced. More recent writings in the arena have focused on patent races and waiting games, in which two or more firms are striving toward what is an essentially common invention, and deciding whether to attempt to reach the goal first (a race) or to let others explore the risks and face the pioneer's dangers (a waiting game). These scenarios, clearly, make sense only if the innovations in question all serve, more or less, the same purpose, that is, if they are substitutes. The firms may, for example, all be hoping to be the first to invent a high-definition television receiver that is economically viable, and whoever is first to get to the patent office will succeed in excluding the others. In a waiting game, firm A may hope that B invents the HD TV receiver, and subsequently goes bankrupt and is forced to sell its patent and equipment to A at a bargain price. In both cases the innovation consists in the creation of what is, essentially, the same given product, sprung forth in its full maturity.

The case upon which I will focus, in contrast, is that of an evolving product, for which innovations take the form of small improvements introduced by different manufacturers of that same product. These improvements are typically complementary. In photography, for example, one camera manufacturer may introduce an improved automatic focus device, another an automatic light adjustment, and a third may invent a way to make the camera lighter in weight and more compact. Each of these three firms has the choice of keeping its invention to itself, but if two of them get together and agree to put out cameras combining the features each has contributed, they will offer a camera that is clearly superior to what each could have produced alone, and they are likely to be in a far better position to meet the competition of the third camera manufacturer. Thus, it is appropriate to consider the automatic focus and the automatic light adjustment to be complementary inventions.

In reality, both types of relationships are encountered. It is not difficult, for example, to recount historical cases of hot patent races. But the day-to-day existence of the large firm in an industry with rapidly evolving technology is more often characterized by the second sort of innovation relationship among enterprises, as their managements seem usually to emphasize. The large firm rarely is the source of revolutionary new products or processes, and the bulk of its innovative investment appears to be devoted to incremental improvements.[3] Thus, when two suppliers of a common product devote R&D effort to that item, they may perhaps be expected only by happenstance to hit upon similar improvements, that is, upon substitute innovations.

However, it is the other, presumably more common, case of complementarity of the innovative results with which the following model deals. This, then, is the one basic premise of the model that follows. It should be emphasized that the model does not assume, in addition, that the world is one of perfect competition or perfect contestability. While there will be an occasional remark in the following discussion about the implications of these market forms for the workings of the model, these are to be interpreted as special cases, rather than the generic form of the construct.

10.3   The Technology-Consortium Model

For concreteness, let us consider an industry containing $n + 1$ firms which are identical in all respects except that firms $1, \ldots, n$ agree to share technical information with one another, while firm $n + 1$ keeps the results of its R&D to itself. Let us assume for simplicity of exposition that each firm routinely spends the same amount on R&D per period, and that the expected return to this expenditure is the same for every firm. Most important, it is assumed that the process inventions of the different members of the consortium are generally expected to be different from one another, and complementary, with none of them usable only as a replacement for one of the others. Finally, it is assumed, also for simplicity in discussion, that this expenditure is devoted exclusively to the pursuit of cost-reducing process innovations. That is, the innovation process is taken to make final products cheaper, but no better. The only purpose of this inessential premise is that it makes the immediate benefits yielded by the innovations quantifiable, thus facilitating their interpretation.

The public-good character of the information derived from the R&D does *not* mean that nothing will be lost in the process of transfer of information from the firm, A, that has produced it, to another enterprise, B, in a technology-sharing consortium. There is, in fact, clear evidence that the process of imitation is rather costly and typically entails expenditures different from those of the earlier innovator (see Chapter 9, section 5). Nevertheless, in the sharing process firm B can expect to derive a considerable net benefit from the information it obtains without payment from the other $n - 1$ members of the technology consortium. Even if it can hope, eventually, to obtain the information by reverse engineering, industrial espionage, or other such means, the empirical evidence indicates that a friendly transfer is typically far cheaper and quicker than a hostile one. In a rapidly evolving field speed is particularly important, since slowly acquired technical information is apt to be obsolete information.

Suppose that B's internal R&D effort can be expected to yield process innovations that contribute a reduction in the cost of manufacturing the firm's final product equal to r percent per year. At the same time, because of transfer costs B can expect a cost reduction from the information it obtains from A, or from any one other single member of the consortium, of only s percent (where $s \leqslant r$). Then, if total R&D outlay by each firm is x per year, and $C_0(y)$ is the initial period's total cost of production of its output, y, its expected cost in the next period will be $C_0(y)[1 - r - s(n - 1)] + x$, that is, its expected future manufacturing costs of final products will be reduced, not only by its own efforts, but also via the R&D carried out by each of the other $n - 1$ members of the consortium.[4] In contrast, the holdout firm, $n + 1$, which refuses to join the consortium and which, by hypothesis, starts off with the same costs as B, will incur in the next period (since by hypothesis $x_{n+1} = x$) the total expected cost, $C_0(y)(1 - r) + x$, which is clearly greater than the consortium member's cost.

Moreover, we will see later that this cost disadvantage will tend to increase relentlessly and cumulatively. Beyond that, if the game is a repeated one and if the market happens to be perfectly competitive or contestable, with entry absolutely free, so that B's expected profit is zero, the holdout firm will be faced with ever-growing expected losses.

The logic of the argument, then, is clear. So long as the firms are similar in terms of expected value of information output and technological changes are predominantly complementary, membership in the technology consortium will offer them a marked competitive advantage *ex ante*. It apparently will pay a firm, X, to hold out from membership only if its large size or other special circumstances lead it to spend so much more on R&D than its rivals do that the cost reduction it expects to achieve for itself will enable it to stay ahead of the cost reductions its competitors can achieve in aggregate and that they can each attain for themselves through the formation of a technology consortium that does not include firm X among its members.[5]

10.4   The Cost of Nonmembership in a Technology Consortium

Let us now examine formally the penalties that the market mechanism imposes upon the nonmember firm.

PROPOSITION 10.1   A firm that does not join a technology consortium of members otherwise identical with itself is subject to automatic imposition by the market mechanism of financial penalties in the form of expected profits lower than those of a consortium member. That is, if two firms are in all other respects identical—in the market demand they face, the structure of their costs, and the returns to their R&D investment—but one has access only to the innovations it introduces itself, while the other has access to the proprietary innovations of other firms, then the latter will be more profitable than the former.

This proposition is virtually self-evident, and it will be formalized only as an introduction to the workings of our model. But the exclusion of nonmembers from the benefits of the consortium that the proposition describes does differentiate technology consortia from the standard varieties of cartel. For example, Great Britain's refusal to join the Organization of Petroleum Exporting Countries has, nevertheless, permitted it to enjoy whatever augmentation in oil prices may have been achieved by the restriction of output undertaken by Saudi Arabia and other OPEC members. Indeed, the sellers of North Sea oil may have profited more than they would have had they joined the cartel, since they were not subject to rules, however ineffective, limiting the quantity of oil any particular member is permitted to sell. In contrast, Proposition 10.1 asserts that the nonmember of a technology consortium is deprived of all of its benefits.

To prove Proposition 10.1, as well as several subsequent results, we use the following notation, for simplicity suppressing subscripts that identify particular firms wherever that information is self-evident:

$x_k = x =$ the R&D expenditure per period of firm k, here assumed identical for all pertinent firms;[6]

$y_k =$ output per period of firm k;

$i = 1, \ldots, n$, the indexes identifying individual consortium member firms;

$j = n + 1, \ldots, N$, the nonmember firms;

$\pi^i(y_i, x_i, n) =$ the total profit function of consortium member i;

$\pi^j(y_j, x_j) =$ the total profit function of nonmember j;

$R^k(y_k) =$ firm k's total revenue per period;

$C^k(y_k) =$ firm k's total non-R&D cost *in period zero*;

$f^k(z_k) =$ the cost reduction factor for firm k in the subsequent period, where $\partial f^k / \partial z_k < 0$ and where

$z_i = nx_i$ for consortium member i and

$z_j = \alpha n x_j$ for nonmember j (so that z_k is a measure of the new information to which firm k has access);

$\alpha < 1$ is the loss in benefits from a "hostile" information transfer relative to the benefit from a "friendly" transfer; and finally,

s and p are superscripts referring to profit-maximizing values of the variables in question, respectively, for those firms (s) that *share* their information and those that hold it *proprietary* (p).

Here we use $\alpha < 1$ to represent the fact that though the spillovers of innovative activity bring benefits to nonmembers of the technology consortium as well as to members, the costs and benefits to the former are generally smaller, because it is more difficult to obtain technological information without the cooperation of its proprietor, and because such hostile technology acquisition takes longer and therefore is closer to obsolescence when the information is finally obtained by the nonmember. We may note also that we can, if we wish, take the variables in the model to refer to *expected values*, so that all of the calculations become *ex ante* in character.

Proof: Since, generally, for a technology sharing firm, i, y_i^p, and x_i^p are not the profit-maximizing values of y_i and x_i, we now have immediately

$$\pi^i(y_i^s, x_i^s, n) \geqslant \pi^i(y_i^p, x_i^p, n)$$

$$= R^i(y_i^p) - f(nx_i^p)C(y_i^p) - x_i^p$$

$$> R^i(y_i^p) - f(\alpha n x_i^p)C(y_i^p) - x_i^p$$

$$= \pi^i(y_i^p, x_i^p). \tag{10.1}$$

This is our desired result; the firm will lose out in terms of profits (or expected profits) if it declines to become a member of the technology consortium when all members spend the same amount on R&D.

The profit (opportunity) loss of the firm that finds itself excluded from the consortium is not just a once-and-for-all affair. Rather, it constitutes an intertemporal stream that grows cumulatively with the passage of time. This is easily proved by rewriting the two central expressions in (10.1) with the addition of the pertinent time subscripts (and the omission of subscripts and superscripts that are obvious). We obtain for the consortium member and nonmember, respectively,

$$C_t = f(nx_{t-1})C_{t-1} \quad \text{and} \quad C_t = f(\alpha n x_{t-1})C_{t-1}, \tag{10.2}$$

so that $\Delta \pi_t$ and $\Delta \pi_{t+1}$, the profit loss in periods t and $t+1$ resulting from ejection from the consortium in period $t - 1$, become

$$\Delta\pi_t = [f(\alpha n x_{t-1}) - f(n x_{t-1})]C_{t-1}$$

$$\Delta\pi_{t+1} = [f(\alpha n x_t) - f(n x_t)][f(\alpha n x_{t-1}) - f(n x_{t-1})]C_{t-1} > \Delta\pi_t,$$

(10.3)

as we wanted to show.

The preceding discussion has several times referred to the model as one involving *ex ante* sharing, in which each consortium member agrees to supply information on the output of its R&D activities over the future period that has been agreed upon. However, it should be noted that the mathematical discussion is not dependent on that assumption in any way. It is equally applicable, for example, to a consortium that operates through cross-licensing of the patents it holds on its past inventions. Thus the results derived so far, and (except where otherwise noted) those that follow, apply to the broad spectrum of technology-sharing consortia, and not only to those of the *ex ante* variety.

It should also be emphasized that while there may be reason to believe that the motivation for membership in a technology consortium that has just been described is important and pervasive, the literature has offered other reasonable explanations for technology sharing. Reduction in the cost burden of R&D to each of the sharing enterprises has already been mentioned. This incentive is clear in the case of research joint ventures, but in arrangements such as royalty-free cross-licensing of patents its role is less obvious. The literature also mentions sharing incentives such as network externalities that only a group of enterprises can achieve, the benefits of standardization and compatibility that a consortium can arrange to have built into the new products of its members, and the possibility that the mutual benefits of an outward shift of the demand curve facing the industry as a whole may only be achievable by products that share all of the available improvements. For further discussion the reader is once again referred to the admirable overview of the subject by Katz and Ordover (1990).

10.5   Welfare Consequences

We come, next, to the welfare consequences of technology consortia. The contrast between horizontal and vertical price cartels shows that such organizations are not all detrimental to the public interest. It is, of course, true that price raising by a cartel of horizontal competitors is likely to cause a welfare loss, but the reverse is clearly true of the Pareto superior price reduction that can be expected of a vertical price cartel (see section 6, below).

In a sense, it is also obvious that a technology consortium can generate welfare benefits, at least unless the sharing of information undercuts the incentive for investment in the process or leads horizontal competitors to engage in monopolistic types of behavior. What will be proved next is that, if the innovations of the firms in question are complementary, in the sense about to be specified, then information sharing will lead the profit-maximizing Cournot oligopolist to *increase* its outlay on innovation.[7] Moreover, the cost saving, in turn, will necessarily lead to an increase in the profit-maximizing output per firm.

It is to be emphasized that neither Proposition 10.2 nor 10.3, which follow along the same lines, implies that a technology consortium elicits a socially optimal outlay on innovation by the firm. It still remains true that the externalities of innovation can be expected to lead to outlays that are generally less than optimal. The contention here is only that the technology consortium moves matters in the right direction by internalizing part of the externality, that is, by ensuring that an innovating firm, A, can internalize a significant portion of the externality, by obtaining the reward of cheaper and quicker access to the innovations some of the other enterprises that benefit from A's technology. We then have:

PROPOSITION 10.2   With a fixed number of profit-maximizing firms producing a single product and investing in cost-reducing R&D, if each firm in the consortium behaves as a Cournot oligopolist and there is complementarity among the research outputs of the technology-sharing firms, then a rise in the number of consortium members will increase each member's outlay on innovation as well as its output of the final product, and lead to a downward shift in its total cost function.

Here we will assume that the number of firms in the industry is expected by the Cournot firm to be fixed, so that an increase in $n + 1$, the number of consortium members, entails an equal reduction in the number of non-members. On the Cournot assumption, this means that each firm will expect the total output of the remainder of the industry to be unaffected by a change in n. For convenience, n will, unrealistically, be treated as a continuous variable.

Proof: Let the profit function of a consortium member (firm 1) be given by

$$\pi = R(y, Y) - f[x + \alpha X(n)]C(y) - x, \tag{10.4}$$

where R, C, y, x, and f have the same economic connotation as before, and

Y = the total output of all firms in the industry other than 1, and which Cournot firm 1 assumes to be constant,

$X(n)$ = the sum of the expenditures on innovation of the n other members of the consortium,

α = a constant, $(0 < \alpha < 1)$, and

D = the Jacobian determinant of the derivatives of π.

Then we expect, by assumption,

$$R_y = \partial R/\partial y > 0, \quad f_x < 0, \quad f_n < 0 \quad \text{and} \quad C_y > 0. \tag{10.5}$$

Moreover, by the second-order conditions

$$D > 0, \quad \pi_{yy} < 0, \quad \pi_{xx} < 0. \tag{10.6}$$

Finally, we define complementarity between x and $X(n)$ (where $dX/dn > 0$) as

$$f_{xn} < 0, \tag{10.7}$$

that is, a rise in $X(n)$ increases the marginal cost saving yielded by a rise in x, firm 1's expenditure on innovation.

Then the first-order maximization conditions for (10.4) are

$$\pi_y = R_y - fC_y = 0, \quad \pi_x = -f_x C - 1 = 0. \tag{10.8}$$

Setting the total differential of each of these equal to zero to determine what changes in y and x are needed to restore equilibrium after an exogenous change in n, we obtain

$$d\pi_y = \pi_{yy}\, dy - f_x C_y\, dx - f_n C_y\, dn = 0 \quad \text{and} \tag{10.9a}$$

$$d\pi_x = -f_x C_y\, dy + \pi_{xx}\, dx - f_{xn} C\, dn = 0. \tag{10.9b}$$

Thus,

$$\partial y/\partial n = (f_n C_y \pi_{xx} + f_{xn} C f_x C_y)/D \quad \text{and} \tag{10.10a}$$

$$\partial x/\partial n = (f_x C_y^2 f_n + \pi_{yy} f_{xn} C)/D. \tag{10.10b}$$

By (10.5), (10.6), and (10.7) it follows directly that (10.10a) and (10.10b) are both positive.

Moreover, the effect of a rise in n on firm 1's total production cost for a given volume of output, y, is

$$dfC/dn = Cf_n + Cf_x \partial x/\partial n < 0. \tag{10.11}$$

This completes the proof of Proposition 10.2. It is also clear that the same results all hold if the inventions are very weak substitutes, so that f_{xn} is positive but relatively small. We can also prove, analogously:

PROPOSITION 10.3   Under the circumstances of Proposition 10.2, but if each consortium member acts on the expectation that every other member will make exactly the same decisions that it does,[8] any increase in n, the number of firms that share the results of one another's R&D, will shift the production cost curve of each such firm downward. Moreover, *each* information-sharing firm will increase its output when n rises,[9] and if the marginal cost reducing returns to x, the firm's investment in R&D, are increased by an increase in the technical information it receives from other consortium members (complementarity in their innovations), a rise in n will increase the firm's R&D outlays.

Proof: For simplicity, rewrite the profit function of a member of the technology consortium as

$$\pi = R(y) - f(z)C(y) - z/n, \quad C' > 0, f' < 0, \tag{10.12}$$

where $z = nx$ is the total outlay on R&D by all the members of the consortium together. Differentiating in turn with respect to z and y, we have the first-order maximum conditions

$$-f'C - 1/n = 0, \quad R' - fC' = 0. \tag{10.13}$$

Equating to zero the total differential of the LHS of each equation yields

$$\pi_{zz} dz - f'C' dy = -dn/n^2 \tag{10.14a}$$

$$-f'C' dz + \pi_{yy} dy = 0. \tag{10.14b}$$

We obtain our comparative-statics results directly, using inequalities corresponding to (10.5), (10.6), and (10.7),

$$dz/dn = -\pi_{yy}/n^2 D > 0, \quad dy/dn = -f'C'/n^2 D > 0. \tag{10.15}$$

Recalling that C is the initial total cost function for the firm and that f is the function indicating the proportion by which that cost is reduced by invention, we also have $\partial fC/\partial n = (\partial fC/\partial z)(\partial z/\partial n) = f'C\partial z/\partial n < 0$, so that the firm's production cost, fC, is, *ceteris paribus*, a decreasing function of n. We can complete our proof by substituting $x = z/n$ in (10.12) and obtain, by then repeating all the preceding steps, the result that $\partial x/\partial n > 0$ iff f'' is negative, zero, or positive and sufficiently small. This can be interpreted as the premise that the innovations are complementary, independent, or very mild substitutes. That is, in all such cases, technological information exchange will actually stimulate each firm's outlays on innovation.

The fact that, under the circumstances of either of our propositions, an expansion in the number of members of the consortium reduces *production* cost is not, by itself, conclusive evidence that efficiency has been increased. For with a given y it is conceivable that the outlay on R&D will increase by more than the cut in production cost. When n increases, so long as the resulting rise in x, the firm's innovation outlays, does not exceed the reduction in its cost contributed by access to the technology of the new consortium member(s), this, obviously, will not happen. However, if a larger value of x were to be selected, this would presumably indicate that the yield of the incremental R&D outlay more than covers this enhanced expenditure. Certainly that must be true if the pertinent markets are perfectly competitive or contestable, and there is at least a presumption that the same conclusion holds in a considerably broader range of market conditions.

This, then, is the sense in which a rise in the number of members of the consortium can be presumed to be welfare-increasing. It should be noted that the same conclusions as well as the specific results contained in Proposition 10.2 or 10.3 must necessarily also apply to the formation of such a consortium. For the decision of n firms to create a technology-sharing consortium can be interpreted simply as an increase in the number of its members from zero to n, and the result then follows directly.

None of the preceding material is to be taken to imply that it is impossible for a technology consortium to be detrimental to the general welfare. On the contrary, it raises at least two (closely related) dangers. If such a group is formed and learns to coordinate its decisions closely, one cannot simply rule out the possibility of perversion of the technology consortium into a conspiracy either to fix prices or to suppress innovation outlays, or both.

There is one apparently characteristic feature of such consortia in practice that seems to reduce these dangers substantially. In every technology-exchange program of which I am aware, the negotiation and supervision of these arrangements are strictly bilateral. That is, even though firms A, B, C, and D are members of the same consortium in the sense that all trade information with each of the others (and each is well aware that the others are doing so), A, for example, will have a separate arrangement with each of the others. Its exchange contract with B may be very different from that with C or D. The four firms will never meet together nor will the group as a whole share communications. Such a mode of operation seems very unlikely to permit the degree of coordination among the majority of the firms in a market that is necessary for effectiveness in fixing prices or in agreeing to hold down R&D outlays.

10.6   Cheating: Incentives and Disincentives

The economic literature is replete with discussions of the inherent instability of price cartels—the difficulty of securing agreement on the output quotas for the individual members, the incentives for cheating, the monitoring difficulties that encourage cheating, and the resulting vulnerability of the entire enterprise.

To get at the stability issue for technology consortia it is convenient to contrast these groupings with price-setting cartels. It may, therefore, be helpful, first, to recall very briefly two standard propositions about what will be referred to as "horizontal and vertical price cartels," that is, cartels composed, in the one case, of horizontal competitors and, in the other, of vertically related firms (that is, firms at least one of which supplies inputs to the other):

1. If firms i and j are horizontal competitors, a rise in j's price will add to i's profits. Collusion will, therefore, lead to (joint profit-maximizing) prices higher than those that emerge under competition.

2. On the other hand, where the enterprises have a vertical relationship or, more generally, if their products are gross complements in market demand, a rise in p_j will reduce i's profits. Hence the price that emerges under joint maximization will in this case be *lower* than that under independent decision making.

That is, of course, why antitrust authorities have tended to have little concern over the merger of vertically related firms, and the law and the regulatory authorities have sometimes explicitly sanctioned joint decisions on prices among vertically related firms (as in the case of railroads in the United States).

Despite the loss of profit from exclusion from a technology consortium it does not follow that incentives for cheating are absent. As a matter of fact, such incentives arise, at least in the short run, in all three cartel types. But in the long run their stories are very different. In the horizontal pricing cartel, as we know, a member can profit by sub-rosa price cutting and sales above its quota, shaving the monopoly profits offered by the cartel price in order to expand its lucrative volume. The opposite temptation clearly besets the member of a vertical pricing cartel, who can gain by setting a price higher than the one agreed to, letting its partners bear the cost of the resulting loss in sales volume. In the case of the technology consortium, the obvious cheating scenario entails total or at least partial withholding of technical information by a member that hopes to be able to profit from the information that the other members provide to itself, while retaining the differential competitive advantage conferred by its proprietary technology. Thus in all three cases it can perhaps be said that dishonesty is the most (immediately) lucrative policy.

At the same time, it should be obvious that the prospects for success in cheating are far from identical. The clearest contrast is that between the horizontal and the vertical price cartels. In the former it pays the customer to act as coconspirator with the cartel member who wishes to cheat. The reduced price that is entailed will be reason enough for the customer to avoid revealing the defector's secret. The opposite is true of a vertical pricing cartel, where the customer has everything to gain by complaining loudly and visibly about a cartel member's attempt to raise its price above the level that had been agreed upon. Thus, a vertical cartel possesses a self-monitoring mechanism that may effectively prevent cheating.

A member of a technology consortium is in a position that must, perhaps, be judged intermediate between those in the other two cases. There is no counterpart to the customer whose cooperation must be secured by a price cartel member who wants to cheat. A technology-consortium member, whose cheating consists of the withholding of information, requires no partner to carry out such a program and there may, consequently, be some hope of short-run success in the undertaking. However, technology exchange is normally a game that is played many times, and here matters change substantially in the direction of stability. Firms have many ways to monitor one another's technology, and a variety of clues—low prices as an indicator of cost reductions, changes in product characteristics, industry gossip, and so on—can arouse the suspicion that the firm in question is not giving out all the information it claims to be ready to provide. In such cases other members of the technology consortium can readily reciprocate: by becoming more selective in passing information about their own technological advances to the suspect enterprise, or ceasing to do so altogether. As in so many places, reputation becomes an invaluable asset in a much repeated game of technology exchange (see below).

From what has been said so far there is little that is distinctive about the case of the technology-consortium member that cheats. It has merely been pointed out that the cheating is apt to be discovered eventually, and that the firm that does so is likely to be deprived of the benefits promised by consortium membership when that happens. But that is also true of both types of price cartel. However, there are at least two special features of a technology consortium that may be effective in discouraging cheating and another that protects the consortium from collapse, even when some cheating occurs.

The first of these special features is the option available to the consortium members of abandoning an informal information-exchange arrangement that relies largely on mutual trust, substituting a more formal program in which the trades are specified explicitly. Perhaps the most straightforward form this can take entails cross-licensing of patents, so that each party knows exactly what it is getting from the other. Such an agreement clearly restricts the opportunity for cheating, and may help to explain the apparent recent rise in patenting.

An alternative approach to prevention of cheating is the arrangement that will be described later in somewhat more detail, in which two firms, A and B, participating in a technology-exchange process negotiate annually the compensation to be paid by A to B (or vice versa) for the shortfall in the innovations that A *expects to provide to B next year*, in exchange for B's innovations given to A. Obviously, such an arrangement provides each firm a strong incentive to reveal all or most of the inventions currently being worked on in its R&D facilities and almost ready for direct use or commercial introduction. For any such invention whose existence is held back by A simply increases the amount it must pay to B on the balance equalization account, and increases A's payment obligation to B by an amount approximating the expected value of the innovation concealed. There is, of course, an adverse selection problem here, because the innovating firm is apt to know more about the value of the invention than the purchaser of its technology does. Yet if such negotiations are repeated at regular intervals each firm will come to learn how trustworthy are the evaluations by the other party of its own inventions. The value of a reputation for integrity in such a bargaining process may, then, reduce the magnitude of the adverse selection problem.

The second attribute of a technology consortium that serves to discourage cheating is more automatic than the option of formalization of the exchange arrangement. Proposition 10.1's proof that nonmembership in the consortium constitutes an ever-growing opportunity loss implies that ejection from the consortium in a repeated game is apt to be very costly, particularly in the longer run. Indeed, in those special cases where markets are highly competitive or highly contestable, so that maximum long-run profits are close to zero, the ejected member will be condemned to growing losses and to eventual insolvency. In such circumstances, firms with a considerable investment at stake and with an ambition for the long-term future will find it advantageous to cultivate a reputation for integrity, just as is pointed out in the literature on product quality in markets with imperfect consumer information. Thus, technology consortia carry with them a substantial and cumulatively growing incentive against cheating, though one that is certainly not foolproof.

This leads us immediately to the third distinctive and pertinent feature of technology consortia: their striking invulnerability to defection, in sharp contrast to the circumstances of a horizontal price cartel. In the latter, as is well known, once the members begin to suspect cheating on the part of the others, it becomes dangerous for them to hold out against joining the defectors. The horizontal cartel member who continues to insist on the high product prices selected in the cartel agreement is likely to find itself without customers, all attracted away by the defecting sub-rosa price cutter. That, ultimately, is why the horizontal price cartels of reality are considered to be so unstable.

In a technology consortium, in contrast, we see that *even when some members defect, each remaining member will continue to enjoy the benefits of access to the R&D of the other remaining members.* That is the obverse implication of Proposition 10.1—that the members of even a small consortium will derive a differential advantage relative to nonmembers. If one member is suspected of cheating, the rational reaction is, therefore, to eject that firm from the consortium, and to continue exchanging information with the remaining members. And certainly, a defection by one member does not eliminate the danger to another member when it does anything to risk ejection from the consortium. In sum, a technology consortium can easily survive a case of (discovered) cheating and so is far less vulnerable to the prospect that one or a few members will succumb to this temptation.

This is not meant to imply that technology consortia are absolutely immune from destabilizing cheating. A prime source of temptation is the fact that even routine R&D can sometimes turn out *ex post* to yield a breakthrough of enormous value. Even where the firm had no reason to believe *ex ante* that its activity in this area would provide results of greater value than those of other firms in the field, when such an extraordinary advance emerges the innovator firm will face the very strong temptation to avoid sharing it with others, particularly with its horizontal competitors. Two considerations will weaken this temptation to some degree: first, the fact that the imitation process usually entails some lag means that the original innovator often can enjoy a considerable benefit from its valuable novelty, even if it provides the pertinent information to the other consortium members promptly and fully. In addition, as we have seen, the costs of permanent exclusion from the consortium as the penalty for failure to abide by its procedures can be very great. Consequently, only if the value of the development is *very* substantial will it be rational to succumb to the temptation to defect because it transpires *ex post* that the R&D investment has been unexpectedly successful.

10.7   Toward Formal Study of the Stability Issue

The stability of a technology-sharing consortium can be investigated somewhat more formally in a repeated-game framework. In a first round of description its structure can be assumed to resemble that of a prisoner's dilemma game. If the members share information they all get higher payoffs than if they all fail to do so. However, firm i will obtain a reward that is even higher if the other firm, k, really shares while i succeeds in hiding its invention and concealing the fact that it is doing so. This situation is illustrated in the payoff matrix of the stage game, table 10.1, in which the notation, as well as the discussion that follows directly after the matrix, are based on the work of Abreu, Milgrom, and Pearce (1991).

Here the two available strategies for each player are Share (S) and Hide (H). π is the return to each sharer if both players share, and excess profit, g, is earned by the firm that is able to exploit the other enterprise's sharing of its technology, but succeeds in hiding its own. Let us take π, g, h, and b all to be strictly positive, with $-b < -h$. Then the symmetric pure strategy profile (S, S) clearly yields payoffs that dominate or Pareto dominate the other symmetric pure strategy profile (H, H). However, the mutual conceal-

Table 10.1
Payoff matrix 1

		Firm k	
		S	H
Firm i	S	π, π	$-b, \pi + g$
	H	$\pi + g, -b$	$-h, -h$

ment strategy profile (H, H) is the unique dominant strategy equilibrium, that is, either firm will do better by choosing H, given any fixed decision by the other enterprise.

But if this is a repeated game that is played at $t = 1, 2, \ldots$, and the payoffs in the Matrix 1 are per period payoff values, then the payoff (π, π) can be sustained in the long run. One equilibrium strategy pair in the repeated game that can in suitable circumstances yield the collusive payoff (π, π) is the trigger strategy profile.[10] This strategy entails the decision by both firms to play Share so long as the other does so, but to play Hide, forever after, once the other enterprise fails to share. If one firm, say i, expects to conceal in some period, call it the initial period, and it believes that the other firm has adopted the trigger strategy that will come into play after period 1, when i's concealment is discovered, then it will no longer earn $\pi + g$, nor even π, per period forever. Instead, taking δ as the pertinent discrete period discount factor, i can expect a stream of earnings whose net present value is

$$NPV = (\pi + g) + (-h) \sum_{t=1}^{\infty} \delta^t = (\pi + g) + (-h)\delta/(1 - \delta), \qquad (10.16)$$

so that, taking this to be equivalent to the constant per period flow of earnings, E for $t = 0, 1, 2, \ldots$, we obtain

$$NPV = E \sum_{t=0}^{\infty} \delta^t = E(1/(1 - \delta)), \quad \text{or}$$

$$E = (\pi + g)(1 - \delta) - h\delta. \qquad (10.17)$$

The adoption of the trigger strategy will induce two profit-maximizing firms to act in a manner that yields the sharing equilibrium and renders it stable if $E < \pi$, that is, if the earnings expectable from this course of action exceed those that can be expected from concealment of proprietary technical information.

From the point of view of the potential defector, the story, so far, can be summarized in Table 10.2.

Table 10.2

	Inclusion in consortium	Exclusion from consortium
Share	0	—
Hide	g	$-b$

This applies where g represents a "one-shot" gain. However, as it stands, with no explicit role assigned to the other members of the consortium, the logic of the construct is the same as that of the prisoner's dilemma game. It is only the presence of the other consortium members that changes the argument and carries it beyond the prisoner's dilemma—repeated-game story which asserts merely that the one-shot gains from cheating do not exceed the future loss from punishment.

One drawback of the preceding construction is that it is not "renegotiation proof" (on this, see, e.g., Bernheim and Ray [1989], Farrel and Maskin [1989], and Pearce [1987/1990]). After a defection in the two-player case, both firms receive low noncooperative payoffs in the punishment phase that follows. May they not then be tempted to promote their mutual interests by renegotiating to achieve a more cooperative mode of operation? But if that is anticipated, the entire incentive structure of the supposed equilibrium unravels. More sophisticated structures are needed to evade this problem (see the papers just cited).

However, in our setting the issue has a nice resolution that rests on the presence of a multiplicity of other firms in the consortium. A defecting firm is punished upon detection (though this may occur only with a lag) simply by exclusion from the consortium. The special feature that characterizes this case is the fact that the nondefecting firms have no need to break up their profitable sharing arrangement. They can go on indefinitely, sharing their information, while the defector continues to suffer the consequences of exclusion. In contestable markets this argument can be strengthened further; for the place of the defecting firm can be taken over by a new entrant.

In short, this formal analysis lends some systematic support to an assertion, in the previous section, about sources of the stability of a technology-sharing consortium. This is the argument that the likelihood of continued profitability of membership in a technology consortium even after defection of one or even several of its members contributes stability to this form of association of a sort that a horizontal price cartel does not enjoy.

Obviously, the preceding discussion is a simplified treatment of its subject. A richer model is a dynamic Markov game in which the state variable (the accumulation of each firm's technical information) increases during periods when sharing goes on. The other main oversimplification is that concealment of information is treated here as though it were perfectly or nearly perfectly observable, though it is in fact likely to be recognized by other firms only imperfectly and only after some delay. Exploration of these effects leads us to the analysis in Abreu, Milgrom, and Pearce (1991) to which the reader is referred for further details.

10.8   On Technology Consortia in Practice

So much for the theory. Let us turn to some empirical evidence on the existence of voluntary exchange of technology. There are studies that confirm that the behavior of firms does not always fit the common picture of the enterprise which is determined to keep its proprietary technological information from all others, and particularly from its horizontal competitors. For example, Von Hippel (1988, ch. 6) studied a sample of eleven (of the forty-firm U.S. total) American steel minimills. These enterprises, which use electric arc furnaces to recycle scrap steel, are regarded as world leaders in labor productivity. They have outperformed Japanese rivals and now account for a very substantial proportion of the steel output of the United States. Von Hippel found, through a series of interviews, that all but one of the firms in his sample regularly and routinely engaged in the interchange of information with the others: "Reported know-how trading often appeared to go far beyond an arm's length exchange of data at conferences.... Sometimes, *workers of competing firms were trained (at no charge), firm personnel were sent to competing facilities to help set up unfamiliar equipment*, and so on" (p. 79; italics added). The know-how traded was, indeed, valuable. It often entailed exchanges with direct rivals, and though engineers and technicians normally carried out the exchanges, it was done with the knowledge and approval of management. The implicit arrangement described in this study is interpretable as a predominantly *ex ante* exchange. Each firm stands ready to reveal technical information to the others, with the implied understanding that the others will reciprocate by providing it with information on the new ideas they acquire in the future, ideas whose nature is as yet likely to be unknown.

Several other studies of the subject are reported by Von Hippel. Thus, Allen et al. examined a sample of more than one hundred Irish, Spanish, and Mexican firms and found exchanges at trade shows followed by plant visits and direct supply of technical information in response to inquiries. Such studies show that technical information exchange does actually occur. However, their limited samples and the relatively small sizes of the enterprises involved may leave open the possibility that the phenomenon is comparatively isolated. There is reason to believe it is much more than that.

Since I began studying the general subject of technology transfer, some five years ago, I have made it my business to raise this issue with every business firm that has engaged me as a consultant. This has entailed perhaps twenty firms, including some of the giant enterprises of the American economy. In each case the existence of some form and degree of technology exchange between the firm and its rivals was readily acknowledged by the firm's management. In several cases managements indicated that they agreed to it rather reluctantly, ascribing it to regular exchange of information among the scientists and engineers employed by them. Indeed, the managerial personnel giving this report indicated that they were uncomfortable or even indignant at the giveaway of valuable information produced at company expense. However, they claimed to have little choice since, according to them, retention of their competitive position required employment of scientists and engineers of high quality, and such able persons were unwilling to work for companies that did not permit communication with their counterparts in other enterprises (compare the quote by J. B. Say at the beginning of the chapter).

In another instance, a retired vice president of one of America's most innovative firms described a technology-sharing arrangement with a Japanese enterprise. Representatives of the two companies meet annually to settle their "balance of payments," with a sum decided by negotiation paid by the firm providing the less valuable innovations to its "consortium" partner, as compensation for the latter's more valuable contribution. A curious feature of this arrangement is that the two firms do not bargain over the value of the innovations provided in the current year, or in the previous year, but over the innovations each *expects* to provide, in the following year. A possible explanation of this *ex ante* orientation of the arrangement as a means to discourage cheating has already been offered.

A consulting assignment, in which I was engaged as this chapter was being written, entailed work for Perkin-Elmer Corporation, a firm that manufactures and sells analytical (scientific) instruments (notably those entailing precision optics) throughout the world. Since World War II, Perkin-Elmer has entered into numerous agreements with domestic and foreign firms for the *ex post* transfer of technology under license, the most interesting of which (for our purposes here) was an agreement in 1960 with the Hitachi Corporation for the systematic exchange of technical information (for other examples of technology-sharing arrangements involving Perkin-Elmer see the appendix to this chapter). In the Perkin-Elmer–Hitachi contracts, the two firms undertook to supply regularly to one another a full menu of technical developments that had come into their possession. Each firm was authorized to produce, with full technical assistance by the other, any item on any such menu it had received, paying a royalty rate of 6 to 7.5 percent for items that had been invented by the other firm, with lower royalty payments called for on items for which the licensing firm had made a smaller innovating or development contribution. In 1971 the contract was modified to restrict the amount of information each firm was expected to supply along with its menus before the other firm had committed itself to its product selections. Evidently, the firms felt that they had been giving away too much information without compensation.

Quotations from their contract of 10 December 1968 illustrate the spirit of the agreements:

Perkin-Elmer ... and Hitachi desire to insure a continuous exchange of technical information in agreed-upon fields of analytical instrumentation.... 3.1 To the extent permitted by other agreements to which one of the parties hereto ... is a party, and in conformity with government security or other restrictions, (a) Perkin-Elmer agrees to make available to [Hitachi] and (b) [Hitachi] agrees to convey to Perkin-Elmer all information each has available to it during the term of this Agreement within the Product Principle List.... 3.2 Upon request [the firms will supply to one another] copies of all drawings available to each containing information relating to such Product Principles. 3.3 Each party may send technical representatives to the other party's premises at its own expense and at times convenient to the other party to obtain technical information related to such Product Principles. 3.4 Upon request [either firm] will send technical experts to [the other] at times and places mutually agreeable for periods not to exceed thirty (30) days.... In each case, the requesting company will be required to pay all travel and maintenance expense of such technical experts but not salaries.   (pp. 1, 5–6)

The contract of 8 April 1971 also states, "Each party covenants and agrees that it will at all times hereafter ... take all reasonable steps to keep all Technical Information communicated to it by the other party secret and confidential and will not divulge any of the said Technical Information to any person or corporation other than those sub-licensed hereunder" (p. 8).

In other industries the technology-sharing arrangements differ, but they are often there. The vice president of IBM in charge of its patent portfolio[11] wrote to me that many firms in his industry licensed their patents, either in cross-licensing contracts with one another, or in limited exchanges with smaller participants in the industry. The contracts usually cover some defined field such as semiconductors or input-output devices. They are formulated in a bargaining session in which the two negotiating firms compare what each has to offer the other (larger firms being expected to provide more patents, but to benefit more from each patent provided by its smaller partner) and the difference in the value of the patent offerings of the two firms is made up by a monetary "balance payment." The contract, which normally runs over several years, entitles each firm to use of the other firm's current patents in the field covered (the *ex post* component of the arrangement), as well as other patents that will later be issued during the life of the contract (the *ex ante* component). The contract covers patents, but not know-how, which remains proprietary.

According to the supplier of this information, the reasons IBM believes such cross-licensing contracts are important is that they "level the playing field," save wasteful costs such as outlays on reverse engineering or on inventing around patents of a rival, and enhance the firm's freedom of action by permitting it to introduce new products without fear that it will be accused of infringing someone's patents.

Other examples are easily found. United Technologies Pratt and Whitney, which manufactures aircraft jet engines and associated products, has acted as a partner with one of its principal competitors, General Electric, "in the development of an engine to power a very high speed future aircraft" (letter to the author by the vice president in charge of management information systems at Pratt and Whitney).

A newspaper report tells us that winemaking in California has been characterized by a "spirit of cooperation and communication.... While different wineries compete fiercely for sales, winemakers have commonly shared their technical knowledge and tricks of the trade, to their mutual benefit" (*New York Times*, 2 July 1992, p. 1).

Even in the fierce race to produce practical high-definition television technology two of the rival groups (one consisting of the General Instrument Company and MIT and the other consisting of the Zenith Electronics Corporation and AT&T) have recently agreed to pool their efforts, and to share the rights that would be provided by the U.S. patents that result from their combined efforts (*New York Times*, 8 May 1992, p. D1).

It is clear, then, that firms, large and small, do in many cases exchange technological information, sometimes reluctantly, perhaps more often very deliberately.[12] It is obviously incorrect to depict the typical firm as a determined guardian of its technology against all use by others. That this is so is perhaps most strikingly illustrated by a recent conference organized for business firm participants by the MIT Enterprise Forum. The conference, held in May of 1992, was entitled "Entrepreneurial Technology Transfer." It offered participants the opportunity to "learn from the leaders in taking innovative technology to market." Surely, this implies eloquently that enterprising distribution of technology has become a widespread feature of business reality.

10.9   Why Some Firms Refuse to Exchange Information

Everything said in this chapter so far seems to suggest that firms have every reason to join in a technology-consortium arrangement, tacit or overt. Yet in practice, a substantial number of firms seem to hold out and try to keep the results of their R&D proprietary. There are several reasons why this can sometimes be rational.

First, there are industries in which innovations tend preponderantly to be substitutes rather than complementary. We have already noted why this encourages unwillingness to share technology. The pharmaceutical industry appears to be a prime example (despite the report in the preceding footnote). An improved drug product seems likely simply to replace its predecessor (as for example, the Sabin treatment for polio replaced the Salk vaccine), and it is apparently rare for the meritorious features of two new medications to be combined into a product representing an improvement over both of its predecessors. Reports on the industry generally indicate that technology sharing, even in the form of cross-licensing, is comparatively unusual, and it is plausible that rarity of complementarity among new product innovations in that industry is a major part of the explanation.

Firms may also be unwilling to enter into an unrestricted sharing arrangement because they recognize that in the future they can happen upon a major breakthrough that offers them a substantial competitive advantage, and which they will then be unwilling to share. The very possibility that this will occur, a possibility likely to be recognized by all the firms in the field, can (as the lawyers say) have a chilling effect upon any information-exchange arrangement. This, then, may be another consideration that helps to explain why technology consortia are apparently far from universal.

A third reason why a firm may hold out from membership in such a consortium is that management may believe its R&D organization to be more capable than that of the other prospective consortium members, so that the innovations expected to emerge from it are likely to be extraordinarily valuable. This, of course, means that the terms of the information trade with the other consortium members is expected by the management of this firm to be in perpetual imbalance. That will be true even if the expectedly superior information value that emerges from the firm's R&D division is captured entirely in the form of rent to the talented personnel who are responsible for its superiority. For that rent payment will have no counterpart cost to the imitator firms that acquire the superior information through the operation of the consortium, so that the information those other firms get will (to them) have a higher anticipated value than the information they supply in exchange. But this influence becomes far more powerful if the input market is sufficiently imperfect to permit firms to capture part of the rents that in a regime of perfect competition would accrue to their more talented R&D staff. Where such exploitation occurs (to use Joan Robinson's term) and where the firm's R&D is an ongoing process, so that the rental payments are not once-and-for-all sunk costs, then superior innovation prospects translate into superior profitability if the differential advantage they promise is not just given away by voluntary information exchange.

Finally, some very superior R&D staff members themselves may choose to go their own way either to form a specialized R&D firm (such as the one operated by Thomas Edison), or the staff may instead choose to open an operating company that can profit by exclusive use of the expected flow of superior innovations in the future. In a market in which staff members with superior ability are vulnerable to exploitation these two courses of action may represent the only means by which they can capture the rents attributable to their performance. And certainly such enterprises, set up to retain the benefits of superior ability to invent and innovate, will be reluctant to join a technology-sharing consortium.

These, then, are some of the reasons why firms may consider it to be in their interests to stay out of technology consortia. Still, enough has been said in this chapter to suggest that self-interest may often dictate membership in the consortium. Even the firm with superior innovation prospects may well find membership attractive if the consortium contains a sufficiently large number of members so that the size of their combined innovation output makes up for the inferiority of the contribution of each individual member. Using illustrative numbers, a firm whose superiority offers it an expected saving of $20 million on its own will nevertheless find itself outcompeted by a consortium of more than five members if each expects $6 million from its own efforts and $6 million from the information it derives from each of the others.

All of the preceding observations apply both to process and product innovations. But when product innovations are the main issue, the array of possibilities grows richer, because competition in new products or in the features of a common product necessarily brings with it product heterogeneity and all the complications of monopolistic competition theory. Since it can permit the coexistence of several islands of (perhaps moderate) monopoly power, product innovation may provide another reason for unwillingness to share. If the innovation process yields distinctive products to each firm in the industry and each of the products commands some degree of customer loyalty, then every firm may be able to charge a price above its competitive level, even where difficulty of collusion rules that out for homogeneous products offered simultaneously by several enterprises. Indeed, this may be one of the more compelling explanations for unwillingness to join a technology consortium. Holding on to one's own differentiated products in a repeated innovation game with difficulty of collusion may be the only way of acquiring a degree of market power sufficient to yield continuing and positive economic profits.

Still, even product innovation often seems not to undermine the incentives for consortium membership, as most of the empirical examples in the previous section confirm. When innovation takes the form of an addition of *improvements* to a common product, and when customers are not particularly loyal to one improvement as against another, a consortium member whose products offer all of the multiplicity of improvements that emerge from the R&D efforts of its fellow members, as well as its own, may have an unbeatable competitive edge over the nonmember of the consortium whose product benefits only from the improvements provided by its own R&D activities.

There is much more to be said about technology consortia and the market's role in the dissemination of productive technology among firms and nations. For example, this discussion has ignored entirely the contribution of multinational corporations, which may yet be shown to play a very substantial role in carrying technical information from one country to another,[13] or of suppliers of technical equipment who sell their products to a number of horizontal competitors, often in different countries, and provide information on current innovations to them all.

But enough evidence has been reported here to give credence to the view that the market does a far better job of technology transfer than is, by implication, credited to it in the literature of economic theory. It has also been shown that, by internalizing the spillovers of knowledge production, technology consortia can even help to reduce the market's incentives for underinvestment in innovation.

All in all, the analysis suggests that we need to reconsider what seems to be the more common position in the economic literature, which holds that the market performs quite well in terms of static economic efficiency, but that, because of inadequacy of expenditure on innovation and unwillingness to share technology, it is rather more defective in the intertemporal sphere. Instead, the truth may perhaps be closer to the opposite view that seems to be common among intelligent nonspecialists—that monopoly, taxes, and other interferences materially inhibit the static workings of the market mechanism, but that the market is completely unmatched in historical or current experience by any other economic arrangement in terms of its *growth* achievements.

Appendix: Some Other Perkin-Elmer Patent-Sharing Arrangements

Besides its contracts with Hitachi, the Perkin-Elmer Corporation participated in about one hundred other such arrangements during the course of
the postwar period. The following are a few examples:

1. *CSIRO.* Spectroscopy employs instruments that fall into two general
categories: infrared spectrophotometers, which are particularly useful for
analysis of the composition of a sample whose makeup is not known in
advance, and the atomic absorption (AA) instruments, which are better
adapted to precise measurement of components previously known to be
contained in a sample. The AA technique was invented in Australia and
was patented in the early 1950s by a firm whose acronym is CSIRO. Before
the availability of AA equipment that was commercially viable, CSIRO
began to license its patents, first on an exclusive basis, then after 1959, to
companies throughout the world. Perkin-Elmer was among the licensees,
agreeing to pay CSIRO's standard royalty (depending on the country of
spectrometer sale) of £25 sterling or $70 per instrument sold, a fee amount-
ing to about 2 percent of the value of the instrument. The relatively low
fee reflected the substantial amount of development work that had to be
undertaken by the licensees to produce a saleable AA instrument.

2. *Advanced Radiation.* In the 1970s Perkin-Elmer patented a process for
the manufacture of the Microalign instrument, which uses a mercury capil-
lary lamp to etch away circuit patterns on photoresistant semiconductor
wafers. Having been a successful sole producer of the item for some period,
in 1977 the firm encountered pressure from its customers to arrange for a
second supplier of the Microalign lamps to ensure their continuous availability. Perkin-Elmer selected a firm, the Advanced Radiation Corporation
(ARC), which it described as "a small, flexible supplier," entering into an
agreement with ARC to allow the latter to produce the lamp and sell it
directly to customers. Because of its blocking patent, Perkin-Elmer was able
to arrange for a royalty of 48 percent of the value of ARC sales, with the
arrangement apparently proving extremely profitable to the licensee.

3. *Laser Precision.* In the late 1970s infrared spectroscopy underwent a
major improvement permitted by the growing power of computers. The
new approach utilized the Fourier transform to make more effective use of
the data generated by the spectroscope. Perkin-Elmer undertook its own
development effort, seeking to design a Fourier transform instrument of its
own. Because the effort proceeded too slowly, to avoid a major gap in its
product line and tardy entry into the field, in 1981 Perkin-Elmer undertook
negotiations with the Analect Division of the Laser Precision Corporation

for access to Analect's Fourier transform instrument. Analect at the time was a tiny concern with three full-time employees, but it held the patent on a viable technique for the purpose. The license called for a payment of $1 million plus a royalty of 4 percent of sales. However, Perkin-Elmer never exercised its option to acquire the license. Instead, it chose to buy the instrument from Analect until Perkin-Elmer came up with a later-generation instrument of its own.

4. *Perkin-Elmer Puerto Rico.* In 1970 Perkin-Elmer founded a wholly owned subsidiary in Puerto Rico, and licensed it to produce a number of the products for which Perkin-Elmer held the patents. The Puerto Rican output was sold entirely to the parent company, which carried out the distribution. The transfer prices seem to have approximated the figures in the license agreement with other firms, though the IRS, predictably, challenged them.

11   On Efficiency and the Pricing of Transferred Technology

This book has emphasized the contribution to productivity that can be provided by dissemination of technology. Here as in many economic arenas, the price mechanism can help matters. This chapter examines this role of pricing as a step between theory and policy.

In recent years, the analysis of a number of important economic policy issues facing the courts and the regulatory agencies, in dealing with monopoly and market power, has been placed on a firm theoretical foundation. However, one arena in which the pertinent economic principles seem not to have been investigated theoretically is the circumscription of monopoly power deliberately granted to innovators under the patent laws. The courts have, not infrequently, compelled the holders of patents to license to others the products or technology in question.[1] However, a decision to compel licensing is no decision at all unless the license fee is specified or, at least, limits are placed on its magnitude. If the patent holder is free to demand any price, without restriction, then the licensing requirement can be undermined completely by the imposition of a fee that is sufficiently high to drive away any takers. It is equally true that if the prospective user of the patented product can induce the courts to require a royalty fee that is extremely low, then the net effect will be tantamount to imposition of a subsidy from the innovator to the imitator, giving a significant competitive advantage to the licensee.

This chapter examines the principles that should govern the choice of royalty rate for a patent license—the price for supply of proprietory technology to others. Is there a price that is socially optimal and, if so, what determines its magnitude? I will argue here that there is such an optimal amount, and its nature will be described. I will also argue that there are circumstances under which arm's length negotiation in a free market can be expected to lead to adoption of something approximating that amount, provided that the patent system gives to the innovator an appropriate degree of market power, no more and no less, however that may be defined or determined.

11.1   Efficiency Implications of the Royalty Rate

Allocative Influences

To determine which levels of royalty rates are consistent with economic efficiency it is necessary to identify the activities that are influenced by the magnitude of those rates. Just what resources will be misallocated if an inappropriate royalty is selected? Three activities are directly affected by royalty rates: (1) the allocation of resources to research and development and other components of the innovation process, (2) the allocation of resources to technology transfer—that is, imitation and dissemination of innovations, and (3) the allocation of production of goods and services making use of the innovations among the firms that supply those items— that is, which firm, the licensee or the licenser, will produce how much of which of the information-using final products?

The first of these—the economy's innovating activity—has been discussed extensively in the literature, and I will offer only a few further comments on the subject. Here the major point is self-evident: if innovators are forced to license their discoveries and to do so at bargain prices, the result will be a marked disincentive to investment in research and in the remainder of the expensive and risky innovation process. However, the other two activities do not seem to have received the attention they merit, and they will require our consideration.

That there is a trade-off between technological innovation and dissemination seems clear, but its source is not always the obvious one. It is widely recognized in the literature that spillovers from technological advances can lead to substantial underinvestment in innovation. If free riders derive a significant share of the benefits, private marginal returns to investment in innovation may be driven to zero well before the social returns have fallen to that level. Anything that facilitates the diffusion of technology would then appear, automatically, to aggravate the free-rider problem; this is the first (and well-recognized) source of trade-off between innovation and technology transfer. Chapter 10 has already shown that technology exchange among firms can help to reduce this conflict. We will see presently that a proper royalty rate on a patent license also can sometimes eliminate or substantially alleviate the free-rider problem.

There is a second attribute of technology transfer that also renders it competitive with innovation. This is the fact, already documented in Chapter 9, section 5, that dissemination is far from costless. It uses substantial quantities of resources and any such use is, prospectively, a reduction in the stock of resources available for innovation (or any other purposes). This, then, is the second component of the trade-off to be examined presently.

Allocation of Innovation Use among Final-Product Producers
Besides its role in influencing the allocation of resources between innovation and dissemination, the royalty rate has a second allocative task. When an innovation has been licensed, there will generally be two or more firms who consider using it to produce similar or identical outputs. The matter to be decided is the share of that final output to be produced by each of those firms or, if its production is carried out only by a single firm, the question is to which of the candidate firms that task will fall. The efficiency of the industry's activities will obviously be affected by this allocation. It is, for example, not necessarily true that the innovator will be a more effective user of the invention than one of the licensees.

Now it is clear that the royalty rate will influence the allocation of the task between innovator and licensee. The lower the rate (which is commonly expressed as a percent of the price of the final innovation-using product) the larger we can expect the final product output of the licensees to be, because a reduction of the royalty rate has the same effect as a fall in an excise tax on that output. In addition, if royalty rates are negotiated separately with each licensee, the allocation of final output production among those firms will also be affected. An optimal set of royalty rates will, then, be one that is consistent with efficient allocation of the task of final-product production among the firms that carry it out. We will see presently what rates this requirement calls for and we will find that it is not precisely the sort of arrangement that unguided intuition has elsewhere suggested to regulatory agencies.

11.2   Digression: Increasing and Decreasing Cost, Marginal vs. Average Cost Pricing, and the Role of Opportunity Costs

The economic literature has reiterated two pertinent propositions which together constitute the foundation of much of the discussion that follows. These familiar propositions are the assertions that: (1) subject to the well-known qualifications, economic efficiency requires the price of each product (including a license giving the holder the right to employ an innovation) to be set equal to that item's marginal cost, and (2) the pertinent marginal cost must include all *opportunity costs* incurred by the supplier in providing the product. It will be convenient to use the term *direct costs* to refer to all costs that, from the point of view of the supplier firm, are not opportunity costs.

The licensing of an innovation would seem to incur neligible direct costs to the licenser. That is, as the public-good attributes of information indicate, technology transfer may entail very little direct cost to the supplier. However, the opportunity costs may well be substantial. This is clearly true if a patent holder's grant of the license to actual or prospective rivals permits those rivals to take profitable business away from the patent holder. It is equally true if the ensuing rivalry forces prices downward or if it adds materially to advertising and other outlays. Thus the marginal costs pertinent to the efficient pricing of a patent license may plausibly be expected to consist largely, perhaps even almost entirely, of the sort of opportunity costs that have just been described. These observations provide much of the logical basis of the discussion of efficient patent licensing fees in the sections that follow.

However, there is a subtle complication of rather substantial importance that does not seem to have been recognized in much of the literature. There are circumstances in which, while total opportunity costs are substantial, they can be expected to be close to zero at the margin. The marginal opportunity cost of the sale or lease of some good or service can, of course, be positive if the item is limited in supply or entails some fixed capacity, so that the more the seller supplies to others, the less it has available for its own use. A firm that lets others use a bridge whose capacity was already fully employed in transporting its own products will thereby incur an opportunity cost. But the public-good attributes of an innovation mean that the grant of a license to others does not run into any such capacity limitation. Indeed, even where the product in question has no public-good attributes, its provision to others need not incur any marginal opportunity costs in the long run on account of capacity restrictions, if the supplier can add to capacity and is prepared to do so up to the point at which the marginal profit yield of further additions to capacity is zero.

An opportunity cost can arise also if the recipient of a license or some other valuable asset can use it to take profitable business away from the supplier. But as we have noted earlier, as the innovative activity of business firms has become routinized, their investment in innovation, as in every other activity, may be expected to be carried to the point where every such activity yields zero economic profit at the margin, and so it can be argued that the opportunity cost of loss of the marginal unit of any product of one of its activities may also be expected to disappear.

This argument is not quite valid as it stands because it misses the nature of the pertinent margin, and the character of what appears to be the most common pricing arrangement for a patent license. Such a license is usually granted in return for a fixed royalty payment per unit sold of the final product that uses the innovation in question. A license to use a remote-control tuner for television sets may call for a payment of, say, 5 percent of the value of each such device manufactured and sold by the licensee. And if that price is set so low that the licensee is able to take away a high proportion of the sales of a similar product by the patent holder, more than just the zero-profit marginal unit of its original sales volume is likely to be lost. That is, a substantial opportunity cost may well be borne by the licenser firm if it permits the licensee to sell still another unit of the product (and arguably, this is the meaning of the marginal use of the license).

But there is yet another reason—scale economies—why the opportunity cost incurred in the licensing of a patent can often be expected to play a substantial role in the determination of an efficient price for use of that asset. As we know, in an output-producing activity that is characterized by declining average incremental cost[2] the market will, in equilibrium, assign the entire output to a single producer, because if production of the output were divided up among several enterprises the total resources cost must be greater than if it is carried out exclusively by the most efficient of the candidate producers. On the production side, then, the efficiency issue is not how much of the total output should be produced by each participating firm (as in the interior solution that one expects in the diminishing returns case most often considered in the literature). Rather, the issue is, which of the firms can produce the entire output at lowest resources cost (in the corner solution that will now apply). The most efficient firm must now be defined as the one that produces the entire output at minimum total incremental cost or, what amounts to the same thing, at lowest average incremental cost.[3] Thus, where production of the particular commodity is characterized by scale economies, average incremental cost replaces marginal cost as the cost standard pertinent for efficiency in production.

More than that. Efficiency in production requires, in the case where the product in question is characterized by declining average incremental cost (AIC), that price be set no lower than average incremental cost. For if firm A sets the price of Y below its AIC (and presumably finances this output by cross-subsidy) it may preclude production by more efficient firm B whose AIC for Y is less than A's but is above A's price (this assumes that B either has no source out of which to cross-subsidize the production of Y, as A does, or that B is unwilling to engage in cross-subsidization). The conclusion that an efficient price must in this case equal or exceed AIC means that an efficient price must then be *higher* than marginal cost because, where AIC declines with output, marginal cost must, of course, be less than AIC. In other words, the efficiency rules are modified profoundly in this case, with AIC playing at least part of the role normally acted by marginal cost (MC) in the case of diminishing returns.[4]

What is the pertinence of this argument to the issue that is crucial to us here—the role of opportunity cost in the determination of efficient price? We saw in the previous section that in some circumstances, notably when opportunity cost is created by capacity limitations, that marginal opportunity cost can be driven to zero if the supplier of the facility at issue can expand its capacity to the point that enables him to use as much as he wants for his own purposes and to sell or lease to others as much of it as he desires. But in such a case, even though *marginal* opportunity cost will be zero (because capacity will be expanded by a profit-maximizing firm to the point where it gains nothing by adding another unit), it does not follow that the opportunity cost on inframarginal units of capacity will also be zero. If inframarginal units do yield positive benefits to the owner when used for his own purposes, and if some substantial proportion of that capacity is nevertheless rented or sold to someone else, that transaction will clearly entail a nonzero opportunity cost. That is, the average incremental opportunity cost will be positive, and the efficient price, which must at least equal AIC, as we have seen, must of course cover the opportunity cost component.

We thus return to the basic and elementary principle on which our discussion of efficient royalty rate for technology transfer is based. It asserts that any *fixed* royalty rate must (at least) equal the higher of the two numbers, MC or AIC, with each of these figures including the appropriate opportunity cost component if the value of that component is zero. In the case of increasing AIC, MC will be the pertinent floor and, of course, in that case MC > AIC. The reverse will be true where AIC is decreasing with output, so that efficiency requires $p \geqslant$ AIC > MC. Thus in either case, $p \geqslant \max(\text{MC}, \text{AIC})$ as the proposition asserts.

Let us now specialize the proposition somewhat, treating the granting of a patent license to another firm as if it were the sale of an input, thereby getting a clearer picture of the efficiency properties of the pricing rule. We have already noted that in the grant of a patent license it seems plausible that both the marginal and average incremental direct costs (that is, the nonopportunity costs) to the holder of the patent are likely to be very close to zero. However, both the marginal and average incremental opportunity costs would appear to be substantial but, perhaps in many cases, diminishing—as use of an invention by rivals increases and spreads, the economic profits of the patent holder (other than those derived from patent rental) are apt to fall toward zero and then level off. Thereafter the marginal opportunity loss from still further dissemination and use of the patented material should be close to zero. If so, patent licensing would constitute a case of declining AIC, with all the implications we have just seen that this situation entails.

11.3   The Innovation as Input and the Efficient Component-Pricing Rule

The literature on the economics of price regulation provides a pricing principle that offers guidance for the choice of efficient royalty rates. This pricing principle has been referred to as the *efficient component-pricing rule*. We will see that, despite the nomenclature, it is merely a variant of the elementary principles for efficiency in pricing that have just been discussed.

The rule applies to the sale of an input—a component, K, of a final product—by a manufacturer, X, of both the component and the final product, to another firm, Y, which also wants to use the component to produce the same final product. Here Y is itself assumed to be a maker of the remaining components (other than K) of the final product. If X sells the component in question to Y, the two firms then become competitors in final-product selling.[5]

In the regulatory arena the problem arises, for example, when two railroads, X and Y, operate along parallel routes from an origin point, A, to an intermediate point, B. Railroad X owns the only tracks that go on from B to terminal point C. In this case, the final product is transportation all the way from A to C. Competing railroad Y, which is the proprietor of tracks from A to B, can be expected in these circumstances to apply for "interconnection" from B to C, seeking to rent "trackage rights" along that route from its rival, X. If the transaction is completed, then X is described in regulatory parlance as "the landlord railroad" and Y is referred to as "the tenant."

Regulators have commonly been requested by prospective tenants to force the landlords to grant them trackage rights. In addition, for obvious reasons, the regulatory agency has usually been asked to decide on the rental fee.

A. The Regulatory Approach to Rental Fee Determination. Roughly speaking, regulators have often approached the rental fee decision in the manner suggested by the following example. Let the average incremental cost incurred by landlord X as a result of Y's use of its track be AIC dollars per train.[6] That is, let X's total cost be increased by (N)(AIC) dollars (track wear and tear, additional planning, and administrative cost) as a result of Y's use of its tracks, where N is the number of trains Y runs over X's tracks.

Suppose that, because of economies of scale, total revenues must exceed the sum of the incremental costs of the two types of traffic (just as it must exceed marginal cost multiplied by output) if X is to break even, and that in the absence of trackage rights the traffic from A to C had earned X a net contribution (total incremental revenue minus incremental cost) toward the shortfall of T = $90 million per year. Suppose also that after grant of the trackage rights X is expected to retain two-thirds of the traffic from A to C, with the remaining traffic going to the tenant, Y.

Then regulators, assuming freight rates for shipments from A to C to be fixed, have generally taken the proper rental fee for the trackage rights to be made up of two components: (1) a charge per train of railroad Y, which is set equal to AIC dollars, the average (direct) incremental cost to X of handling Y's train, and (2) an adjustment supplement designed to leave X with exactly two-thirds of the $90 million contribution the traffic formerly provided. That is, under this regulatory rule the landlord is granted its pro rata share of the contribution, in this case corresponding to its two-thirds expected share of the total traffic.

We will see presently that this regulatory rule is in fact inconsistent with economic efficiency. But first let us indicate briefly in what respects the setting of the royalty rate for the license of a patent is analogous to the setting of the rental fee for trackage rights or the pricing of any other product component in comparable circumstances.

B. *Patent License Fees and the Pricing of Product Components.* Up to a point, the analogy should be readily apparent. Improved technology or product design is an input to the final product, an input not essentially different from the purchase of a bigger or better machine which was previously available on the market but which the firm had not previously decided to acquire. The purchase of the machine is equivalent to the required investment in R&D by the innovating firm, and the acquisition of a license to use the new technology is equivalent to leasing of the machine. Taking this reasoning one step further, the granting of a patent license by innovating firm X to the horizontal competitor firm Y is precisely analogous to the grant of trackage rights by the landlord to the tenant railroad. Both features requisite for the applicability of the component-pricing principles are satisfied by the patent-licensing issue. First, the license entitles the recipient firm, Y, to use a component of a final product, a component that is the property of another firm, X. Second, the two firms are horizontal competitors in the sale of the final product.

Let us examine what is required for optimal pricing in such a case.

C. *The Optimal Component-Pricing Rule.* In brief, the optimal component-pricing rule asserts that the rent Y should pay per train is the entire average incremental cost incurred by each train traversing X's route BC, *including any incremental opportunity cost* that the passage of Y's train imposes on X. Expressed in this way, the rule is entirely familiar to economists, as we have seen, and its logic will be virtually self-evident to them, except for its focus on average incremental cost rather than marginal cost. However, it may be useful to restate the rule in the form in which it has been presented in the regulatory arena. There, the same rule states that the appropriate per-train payment by Y is AIC, the per unit incremental cost (excluding opportunity cost), plus T/M, where T was the total contribution X earned from the AC traffic before the grant of trackage rights and M is the total number of trains going from A to C. Thus X will receive from Y for Y's N-train traffic a total payment equal to

$$(N)(AIC) + NT/M, \tag{11.1}$$

giving it a contribution to profit equal to

$$(N)(AIC) + NT/M - \text{the cost to X of Y's traffic}$$
$$= (N)(AIC) + NT/M - (N)(AIC) = NT/M. \tag{11.2}$$

The contribution X will receive from the M − N trains of its own that continue to traverse the route will equal

$$(M - N)T/M = T - NT/M.$$

The landlord's gain from the combined traffic after expending (N)(AIC) on Y's trains will then be

$$NT/M + T - NT/M = T. \tag{11.3}$$

In other words, under the optimal pricing rule the landlord will gain the same total contribution, T, whether or not it grants the traffic rights, and despite the fact that X now runs fewer trains of its own.[7] This is very different from the standard regulatory arrangement that assigns both X and Y a share of T, prorated in proportion to their respective shares, M − N and N, of the total traffic, M.

To begin to see why this solution is efficient we note that in an effectively competitive (perfectly contestable) market that is how the rent level will in fact be set. No landlord who can use a piece of property for her own business purposes will rent it to a competitor for less than the direct incremental cost of the tenant's occupation of the property *plus the opportunity cost to the landlord* of the rental arrangement. If the landlord can earn $90,000 by using the property for her own business purposes, she will require the tenant to make good that $90,000 she forgoes by renting the property to him. That opportunity cost payment is, of course, the NT/M portion of the tenant's payment in our general statement of the optimal component-pricing rule. Consequently, even in the most competitive of markets no landlord will rent for a fee less than (11.1). Moreover, if there is plenty of competition, that is, a profusion of alternative properties are available to the tenant on comparable terms, he will pay no more then that.[8]

Since, in the absence of externalities, we expect competitive prices to be consistent with economic efficiency, the preceding argument can be taken to establish a presumption that the component-pricing rule is indeed optimal. However, this can also be shown more directly.

The issue in the railroad example is that the freight can be carried over competitive route segment AB by either X or Y. Let AIC_x and AIC_y, respectively, be the per train incremental cost if this portion of the service is performed by X or Y. Then it will be more efficient for the landlord, X, to do the job if $AIC_x < AIC_y$, and it will be more efficient for the tenant, Y, to do so if the equality is reversed.[9]

To prove that the component-pricing rule automatically apportions the task to the more efficient carrier we first provide an explicit expression for the contribution, T, of the total AC traffic. For this purpose let P represent the price the shippers pay for transportation of a trainload of freight over the entire route, AC. Then clearly, X obtains from its M-train traffic (in the absence of a grant of trackage rights to Y),

$$T = M(P - AIC - AIC_x),\tag{11.4}$$

where AIC is, as before, the incremental cost of taking a train over noncompetitive route segment BC, and AIC_x is X's incremental cost of carrying the train the remainder of the way. Now if Y acquires trackage rights and sends N trains over the route, the profit it will earn is its total revenue PN, minus its rental payment, given by (11.1) minus $(N)(AIC_y)$, the incremental cost it incurs by carrying the N trains over route AB. That is,

$$\text{Y's profit} = N(P - AIC - T/M - AIC_y)\tag{11.5}$$

or, substituting the value of T/M obtainable from (11.4),

$$Y's\ Profit = N(AICx - AICy). \qquad (11.6)$$

This tells us that Y will make a profit by renting the trackage rights if and only if it is the more efficient carrier, so that $AICy < AICx$. Indeed, its profit will then be equal to the net resources saved by use of Y rather than X. However, (11.6) shows that when pricing follows the component-pricing rule firm Y will lose money by the acquisition of trackage rights if it is the less efficient carrier.

In sum, in terms of allocation of the traffic between X and Y, rent-setting rule (11.1) is, indeed, the optimal component-pricing rule.[10] The same logic clearly applies without modification to the fee for a patent license.

11.4   On the Innovation-Dissemination Trade-off

There remain for discussion the requirements of efficiency in the allocation of resources between innovation and dissemination. The royalty rate by itself cannot carry out this task since it is already determined by the requirement of efficiency in the allocation of output among the innovation-using firms, as the previous section described. It is convenient, then, that another price, P, that of the final product, remains to be determined. We will see that P together with the royalty rate can do the job, at least in principle.

The Royalty Rate and the Innovation-Dissemination Trade-off
A royalty rate that follows the optimal component-pricing rule already makes some contribution toward solution of the problem by moderation of the conflict between dissemination and innovation. If the innovation could be used by anyone who wished to do so, without any royalty payment, competition among the imitators could drive prices so low that those prices would offer little or no reward to the innovator. Without a royalty or some equivalent payment the licensee will bear no part of the innovation cost and competitive pressures can drive prices down to cover only the costs the competitors do bear, leaving no incentive payment for innovation.

The royalty rate helps substantially to resolve the difficulty. By creating a component of the licensee's costs that corresponds to the costs entailed in the innovation process it drives a wedge between the competitive market price of the final product and the costs other firms incur when they make use of the innovation. The net result is that the innovator can obtain compensation as an incentive for further innovative effort, and it can obtain this compensation from two sources. First, despite the use of the technology by others, the innovator is enabled to continue getting from the sale of his own products what can be interpreted as virtuous (but temporary) monopoly profit as a result of the fact that the licensed competitors cannot afford to drive prices down to what would otherwise be their own average costs—the competitive price levels. Second, because the license fee compensates the innovator for the opportunity cost of production by the licensees, the rental fee becomes a source of compensation designed to be perfectly compatible with the returns the innovator obtains from its own production. This compatibility feature has led to the optimal component-pricing rule being described as the "principle of indifference" (or as the "parity principle"). That is, it calls for the royalty rate to be set at the level that makes the innovator indifferent between production by licensees and production by himself; it imposes financial terms for the licensees' use of the technology that are on a par with the patent holder's implicit charges to itself.

The Role of the Final-Product Price
To complete the story, however, we must determine the value of T, the total contribution (incentive payment) received by the innovator or, what is equivalent, by (11.4), the value of P, the final-product price. It is clear that, *ceteris paribus*, the greater the strength of the monopoly power possessed by the innovator the higher the value of T that it can hope to collect, and the stronger the incentive for investment in innovation will be.

Policy can clearly contribute to this power, for example, by facilitating the grant of patents, by strengthening their enforcement, by extending the life of the patent, and so on. All this is rather obvious and it is only worth pausing to note that what policy can accomplish here is limited by market conditions and the value to the public of the innovation at issue. No matter how rigorous the patent laws, the public cannot be forced to pay a price for the final product higher than the figure that reduces demand to zero.

This means that if patent laws are uniform, T cannot be set at any one value that is deemed to be universally optimal. Rather, the optimal value will vary from one innovation to another, depending on its reception by the market. But that is as matters should be, and the differential in returns is the incentive for the innovator to try harder—to seek to come up with an innovation that yields a value of T well above the norm because it is attractive to consumers.

Remarks on the Optimal Value of T

But as we have seen, changes in policy can affect the *expected* value of T, the mean reward for innovation. This suggests that there may be an optimal expected value of this parameter. It is even easy to state what it is, at least in abstract terms, though the result is hardly likely to be very helpful for policy design. Since an increase in T will presumably add to the resources devoted to innovation, T should be set so that the expected marginal social yield to (added) investment in innovation is equal to the marginal opportunity cost of those resources.

This proposition of elementary economic theory appears to tell us only one thing of any value. It makes clear how difficult it is to calculate that efficient value of T or even to shed any light on its quantification. Who can calculate the expected marginal yield of current or future investment in innovation *in general*, without reference to any particular prospective innovation? The conclusion is that, at least for now, formal economic analysis has little to offer the decision maker in this arena. Decisions on the proper strength of patent protection must continue to be based on an amorphous blend of judgment, equity considerations, and political pressures.

11.5   The Market, the Royalty Rate, and Efficiency

Given the policy decision on the strength of legal protection to be accorded to the innovator, if royalty rates are set in accord with the optimal component-pricing rule, everything will fall into place. A set of resources commensurate with the selected innovator-protection policy will flow into the creation of innovations. Patent licenses will be acquired only by firms that can make efficient use of them, and the production of innovation-using final products will be allocated efficiently among firms.

There remains only the question whether something need be done to ensure that royalty rates are set in accord with the efficient component-pricing rule. There is some a priori reason to suspect that the market mechanism can produce that result. For we saw earlier that this is the way that component prices will be set in a market that is perfectly contestable or highly competitive. Yet casual observation suggests that in reality patent-license fees are not always set in this way. Many a firm pays for permission to use another's technology by means of reciprocation. Some have *ex ante* arrangements under which each expects free access to the other's technological developments as they emerge in the future. Other firms exchange technology *ex post* by cross-licensing of patents, often at a negligible, or even a zero, royalty rate (see Chapter 10, section 8).

Now one can understand why that is done if two such firms expect the exchange to turn out approximately equal year by year or even only in the long run. If a royalty rate set in accord with the component-pricing rule were to mean that each firm expected to owe the other approximately $2 million at the end of the year, collection of the reciprocal debt would not be worth the cost, and cancellation of the debt would be attractive. Not only will the firm's profits be unaffected if it ends up paying and receiving $2 million. In a competitive market its prices will also be unaffected since, on balance, its costs will be unchanged by the choice between reciprocal payment and cancellation of the payment obligation.

Still, the choice between the two arrangements *does* matter, because it will affect the allocation of outputs among the firms. A zero royalty means there is that much more incentive at the margin for the licensee to expand output. The situation is similar to that of a restaurant that offers diners all they can eat at a fixed price. Even if profits are the same as those of a restaurant run on the more usual pricing arrangement, the regular customers of the fixed entry fee restaurant are apt to gain more weight.

Analogously, imagine two firms, each of which produces two goods, A and B; suppose that firm 1 provides an innovation usable in the production of good A, while firm 2 comes up with an innovation pertinent to B's production. If each firm grants the other a license to use its own innovation, the amounts of the two goods produced by each firm will surely vary with the magnitude of the license fee. A low or zero fee will encourage provision of a larger share of each output by the licensee. If, when the fee is zero, we let $a_1(0)$ represent the output of good A by firm 1 and so on, we expect that the ratio $a_1(0)b_2(0)/a_2(0)b_1(0)$ will be lower than the corresponding ratio, $a_1(z)b_2(z)/a_2(z)b_1(z)$, with a fee, z, that satisfies the optimal component-pricing rule. Clearly, in general these two ratios will not both satisfy the requirements of economic efficiency. Since as we have seen, it is the fee, z, that satisfies the requirement of efficiency, a zero fee will generally not be optimal.

This immediately raises two important questions. First, is there some persistent impediment to the working of the market mechanism that prevents it from driving the royalty rate toward its optimal level? Second, if this is so, is it appropriate for the public sector to intervene, and in what manner? Unfortunately, the answers are far from clear. Their pursuit is a task that remains to be carried out.

The theory of pricing for allocative efficiency in innovation and technology dissemination is quite straightforward when expressed in general terms.

Indeed, we know much more than that about the optimal value of the license fee. When a court or a regulatory agency chooses to intervene, economic analysis is in a position to offer concrete guidance for the determination of the fee and to show how the choice of fee affects economic efficiency. Here, as so often happens, the economist's rules turn out to call for fees very different than those regulators have tended to favor in analogous arenas.

The basic conclusion is that, while managerial and entrepreneurial contributions to technology transfer undoubtedly serve the public interest, they can be carried out in a manner that is efficient or one that is inefficient. Price, as usual, plays a key role here, and in this chapter we have obtained some insight into the character of the price arrangement that serves efficiency.

12

Toward Improved Allocation of Entrepreneurship

Although critics complained that democracy made the [ancient] Athenians litigious, the system contained a device meant to promote restraint. If the plaintiff did not win a stated percentage of the jurors' votes he was required to pay a considerable fine—to the state in public prosecutions, to the defendant in private ones. This must have served as a significant deterrent to the frivolous, malevolent, and merely adventurous suits.

Kagan (1991, p. 57)

The central theme of this book is the entrepreneur's vulnerability to misallocation, when evaluated in terms of the interests of society. We have taken the typical entrepreneur to be driven by the desire for wealth, power, and prestige, and have assumed that he is tempered in the pursuit of his goals by morality and idealism no more and no less than other humans are. But when entrepreneurs succumb to temptation, and particularly when they do so in droves, the cost to society is likely to be high because the activities of entrepreneurs have such a substantial effect on the performance of the economy. Thus, when entrepreneurs flock into the business of providing the services of mercenary armies, or the production and supply of illegal narcotics, or the seeking of rents, the output of the economy is likely to suffer, and at times it appears to have suffered substantially.

But it seems plausible that if entrepreneurs are lured by the prospect of rich rewards into unproductive or even antiproductive activities, then similar rewards or penalties should also be capable of tempting them in the other direction. The purpose of this chapter is to explore with the aid of illustrations whether this can be done and, if so, by what means.

12.1 Japan, Patent Licensing, and the Rules of the Game

In Chapter 4 we saw that, in Japan, the rules of the game have been designed to discourage the allocation of entrepreneurial talent into rent-seeking litigation. That same society possesses still other rules that serve to *encourage* productive entrepreneurial activity. As an example, let us consider some Japanese patent provisions that, rather than impeding the flow of proprietary technology, appear to stimulate its dissemination and to reduce the costs of imitating entrepreneurial activity. Thus, even if Japanese firms do have an unusual cultural propensity to imitate and to share the results of innovation, their behavior is also strongly influenced by Japan's patenting rules.[1]

Provision 1. Award of the Patent to the First to File. In the United States and Canada, a patent is awarded to the party that provides evidence that it was the first to *discover* the invention in question. In Japan and most other countries, in contrast, the patent goes to the party that is first to *file* its application. This has two consequences, both of which serve to stimulate dissemination: first, the rule encourages early filing, making the technical information available sooner, and perhaps far sooner, than under the U.S. system, and giving rivals an earlier opportunity to profit in their own innovative efforts from the knowledge that is required to be disclosed along with the application (see below). Second, applications filed in haste tend to be imperfect and incomplete, making them more vulnerable to challenge and to conflicting claims. This can pressure the parties to arrive at a settlement, with the successful patent applicant precommitted to provide licenses to rivals in exchange for agreement by the latter not to challenge the application.

Provision 2. Prepatent Disclosure. In the United States, public disclosure of the technical details of a patented invention is required, but only after the patent has been granted. In Japan, in contrast, the details must be published in the official gazette where anyone can examine them, immediately after the filing of an application. The information must remain available for eighteen months thereafter, even if the patent has not been granted in the interim. Obviously, this too gives an early helping hand to rivals seeking to provide themselves with a similar invention, and strengthens their position in bargaining for a license.

Provision 3. Prepatent Challenges. In the United States, opposing parties can intervene only after a patent has been granted, and the patent holder can deal with one challenger at a time. In Japan, the patent application can be challenged before the authorities have made their decision, and there is no limit on the number of opponents who have standing to argue simultaneously that the patent should not be granted because the invention is obvious, or insufficiently novel, or lacks industrial application. The patent applicant has only a brief period to respond, and the application may be rejected if even a single challenge is deemed not to have been answered adequately. This seems clearly to encourage early licensing as a means to prevent challenges, and not only because there is so great a risk that one of the challenges will prove successful. For even if no opponent succeeds in preventing the grant of the patent, a protracted challenge can be very damaging to the applicant's interests since it cuts effective patent life, which is limited to twenty years after the date of application.

Provision 4. Prepatent Royalties Imposed Only for "Knowing Use." Under the Japanese rules, others can generally use a prospectively patentable invention during the period after a patent application has been filed. They are simply obligated to pay royalties that are deemed "reasonable." Moreover, the user is obligated to pay such royalties only if the applicant's invention has been used *knowingly*. Thus failure by the applicant to reach early agreement with prospective users is risky and can prove costly if it turns out to be difficult to provide evidence that a user employed it knowing that the patent had been applied for.

Provision 5. Patentability of Minor Modifications. Under Japanese patenting practice, the coverage of a patent is generally very narrow—that is, only the unsanctioned production of items whose technology is extremely similar to the patented item is prohibited. In addition, the requirement, found in any patent system, that the patented idea be novel is interpreted relatively loosely in Japan. As a result, rivals who have learned the technology of an innovation during the disclosure period following the patent application, and have used the knowledge so acquired to design minor modifications of the original invention, are entitled to apply for patents of their own to cover their variations on the original invention. This clearly weakens the power of a patent to exclude use by others. In addition, the original inventor may find herself boxed in by the derivative patents and prevented from using her own invention in her production process for fear of violating imitators' "improvement patents."

All these apparently idiosyncratic patent provisions contribute strong pressure on Japanese innovators to enter into cross-licensing arrangements with rivals. The mere presence of these rules constitutes a threat not only to the success of the initial patent application (via the prospect of direct opposition), but also to the right to use the patent if it should be granted but immediately hemmed in by patented improvements. In Ordover's words, "The Japanese patent system subordinates the short-term interests of the innovator in the creation of exclusionary rights to the broader policy goals of diffusion of technology" (1991, p. 48). The legislators and administrators of the Japanese patent mechanism seem to have been determined not to leave the encouragement of dissemination to the market, to cultural propensities, or to chance. They have organized the institution in a way that imposes strong pressures for rapid and effective spreading of new technology among domestic users and facilitates the work of enterprising imitators. One also has the impression that the arrangements have had the apparently intended effect. In short, the Japanese model shows once more that the rules of the game *can* be designed to provide the incentive for entrepreneurs and managements to increase their contribution to the economy's productive capacity and to its output.

Let us now proceed to some illustrative policy proposals designed to take advantage of this option. It is hardly necessary to say that these proposals are mostly preliminary, that most of them require considerable further exploration, and that they are by no means meant to be exhaustive. In any event, the brevity of our discussion of each proposal will, by itself, suggest how much more investigation of its details and implications remains to be done.

12.2   Policy Measures to Discourage Litigative Rent Seeking: The Use of the Antitrust System to Subvert Competition

The present American system of antitrust statutes and regulations, it was argued in Chapter 4, is often subverted by rent preservers who seek to use these laws to protect themselves from effective competition. We begin here with some proposed amendments of these rules and practices, which are intended to discourage such enterprising rent-seeking activity, and thereby provide an incentive for the reallocation of entrepreneurial effort into more productive channels. The proposals are grouped into three broad categories: (1) measures designed to prevent misuse of antitrust statutes and regulation as protectionist instruments that weaken the competitive process, (2) measures that inhibit their use for rent-seeking purposes, and (3) measures that address themselves to the conventional concerns about the issue of antitrust and intertemporal efficiency.

Preventing Use of Antitrust to Inhibit Competition
It is in the arena of misuse of antitrust by runners-up who hope to shield themselves from the effectiveness of competition that the theoretical model of perfect contestability can make its main contribution. A regime of perfect contestability can be defined, roughly, as one in which all barriers to entry and exit are completely absent—it is the most powerfully competitive situation that is viable for the large enterprises that one expects to

emerge under conditions of economies of scale and scope. The ideal of perfect competition, despite the exemplary economic performance welfare theory has shown it to elicit from producers and consumers, has long been recognized as something so far removed from the practicalities of the pertinent economic arenas that it was largely ignored in the design of policy. But taken as an ideal to be emulated, the contestability model is different. It has been shown, like perfect competition, to meet the requirements of static economic efficiency (see Baumol, Panzar, and Willig [1988, ch. 2 and 12]) and it seems to comport workably, if imperfectly, with intertemporal efficiency. Yet it does not require industries to be transformed into the collections of diminutive enterprises that, by definition, populate the world of perfect competition—small firms that are inconsistent with and rendered undesirable by the presence of economies of scale and scope.

Once it is agreed that the proper role of antitrust regulation is to promote competitiveness where it is prospectively viable, and to act as a surrogate for competition where it is not, a general course of action recommends itself. Of course, it is only enterprises that are relatively large relative to the size of their industries to which regulatory attention to pricing, investment, and other related decisions is normally directed. These are precisely the sorts of business firms to which the ideal of perfect competition is inapplicable. The standard of acceptable conduct by the firms at issue, then, becomes what their behavior would be if they *were* operating in a market that was (hypothetically) perfectly contestable.[2] Such behavior should, ideally, be expected of all firms subject to antitrust rules or regulatory scrutiny. But those firms should never be constrained any further than that, since any further circumscription of the range of decisions open to them must represent governmental intrusion that threatens efficiency by requiring firms to act differently from the ways in which effectively competitive market forces would force them to behave.

Three specific examples will illustrate the policy implications of these observations:

i. Abandonment of Fully-Allocated Cost as a Guide to Price Evaluation. The history of regulation and the antitrust system is replete with the use of "fully allocates cost" calculations by protection-seeking competitors. The *fully allocated cost* (FAC) of some product, X, is an accounting concept for a multiproduct firm, which attributes to X, in addition to its own marginal or incremental cost, some prorated share of the fixed costs incurred in common on behalf of X and the other products of the firm. The share of those common costs attributed to X admittedly and unavoidably is always determined on some arbitrary basis. Protection-seeking competitors, arguing before the courts or at regulatory hearings, have often proposed these costs, suitably calculated to produce a high FAC figure, as the appropriate price floor for their competitors, claiming that prices lower than this are destructive or predatory. Similarly, firms seeking to extract subsidies for the inputs they purchase have urged the use of these same FAC costs (but, predictably, calculated in a manner that yields a low FAC value) as ceilings for their suppliers, claiming that prices higher than this are unfair.

But economic analysis shows that neither perfect contestability nor even perfect competition calls for firms to satisfy these arbitrary standards. Market forces simply make no rules linking prices to fully allocated costs, which are also, demonstrably, an impediment to economic efficiency of any sort. Moreover, because the FAC figures are fundamentally arbitrary, they invite endless and inventive litigation over which of the available arbitrary standards to use in calculating the FAC figures to govern the outcome of any particular case at issue.

An explicit commitment to eschew any and all further reliance on fully allocated cost in antitrust actions related to pricing and in regulation of rates would close off an important avenue for subversion of the antitrust laws by those who would use them to reduce the severity of the competitive process, thereby discouraging this widespread form of enterprising litigative effort.

ii. Use of Areeda-Turner-like Rules. The obverse of the preceding point is that criteria of acceptable pricing behavior should be derived from careful economic analysis of the behavior of competitive and contestable markets. The so-called Areeda-Turner criterion of predatory pricing, which calls for prices to be judged predatory if and only if they fall short of the corresponding marginal costs, is an example of such a standard.[3] Despite all the criticism to which it has been subjected, and all the modifications that have been proposed by very competent economists, this criterion must nevertheless be recognized as a very commendable and basically defensible step in the right direction, one that should considerably narrow the scope for inventive rent-seeking litigation.

iii. Incremental Cost Floors and Stand-alone Cost Ceilings. A further step in this direction was taken by the Interstate Commerce Commission in 1985 when it adopted what it called "constrained market pricing" as its guide for the regulation of rates for the transportation of coal by railroads.[4] Explicitly acknowledging contestability analysis as the basis for its decision, the ICC adopted the incremental cost of any type of shipment as the proper floor for its price, and stand-alone cost (the price that would make entry just barely profitable in a hypothetical, and otherwise similar, market from which entry barriers were totally absent) as the corresponding ceiling. The point is that in a perfectly contestable market, depending on demand conditions, price can sometimes go as low as incremental cost, and sometimes as high as stand-alone cost, but any price that is outside those bounds will rapidly be undermined by market forces. Such pricing clearly offers both consumers and rival suppliers of the products in question all the protection against exploitative pricing practices that an effectively competitive market would provide to them. These pricing rules can also be shown to be compatible with the requirements of at least static efficiency, and surely contribute to intertemporal efficiency by discouraging the diversion of entrepreneurship into attempts to use antitrust regulation as a means to protect firms from effective competition.

Discouragement of Use of Antitrust Regulation for Rent-Seeking Purposes
We can be briefer in the discussion of the second category of our policy suggestions, since the points are fairly straightforward and have been dealt with elsewhere in the literature. The essence of the matter is to take steps to discourage the use of private antitrust actions as prospective "cash cows," ready for milking by rent seekers.[5] Here several policy measures seem clearly to merit consideration:

i. Symmetry of Responsibility for Costs Imposed on the Victor. In the current legal arrangements, the defendant in an antitrust case can be required to bear the costs incurred by the plaintiff in bringing the suit, if the defendant is found guilty of violating the antitrust laws. But if the suit is found to have no merit the defendant generally cannot recover its costs from the plaintiff—at least not without going to the trouble and expense of instituting a countersuit. This asymmetric and favorable treatment of the plaintiff is a clear incentive for rent seeking; a change in this arrangement consequently seems to have much to be said for it.

ii. Restrictions of Contingency Arrangements with Lawyers. The argument for amendments to restrict the use of contingency arrangements by attorneys in private antitrust suits is similar. There may be exceptional cases in which contingency arrangements are indispensable, but these circumstances should be spelled out clearly, and restricted narrowly. Perhaps a simple ceiling on contingency fee payments, limiting them, say, to $1 million, would preserve this instrument for use by less affluent clients, while making it unavailable to any "megacase" treasure hunt.

iii. A Clear and Rational Criterion for Class-Action Designation. The class-action suit has a very legitimate social purpose and it sometimes contributes to the efficiency of the legal process. However, the basis on which class-action designation is granted or denied is far from clearly spelled out, and it seems often to be granted where it serves no discernible social purpose.

But it can also serve as an instrument of what is not quite blackmail by the rent seeker, who uses the enormous risk borne by the defendant in a class-action case to extract a lucrative settlement. Often such cases never go to trial, the legal battle centering, instead, on whether the plaintiff's request for class-action status will be granted or denied. Defendants usually lose this preliminary skirmish, in which the real charges against them are never even examined. Then defendants commonly elect to settle out of court even if they believe themselves to be completely innocent. The implication is that some effort needs to be devoted to reexamination of the logic of class actions to determine the circumstances in which they serve the public interest and those where they do not, and corresponding amendment and spelling out of the pertinent legal rules should be given serious consideration.

iv. Uncoupling of Trebled Damages. Since it is clear that violators of antitrust rules sometimes succeed in escaping detection, prosecution, or punishment, it would not provide an adequate deterrent to make them subject to payment of only the amount of damage their conduct has caused. Effective deterrence, therefore, does require some multiplication of the damage figure as the amount for which they are liable if found guilty, even if the number three, which is commonly used for this purpose, is a bit arbitrary. But by multiplying the prospective reward, trebled damages also serve as an added incentive for rent-seeking private antitrust suits.

The compound goal of effective deterrence without encouragement of rent seeking can be served by continuing the trebled damages as the amount for which the defendant is liable if found guilty, but limiting the amount the plaintiff is permitted to recover to actual damages plus, perhaps, some small addition. The resulting surplus can then, perhaps, go to the federal government.

Measures to Insulate Innovation from Antitrust Inhibition

Other appropriate modifications of the antitrust rules build on the well-known observation, discussed in earlier chapters, that social rates of return to investments in R&D tend to exceed private rates of return to such activities. Consequently, antitrust policies should be designed carefully to avoid steps that increase the gap even further and invite legal intervention by competitors who are less successful at inventive activity, and who seek protection in the antitrust laws from the competition of innovative firms. In particular:

i. The antitrust rules should avoid discouragement of cooperative innovative effort unless there are clear grounds for the suspicion that the effect will be to hamper or destroy competition. Antitrust statutes should take account of the benefits from cooperation in technology production. Research joint ventures, research consortia, and even mergers in high-technology industries are frequently a socially optimal response to market failures that beset the production and dissemination of knowledge. Consequently, a relaxed rule-of-reason approach to interfirm coordination may well prove to be the best way to deal with the legitimate concerns apt to be raised by such coordination. In this process consortia, joint ventures, information interchange, and even mergers of firms with substantial current market shares in high-technology industries can be presumed to be conducive to dynamic efficiency—more so than in industries that are less driven technologically.

ii. Antitrust policy should avoid inhibition of the dissemination of information. Firms should be permitted great latitude in their patent-licensing policies in order to increase returns to innovative effort and facilitate dissemination. Consequently, licensing schemes employed by patent holders must not be subject to more stringent antitrust constraints that those affecting exploitation of other property rights. Such restraints on the use of the antitrust laws to prevent them from imposing unjustifiable inhibitions upon cooperation in invention and dissemination should be made as explicit and binding as possible. Only in this way is it possible to prevent ambiguity and uncertainty from fostering the fear of prosecution, which at least some observers believe to be a major impediment to such ventures and an invitation to private lawsuits undertaken for anticompetitive purposes.

The preceding discussion does not pretend to constitute anything like a coherent and exhaustive program for the future directions of antitrust activities. However, it illustrates policy measures suggested from years of my personal observation and direct participation in such litigative affairs— measures that seem to promise to reduce the incentives for rent-seeking litigation without inhibiting legitimate private antitrust initiative to a degree unjustifiable as a trade-off serving the general interest. There is some reason to believe that these measures are not unworkable, particularly since some of them are in fact in force, and apparently have caused no serious side effects, in one or more countries that are industrialized and prosperous.

12.3 Policy Measures to Discourage Other Forms of Rent-Seeking Litigation

The antitrust arena is clearly not the field of litigation that has been the main focus of public attention. Debate over the "litigation explosion" has, rather, been concentrated on damage and personal injury suits that have so drastically complicated the lives of doctors and the workings of insurance companies, pharmaceutical manufacturers, producers of playground equipment, and suppliers of many other goods and services. Though the matter is by no means open-and-shut, there is good reason to believe that the arena has attracted a considerable amount of innovative legal talent that has succeeded in extracting large jury awards, lucrative out-of-court settlements, and handsome incomes for the attorneys themselves. Whether these financial rewards have, on the whole, been inappropriately large is a subject that still elicits a great deal of argument, much of it appealing more directly to the emotions than to dispassionate evaluation. This is no place to enter the lists on one side or the other.

However, it does seem clear that the evolution of tort law and other related branches of legal doctrine, under the interpretation of the courts, has generally gone in a direction that facilitates and encourages rent seeking and damages the public interest. Lack of experience in the area limits the amount that I can usefully venture to propose on the subject, but a few plausible principles do suggest themselves.

A. Only defendants shown to be at fault should be penalized. Until recent decades it was taken for granted that, unless the defendant in a malpractice or product-liability suit was actually shown to have been at fault, that defendant normally bore no responsibility for reimbursement of the plaintiff for damage suffered, let alone for any additional payment intended as a penalty. Of course, this did not free insurance companies of the obligation to pay for any damages covered under the terms of a contract with the plaintiff, nor did it exempt the former from any other pertinent contractual obligation. However, it did not obligate any defendant to pay any more than that unless it could be shown to have contributed to the damage either deliberately or through negligence in failing to take reasonable precautionary measures that were either promised explicitly or could reasonably have been expected by the victim.

To the extent that juries, courts, and regulatory agencies have departed from this standard and, as is often alleged, have been prepared to impose penalties upon a defendant in the absence of strong evidence of culpability and negligence, they have undermined economic efficiency in at least three ways. First, they have distorted the prices of drugs, medical services, insurance, and other products by imposing on the suppliers of these items costs that more properly represent an obligation of society as a whole, rather than of a particular industry, and this has undoubtedly caused some resource misallocation. In particular, they have reduced the supply of some of these products, sometimes risking total elimination of the provision of the items subject to the risk of heavy penalties and the high insurance costs that resulted. Second, they have introduced moral hazard by reducing the incentive for prospective victims to undertake reasonable risk-avoidance measures. Just as full insurance coverage reduces the incentive for the owner of valuable jewelry to undertake reasonable but costly burglary-prevention steps, the prospective victim of risky products may be led to carelessness in their use by the prospect of generous damage awards. Finally, any such changes in the rules have increased the incentives for rent-seeking litigation, with all of its associated wastes, and have stimulated the allocation of entrepreneurial resources into such activities and out of more productive endeavors.

The implication is that the social interest would be served by a firm commitment under new legislation to exempt all defendants from penalty in the types of cases in question unless culpability or negligence is proved beyond reasonable doubt.

B. *Plaintiffs who have been shown to have contributed to the damage at issue should not be compensated or their compensation should be reduced commensurately.* At the same time that, according to allegations by critics, the developments described in the preceding paragraphs were taking place, plaintiffs were, reportedly, often exempted from the requirement, previously in force, that they had not contributed to the damage at issue. For example, the fact that the plaintiff had drunk a preparation clearly labeled, "Danger! For external use only!" or that this individual had violated the law by driving without a seat belt when involved in a car accident, may now no longer constitute grounds for exempting the defendant from payment of damages, or even from penalties, or even for reducing the amounts of such payments. The costs to society are precisely of the same sorts as those described in the preceding paragraphs, and need not be repeated here.

The implication, once again clear, is that economic welfare can be served by adoption of unambiguous rules that reduce or eliminate the defendant's liability if the plaintiff can be shown to have contributed to the damage in question. The reduction, of course, should be proportioned to the extent that the plaintiff's contribution can be shown, again beyond reasonable doubt, to have contributed to the risk and magnitude of the damage.

C. *Defendants should be responsible for damage resulting from their actions only if the risks entailed were known or reasonably knowable at the time of the actions.* Frequently, only extensive experience in the use of a product or improved methods of research can reveal any risks entailed in use of that product, risks that may not even have been suspected at the time it was introduced. If the firm that supplies the product devoted a reasonable amount of effort and expenditure to testing its safety at the time, and no evidence of any dangers emerged from that effort, the firm should not be held responsible at a later date if previously unsuspected risks should then emerge. This is not merely a matter of equity. If one holds firms liable in this way they may be intimidated into holding back the introduction of valuable products and into spending wastefully large amounts on pretesting.

Aside from the wastes entailed, the delay in introduction of new products may itself constitute a peril to the public welfare. It has been argued persuasively with the aid of statistics that strict safety rules for the introduction of new medicines have, on balance, cost a significant number of lives among patients who were deprived of the use of effective medication which had not yet been tested sufficiently to satisfy the standards. The old film biography of Louis Pasteur provides an apt parable in the scene in which he injects a small boy bitten by a rabid dog with an untested vaccine. The vaccine saves the boy's life—but would Pasteur have dared to use it under today's liability rules?

For our purpose, however, the main issue is the stimulus to rent seeking provided by inadequate protection of defendants in liability cases. Thus on all these grounds, it would appear to serve the public interest to provide explicit immunity from liability to suppliers of goods or services from any risks that could not have been known to them at the pertinent date with the aid of an appropriate outlay of funds and effort.

D. *A prospective plaintiff should not be deprived of the opportunity to undertake a voluntary, but binding, commitment not to sue if the product consumed by her turns out to cause damage, but she was fully informed at the pertinent time of all risks that were known (and reasonably knowable).* It has long been recognized in the economic literature that the right to enter into a binding commitment is a valuable asset. Thus contrary to appearances, deprivation of that right often constitutes a loss, rather than a protection to the individual. It has been claimed, as an illustration, that the interest rates that medieval kings had to pay on their loans were far higher than those currently charged to others, simply because there was no way in which the king could commit himself to pay—no court had the power to penalize him for lateness or default. Today physicians tell us that they are reluctant to provide risky but promising treatments to patients, who cannot legally undertake a binding commitment not to sue if something goes wrong. Thus while some damaged patients may benefit *ex post*, many more may be harmed because the inability to commit themselves deprives them of a valuable treatment or, at least, deprives them of the opportunity to make a rational choice on whether to undergo the treatment on the basis of a dispassionate and informed assessment of the risks.

As a device that facilitates lawsuits that are not in the *ex ante* interests of either prospective plaintiffs or prospective defendants as a class, inhibition or prohibition of binding precommitment constitutes yet another means to facilitate litigative rent seeking, and to encourage the allocation of entrepreneurial talent in that direction.

E. Courts, juries and regulatory agencies should be precluded from considering the availability of "deep pockets" to the defendant in liability cases. There is reason to suspect that a defendant believed to have substantial resources at its disposal is more likely to be found guilty than a defendant with more limited wealth, and if found guilty, the imposed payment for damages or any associated financial penalty is likely to be larger. This clearly serves to misallocate resources by tending to assign riskier tasks to less affluent suppliers, regardless of whether they are the more efficient performers of those tasks.

Moreover, by enabling enterprising lawyers to be selective in their choice of targets—picking defendants particularly vulnerable to large damage payments—those lawyers can increase both their probability of victory, at least in the form of a favorable out-of-court settlement, and the amount of income they can hope to derive in the process. This, too, constitutes an incentive for rent-seeking activities, to which the relevant remarks in the preceding paragraphs clearly apply.

All of the discussion in this section has been intended to provide some illustrative modifications in current rules and procedures that will not *prevent* appropriate litigation, but will serve to discourage the use of litigation as a rich arena for rent seeking. The proposals undoubtedly betray the author's lack of legal training and consequently are surely tinged at more than one point by naïveté. But they are intended primarily to show that there are things that can be done to impede the misallocation of entrepreneurial talent, rather than to provide a set of finished and fully defensible proposals.

12.4 Some Proposals on Corporate Mergers and Acquisitions

The second of the primary examples offered in this book of recent and current activity that is widely suspected to encompass substantial rent-seeking elements is the takeover of firms by others, at least when the activity becomes strikingly intensive, as it did during the 1980s. It is generally agreed that corporate mergers and acquisitions can be benign and promote the social interest by getting rid of incompetent managements, by serving to spur competent managements to greater effort on behalf of stockholders, and in a variety of other ways. However, the rent-seeking side of the activity can be costly to society, if in no other way, by draining off valuable entrepreneurial resources. The issue, then, is once again how one can inhibit the socially damaging side of takeover activity without seriously inhibiting its benefits. Having gone into such detail on the subject of rent-seeking litigation, the discussion of policy for mergers and acquisitions will be confined to a few illustrative suggestions.

A. Graduated Capital Gains Tax Rates Based on Holding Period. It has widely been suggested that one effective way to discourage rent-seeking use of mergers and acquisitions is to separate out the "true investors," who undertake these activities for the long-term gains they promise through enhanced economic efficiency. The idea is to arrange for these more dedicated investors to be treated better than the others, the "raiders," who seek control of the threatened firm merely for quick financial gain, perhaps in the process weakening or destroying an enterprise which, with time and suitable outlay of effort, might have become a more valuable asset to society. Such a focus on rapid financial gains in leveraged buyouts and other forms of takeover activity may be one manifestation of general and excessive preoccupation with the short run in recent U.S. business decisions. It has proved difficult to find definitive evidence on this widely believed hypothesis about current business behavior, one way or the other, but the fact that it is accepted by many business leaders suggests that it should not be dismissed lightly.

In any event, a proposal that has repeatedly been offered to deal with the problem, both in its general form and so far as takeovers are concerned, calls for drastic modification in the rules for taxation of capital gains. It is suggested that capital gains on assets held for long periods, say five years or more, should be taxed at very low rates, and that only the real, inflation-adjusted, capital gains from such investments should be taxed at all. For shorter holding periods the tax rates should be higher, and for extremely brief holding periods, perhaps under a month, tax rates approaching prohibitive levels should be considered.

Such a measure might well discourage some, but not all, forms of rent-seeking acquisition. Obviously mergers whose primary purpose is the acquisition of enduring monopoly power have an objective that is as long-term as those that are intended to assemble a productive enterprise whose enhanced scale and scope make it far more efficient than its unintegrated components were previously. Still, judicious but vigorous enforcement of the antitrust laws to prevent such mergers, along with the incentives provided by the graduated capital gains tax that has just been described, can go far to discourage or even prevent rent seeking by corporate raiders.

B. Prohibition of Poison Pills and Related Protectionist Devices. The proposal of the preceding paragraph is designed to strengthen the defenses of the prospective target firm against attack by any who seek to acquire it (or threaten it) for purposes other than long-term profits through productive activity. But care is required to prevent the playing field from being tilted too far against acquisition attempts, including those that are unwelcome to the target firm's current management. Since the productive contribution of takeover activity in general seems clearly beyond dispute, it is appropriate to take steps to ensure that balance is maintained. In particular, some of the defensive measures commonly adopted by a firm's current management may well impede the productive role of mergers and acquisitions and can often be interpreted persuasively as rent-preservation devices that serve only the interests of those entrenched executives.

It would, consequently, appear appropriate to couple the graduated capital gains regime with rules depriving managements of some of the more questionable of their defensive instruments, the poison pill constituting a clear example of a candidate for prohibition. These defensive instruments have already been discussed in Chapter 3, and there is nothing to be gained by going over the same ground here.

The basic point is that methods are available to curtail the rent-seeking elements in merger-and-acquisition activity without seriously damaging its capacity to provide beneficial contributions. The two steps just described are meant only to show that appropriate changes in the rules of the game are possible and that they offer some prospect of proving effective in eliciting a productive reallocation of entrepreneurial talent.

12.5   A Government Role in Acquisition of Foreign Technology

Up to this point the discussion of policy has been concerned with changes in the rules of the game that can be expected to modify the incentives underlying the market's allocation of entrepreneurial talent in directions that encourage productivity growth. No direct role has been proposed for government; the emphasis has, rather, been on the workings of the market mechanism, and on removal of incentives that may be considered to lead it to work in undesirable directions. There may, however, be some room for direct contributions by government in such a program. This section will provide one pertinent example. Economists generally agree that government can play a useful role in the provision of public goods (defined by economists as goods or services which [like the proverbial example, a lighthouse] can serve additional users at zero additional cost), because private enterprise lacks the incentive to supply optimal quantities of such outputs. Indeed, private enterprise may not be able to supply them at all where, as is often apparently true of public goods, the outputs lack the attribute of excludability, meaning that persons who are unwilling to pay for them nevertheless cannot be prevented from enjoying their benefits.[6]

The encouragement of technology transfer provides an example. Chapter 8 emphasized the importance of the contribution of technology transfer to productivity growth. In particular, it stressed the significance for the growth of any particular economy of the acquisition and absorption of technological information from abroad. But the transfer process has significant public-good characteristics. For example, the work of monitoring foreign technical journals and of providing English translations of pertinent articles can be carried out nearly as cheaply for a multiplicity of U.S. firms, or even for a considerable number of industries, as it can on behalf of any single business enterprise. Japan has been particularly adept at the importation and adoption of new technology, as the United States had been in the nineteenth century. Mansfield (1990, p. 343) reports, on the basis of a survey of one hundred American firms in thirteen industries, that these respondents believed only 29 percent of U.S. firms spend as large a percentage of their sales on the monitoring of foreign technology as the average amount spent by the Japanese, only 47 percent as much as the Germans do, only 51 percent as much as the French do, and only 70 percent spend as much as the average British enterprises in the corresponding industries. If these impressions by American businesspersons are correct, the United States has a long way to go in terms of monitoring and, presumably, effectively adopting foreign technology.

This is an area in which it seems plausible that the federal government can make a useful contribution, and the materials that follow are intended to indicate promising avenues for such a contribution.

The general proposal in this area is, then, straightforward, and of a type that is entirely standard in applied welfare economics. It simply calls for exploration of the significant public-good properties that arise in the transfer of foreign technology to the United States, and consideration of those among them that justify governmental financing or actual provision of the pertinent service. For example, it may prove to be profitable socially for the federal government to establish a special "office of technology transfer," with a staff of specialists qualified to monitor, translate, and disseminate pertinent materials in foreign publications. This, surely, constitutes a form of "industrial policy" that should make sense even to those economists who are most suspicious of public-sector intervention. It should be noted, also, that if such a step does succeed in speeding technology transfer, while it will at first mostly benefit this country (or any other country that adopts it), in the long run it should contribute to productivity growth of the world economy and offer advantages that extend well beyond the borders of the nation that undertakes the program.

The following, more detailed proposals, are designed, in effect, for policymakers to "learn by doing," since, it must be admitted, we have very little firm knowledge on which to base a definitive program for the promotion of technology acquisition. It is, of course, easy for a government to assemble and disseminate masses of information, but there remains the question whether industry will put that information to use, and whether it will do so quickly and effectively. In short, we cannot be certain from intuition alone what technical information will really prove attractive and useful to industry, and what incentives will induce industry to put more such information to use. Thus it is proposed that every step in the program: (1) be launched on a limited scale, (2) be accompanied by the collection of evaluation data whose nature is carefully specified in advance, (3) be conducted, wherever practical, in accord with the principles of experimental design, and (4) be subjected to careful and systematic qualitative and quantitative evaluation before the step is extended beyond the group of participants in the experiment. In this way the program can be expanded with reasonable confidence that it is founded on evidence and offers as great a prospect of accomplishing its purpose as analysis can promise.

Finally, it should be emphasized that an undertaking such as that proposed here is not entirely novel in the United States. For many years the Agricultural Extension Service worked to disseminate up-to-date technical information to U.S. farmers, and the program is reputed to have been very successful. Thus experience suggests that the approach is not impractical. Let us, then, turn to some illustrative specific proposals.

A. *Education and Training*. The United States should establish a set of well-funded scholarships for the study of engineering and other pertinent subjects by American students studying in Japan, Germany, and several other countries that are leading producers of innovation. This program would include funding of an intensive set of language courses that would prepare the American students for their studies abroad. The students would be obligated, upon completion of their courses, to take suitable jobs in U.S. industry or government for a period of five years after completion of their studies.

B. *Immigration of Foreign Technicians and Related Personnel*. A fund should be established to provide subsidies for the immigration, permanent or temporary, of foreign scientists, engineers, and technicians who can provide knowledge to American industry about current foreign technological developments. To be eligible for such a subsidy, a prospective immigrant must be sponsored by an American firm, university, or government agency, with the sponsor obligated to provide employment to the immigrant, and to make a case that the immigration of the individual in question will make a substantial contribution to absorption of useful technological information by U.S. industry.

C. *Establishment of Observer Staff in U.S. Embassies*. At several countries that are leaders in innovation, the U.S. embassy should be provided with a special technology-monitoring staff of a size that can be deemed adequate. This staff would keep track of technical journals, company newsletters, and other available published materials, and arrange for translations where desirable, making those translations available to U.S. firms. In addition, the staff members should seek to arrange interviews with suitable persons in firms in the foreign country in which they are stationed, to elicit all information that can be obtained legitimately and voluntarily. They can also help to facilitate technology transfer agreements between those firms and American enterprises. There would be frequent contact between these embassy staff members and suitable representatives of U.S. industry to ensure that the efforts of the embassy observer staff are directed in a manner that is as useful as possible.

D. *Study of Measures Taken by Governments in Other Countries to Facilitate Absorption of Foreign Technology by Their Industry*. The National Science Foundation or some other suitable agency should be given funds to support an extensive and systematic study of the programs of other governments to encourage the acquisition of foreign technology. The study should provide extensive descriptions of the programs, their funding, their modifications over the years, and their legal status and administrative arrangements and practices. Interviews with businesspersons in the countries in question can be used to provide analysis of the effectiveness and shortcomings of each of the programs. The study should provide a report and a set of recommendations based on foreign experience to the appropriate committees of the U.S. Congress and to suitable agencies of the executive branch.

E. Loan Guarantees to Industry for Funding of Rapid Adoption of Critical Technology from Abroad. A fund should be established to provide loan guarantees to small U.S. firms undertaking substantial investment in products whose production depends critically on newly imported technology. Basic criteria to be followed in determining the eligibility of an applicant firm for a loan guarantee under this program are: (1) evidence that the products at issue show promise for rapid output growth in both foreign and domestic markets, (2) evidence of the presence of economies of scale and scope in the production process, requiring the investment of relatively large amounts of capital in order for the firm to become competitive, and (3) some evidence of entrepreneurial accomplishment, or at least of prospective entrepreneurial ability.

F. Explicit Grant of Antitrust Immunity to Industry Consortia Dedicated Exclusively to Transfer and Sharing of Technology. Because of the large capital requirements imposed by economies of scale and scope, accomplishment in this arena may well require or at least be facilitated by joint or coordinated action by a multiplicity of firms. Though the Department of Justice seems to have been forbearing on coordinated effort where it promotes American technology,[7] there is no guarantee that firms will be safe from legal difficulties as the result of participation in such an undertaking. This has been reported to exert a chilling effect upon joint undertaking in the arena. A congressional measure explicitly exempting from the antitrust laws coordinated action by firms for the acquisition of technology abroad, as well as for the development of new technology at home, should therefore considerably encourage and facilitate such efforts.

The preceding list is intended only to suggest some plausible avenues for policy to follow. Obviously, more study and consideration will be required before any of the recommendations can be advocated with confidence.

There has been little in this chapter that resembles any systematic exploration of detailed policy or even an attempt at exhaustive investigation of some of its subareas. The aim, rather, was to offer prolegomena to the study of policy along the lines that this book invites. This remark is not to be interpreted as a manifestation (or as the pose) of undue modesty. On the contrary, the basic claim that the materials in this chapter were intended to support is highly immodest. Defining entrepreneurs as the movers and the shakers in the process of economic change, and not simply as the founders or the operators of business firms, it has been contended here that until now there has been little or nothing in the theory of entrepreneurship that can serve as a foundation for the design of workable policy related to the contribution of this critical resource. The interpretation of entrepreneurship as an allocable resource; the identification of the economic forces that appear to govern that allocation; the discussion of productive and unproductive entrepreneurial occupations; and that of the consequences of the allocation of productive entrepreneurship between innovation and imitation, all seem, probably for the first time, to provide the beginnings of such a foundation. There is, clearly, much more to be done, and I hope for nothing more of this book than that it should move others to undertake the tasks that remain.

Epilogue:
The Entrepreneur in a
Model of Growth

Economic modeling of competition through innovation [must] treat disequilibrium dynamics explicitly.

Nelson (1992)

Entrepreneurship is but one of the influences that shapes the growth of an economy. Since it was proposed at the outset to bring to an end to the entrepreneur's ostracism from economists' growth models, this epilogue undertakes to review the materials provided in this book in order to see to what extent we have made progress toward that goal. For that purpose we will have to go further and begin to describe the general outlines of an operational model of growth. However, the bulk of the task of provision of a more formal model will be left to the next volume in this series of books on productivity.[1] This epilogue, then, can be viewed as transition between the present volume and the next.

It seems generally to be agreed that the key to growth in economic welfare, as measured by some index such as GDP per capita, is the degree of success of an economy in enhancing its productivity. Productivity, in turn, is taken to be stimulated by a number of variables, including, among others, investment in capital equipment, education, and expenditure on R&D. While there is some powerful econometric evidence consistent with the hypothesis that these factors play an important role in productivity growth, from our point of view what is noteworthy is the absence from this list of the three variables emphasized in this book: entrepreneurship, investment in the innovation process, and technology transfer.

It will be argued in this epilogue that the variables emphasized in the econometric studies play a role in the productivity growth process that is substantially different from the role of the elements that have been focused upon here. I will suggest that so far as capital investment, education, and the like are concerned, one can best proceed by treating them as *endogenous* variables in a sequential process—in other words, these variables affect productivity growth, but productivity growth, in turn, itself influences the values of these variables, after some lag. These endogenous influences are, then, critical components of a feedback process. To some degree, the same story can be told about the exercise of entrepreneurship, investment in innovation, and the magnitude of activity directed to the transfer of technology. These too, clearly, are influenced by past productivity growth achievements and they also, in their turn, influence future growth. Yet it would seem plausible that there is a strong streak of exogeneity in these variables, which can help to account for the outbreak and spread of industrial revolutions and for the relative decline and even for the collapse of economies that formerly were models of success.

The models we will provide are clearly quite distinct from the two currently most noted growth constructs, that of Solow (1956) and the more recent model introduced by Romer (1986). It should be emphasized at once that the differences among the models do not mean that if one of them is reasonably close to the pertinent facts, then the others must be wrong. The art of model building entails the design of simplified constructs, each of which, if successful, sheds light upon some facet of reality. Consequently, two disparate models, designed to explain two different sides of one phenomenon, can be equally valid.

E.1   On the Role of the Entrepreneur

It should be clear that, in terms of the standard list of the variables affecting economic growth, entrepreneurship enters only indirectly. Innovation and technology transfer are the variables affected by the exercise of what has been referred to here as "productive entrepreneurship." It has long been recognized in the economic literature that innovation is encouraged by the work of the entrepreneur. The notion that imitative entrepreneurship—or innovative technology transfer—is also part of the entrepreneur's accomplishments, and that this work of dissemination can make contributions to productivity not systematically inferior to those provided by innovation, are ideas that are rather less common. In any event, it is indirectly, through the entrepreneur's role in promoting these two activities, that she influences productivity in the model that is envisioned here.

A central theme of the preceding chapters has been that the nature and intensity of the productive activities of entrepreneurs are determined by current economic circumstances and, in particular, by the relative size of the rewards offered to different allocations of entrepreneurial activity. Entrepreneurs tend to devote their talents to lines of activity that offer the largest returns in terms of some blend of wealth, power, and prestige. This argument has a double purpose: first, to dispute the notion that the exercise of entrepreneurship is directed by mysterious exogenous forces that are difficult to identify or even describe, and therefore impossible to influence. Second, the objective is to provide some foundations for rational public policy directed to facilitation and encouragement of *productive* entrepreneurial activity. I have argued that changes in the reward structure can influence the allocation of entrepreneurial activity between productive and unproductive uses, and between innovation and its dissemination, presumably among many other options. In this respect, the determination of the foci of entrepreneurial activity is assuredly endogenous, perhaps no less than the determination of the amount of investment carried out by the economy.

E.2   Feedback and "Ancillary Variables" that Affect Productivity

But there appear to be crucial differences between the behavior of the variables that describe the role of the entrepreneur and the behavior of those other variables that affect productivity growth. Elsewhere (1993), I refer to these as the "ancillary variables" in a discussion surveying the many recent empirical studies of the productivity convergence hypothesis, which claims that the economies of the world that are not exceedingly underdeveloped are subject to some common forces that are driving them ever closer together in terms of their productivity levels, GDPs per capita, and other performance measures. There the variables in question were called "ancillary" because they constitute supplements to the small set of variables considered in the earliest empirical convergence studies—the variables that deal with the issue most directly, if perhaps a bit naïvely.

First, the behavior of the ancillary variables and those that can be taken as measures of entrepreneurial activity differ because innovation seems to be subject to exogenous influences far stronger than is true of investment. One can hardly feel confident that we can account fully for the appearance of the "wave of gadgets" that constituted the Industrial Revolution of the eighteenth century, and one can feel even less sure of any economic explanation of the earlier industrial revolution of the twelfth and thirteenth centuries (see Chapter 2). In contrast, while year-to-year variations in investment can arguably be ascribed to indefinable influences such as the ebb and flow of "animal spirits," its longer-term trajectory can surely be accounted for to a very large degree by influences such as the stage of the business cycle, the rate of growth of per capita GDP in the economy, and the rapidity of its acceleration.

Specifically, our analysis will proceed on the following basic hypothesis: there are a number of variables that are among the main influences encouraging productivity growth. But productivity growth, and the resulting enhancement in GDP per capita, are, in turn, among the main stimulants serving to enhance the values of those same variables. For example, there seems to be general agreement that investment, with its contribution to the capital-labor ratio, is a prime stimulant of labor productivity. But the data suggest also that investment itself is heavily influenced by output per capita, being systematically higher in countries whose GDP per capita is higher than in countries that are impoverished, on the same criterion. The data also indicate (see Baumol, Blackman, and Wolff [1989, pp. 180–84]) that rapid acceleration of per capita GDP is extremely effective in enhancing rates of saving and investment.

Similar remarks apply to a country's expenditure on education, its investment in R&D, and a number of the other variables usually cited as stimulants of productivity growth. Casual empirical observation suggests that if a country's productivity level takes off from a path of relative stagnation, then during the stage of initial acceleration, outlay on R&D (much of it devoted to adoption and necessary modification of foreign technology) tends to rise substantially. After that, as growth in productivity ceases to accelerate, the expenditure on R&D as a percent of GDP tends to level off. The same sort of pattern appears to apply to education and, perhaps, to a number of other variables that are major determinants of productivity growth.

Several implications follow. The first is a consequence for econometric testing of the influence of these variables. My recent survey (1993) reports the results of a number of econometric studies of the convergence hypothesis. In these studies it has been shown consistently that the statistical results are considerably enriched by the addition of one (or several) variable(s) (such as investment in capital equipment or outlay on education) to the regressions used earlier to test whether countries are growing more similar in terms of productivity level or level of GDP. Calculations using the added variable show that the forces of convergence encompass far more countries, and extend over a longer period than the earlier, and simpler, studies had indicated. That, however, is not the significant matter for our discussion at this point. Rather, the issue is brought out by the rather startling observation that the half dozen or so empirical convergence studies using ancillary variables such as equipment investment or education yield virtually identical qualitative results *even though the ancillary variables employed vary from study to study*. For example, several of the investigations use some measure of education (e.g., Baumol, Blackman, and Wolff [1989, pp. 203–6], and Mankiw, Romer, and Weil [1990]). Another employs as ancillary variable only equipment investment (De Long and Summers [1990]). Still another employs several ancillary variables including a measure of political stability (Barro and Sala i Martin [1990]). A fifth uses a number of variables that include a measure of openness of the economy to foreign trade (Dollar [1991]). The remarkable fact is that all of these analyses reach qualitative conclusions that are essentially the same no matter what set of statistics they have employed as ancillary variables. Surely the most plausible explanation of this rather implausible result is that many, if not all, of the ancillary variables selected for inclusion in the analyses have behavior patterns that are exceedingly similar. If this is so, then any one of them can, statistically speaking, serve as a proxy for the others. That is, the numbers alone, on this hypothesis, are incapable of distinguishing among them in terms of their influence upon growth in variables such as labor productivity. The similarity in their intertemporal trajectories means that as far as a regression analysis is concerned they are all virtually the same variable.

It is noteworthy that none of these studies seems to include a variable that can serve as an indicator of the level of productive entrepreneurial activity. My conjecture here is that such a variable, if a reliable one can be found, will follow a time path rather different from that of the variables that serve as the ancillary influences in the convergence studies just discussed. That is, had such a variable been included in one of those studies, we might have expected results rather different from those of the investigations that were actually carried out. The second and more important point for our present discussion is that, since the empirical evidence supports the hypothesis that the ancillary variables are profoundly affected by an economy's productivity growth, while those variables, in turn, substantially affect that productivity growth path, then one is driven to describe this set of relationships with the aid of a *feedback model*. Indeed, one can conjecture that productivity growth may well constitute one of the most powerful and unambiguous examples of feedback in the workings of the economy. The next section of this epilogue will illustrate the nature of such a feedback relationship. However, the bulk of our discussion of productivity growth as a feedback process must be left to the next volume of this series.

E.3   A Rudimentary Model of Investment-Productivity Feedback and the Role of Innovation

The preceding discussion virtually spells out the structure of the most primitive of feedback models that encompasses both ancillary and entrepreneurial variables. In the paragraphs that follow we will use investment, I_t, as our sole (illustrative) ancillary variable.[2] Assuming linearity for the sake of simplification, we will arrive at a model whose most elementary variant has a formal structure remarkably similar to the justly celebrated Samuelson accelerator-multiplier model.

The basic premise from which our analysis begins (one that has some support in empirical evidence; see, for example, Baumol, Blackman and Wolff [1989, pp. 180–184]) is that rapid *growth* in a nation's per capita output (or in its productivity) is associated with a high *level* of investment. This acceleration principle type of relationship provides a component of investment which can be described by

$$I_t^* = a + b(Y_{t-1} - Y_{t-2}),\tag{E.1}$$

where Y_t represents a variable such as per capita income or labor productivity (output per work-hour) in period t. For concreteness we will henceforth refer to it as "per capita income." The component of investment induced by *growth* is supplemented by the added investment generated by a higher *level* of per capita income (the higher per capita investment found in the wealthiest countries relative to that in impoverished countries),[3] yielding a relationship such as

$$I_t^{**} = c + rY_{t-1}.\tag{E.2}$$

If in addition, one assumes that a linear relationship describes the influence of investment on income, so that

$$Y_t = s + vI_t, \quad \text{where} \quad I_t = I_t^* + I_t^{**},\tag{E.3}$$

then the three relationships together give us an equation that is formally identical with that of Samuelson:

$$Y_t = k + v(b + r)Y_{t-1} - vbY_{t-2}.\tag{E.4}$$

There is no point in repeating the well-known analysis of the behavior of the trajectory generated by this second-order difference equation, with its possibilities of monotonicity or oscillation, stability or explosiveness. This is so particularly because the model immediately requires some complication. The k in the preceding relationship cannot legitimately be interpreted as a constant if innovative activity and other ancillary variables are to play a role, as they surely must, in any plausible analysis of the time path of productivity and per capita output. Thus k cannot be taken to be a constant or a parameter, but must itself be assumed to be a function of a number of variables, perhaps including time. Most of this must be left to the next volume, but a way in which one of the variables, innovation, can be included will be indicated.

Before doing so, however, we must consider briefly two possible complications of the preceding relationships that may prove desirable. First, we may take note of the hypothesis that the rate of saving is stimulated by *acceleration* of per capita income, in addition to its rate of growth, as in (E.1). The argument is that consumption habits are lagged, and tend to be based on the per capita income and rate of growth that were experienced in the past. Thus, when an economy experiences a sudden acceleration of growth (a takeoff) such as happened to Japan or Taiwan, consumption lags, and savings rates, as a residue, attain unprecedented levels. If mobility of capital is limited, the economy's investment level can be expected to follow the same pattern.[4] This would give us a third investment component that follows a relationship such as[5]

$$I_t^{***} = u(Y_{t-1} - Y_{t-2}) - w(Y_{t-2} - Y_{t-3}). \tag{E.5}$$

A second complicating modification entails interpretation of the growth rate not as an absolute change, as in (E.1) or (E.5), but as a percentage change, so that one may prefer to replace (E.1) by

$$I_t^* = a(Y_{t-1} - Y_{t-2})^b / Y_{t-2}^c, \quad \text{or} \tag{E.6}$$

$$\ln I_t^* = \ln a + b\ln(Y_{t-1} - Y_{t-2}) - c\ln Y_{t-2}, \tag{E.7}$$

thus replacing all of our earlier variables with their logs, with suitable modification of all of the preceding relationships.

These considerations yield simple variants of the way in which the feedback relationships, such as that between investment and per capita income can be incorporated into the analysis. It need hardly be said that one can proceed directly from such a formulation to investigation of the resulting time path.

E.4   Convergence as Entrepreneurial Accomplishment

We turn, next, to illustration of the manner in which one can incorporate relationships in which the feedback properties are less direct, entailing concepts such as entrepreneurial technology transfer and the convergence phenomenon. The paragraphs that follow will, for this purpose, describe the Chatterji (1992) formal model of a possible mechanism of the convergence phenomenon, following an analysis by Gomulka (1986). That model is based on the hypothesis associated with the work of Alexander Gershenkron, Simon Kuznets, and Moses Abramovitz, asserting that for countries that are (moderately) behind the leader in terms of technology, productivity, and per capita income, the farther behind they are the more rapidly they can grow because they are in a position to profit most from technology transfer from the leader(s). This explanation of the convergence hypothesis, along with some statistical evidence, has already been described in Chapter 8.

In the Chatterji analysis this is expressed in the equation

$$y_{t+1} - y_t = A + B(y_t^* - y_t) - C(y_t^* - y_t)^2, \tag{E.8}$$

where y_t is the natural logarithm of per capita income in the country in question in period t, and y_t^* is the corresponding value for the leader country. Thus

$$z_t = y_t^* - y_t \tag{E.9}$$

measures the gap between the country in question and the leader country in period t. For the leader country, since z is, by definition, always zero, we obtain from (E.8)

$$y_{t+1}^* - y_t^* = A. \tag{E.10}$$

Here A can be interpreted as the leader's autonomous rate of technical change, determined by its entrepreneurial activity. From the two preceding equations we have at once

$$y_{t+1} - y_t = z_t - z_{t+1} + A. \tag{E.11}$$

Substituting this into (E.8) we get Chatterji's basic equation

$$z_{t+1} = (1 - B)z_t + Cz_t^2. \tag{E.12}$$

As Chatterji points out, since in equilibrium $z_t = z_{t-1}$, there are two possible equilibria, $z_e = B/C$ and $z_e = 0$. The latter, of course, entails perfect catch-up with the leader, while the former involves an equilibrium with a permanent and constant relative income gap, $B/C > 0$, between leader and follower. As is well known, an equilibrium will be stable when the slope of the phase curve, the graph of (E.12), is less than unity in absolute value at the equilibrium point. This slope is

$$dz_{t+1}/dz_t = (1 - B) + 2Cz_e,$$ (E.13)

so that the convergence equilibrium point $z_e = 0$ will be stable iff $0 < B <$ 2. Similarly, substituting $z_e = B/C$ into (E.13), we see that this permanent gap equilibrium point will be stable iff $0 > B > -2$.

The value of B can be determined by the initial conditions. That is, by using three (observed) values of y_t, preferably consecutive, and by inserting them into (E.12), they will yield two simultaneous equations that can, normally, be solved for the values of B and C. However, rather than pursuing this process for the Chatterji equations, it is preferable for our purposes to turn to a qualitative discussion, thereby avoiding the very sensitive dependence on the functional form that happens to have been selected as an implicit hypothesis of the model, a rather inconvenient attribute of difference equation models such as this.

Figure E.1 shows the phase graph in z_t, z_{t+1} space of a difference equation such as (E.12). It depicts two possible graphs of (E.12), labeled $F(z_t)$ and $G(z_t)$. Which of them is applicable depends on the values of the two parameters. In the graph there are two equilibrium points, the origin and E, for at both these points the graph cuts the 45-degree ray, where $z_t = z_{t+1}$. Since between 0 and E the graph of G lies below the 45-degree ray, if G, rather than F, happens to be the true phase curve (the graph of the difference equation) the time path, $ABCD \ldots$, in this zone must go monotonically downhill, away from E and toward 0. Thus if G is the phase curve, E

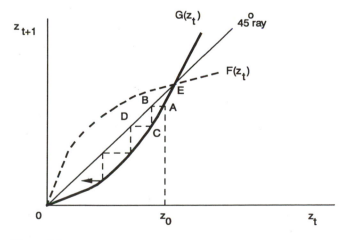

Figure E.1

must be an unstable equilibrium,[6] while the origin is stable. This means that any country will be driven toward the point of parity with the leader (since z measures the country's shortfall behind the leader). Thus, in this case the model is one of asymptotically *perfect* convergence (catch-up) of the two economies in question. But that is only so because the graph of the difference equation happens to cut through the origin. As we will see presently, when we discuss figure E.3, it can happen that no intersection of that curve with the 45-degree ray passes through the origin. An intersection can, instead, lie near the origin, for example, meaning that the corresponding long-run equilibrium entails a permanent but slight gap between the two countries. We can, then, perhaps interpret G as the phase graph governing the growth path of an economy such as that of France or Germany.

Similarly, it is easily confirmed that if the phase curve in figure E.1 is F, which lies above the 45-degree ray between the origin and E, then the origin will be an unstable equilibrium, while E must be stable. Here the two economies are moving toward a substantial and permanent gap, the magnitude of z at point E. This can, perhaps, be taken to describe the history of a stagnant LDC.

It should be noted that an initial position such as point A, one that lies below the 45-degree ray, means z_{t+1} must be less than z_t, that is, the follower country must be gaining on the leader. Any two successive periods in which the follower moves closer to the leader must yield a data point such as A, below the 45-degree line. But a point such as A on the time path (interpreted as the "initial position," that is, the position used to determine the values of the parameters of the governing difference equation) also means that if the graph is to be consistent with that point's position, the parameter values must be such that the graph has the shape of G rather than that of F. In other words, if the assumed structure of the model is such as to constitute curves such as F or G as the two qualitative possibilities, then an initial relative position such as A for the follower vis-à-vis the leader implies that the follower will be driven toward the origin, moving it ever closer to the leader. The reverse will clearly be true of a follower whose performance puts it in an "initial position" represented by a point above the 45-degree line somewhere between the two equilibria.

However, figure E.1, corresponding to equations (E.8) and (E.12), does not represent the only possible relationship. Figure E.2 shows another possibility, also discussed by Chatterji. Here, there are three equilibrium points represented by 0, A, and B. Noting that a segment of the phase graph that lies above the 45-degree ray moves the time path of z toward the right and that a segment below that ray moves z on a time path toward

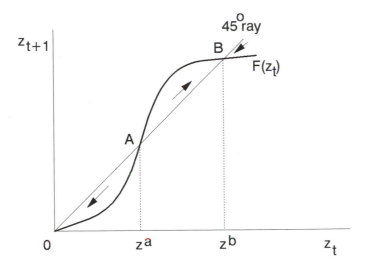

Figure E.2

the left, we obtain directions of movement indicated by the arrows. This means that the intermediate equilibrium point, A, must be unstable, while the two outer equilibria, 0 and B, must be stable. Here an economy will have entered a successful process of convergence if it begins with any initial z value to the left of unstable equilibrium point A, while it will be forced to move toward a permanent gap equilibrium, B, if it starts off with any value of z between z^a and z^b, corresponding to equilibrium points A and B, respectively.

The substantive difference between the cases represented by the two figures is that, in the former, a country that is falling behind can get out of its difficulties only by a change in the underlying economic relationships that govern its fate. It must somehow change its phase curve from F to G. In contrast, in the circumstances represented by figure E.2, the country can reverse direction if it is able to improve its relative performance just once, moving z_t from a position between z^a and z^b to one anywhere between 0 and z^a. That is, it can reverse its fate just by a single period of substantial catch-up, or a reduction in that period's value of z.

Finally, figure E.3 shows a very different way out of the trap in which a country unable initially to move closer to the leader finds itself. Here, at the equilibrium point E'', the phase curve has a negative slope, leading to cobweblike oscillatory movement that drives it below the 45-degree ray, and so back to the stable equilibrium point E, close to the origin. This may, perhaps, resemble the story of some of the Far Eastern "miracle economies."

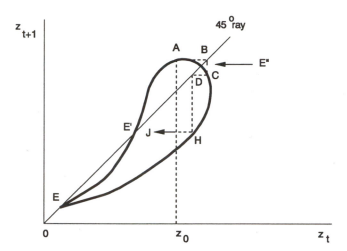

Figure E.3

Empirical investigation can, perhaps, indicate which of these pictures applies to which economies. More important, by including the behavior of ancillary variables, it may suggest how a country can change the regime governing the trajectory of its economy from that represented by one of the graphs to another.

The two preceding sections laid out prototype models illustrating possible formalizations of both the role of the productive entrepreneur (as embodied in innovation and technology transfer) and the variables such as R&D expenditure, educational outlays, and investment that we believe to be encompassed in the feedback process that characterizes productivity growth. These two types of relationships will still have to be combined, their characteristics explored empirically, and their behavior investigated analytically. That is the task to which we intend to turn our attention in the next book in this series.

Notes

Chapter 1

1. Solow's quantitative estimate and other similar conclusions were challenged in an article by Jorgenson and Griliches (1967). However, their contention does not necessarily imply any denigration of the role of the entrepreneur. Jorgenson and Griliches undertook to reevaluate the magnitude of the role of technical change by treating it as a residual, estimating the remaining contributions to labor productivity by investigating directly how much of growth in output per worker can be accounted for by sheer expansion in the quantities of inputs that are measurable by conventional methods. It is undoubtedly true that growth in output contributed by entrepreneurship and innovation often requires corresponding increases in input quantities, but that does not mean that the entrepreneur has played little or no role in the generation of such output increases. It merely means that, since the amount of entrepreneurial activity is difficult to quantify, the correlation between that activity and the quantities of conventional outputs makes the role of the former even more difficult to measure.

Moreover, even the very recent work by Jorgenson, Gollop, and Fraumeni (1987) which, on the basis of highly sophisticated econometric analysis, assigns a primary role to the capital stock in the remarkable postwar rise in U.S. labor productivity, nevertheless calculates that more than one-third of the annual growth rate in labor productivity is attributable to innovation (improvements in productivity) (pp. 1–2).

2. In practice there is considerable evidence showing that transfers almost never mean mere transport of an idea without any modification. Rather, imitative entrepreneurship has almost always required inventive changes to adapt the transferred process to local customs, climate, input characteristics, and so on. Sometimes these modifications (like the substitution of ferrous metal for wooden rails in U.S. railroading) have then been retransferred back to the invention's country of origin.

3. There is one residual and rather curious role sometimes left to the entrepreneur in the neoclassical model. Here he has become no more than the indivisible and nonreplicable input that accounts for the U-shaped cost curve of a firm whose production function is linear and homogeneous. How the mighty have fallen!

4. It should be emphasized that there is a growing and very promising body of theoretical literature dealing with analytical tools that seem useful for the study of entrepreneurship. See, for example, Nelson and Winter (1982), the essays by Ursprung and others in Bös, Bergson, and Meyers (1984), and Schmitz (1988). See also the survey of theoretical literature pertinent to entrepreneurial activity in Casson (1982), especially Chapter 19. There has

also recently emerged a very powerful body of analysis investigating the process of invention and innovation in terms of races and waiting games, a subject to which we will return
in a later chapter. For references and a very illuminating discussion, see Dasgupta (1988).

5. The problem was recognized long ago by Thorstein Veblen. One may recall the characteristic passage in which he described the economic man as

a lightning calculator of pleasures and pains, who oscillates like a homogeneous globule of
desire of happiness under the impulse of stimuli that shift him about the area, but leave him
intact. He has neither antecedent or consequent. He is an isolated, definitive human datum,
in stable equilibrium except for the buffets of impinging forces that displace him in one
direction or another. Self-imposed in elemental space, he spins symmetrically about his own
spiritual axis until the parallelogram of forces bears down upon him, whereupon he follows
the line of the resultant. When the force of the impact is spent, he comes to rest, a
self-contained globule of desire as before.... [He] is not a prime mover. He is not the seat
of a process of living, except in the sense that he is subject to a series of permutations
enforced upon him by circumstances external and alien to him   (1919, pp. 73–74).

6. My former colleague, the late W. Arthur Lewis, adduced yet another reason why the
current theory does not help us to understand the entrepreneur. He remarked in a note to
me, "The entrepreneur is doing something new and is therefore to some extent a monopolist.... We have no good theory of entrepreneurship because we have no good theory of
monopoly. Our theory that monopolists [act] to maximize profit is obviously absurd, given
the low elasticity of demand of most monopolized products." I agree that this observation
points to a most fundamental gap in the theory of the firm.

7. For a remarkable study of entrepreneurship by a social psychologist, see D. C. McClelland
(1961). While the book can be accused of being naïve in spots, particularly in its literal
interpretation of economists' theoretical models and the crucial role they assign to the profit
motive, it provides a rich set of illuminating hypotheses and supports them with quantities
of psychological test results for a great variety of cultures. In what is perhaps the most
interesting part of his discussion from our point of view, the author claims to show that
entrepreneurs are motivated by n-achievement (the need for achievement) and not by desire
for money (pp. 233–37). In his tests, people with high levels of n-achievement do no better
when offered larger amounts of money for success, whereas people with low n-achievement
scores do much better when offered money. However, it should be noted that while a rise
in absolute income levels does not seem to stimulate n-achievers, a rise in marginal returns
does seem likely to spur them on, according to the author, because it provides a clearer
measure of accomplishment. (The economist would no doubt propose a different explanation.) He also claims to show that n-achievers choose smaller risks than the average person:
they are not gamblers, but are calculators and planners. The entrepreneur is not essentially
an individual who chooses to bear risks—that is the speculator, a person with quite a
different personality (pp. 210–25). Another interesting claim by McClelland is that the
n-achiever is not an individualist and does not depend for success on private enterprise
(pp. 292–300). Such persons get just as much satisfaction from the manipulation of a com-
mittee, or from working for a government, since their interest is in results rather than in
considerations such as profit or status. This is perhaps one reason huge committee-run
corporations can be successful.

8. I believe a key element of Schumpeter's contribution to the theory of entrepreneurship is
precisely of this variety. In its discussion of the activities of the entrepreneur, *The Theory of
Economic Development* (1911, 1934) offers us little more than a taxonomy. But enormous
illumination is provided by Schumpeter's analysis of the process whereby the rewards of
innovation are only gradually eroded by the competitive process, and the corollary obser-

vation that some imperfection in the market mechanism is essential to permit a financial reward for innovation.

9. Of course, this is a considerable oversimplification. Individual entrepreneurs can have talents that suit them only for particular lines of endeavor, or they may have preferences that wed them passionately to particular industries or products, and the mobility of such persons will obviously be correspondingly limited. The same is, however, obviously true of individual members of the labor force, perhaps even to a greater degree than is typical of entrepreneurs. But despite such frictions, labor theory does not deny that some reallocation of the labor force as a body will occur in response to changes in the patterns of wages and job opportunities. It is no more than this that is claimed here about the mobility and movement of entrepreneurs.

10. Rosenberg also comments in a letter to me that, "The remarkable success of the Japanese economy in the past 30 years is confirmation of the economic importance of the improvement process. Moreover, the Japanese firm seems more appropriately structured than the western one for the purpose of generating such improvements."

11. The point is also underscored by the difficulty of providing an illustrative quotation of reasonable length from that decision. The problem is that, in order to distinguish whether the prior-art argument is or is not valid, many pages of closely reasoned technical discussion are required in each case where that argument is invoked.

Chapter 2

1. A very similar viewpoint, stressing the allocability of persons with innovative talent among productive and less-productive activities, is taken by Murphy, Shleifer, and Vishny [1990] in a very illuminating theoretical and empirical analysis. The same general idea, albeit in more specialized terms, appears in the writing of Leijonhufvud and that of Myhrman.

2. There has, however, recently been an outburst of illuminating writings on the theory of the innovation process, analyzing it in such terms as races for patents in which the winner takes everything, with no consolation prize for a close second, or treating the process, alternatively, as a "waiting game," in which a patient second entrant may outperform and even survive the first one in the innovative arena, who incurs the bulk of the risk. For an overview of these discussions as well as some substantial added insights, see Dasgupta [1988].

3. It is true that Schumpeter's list includes the opening up of new markets as one of the five prime entrepreneurial activities. But here he is presumably referring to markets for goods in general, rather than for innovations, including technological developments, in particular.

4. In chapter 4 the connotation of the rather imperfectly defined term, "rent seeking," will be discussed. For the moment it suffices to say that "rent" is here defined as a payment whose recipient provides no added output to society in return. The term is chosen as an analogue to the payment extracted by a landholder for the use of his property, a payment that results in no net addition to the total number of acres of land in existence. Rent seeking, then, can be defined as a normal business activity, but one devoted to pursuit of the sort of unproductive earnings just described. Commonly cited examples are lobbying for legislation that protects an industry from competition and litigation over monopoly licenses (as in the license to operate an electric utility or a local telephone company).

5. Note that here Schumpeter is not referring to the temporary monopoly achieved by the successful innovator—essential as an incentive for further innovation—that plays so cen-

tral a role in his model. Rather, he clearly is writing about the "new combination" that is constituted by reduction for the indefinite future of competition in some market, not necessarily with the aid of a better product or a superior productive technique.

6. For a very illuminating recent study that employs a more Marxian connotation of "unproductive activity," see Wolff [1987]. That volume also provides empirical evidence indicating that unproductive activity so defined has been rising significantly in the period since the Second World War (see chapter 5).

7. To be fair to Finley, we may note that he concludes that it is *not* really interesting. North and Thomas [1973, p. 3] make a similar point about Harrison's invention of the ship's chronometer in the eighteenth century (as an instrument indispensable for the determination of longitude). Those authors point out that the incentive for this invention was a large governmental prize rather than the prospect of commercial profit, presumably because of the absence of effective patent protection.

8. The conquest has at least two noteworthy entrepreneurial sides. First, it involved an innovation—the use of the stirrup by the Normans at Hastings, which enabled William's warriors to use the same spear to impale a series of victims with the force of the horse's charge, rather than just tossing the spear at the enemy, much as an infantryman could. Second, the invasion was an impressive act of organization, with William having to convince his untrustworthy allies that they had more to gain by joining him in England than by staying behind to profit from his absence by trying to grab away his lands as they had tried to do many times before.

9. In saying all this, I must not be interpreted to take the conventional view that warfare is an unmitigated source of impoverishment of any economy that never contributes to its prosperity. Careful recent studies have indicated that matters are more complicated (on this see, e.g., Milward [1970] and Olson [1982]). Certainly the unprecedented prosperity enjoyed afterward by the countries on the losing side of the Second World War suggests that warfare need not always preclude economic expansion, and it is easy to provide earlier examples. The three great economic leaders of the Western world preceding the United States—Italy in the thirteenth to sixteenth centuries, the Dutch Republic in the seventeenth and eighteenth, and Great Britain in the eighteenth and nineteenth—each attained the height of their prosperity after periods of enormously costly and sometimes destructive warfare. Nevertheless, the wealth gained by a medieval baron from the adoption of a novel bellicose technique can hardly have contributed to economic growth in the way that resulted from adoption of a new steel--making process in the nineteenth century or the introduction of a product such as the motor vehicle in the twentieth.

10. Bloch notes that the monasteries had both the capital and the large number of consumers of flour necessary to make the mills profitable. In addition, they were less likely than lay communities to undergo military siege, which, Bloch notes, was (besides drought and freezing of the waterways) one of the main impediments to adoption of the water mill, since blocking of the waterway that drove the mill could threaten the besieged population with starvation (see Bloch, pp. 550–553).

11. The best story I have been able to reconstruct to account for the apparently superior entrepreneurship of the Cistercians is that by the time in question other monastic orders had adopted the position that the labor the monk was required by religious doctrine to perform could legitimately consist entirely of religious work, for example, the work of scribes and illustrators of religious manuscripts. The more onerous work in the fields and elsewhere that was needed to keep the monastery going could then be performed exclusively by hired "lay brothers." According to this account, the Cistercians lagged in acceptance of this view of

the matter and continued to demand hard physical labor from the members of the order, and that provided the incentive for them to seek labor-saving technical improvements, because they *were* permitted to devote any time saved in this way to more pleasant religious labor. I must admit that this hypothesis is not overwhelmingly convincing, and that the evidence for it is marginal.

12. The evidence indicates that the wealth of affluent families in Great Britain continues to be derived preponderantly from commerce rather than from industry. This contrasts with the record for the United States, where the reverse appears to be true (see Rubenstein [1980, pp. 22—23, 59—60]).

13. It has been suggested by historians (see, e.g., Bloch, p. 547) that an abundance of slaves played a key role in Roman failure to use the water mill widely. However, this must imply that the Romans were not efficient wealth seekers. As the cliometric literature has made clear, the cost of maintaining a slave is not low and certainly is not zero, and slaves are apt not to be efficient and dedicated workers. Thus, if it had been efficient to replace human or animal power by the inanimate power of the waterways, failure to do so would have cut into the wealth of the slaveholder, in effect, saddling him with the feeding of unproductive persons, or keeping the slaves who turned the mills from other, more lucrative, occupations. Perhaps Roman landowners *were* fairly unsophisticated in the management of their estates, as Finley [1985, Chapter IV] suggests, and, if so, there may be some substance to the hypothesis that slavery goes far to account for the failure of water mills to spread in the Roman economy.

14. The classic description and analysis of Chinese technology and invention is Needham [1965, 1981]. A briefer but excellent discussion is provided by Mokyr [1990, Chapter 9].

15. Also, as in Rome, none of this was associated with the emergence of a systematic body of science involving coherent theoretical structure and the systematic testing of hypotheses on the basis of experiment or empirical observation. Here, too, the thirteenth-century work of Grosseteste, William of Henley, and Roger Bacon was an early step toward that unique historical phenomenon—the emergence of a systematic body of science in the West in, say, the sixteenth century (see Needham [1956]).

16. As was already noted, science and scientific method also began to make an appearance with contributions such as those of Bishop Grosseteste and Roger Bacon. Walter of Henley championed controlled experiments and observation over recourse to the opinions of ancient authorities, and made a clear distinction between economic and engineering efficiency in discussing the advisability of substituting horses for oxen. And Roger Bacon displayed remarkable foresight when he wrote, circa 1260:

Machines may be made by which the largest ships, with only one man steering them, will be moved faster than if they were filled with rowers; wagons may be built which will move with incredible speed and without aid of beast; flying machines can be constructed in which a man ... may beat the air with wings like a bird ... machines will make it possible to go to the bottom of seas and rivers.   (as quoted in White, p. 130)

17. But then, much the same was true of the first half century of "our" Industrial Revolution, which until the coming of the railways was centered on the production of cotton that perhaps constituted only some 7 to 8 percent of national output (Hobsbawm, p. 68). Initially, the eighteenth-century Industrial Revolution was a very minor affair, at least in terms of investment levels and contributions to output and to growth in productivity (perhaps 0.3 percent per year). On this, see Williamson [1984, pp. 2—7], Landes [1969, pp. 64—65], and Feinstein [1978, pp. 40—41].

18. The restraints imposed by the church had another curious affect—they apparently made bathing unfashionable for centuries. Before then, bath houses had been popular as centers for social and, perhaps, sexual activity; but by requiring separation of the sexes and otherwise limiting the pleasures of cleanliness, the church undermined the inducements for such sanitary activities. On this, see Gimpel, pp. 87–92.

19. More will be said in chapter 5 on Japanese institutional arrangements that are designed to keep litigiousness in check.

Chapter 3

1. I am extremely grateful to Burton G. Malkiel and Louis Lowenstein for their many useful comments on the remainder of this chapter. Of course, neither of them can be held responsible for my conclusions, and Professor Lowenstein has expressed strong reservations about some of them. In particular, he takes the position that in the longer run, despite what he and I both regard as its imperfect efficiency, the stock market can be relied upon to price stocks reasonably closely to the true value of the business firm, without the intervention of takeovers: "Given the huge cost of takeovers, the inaccuracy with which targets are targeted, etc., the best cure for a too low stock price is to buy the stock, not sell the company ... [because] the Graham-Dodd point of view would be that the shortfall of stock prices is not likely to endure very long" (letter to me, dated October 24, 1990).

2. One reader of the manuscript, a deservedly noted member of our profession who is, however, admittedly partial to the financial activities in question, commented that while those named in the text who were occupied in mergers and acquisitions probably contributed to productivity, Lee Iaccoca, by saving a firm that arguably should better have gone bankrupt, actually acted as a drag upon output. It is not my purpose here to prejudge the matter; the argument does suggest how much care is required before concluding whether an activity is productive or unproductive. But whichever way the evidence leads us, it does not undermine the hypothesis that the structure of the financial rewards offered by the economy affects the allocation of entrepreneurial talent between productive and unproductive occupations.

3. Actually, none of this is new either. The firms bought by John D. Rockefeller were not always willing sellers, and Rockefeller was surely inventive in the ways he found to secure their acquiescence. The ingenious buccaneering battles of Gould, Vanderbilt, Drew, and Fisk for control of the Erie Railroad make marvelous reading precisely because of the daring and inventiveness of the protagonists.

4. The Modigliani-Miller analysis long ago suggested that, in the absence of tax differentials and other such impediments, there is nothing to be gained, one way or the other, from the use of debt rather than equity financing. But as was demonstrated in Baumol and Malkiel (1967), the double taxation of stock dividends does make it profitable to resort to a substantial proportion of debt, as intuition suggests. As Miller recently observed, "A number of recent developments in finance can be seen as confirming the suspicions of many of us academics in the early 1960s that high leverage strategies to reduce taxes were indeed entirely feasible. Among these, of course, is the now large outstanding volume of what are popularly known as 'junk bonds'" (Miller [1988, p. 113]).

5. In addition, Professor Lowenstein informs me, all-cash offers are made in order to avoid the requirement of registration of the junk bonds or other new securities with the Securities and Exchange Commission, thereby eliminating a delay that might weaken the effectiveness of the bid.

6. This section, dealing with the possible productive contributions of the mergers-and-acquisitions movement, is not meant to imply that they never have any damaging effects upon the economy's output. There are, indeed, a number of consequences that may well have such results. For example, it is quite plausible that the heavy debt with which a number of firms were saddled by leveraged buyouts severely damaged those companies and inhibited or even put a stop to growth in their outputs. Since the central purpose of this chapter is to examine one type of damage that takeovers may cause, little attention is paid to other possibly deleterious effects.

7. Those who believe that markets are nearly perfectly efficient and that expectations of stock buyers and sellers are nearly perfectly rational generally hold that this cannot happen. But such a conclusion is surely rendered highly implausible by observation of phenomena such as occasional sharp swings in the prices of stocks when there is little discernible change in any underlying "fundamentals." The claim that there is overwhelming evidence supporting the efficient market hypothesis mistakes persuasive tests indicating that stock movements approximate random walks for tests of efficiency. It is true that in a perfectly efficient market all but random stock-price movements will be eliminated. But that only means that efficiency implies randomness and *not* the converse. Surely, perfectly random *irrational* behavior by the bulk of stock purchasers and sellers can also lead to randomness, especially if rational market participants are forced to behave similarly when they recognize the prevalence of that behavior pattern. And at least some observers would probably regard the latter explanation of the random character of stock-price movements as far more plausible than the hypothesis that participants meet the demanding requirements of rational expectations theory.

8. Of course, the arbitrage process can overcorrect or undercorrect stock prices that are out of line with the prospects of the firm. If the market for small shares in the firm can be inefficient, the same can be true of the other market—that for entire companies. This can lead to phenomena such as speculative "bubbles," in which frenzied bidding drives prices up to levels that have little relation to reasonable expectations for the earnings prospects of the firms being bid for. In a forthcoming book, Lowenstein argues persuasively that this is what did happen in many of the mergers and acquisitions of the 1980s.

9. This argument suggests that a systematic difference between prices in the two markets is perhaps to be expected, with price in the market for small quantities of stock "naturally" tending usually to be the lower of the two. The purchaser who acquires enough shares to control the firm is automatically *guaranteed* access to a return corresponding to the full future earnings of the firm, while in a world in which what we may refer to as the Shubik paradox holds sway, small stockholders may be rational in feeling that they can never confidently expect such a return, unless a raider intervenes and puts the firm "into play."

10. On the definition proposed earlier in this chapter, the illegality of insider trading may perhaps disqualify it as an example of rent seeking, but its spirit is close and its practitioners are usually highly respectable members of society (until they are caught).

11. The view of insider trading associated with the Chicago school is that the problem arises largely because of the "5 percent rule," which requires the raider to disclose himself once he has acquired 5 percent of the target's stock. In order to get hold of enough stock to make the attempt worthwhile, it is asserted, the raider must obtain allies who will also gather up stock for eventual transfer to the raider before the 5 percent rule comes into play. On this view, then, if the 5 percent rule were eliminated the insider trading phenomenon would largely disappear. Others, however, feel that the problem goes deeper, and that a shadow is cast over the integrity of the market if any players are permitted to operate on the basis

of information which has been acquired by whatever means and for whatever reason, but access to which is systematically denied to other participants in the market.

12. In letters to me Professors Louis Lowenstein and Andrei Shleifer have both expressed disagreement with the preceding discussion, the former because my discussion treats the takeover boom too kindly and the latter because the discussion criticizes takeover activity too severely. Professor Shleifer writes, in part, "I don't think that greenmail and investment banker fees are very important. There are many other kinds of rents to be sought in takeovers, but these are not they.... I should say that I am a little skeptical about transfers [rent seeking] in takeovers, having spent a good deal of time on them." The forms of transfer in takeovers that he considers more important are described in an article by Shleifer and Summers (1988). There the authors stress the use of takeovers as a means to get out of costly commitments made by the previous management to the firm's employees, its suppliers, and others. For example, the new management may fire workers with seniority who had thought their jobs safe, impose nonunion wages, or institute a less costly medical or pension plan. In this way, in the wake of the takeover, stockholders acquire rents from those with whom the breach of trust has occurred.

Chapter 4

1. For an earlier discussion of the subject, see Baumol and Ordover (1985).

2. Similar, but not the same. The central issue dealt with in the statute was the grant of monopolies to favorites and others by the monarch (particularly by Queen Elizabeth I and King James I, during the last year of whose reign the act was adopted). At that period the term *monopoly* referred to such a grant of the exclusive right to provide some commodity, rather than its achievement by a private firm on its own initiative. However, the opportunity to acquire a monopoly from the monarch (or from Parliament, as the statute permitted) clearly constituted, to put it mildly, a very powerful incentive for forms of rent seeking even more blatant than today's.

3. There has, apparently, been little empirical research on the subject. A notable exception is Klein (1989), who conducted a statistical analysis, using as his database all cases in which the court's opinion cited the most recent Supreme Court decision dealing explicitly with "sham litigation." The sample was then reduced further, by restricting it to "cases which alleged sham violations of the Sherman Act in adjudicatory settings," and in which the defendant had filed a countersuit involving these allegations. In the fourteen years covered by the search, Klein found 117 cases meeting his requirements (pp. 46–47). He concluded, "The number of litigated countersuits is smaller, and the recent increase in this number is less, than some in the legal community have claimed" (p. 69).

Of course, this does not necessarily mean that rent-seeking antitrust litigation is infrequent or unimportant. There are several reasons why the actual number of pertinent cases is undoubtedly larger than the 117 found by Klein. In my experience, countersuits often are not undertaken or are dropped in an out-of-court settlement, and all these are excluded from Klein's set. Moreover, the rent-seeking firm, rather than undertaking its own private antitrust suit, may try to persuade the U.S. Department of Justice or the Federal Trade Commission to do so.

It should be noted that, even if such an attempt turns out to have entailed what is indisputably a sham, the firm that undertakes it may be immune from any punishment on the grounds that the First Amendment of the U.S. Constitution "protects most attempts to influence government, even for anticompetitive ends" (Klein, p. 27). This is the doctrine that was enunciated by the Supreme Court in *Eastern Railroad President's Conference v. Noerr*

(1961), which together with a subsequent (1965) case, came to constitute what is referred to as the Noerr-Pennington doctrine.

4. The author participated as "expert witness" in this and the two cases that follow. The reader may, consequently, question the impartiality of the reports.

5. I am extremely grateful to Jonathan Jacobson of the Coudert Brothers law firm for help in assembling these cases. It is easy to multiply the examples, as the following summaries indicate:

1. *United States v. Singer Manufacturing Co.* (1963). An American sewing machine company entered into agreements with Italian and Swiss manufacturers to pool their patents and to maintain patent infringement suits against Japanese manufacturers. The American, Italian, and Swiss companies were concerned because the Japanese companies were offering lower prices. The Supreme Court ruled that the American, Italian, and Swiss manufacturers had violated the antitrust laws. (Reference: 374 U.S. 174.)

2. *Hiland Dairy v. Kroger* (1968). Plaintiffs, independent local dairy processors and retailers, complained because Kroger built its own local dairy processing plant that could supply 20 percent of all local dairy needs and because Kroger would use its self-supplied dairy products as a retail loss leader. The court dismissed the case. (Reference: 402 F.2d 968.)

3. *Telex Corp. v. IBM* (1972). Telex sought to obtain an injunction barring IBM from announcing new product introductions; the appeals court dissolved the injunction. (Reference: 464 F.2d 1025.) In a later proceeding, Telex's contention that IBM's prices were too low was also rejected. (Reference: 510 F.2d 894.)

4. *Brunswick Corp. v. Pueblo Bowl-O-Mat* (1977). A bowling alley operator complained because Brunswick purchased and continued to operate various bowling alleys that would otherwise have gone out of business. The Supreme Court dismissed the case. (Reference: 429 U.S. 477.)

5. Americana Industries v. Wometco (1977). A movie theater complained because a competing movie theater charged a $3 admission price instead of the $4 price that the plaintiff was charging. The court dismissed the case. (Reference: 556 F.2d 625.)

6. *Lormar Inc. v. Kroger* (1979). A supermarket chain sought an injunction preventing Kroger from selling groceries at "unreasonably low" prices. The court refused the injunction. (Reference: 1979-1 Trade Case. 62,498.)

7. *California Computer Products v. IBM* (1979). A manufacturer of IBM-compatible peripheral devices complained because IBM had introduced various new products that were not compatible with plaintiff's and because IBM had lowered its prices. The court dismissed the case. (Reference: 613 F.2d 727.)

8. *Bavon Bottling v. Dr. Pepper* (1984). A Pepsi/7-Up bottler sued to prevent a local Coca-Cola bottler from acquiring a local Dr. Pepper bottler on the grounds that the acquisition would make the Coca-Cola/Dr. Pepper bottler more efficient. The Pepsi/7-Up bottler also complained about low prices being charged by the Coca-Cola/Dr. Pepper bottler. The court dismissed the case. (Reference: 725 F.2d 300.)

9. *Hanguards Inc. v. Ethicon* (1984). The defendants pursued a series of bad-faith patent infringement lawsuits in order to drive the plaintiff, a competitor, from the market. The court sustained the plaintiff's claim that these lawsuits violated the antitrust laws. (Reference: 743 F.2d 1382.)

10. *Cargill Inc. v. Montfort of Colorado* (1986). A meat processor complained because a merger of two of its competitors would lower their costs and enable them to charge lower prices, thereby taking sales and profits away from the plaintiff. The plaintiff sought an injunction barring completion of the merger. The Supreme Court dismissed the case. (Reference: 479 U.S. 104.)

11. *Rickards v. Canine Eye Registration Foundation* (1936). A group of noncertified veterinarians filed an antitrust suit challenging the formation and operation of CERF, a nonprofit organization that collected information concerning eye diseases in dogs. The plaintiff group was complaining because CERF only collected information based on eye exams by certified veterinarians. CERF counterclaimed that the plaintiffs' lawsuit was an effort to drive CERF out of business and that the lawsuit itself was an antitrust violation. The court dismissed the plaintiffs' claims and ruled for CERF on its counterclaims. (Reference: 783 F.2d 1329.)

6. The term seems to suggest fraudulence in the claims, that is, litigation in which the plaintiff makes accusations known to be untrue. However, while the courts have accepted this type of fraud as a sufficient condition for a lawsuit to be considered a sham, the term has been used far more broadly. Thus in *Grip-Pak Inc. v. Illinois Tool Works Inc.* (1982), Judge Posner's decision accepted the possibility that a lawsuit can constitute sham litigation actionable under the antitrust laws even if the claims are "not wholly groundless," provided that the lawsuit makes sense for the plaintiff only if it deters or harms competition, that is, if the plaintiff would have been economically irrational to have brought the case in the absence of a sufficient probability of such an anticompetitive effect. For more on the case law and the definition of "sham litigation," see Klein (1989).

7. The *incremental cost* of a product or service is a generalization of the concept of marginal cost. It refers to the addition to the firm's total cost that results from a given increment in the quantity supplied of the output in question. If no specific increment is mentioned, the term is usually used to refer to the reduction in total cost that would have been realized if the firm had not supplied any of that output. This is also sometimes called "the incremental cost of the entire service." If this figure is divided by the quantity of product that is actually being supplied, the resulting quotient is referred to as the product's "average incremental cost."

8. Actually, there were some earlier methods that enabled information to travel faster than people could, for example, the Native American smoke signals and the French chain of signaling stations.

9. Edison's biographer, Josephson, writes of the "remarkable impudence" of George Westinghouse, Edison's competitor in the incandescent-lighting field. He quotes a Westinghouse advertisement: "We regard it as fortunate that we have deferred entering the electrical field until the present moment. Having thus profited by the public experience of others, we enter ourselves for competition, hampered by a minimum of expense for experimental outlay.... In short, our organization is free, in large measure, of the load with which [other] electrical enterprises seem to be encumbered. The fruit of this ... we propose to share with the customer" (1959, p. 343; Josephson cites a pamphlet issued in 1887 by the Edison Electric Light Company, giving warning to patent violators: *A Warning*, pamphlet of E.E.L.C., 1887, Edison Laboratory Archives).

10. I believe that the role of lawyers in economic growth is also more complex than what is suggested by this regression or, for that matter, by the discussion of the entire chapter. I suspect that without the rule of law economic growth would be reduced to a trickle, as it has so often been in societies with arbitrary powers in the hands of government, or worse still, where political chaos is the normal state of affairs. Thus I believe that the contribution of (a small number of able) lawyers to growth is enormous and perhaps even unequalled by that of any other profession. However, once the number of lawyers grows large, the marginal yield of further additions to their number does become negative.

11. Haley, *supra*, 368–78, n. 232.

12. Id., 371 (citing Dan Fenno Henderson, *Conciliation and Japanese Law: Tokugawa and Modern.* Seattle: University of Washington Press, 1965 (footnotes omitted)).

13. Id., 373.

14. Id.

15. Id., 381.

16. See Meyerson, *Why There Are So Few Lawyers in Japan,* Wall St. J., Feb. 9, 1981, p. 16, col. 3.

17. Haley, *supra,* 386, n. 232, table 9. In part this is a matter of defining "lawyers," a problem that plagues all attempts at cross-national comparison in these matters. An American lawyer who practiced in Japan recently suggested that twelve thousand—often cited as the number of lawyers in Japan—is in actuality the number of lawyers who function as barristers and that more then one hundred thousand law graduates are said to be doing legal work (Shapiro, letter to the editor, *New York Times,* July 4, 1983, p. 18).

18. Haley, *supra* 385—86, n. 232.

19. This means that, over the thirty-year period reported, the number of lawyers grew at an average rate greater than 3.5 percent per year, while the number of lobbyists grew at an impressive rate exceeding 15 percent per annum, continuously compounded.

Chapter 5

1. There is another line of defense that is frequently used by firms which continue to use older techniques even after they face the threat of a rival's innovation. Often innovations stimulate a heightened pace of improvement in the old techniques or products that are threatened by the new—itself a rent-preserving activity. As a result, obsolete products often reach their apex of quality or efficiency *after* the appearance of the substitute that will eventually replace them. The clipper ship as a response to the steam vessel, and improved gas lighting as an answer to illumination by electricity are just two examples. For valuable further discussion, see Rosenberg (1976, ch. 11).

2. It should be clear that the term *innovation* is being used to refer to *productive* innovation, as defined in Chapter 1. Unless noted otherwise, this usage will continue throughout the current chapter.

3. The assumption that low levels of innovative activity are likely to elicit innovation-stimulating (rather than innovation-sabotaging) responses from rivals affects the remainder of the discussion of the chapter in only one way. It introduces the nonlinearity that is capable of eliciting a chaotic trajectory in the time paths of the variables. The reader who considers this result to be of little significance can simply ignore the premise, because it does not affect such implications of the model as the oscillatory behavior pattern of investment outlays one way or the other.

4. In figure 5.2, the coefficient b in (5.5) is set equal to 2a.

Chapter 6

1. Routinization has sometimes even been carried one step further, with the systematic preparation within the firm of a menu of possible inventions from which the preferred

developments are selected by another process that has also been made routine. The company laboratory is then assigned the task of finding the technical means to carry out the desired innovation. For example, at Eastman Kodak, computers are used to simulate systematic qualitative variations in photographic prints (contrast, relative sharpness of foreground and background, brightness and balance of colors, etc.). The computer turns out "pseudo-photographs" which the naked eye cannot distinguish from real camera products, and which embody the contemplated ranges in picture quality—ranges which at that time no one knows how to attain by photographic means. Consumer and professional photographer panels are then used to decide which of the computer-generated pseudophotographs promise to be most saleable, and the company laboratories are assigned the task of inventing a film that will yield the desired results.

2. For a clear illustration of the transfer of the innovation process to managers, see Gary Reiner, "It Takes Planning to Put Plans into Action," *New York Times*, March 12, 1989, sec. 3, p. 3. Reiner contrasts the systematic new product planning in firms like Matsushita (Panasonic) and Apple with that of the "typical corporation." He reports that, "In the typical company the purpose of [new product] planning is for the business manager to get financial approval from the company's senior management team. The business manager presents his case to the senior management and if approved, he is then on the spot to achieve the plan." The Panasonic and Apple procedures, as reported, are at least equally bureaucratic, though perhaps more effectively organized. Throughout the article, the term *management* (and its various hierarchical levels) constantly reappears. How far this all obviously is from the derring-do entrepreneur and the inspired inventor of legend, working away in the cliché basement or garage!

3. Unlike the preceding discussion, in most of the chapters that follow the mathematical models will deal with cost-reducing process innovations rather than with revenue-enhancing product innovations. That focus is chosen because it is easier to quantify the magnitude of a cost saving than the value of a change in product quality, and the discussion becomes correspondingly simpler. Except where noted, my investigations have revealed no qualitative differences between the two cases, so far as the formal relationships are concerned. However, in Proposition 6.2 I have deliberately focused on the product innovation case, to show what modifications in our formal analysis it requires.

4. In a range of small-volume scientific instruments such as spectrophotometers it is reported by one observer that minor "tactical" changes in product design are "generally planned ... approximately every three years for each instrument. These tactical changes ... may involve no more than a cosmetic change in the product." These changes are undertaken in an attempt "to stimulate demand for the instrument, which generally begins to fall in the third year after introduction." The resemblance to the pattern of revision (changes in product design) of basic college textbooks is striking.

5. Proof. Write v for $(k/2) - R_T$. For (6.16) to have a real-valued solution for T, $v > 0$ must hold. Then $T = (G/v)^{0.5}$ approaches zero asymptotically from above as v increases, that is, as R_T approaches zero. Moreover, clearly, $T_v < 0$ and $T_{vv} > 0$, so the result follows.

Chapter 7

1. Nevertheless, it is inappropriate to ignore the important case of product improvement. As Professor Rosenberg has pointed out to me, "When American firms are asked about their R&D expenditure plans, they classify most of it as product innovation or improvement, not process innovation." Consequently, comments will be offered throughout on the pertinent differences in our conclusions that arise under the two types of innovation.

2. Our objective is to show that, as the value of v rises, the curve of the marginal benefit of waiting, B_T, rises with T for small values of T but falls for large T, leading to an intersection with any B_T curve corresponding to a lower value of v, as in figure 7.2. To understand the reason we must first note that with r (the interest rate) greater than v (the rate of improvement of the product), every increase in T must lead to some erosion of the present value of the product improvement. That is, on this score by itself, it would always pay to purchase at date $T = 0$. Of course, other influences incorporated in the remaining terms of the objective function work in the opposite direction—for example, too early a purchase may entail too high a purchase price (too rapid an introduction of the innovation can entail excessive development cost). These influences together normally yield an optimal value of $T > 0$. However, any such positive T entails some loss in the present value of marginal benefit of waiting, as given by the negative last term in (7.7). This loss is proportionate to $(v - r)/r$, which clearly declines when the value of v rises toward that of r. But the loss also erodes with the passage of time because it is divided by $e^{(r-v)T}$. That loss-erosion rate is obviously also cut by a rise in v. Thus an exogenous increase in the value of v will lower the deduction from the marginal benefit of waiting at the lefthand end of the curve, but it will lower the rate at which the present value of the deduction subsequently declines. Consequently, the rise in v will raise the lefthand end of the marginal benefit curve, but will lower its rightward end, just as in the case of cost-reducing process innovation, as illustrated in figure 7.2.

3. This, too, would appear to accord generally with the record of innovation in practice. While imitation seems often to follow fairly closely on the heels of the innovation, usually a few years (perhaps on the order of one to four) do seem typically to separate the two. On the timing of imitation in practice, see Mansfield, Schwartz, and Wagner (1981).

Still, there are cases where the improved model of the imitator followed almost immediately upon the initial innovation. One example is the seventeenth-century introduction by the Rev. Edward Barlow of the repeater watch—the watch which, until about World War I, served as the substitute for an illuminated dial, by striking the current hour any time the pertinent lever was depressed, and in some rather expensive later versions even chiming the current time correct to the minute. The point here is that Barlow's repeater was followed almost immediately by Daniel Quare's improved model. On the other hand, the dramatic few hours that separate Alexander Graham Bell's and Elisha Gray's telephone patent applications are surely an example of an astonishingly close patent race, rather than a Hotelling sort of innovator-imitator timing equilibrium. As a matter of fact, even the Barlow-Quare affair turned into a battle—if not a race—for the patent, which the king awarded to Quare.

4. We ignore the implausible case where the segment of the profit curve to the right of h has a positive slope throughout, so that the optimal launch date may then be infinity.

5. Here if i bids x^* then, if everyone else bids zero, it will receive the payoff $Ax^{*a} - x^*$, by Proposition 7.4. But if some other player also bids x^*, then i still receives the same payoff by the rule of the game covering the payoffs to tied bidders.

Chapter 8

1. There are, of course, noteworthy exceptions to this characterization of the literature. See, for example, the very illuminating pieces by D'Asprement and Jacquemin (1988) and by Katz and Ordover (1990).

2. In section 8.6, in which we examine the evidence on speed of technology dissemination, we will see that this figure is not unrealistic.

3. Excluding Yugoslavia, which participated in the work of the OECD with a special status.

4. The large number of patents in Japan is almost certainly explained at least in part by a feature of that country's patent system that leads to application for a multiplicity of patents to protect what would normally be regarded as a single invention. As Ordover (1991) explains the matter, "Until the beginning of 1988, the Japanese patent law limited each patent application to a single *independent claim* ... (the same restriction existed in Europe as well). Thus ... an inventor of an oversized tennis racket [beside patenting the racket itself] would have to file separate patents for a frame and, possibly, for the method of stringing such a racket. In contrast, in the United States, a single application can include a number of independent claims that together constitute the invention (pp. 47—48).

5. It should also be noted from the figures on the patents-population ratio that the total number of patents is a poor measure of a nation's "inventiveness." In terms of patents per capita in 1988 Switzerland led the OECD, with Japan in second place, and the United States sixth after Sweden, West Germany, Luxembourg, and Austria.

6. For more details on the materials in the following section, see Baumol, Blackman, and Wolff (1989, ch. 5 and 9). For a servey of more recent studies of convergence, see Baumol (1993).

7. My conclusion in an earlier version of this story (1986) has justly been criticized by De Long (1988). He points out that Maddison's sample is inadvertently biased by his inclusion of only the *ex post* successes among the world's economies, those whose productivity levels are most likely to have converged. In 1870, he notes, Japan was highly unlikely to have been included in anyone's list of probable industrial giants of the future, while Argentina would almost certainly have been added to Maddison's list. But elimination of Japan and inclusion of Argentina would certainly have weakened the pattern of convergence, if not eliminated it altogether.

My views have naturally been modified by these cogent arguments and by the analysis of the estimates of per capita GNP by Bairoch (1976) that extend back to 1800. My position now is that the period 1800 to perhaps 1870 was one of marked divergence. This holds statistically for virtually any subsample of the countries in the seventeen-nation list for which estimates are provided by Bairoch. But such early divergence is only to be expected since, as we know, in the first years of the Industrial Revolution England pulled rapidly ahead of everyone else, with Germany, the United States, and France subsequently also pulling ahead of the remaining nations. Then, I still believe, toward the end of the century a sort of "convergence club" of nations—mainly those in Maddison's sample—was formed. To anticipate my later argument, its membership was composed of the group of nations that became adept at learning quickly and putting into practice one another's technological advances. Certainly from 1950 to 1980, as careful and extensive analysis of the Summers and Heston (1984) data for seventy-two countries shows, convergence was the order of the day, for the upper group of nations in terms of GDP per capita, even if this group is picked entirely *ex ante* (that is, from their standing at the beginning of the period covered by the data), just as De Long considers appropriate. However, even here, patterns for intermediate postwar periods are not unambiguous.

8. Actually, at least two serious statistical biases (in the nontechnical sense) account for part of the apparently strong result. First, growth figures were used in the process of estimation of the earlier data, imparting a correlation between the two. Second, the independent variable in the regression is the denominator of the dependent variable, also making for a (negative) correlation. Other sources of statistical bias work in the same direction. For a discussion of other statistical problems that beset this and the following regression, see Baumol (1986, p. 1076n).

9. The probing investigations of Dowrick and Nguyen (1989), Barro and Sala i Martin (1990), and others have recently confirmed that it is nonsense to conclude from such a simple regression exercise that differences in policy, institutional arrangements, and so on virtually do not matter. But that is precisely my point here: if we are to accept the conclusion that their apparent irrelevance is mere surface appearance (as I do), it is appropriate to seek the mechanism that produces the illusion. It is only after we have identified the device that enables a magician to perform a trick that we can rely on more than faith for our belief that it really is not magical.

Chapter 9

1. This excludes cases in which perfect or near perfect replication is literally required of the imitator, by the terms of a licensing agreement or by some other constraint. A classic example is the £20,000 prize eventually (if grudgingly) awarded toward the end of the eighteenth century to John Harrison for construction of a seagoing clock with sufficient accuracy to permit reliable shipboard calculation of longitude for the first time. (The importance of this accomplishment for facilitation of commerce and prevention of shipwrecks is suggested by the magnitude of the prize and of similar prizes offered in France and elsewhere at a time when the income of the highest churchman in Scotland was less than £150 per year). Part of the requirement of the prize was replicability by another clockmaker and, accordingly, Harrison's clock was copied and tested for accuracy. It may amuse the reader to know that the ship selected to test the accuracy of the copy was the *Bounty*, on that famous voyage. Mr. Christian took the clock with him to Pitcairn Island, from where, by a long and roundabout route, it was eventually returned to Greenwich. There, along with Harrison's beautiful chronometers, it continues to run with impressive accuracy.

The story ends up also illustrating Rosenberg's point dramatically. When, soon after, accurate clocks (chronometers) became a standard piece of equipment on valued ships, they followed designs radically different from Harrison's—those of Arnold and Earnshaw. Earnshaw's design served as prototype until after the Second World War.

2. Yet as Professor Rosenberg has emphasized in a letter, "Schumpeter's position with respect to opening of new markets is somewhat ambivalent. He listed it as one of the five different forms of innovation, but he certainly did not give it much emphasis. Perhaps the reason is precisely that it would have involved elevating the role of the mere imitator.'"

3. More recent attempts to prevent the transfer of technology on grounds of military security or in order to preserve a competitive advantage for the home country seem to have been little more effective than earlier efforts to prevent the export of imitative entrepreneurs. These recent prohibitions seem, at most, to have succeeded in increasing slightly the lag in the transfer process, and to have stimulated employment in the craft of espionage, military and industrial. Periodic scandalous revelations about secrets stolen have repeatedly embarrassed governments and provided exciting materials for journalists and writers of popular fiction.

4. See Blomstrom and Wolff, chapter 11, in Baumol, Nelson, and Wolff (1993).

Chapter 10

1. For an illuminating paper that studies learning by firms from one another using a theoretical orientation somewhat similar to that employed here, see Petit and Tolwinski (1993). See also the very illuminating articles by D'Asprement and Jacquemin (1988) and by Katz and Ordover (1990).

2. The special role of complementarity and substitution in innovation has also, independently, been emphasized by Richard Nelson (1990); and see also Merges and Nelson (1991). It has also been studied very recently, in another context, by Young (1992).

3. Thus Levin reports, on the basis of his systematic study, that "technological advance in the electronics industries has been much more 'cumulative' than 'discrete'" (1988, p. 427). Rosenberg's work (e.g., [1976, p. 66ff]) has also emphasized this point, and has provided an abundance of illustrations.

4. In addition, such an *ex ante* sharing arrangement clearly provides the firm insurance against the risk that its own R&D effort will turn out to yield little of value in any given year.

5. Even then, or when a firm's R&D organization is superior in ability to those of its rivals, participation in a technology consortium can be profitable, as will be argued presently, and as the example of IBM clearly confirms (section 10.7, below).

6. The identity of the innovation expenditure of the different firms follows from the simplifying premise that all of the firms have identical cost and demand functions. Since each carries out a profit-maximization calculation or formulates a strategy in the same way that every one of the others does, it follows that they will each select the same value of x. Later, in Proposition 10.2, the choice of value of x is calculated explicitly on the premise that each firm follows a Cournot strategy. Except in the model underlying Proposition 10.3 the premise that the value of x is the same for every firm plays no essential role.

7. Levin's evidence seems to provide some empirical underpinning to this result, even though it has sometimes been suggested in the theoretical literature that (unintended) information sharing should discourage expenditure on innovation by the firm. Thus note Levin's comments on the prediction of Spence's model: "That spillovers discourage R&D investment but may be conducive to rapid technical progress." Levin indicates that his results, "though only suggestive, give some support for the latter hypothesis, but none for the former" (1988, p. 427).

8. This term can be interpreted either to mean that the outcomes are symmetric or that the choices are made jointly. Here I mean the former—that because the firms are all similarly situated, their profit-maximizing decisions on outputs and investment in R&D will be the same, and that long experience will have led each firm to recognize the identity with its own behavior of the behavior of the other members of the cartel.

9. For a similar result for the case of cooperation in R&D activity (in contradistinction to the sharing of the results of independent R&D activity), see the very nice paper by D'Asprement and Jaquemin (1988).

10. Throughout, we measure payoff in terms of a constant per period equivalent. That is, if a stream of payments has an expected net present value which we call NPV, and δ is the per period discount factor, then the constant per period flow equivalent of that stream is an amount, E, whose discounted present value summed for $t = 0.1, 2, \ldots$ is also equal to NPV.

11. I am, of course, deeply grateful to Vice President Howard G. Figueroa for giving me the information described here, and for editing this portion of the manuscript for accuracy.

12. Note also the following observation by Professors Kenneth George and Caroline Joll (1981) about practices in the United Kingdom: "In addition a group of firms in research-intensive industries may operate a patent-pooling and licensing arrangement by which all the firms agree to license one another but no outside firms. Indeed, Silberston and Taylor [1973] found that in the pharmaceutical industry the most important advantage claimed for

the patent system was that it gave the firms something to put into such a patent-pooling system so as to gain access to the other firms' patented drugs" (pp. 231–32).

13. On this see, for example, Blomstrom and Wolff (1993).

Chapter 11

1. See, for example, Scherer (1980, pp. 456–57). Scherer reports that while a number of European countries and Japan, unlike the United States, have laws containing general compulsory licensing provisions, grants of such licenses have been quite infrequent in those countries, while in the United States they have often been granted by the courts at "reasonable royalty rates" (and occasionally free of charge) as a remedy in antitrust cases.

2. In a multiproduct firm or industry characterized by costs that are fixed and common to the various activities involved, the average total cost is not even definable, because the fixed and common costs can only be divided in an arbitrary manner among those activities. However, even then, each activity does have its uniquely defined values for total and average *incremental* costs, that is, the addition to cost that occurs, *ceteris paribus*, as a result of the addition of the product in question to the entire product line.

3. This statement assumes that total industry output of the commodity is fixed so that the most efficient firm is the one that can provide that given output with lowest resources use. In practice, of course, different firms will differ in their cost functions and will consequently vary in the output they provide when assigned the position of exclusive producer of the item in question. This still need create no difficulties in defining and identifying the more efficient of the candidate producers unless there are, say, two firms, A and B, with A having the lower average incremental cost at the output quantity, y_a, of good Y that it would produce if it were sole producer of Y, and with B having the lower average incremental cost at its output level, y_b.

4. One implication is that the Ramsey pricing rule must be changed if there are scale economies in the production of the individual outputs and the allocation of output among candidate producers is to be efficient. Still, it does not follow that AIC will replace MC in the resulting pricing rules, because while a price below AIC may exclude a more efficient producer, a price above MC will exclude consumers or prevent volumes of purchase that entail a marginal benefit that is greater than marginal cost but lower than price. Thus optimal pricing may entail a compromise, an efficient trade-off between the productive inefficiency elicited by a price below AIC and the consumption inefficiencies introduced by a price above MC. In a generalized Ramsey solution, that is, one that is optimal subject to the constraint that the producer's total revenue cover its total cost, if the price of each of its products is set equal to the corresponding AIC, there may still be a financial shortfall, in particular because fixed and common costs will not be covered. Nevertheless, while we must expect some Ramsey prices for the firm or industry to exceed the corresponding AIC values in such a case, others may well fall somewhere between AIC and MC.

5. The decision by X whether or not to sell component K to Y also amounts to a standard make-or-buy decision by X—whether to make the remaining components of the final product for itself or to purchase them from X.

6. The following discussion is framed in terms of incremental cost rather than marginal cost, where incremental cost is defined as the expenditure that the firm would be able to avoid if it were *not* to supply any of the good or service in question. As we have noted, this modification is appropriate where scale economies are present. Because it neglects the

pertinent marginal calculations the discussion in the text is incomplete, since efficiency (optimality) requires that price not fall below *either* marginal or average incremental cost. Standard welfare analysis confirms the part of the statement pertaining to marginal cost, while the pertinence of incremental cost is demonstrated in the text. As has been seen, the price-incremental cost rule is invoked when for some reason a product will be offered exclusively by one supplier, and the task is to ensure that the most efficient of the candidate suppliers gets the job. On the other hand, the marginal calculation comes into its own when two firms offer the same product simultaneously, and the issue is to determine how much is to be supplied by each in an optimal apportionment of the task. The discussion in the text is, of course, readily reformulated in terms of marginal rather than incremental cost, for application to an issue of the latter variety.

7. The rule may, then, appear to conflict with the result contributed by Diamond and Mirrlees (1973), which asserts that in a Ramsey solution it is inefficient for the price of any intermediate good to include any markup over marginal cost. However, there is no such conflict, since true marginal cost must include all of marginal opportunity cost, as we know, and the contribution derived from the tenant by the landlord in the discussion of the text is simply part of the landlord's opportunity cost incurred in providing trackage space to the tenant—it entails no Ramsey markup over that marginal cost.

It should be noted, incidentally, that as is common in discussions in Ramsey analysis, Diamond and Mirrlees do not deal with cases of scale economies, so that the allocation of production among firms entails an interior maximum in whose determination MC rather than AIC plays the key cost role.

8. Actually, in practice the tenant can be expected to spend a small amount, δ, more than that in order to induce the landlord to rent the property to him rather than using it herself.

9. It is easy to extend the analysis to the case where efficiency requires each railroad to carry part of the traffic, apportioned so that $MCx = MCy$, where MCx is the marginal cost to railroad X of carrying an additional unit (carload or ton) of freight over route segment AB.

10. Those who feel that it is inequitable for the landlord to be paid the full opportunity cost of its rental have referred to such pricing as "a perfect price squeeze." But note that the rule does give the tenant all of the fruits of whatever superiority in efficiency it may provide.

Chapter 12

1. Most of content of the following paragraphs is a summary of material in an extremely illuminating paper by Ordover (1991), which describes the pertinent Japanese arrangements and analyzes their consequences.

2. Though a number of critics have raised questions about the frequency with which approximations to perfect contestability are to be found in reality, and about the desirability of the performance to be expected of firms and industries in markets that are imperfectly contestable, no one seems to have raised doubts about the desirability of the use of perfect contestability as a policy benchmark for socially ideal business behavior, in the manner described here.

3. The creators of this criterion, Phillip E. Areeda and Donald F. Turner of Harvard Law School, are among the most distinguished authorities on antitrust law. Their classic article (1975) is one of the most influential writings on predatory pricing.

4. Interstate Commerce Commission, "Coal Rate Guidelines, Nationwide," Ex Parte no. 347 (sub-no. 1), Washington, D.C., Aug. 3, 1985.

5. The Supreme Court has unanimously taken a recent step that can offer powerful protection to rent-seeking litigation. In *Professional Real Estate Investors v. Columbia Pictures*, no. 91–1043, May 3, 1993, the Court held that a plaintiff's lawsuit cannot be rejected as "sham litigation" unless " ... the lawsuit [is] objectively baseless in the sense that no reasonable litigant could realistically expect success on the merits .... [and, in addition, that] the baseless lawsuit conceals 'an attempt to interfere directly with the business relationships of a competitor'" (pp. 10–11).

6. This does not mean that it is efficient for government to *produce* those public goods. It may well be more effective to have them supplied by private firms, with government merely contributing the financing. On the circumstances in which actual production by government serves the social interest, see Baumol (1984).

7. Indeed, as J. S. Metcalfe notes, "Such has been the pressure to develop collaborative R&D in the USA that the National Cooperative Research Act was passed in 1984 to exempt joint research ventures from the provisions of the Sherman Act and to limit the scale of damages which could be claimed by injured third parties" (1992, p. 74).

Epilogue

1. The series includes, in addition to the present volume, *Productivity and American Leadership: The Long View* by William J. Baumol, Sue Anne B. Blackman, and Edward N. Wolff (1989); *Convergence, Competitiveness and International Specialization* by David Dollar and Edward N. Wolff; and *Productivity, Feedback, and Long-Term Growth* by W. J. Baumol and Edward N. Wolff (forthcoming), all published by MIT Press, and based on research supported by the Price Institute for Entrepreneurial Research, the Alfred P. Sloan Foundation, the National Science Foundation, and the C. V. Starr Center for Applied Economics at New York University.

2. For our first formal model of feedback relationships in productivity growth, see Baumol and Wolff (1983). There the subject is the interrelationship between R&D expenditures and productivity, taking account of the behavior of R&D cost as increased productivity elsewhere in the economy increases the opportunity cost of labor spent on R&D.

3. There may be some reason to suspect that this wealth effect on investment tends to peter out once an economy passes beyond intermediate levels of affluence, so that the pertinent relationship should perhaps be assumed to be nonlinear. However, as will be noted presently, an alternative hypothesis can help to account for any leveling off of investment as a function of per capita income beyond some interval of time.

4. Numerous empirical studies, following the work of Feldstein and Horioka (1980), have documented the remarkable association between levels of savings and investment from country to country.

5. If we eliminate the lag in (E.5), thus expressing acceleration as the increase in growth rate from that between $t - 1$ and $t - 2$ to that between t and $t - 1$, it is easy to see that the similarity to the Samuelson equation is not destroyed.

6. It is trivial to see that from a starting point to the right of E the trajectory of z will be monotonically uphill, so that E is unstable in either direction.

References

Abramovitz, Moses. "Catching Up, Forging Ahead, and Falling Behind." *Journal of Economic History* 46, no. 2 (June 1986): 385–406.

Abramovitz, Moses. *Thinking about Growth and Other Essays on Economic Growth and Welfare*. New York: Cambridge University Press, 1989.

Abramovitz, Moses, and Paul A. David. "Reinterpreting Economic Growth: Parable and Realities." *American Economic Review* 63 (May 1973): 428–39.

Abreu, Dilip, Paul Milgrom, and David Pearce. "Information and Timing in Repeated Partnerships." *Econometrica* 59, no. 6 (November 1991): 1713–33.

Allen, Thomas J., Diane B. Hyman, and David L. Pinckney. "Transferring Technology to the Small Manufacturing Firm: A Study of Technology Transfer in Three Countries." *Research Policy* 12 (August 1983): 199–211.

Areeda, Phillip E., and Donald F. Turner. "Predatory Pricing and Related Practices under Section 2 of the Sherman Act." *Harvard Law Review* 88 (1975): 637–733.

Ashton, T. S. *The Industrial Revolution, 1760–1830*. London: Oxford University Press, 1948.

Bairoch, Paul. "Europe's Gross National Product, 1800–1973." *Journal of European Economic History* 5 (1976): 213–340.

Balazs, Etienne. *Chinese Civilization and Bureaucracy*. New Haven: Yale University Press, 1964.

Barro, R. J. "Economic Growth in a Cross Section of Countries." *Quarterly Journal of Economics* 106 (1991): 407–43.

Barro, R. J., and Xavier Sala i Martin. "Economic Growth and Convergence across the United States." National Bureau of Economic Research, working paper 3914. Cambridge, Mass.: NBER, August 1990.

Baumol, William J. *Business Behavior, Value and Growth*. Rev. ed. New York: Harcourt, Brace and World, 1967.

Baumol, William J. "Toward a Theory of Public Enterprise." *Atlantic Economic Journal* 12, no. 1 (March 1984): 12–19.

Baumol, William J. "Productivity Growth, Convergence and Welfare: What the Long Run Data Show." *American Economic Review* 74 (December 1986): 1072–85.

Baumol, William J., and Jess Benhabib. "Chaos: Significance, Mechanism, and Economic Applications." *Journal of Economic Perspectives* 3, no. 1 (Winter 1989): 77–105.

Baumol, William J., Sue Anne Batey Blackman, and Edward N. Wolff. *Productivity and American Leadership: The Long View*. Cambridge, Mass.: MIT Press, 1989.

Baumol, William J., and Burton G. Malkiel. "The Firm's Optimal Debt-Equity Combination and the Cost of Capital." *Quarterly Journal of Economics* 81 (November 1967): 547–78.

Baumol, William J., and Janusz A. Ordover. "Use of Antitrust to Subvert Competition." *Journal of Law and Economics* 28, no. 2 (May 1985): 247–65.

Baumol, William J., John C. Panzar, and Robert D. Willig. *Contestable Markets and the Theory of Industry Structure*. Rev. paperback ed. San Diego: Harcourt Brace Jovanovich, 1988.

Baumol, William J., and Edward N. Wolff. "Feedback from Productivity Growth to R&D." *Scandinavian Journal of Economics* 85 (1983): 147–57.

Baumol, William J., Richard R. Nelson, and Edward N. Wolff (eds.), *International Convergence of Productivity, with Some Evidence from History*. New York: Oxford University Press, 1993.

Baumol, William J. "Multivariate Growth Patterns: Contagion and Common Forces as Possible Sources of Convergence." In Baumol, Nelson and Wolff 1993.

Baxter, William. "The Political Economy of Autitrust." In R. D. Tollison, ed., *The Political Economy of Autitrust*, Lexington, Mass.: Lexington Books, 1979.

Beniger, James R. *The Control Revolution: Technical and Economic Origins of the Information Society*. Cambridge, Mass.: Harvard University Press, 1986.

Berman, Constance H. *Medieval Agriculture, the Southern French Countryside, and the Early Cistercians*. Philadelphia: American Philosophical Society, 1986.

Bernheim, D., and D. Ray. "Collective Dynamic Consistency in Repeated Games." *Games and Economic Behavior* 1 (1989): 295–326.

Bhagwati, Jagdish N. "Directly Unproductive, Profit-Seeking (DUP) Activities." *Journal of Political Economy* 90 (1982): 988–1002.

Bloch, Marc, "Avénement et conquêtes du moulin a eau." *Annales D'Histoire Economique et Sociales* 7 (Novement 1935): 538–63.

Blomstrom, Magnus, and Edward N. Wolff. Chapter 11 in Baumol, Nelson, and Wolff 1983.

Bös, Dieter, Abraham Bergson, and John R. Meyers. *Entrepreneurship*. Vienna: Springer Verlag, 1984.

Braudel, Fernand. *Civilization and Capitalism, 15th–18th Century*. Vols. 2 and 3. New York: Harper and Row, 1986.

Brimelow, Peter, and Leslie Spencer. "The Best Paid Lawyers in America." *Forbes Magazine* (October 16, 1989): 197–219.

Brooke, Christopher. *Europe in the Central Middle Ages, 962–1154*. London: Longman, 1964.

Buchanan, James M., J. R. Tollinson, and Gordon Tullock. *Toward a Theory of the Rent Seeking Society*. College Station: Texas A&M Press, 1980.

Cantillon, Richard. *Essai sur la Nature du Comerce en Général*. London: Fletcher Gyles, 1755. Reprint. Henry Higgs ed., London: Macmillan, 1931.

Carus-Wilson, Eleanor M. "An Industrial Revolution of the Thirteenth Century." *Economic History Review* 11, no. 1 (1941): 39–60.

Casson, Mark. *The Entrepreneur*. Totowa, N.J.: Barnes and Noble, 1982.

Chatterji, Monojit. "Convergence and Growth amongst Rich and Poor." Vassar College, working paper no. 21, March 1992.

Cipolla, Carlo M. *Before the Industrial Revolution: European Society and Economy. 1000–1700*. New York: W. W. Norton, 1976.

Clark, Colin. *The Conditions of Economic Progress*. 3d ed. London: Macmillan, 1957.

Coleman, D. C. "Industrial Growth and Industrial Revolutions." *Economica* 23, no. 3 (February 1956): 1–20.

Coleman, D. C. *Industry in Tudor and Stuart England*. London: Macmillan, 1975. Council of Economic Advisers. "The Market for Corporate Control." *Economic Report of the President*. Washington, D.C.: U.S. Government Printing Office (1985): 187–216.

Cowdrey, H. E. J. "The Peace and the Truce of God of the Eleventh Century." *Past and Present* no. 46 (February 1970): 42–67.

Dasgupta, Partha. "Patents, Priority and Imitation or, the Economics of Races and Waiting Games." *Economic Journal* 98 (March 1988): 66–80.

D'Asprement, Claude, and Alexis Jacquemin. "Cooperative and Noncooperative R&D in Duopoly with Spillovers." *American Economic Review* 78 (December 1988): 1133–37.

David, Paul A. "Invention and Accumulation in America's Economic Growth: A Nineteenth-Century Parable." In *International Organization, National Policies and Economic Development*. K. Brunner and A. H. Meltzer, eds., 179–228. Amsterdam: North-Holland, 1977.

De Long, J. Bradford. "Have Productivity Levels Converged?" *American Economic Review* 78 (December 1988): 1138–54.

De Long, J. Bradford, and Lawrence H. Summers. "Equipment Investment and Economic Growth." *Quarterly Journal of Economics* 106, Issue 2 (May 1990): 445–502.

De Roover, Raymond. "The Commercial Revolution of the 13th Century." In *Enterprise and Secular Change*. F. Lane and S. Riemersa, eds., London: Allen and Unwin, 1953.

Diamond, Peter A., and James A. Mirrlees. "Aggregate Production with Consumption Externalities." *Quarterly Journal of Economics* 87 (February 1973): 1–24.

Dollar, David. "Exploiting the Advantages of Backwardness: The Importance of Education and Outward Orientation." Mimeo, World Bank, December 1991.

Douglas, David C. *William the Conqueror*. Berkeley: University of Calfornia Press, 1964.

Dowrick, Steve, and Duc-Tho Nguyen. "OECD Comparative Economic Growth 1950–85: Catch-Up and Convergence." *American Economic Review* 79 (December 1989): 1010–30.

Easterbrook, Frank H., and Daniel R. Fischel. "Corporate Control Transactions." *Yale Law Journal* 91, no. 4 (March 1982): 698–737.

Easterlin, R. A. "Regional Growth of Income: Long Run Tendencies." In *Population Redistribution and Economic Growth in the United States*. S. Kuznets and D. Thomas, eds., Philadelphia: American Philosophical Society, 1957.

Easterlin, R. A. "Interregional Differences in Per Capita Income, Population, and Total Income, 1840–1950." In *Conference on Research in Income and Wealth, NBER Studies in Income and Wealth*. Vol. 24. Cambridge, Mass.: National Bureau of Economic Research, 1960.

Evans, G. C. "The Dynamics of Monopoly." *American Mathematics Monthly* (February 1924): 77–83.

Farrel, J., and E. Maskin. "Renegotiation in Repeated Games." *Games and Economic Behavior* 1 (1989): 327–60.

Feinstein, Charles H. "Capital Formation Great Britain." In *The Cambridge Economic History of Europe, VIII*. P. Mathias and M. M. Posten, eds., Cambridge: Cambridge University Press, 1978.

Feldstein, Martin, and Charles Horioka. "Domestic Saving and International Capital Flows." *Economic Journal* 90 (June 1980): 314–29.

Finley, M. I. "Technical Innovation and Economic Progress in the Ancient World." *Economic History Review* 18 (August 1965): 29–45.

Finley, M. I. *The Ancient Economy*. 2d ed., London: Hogarth Press, 1985.

Fisher, Franklin M. "The Social Costs of Monopoly and Regulation: Posner Reconsidered." *Journal of Political Economy* 93 (April 1985): 410–16.

Forbes, R. J. *Studies in Ancient Technology*. Leiden: E. J. Brill, 1955.

Friedlaender, Ann F. *The Dilemma of Freight Transport Regulation*. Washington, D.C.: Brookings Institution, 1969.

Galanter, Marc. "Reading the Landscape of Disputes: What We Know and Don't Know about Our Allegedly Contentious and Litigious Society." *UCLA Law Review* 31, no. 1 (October 1983): 4–71.

George, Kenneth D., and Caroline Joll. *Industrial Organization*. 3d ed. London: Allen and Unwin, 1981.

Gilbert, K. R. "Machine Tools." In *A History of Technology*. Charles Singer et al., eds., London: Oxford University Press, 1958.

Gimpel, Jean. *The Medieval Machine: The Economic Revolution of the Middle Ages*. New York: Holt, Reinhart and Winston, 1976.

Gomory, Ralph. "Technology Development." *Science*, May 6 (1983): 576–80.

Gomulka, Stanislaw. *Growth, Innovation and Reform in Eastern Europe*. Madison: University of Wisconsin Press, 1986.

Greenleaf, William. *Monopoly on Wheels: Henry Ford and the Selden Automobile Patent*. Detroit: Wayne State University Press, 1961.

Graves, Ralph H. *The Triumph of an Idea: The Story of Henry Ford*. Garden City, N.Y.: Doubleday, Doran and Company, 1934.

Griliches, Zvi. "Recent Patent Trends and Puzzles." *Brookings Papers on Economic Activity*. Washington, D.C.: Brookings Institution, 1989.

Griliches, Zvi. "Patent Statistics as Economic Indicators: A Survey." *Journal of Economic Literature* Vol. 28 (December 1990): 1661–1707.

Haavelmo, Trygve. "The Statistical Implications of a System of Simultaneous Equations." *Econometrica* 11 (January 1943): 1–12.

Haley, John O., "The Myth of the Reluctant Litigant." *Journal of Japanese Studies*, Volume 4, No. 2 (Summer 1978): 359–90.

Hall, Bronwyn. "The Effect of Takeover Activity on Corporate R&D." In *Corporate Takeovers: Causes and Consequences*. Alan J. Auerbach, ed., Chicago: University of Chicago Press, 1988.

Hanson, Philip, and Keith Pavitt. *The Comparative Economics of Research Development and Innovation in East and West: A Survey*. Chur, Switzerland: Harwood Academic Publishers, 1987.

Hicks, John R. *A Theory of Economic History*. Oxford: Clarendon Press, 1969.

Hobsbawm, Eric J. *Industry and Empire*. Harmondsworth: Penguin Books, 1969.

Hoogenboom, Ari, and Olive Hoogenboom. *A History of the ICC: From Panacea to Palliative*. New York: W. W. Norton, 1976.

Hume, David. "Of the Jealousy of Trade." In *Writings on Economics* 78–80. E. Rotwein, ed., Madison: University of Wisconsin Press, 1955. (First published in 1758.)

Hyman, Anthony. *Charles Babbage: Pioneer of the Computer*. Princeton, N.J.: Princeton University Press, 1982.

Innovation and Achievement. Westvaco Corporation, 1987.

The Inventive Yankee, From Rockets to Roller Skates, 200 Years of Yankee Inventers and Inventions. Dublin, N.H.: Yankee Books, 1989.

Jardim, Anne. *The First Henry Ford: A Study in Personality and Business Leadership*. Colonial Press, 1970.

Jarrell, Gregg A., James A. Brickley, and Jeffry M. Netter. "The Market for Corporate Control: The Empirical Evidence Since 1980." *Journal of Economic Perspectives* 2 (Winter 1988): 49–68.

Jensen, Michael C., and Kevin J. Murphy. "Are Executive Compensation Contracts Structured Properly?" *Managerial Economic Research Paper 86–14* Simon School of Management, 1986.

Jensen, Michael C., and Kevin J. Murphy. "Takeovers, Their Causes and Consequences." *Journal of Economic Perspectives* Vol. 2 (Winter 1988): 21–48.

Jeremy, David J. "Damming the Flood: British Government Efforts to Check the Outflow of Technicians and Machinery, 1780–1843." *Business History Review* 51 (Spring 1977): 1–34.

Jones, Eric L. *The European Miracle*. Cambridge: Cambridge University Press, 1987.

Jorgenson, Dale W., and Zvi Griliches. "The Explanation of Productivity Changes." *Review of Economic Studies* (July 1967): 249–83.

Jorgenson, Dale W., Frank Gollop, and Barbara Fraumeni. *Productivity and U.S. Economic Growth*. Cambridge, Mass.: Harvard University Press, 1987.

Josephson, Matthew. *Edison*. New York: McGraw-Hill Book Company, 1959.

Kagan, Donald. *Pericles of Athens and the Birth of Democracy*. New York: Free Press, 1991.

Katz, Michael L. "An Analysis of Cooperative Research and Development." *Rand Journal of Economics* 17 (Winter 1986): 527–43.

Katz, Michael L., and Janusz A. Ordover. "R&D Cooperation and Competition." In *Brookings Papers on Microeconomics*. 137–203. Washington, D.C.: Brookings Institution, 1990.

Kirzner, Israel. *Competition and Entrepreneurship*. Chicago: University of Chicago Press, 1973.

Klein, Christopher C. "Economics of Sham Litigation: Theory, Cases, and Policy." Washington, D.C.: U.S. Federal Trade Commission, Bureau of Economics Staff Report, April 1989.

Laband, David N., and John P. Sophocleus. "The Social Cost of Rent Seeking: First Estimates." *Public Choice* 58 (September 1988): 269–75.

Laband, David N., and John P. Sophocleus. "An Estimate of Resource Expenditure on Transfers in the United States." Clemson, S.C.: Department of Economics, Clemson University, 1990. Unpublished.

Landes, David. *The Unbound Prometheus*. New York: Cambridge University Press, 1969.

Lefebvre, Georges. *The Coming of the French Revolution*. Princeton, N.J.: Princeton University Press, 1947.

Leibenstein, Harvey. "Allocative Efficiency vs X Efficiency." *American Economic Review* 56 (June 1966): 382–415.

Leijonhufvud, Axel. "Costs and Consequences of Inflation." In *The Microeconomic Foundation of Macroeconomics* (Proceedings of an International Economic Association Conference), G. Harcourt, ed., London: Macmillan, 1977; reprinted in Axel Leijonhufvud. *Information and Coordination: Essays in Macroeconomic Theory*. New York: Oxford University Press, 1981.

Leijonhufvud, Axel. "Inflation and Economic Performance" *Kieler Vorträge* no. 101: J. M. B. Mohr, 1983. Also In *Money in Crisis: The Federal Reserve, the Economy, and Monetary Reform* Barry N. Siegel, ed., Cambridge, Mass.: Ballinger Press, 1984.

Levin, Richard C. "Appropriability, R&D Spending, and Technological Performance." *American Economic Review* 78 (May 1988): 424–28.

Levin, Richard C., A. K. Klevorick, R. R. Nelson, and S. G. Winter. "Appropriating the Returns from Industrial Research and Development." *Brookings Papers on Economic Activity* 3. 783–820. Washington, D.C.: Brookings Institution, 1987.

Lewis, W. Arthur. "International Competition in Manufactures." *American Economic Review* 47, no. 2 (May 1957): 578–87.

Lewis, W. Arthur. *Growth and Fluctuations: 1870–1913*. Princeton, N.J.: Princeton University Press, 1978.

Lichtenberg, Frank R. *Corporate Takeovers and Productivity*. Cambridge, Mass.: MIT Press, 1992.

Lichtenberg, Frank R., and Donald Siegel. "Productivity and Changes in Ownership of Manufacturing Plants." *Brookings Papers on Economic Activity*. Washington, D.C.: Brookings Institution (1987): 643–73.

Lichtenberg, Frank R., and Donald Siegel. "The Effects of Leveraged Buyouts on Productivity and Related Aspects of Firm Behavior." National Bureau of Economic Research, working paper 3022. Cambridge, Mass.: NBER, 1989.

Lindbeck, Assar. "The Advanced Welfare State." University of Stockholm, 1987. Forthcoming in *The World Economy*.

Liu, J. T. C., and Peter Golas, eds. *Change in Sung China*. Lexington, Mass.: D. C. Heath, 1969.

Lopez, Robert S. "Hard Times and Investment in Culture." In Metropolitan Museum of Art, *The Renaissance: A Symposium*. New York: Oxford University Press, 1969.

Lowenstein, Louis. *What's Wrong with Wall Street?* Reading, Mass.: Addison Wesley, 1988.

Maddison, Angus. *Phases of Capitalist Development*. Oxford: Oxford University Press, 1982.

Malone, Dumas, ed. *Dictionary of American Biography*. New York: Charles Scribner's Sons, 1934. Various volumes and supplements.

Mankiw, N. Gregory, David Romer, and David, N. Weil. "A Contribution to the Empirics of Economic Growth." National Bureau of Economic Research, working paper 3541. Cambridge, Mass.: NBER, December 1990.

Manne, Henry G. "Mergers and the Market for Corporate Control." *Journal of Political Economy* 73, no. 2 (April 1965): 110–20.

Mansfield, Edwin. "R&D and Innovation: Some Empirical Findings." In R&D, Patents and Productivity. Z. Griliches, ed. Chicago: University of Chicago Press (1984): 127–48.

Mansfield, Edwin. "How Rapidly Does New Industrial Technology Leak Out?" *Journal of Industrial Economics* 34 (December 1985): 217–23.

Mansfield, Edwin. "Comment." In *Productivity Growth in Japan and the United States*. Charles R. Hulten, ed. Chicago: University of Chicago Press (1990): 341–46.

Mansfield, Edwin, Mark Schwartz, and Samuel Wagner. "Imitation Costs and Patents: an Empirical Study." *Economic Journal* 91 (December 1981): 907–18.

Marris, Robbin. "A Model of 'Managerial' Enterprise." *Quarterly Journal of Economics* 77 (May 1963): 185–209.

Marsh, Robert M. *The Mandarins*. Glencoe, Ill.: Free Press, 1961.

Marx, Karl. *Capital*. Vol. 1, 1867. Vol. 3, 1894. Chicago: Charles H. Kerr & Co., Vol. 1, 1906, Vol. 3, 1909.

McClelland, D. C. *The Achieving Society*. Princeton, N.J.: Princeton University Press, 1961.

McCormick, Robert E. "The Strategic Use of Regulation: A Review of the Literature." In *The Political Economy of Regulation: Private Interests in the Regulatory Process*. Washington, D.C.: U.S. Federal Trade Commission, March 1984.

McCullough, David. *The Path between the Seas*. New York: Simon and Schuster, 1977.

McNeill, William H. *History of Western Civilization*. Rev. ed. Chicago: University of Chicago Press, 1969.

Merges, Robert P., and Richard R. Nelson. "On Limiting or Encouraging Rivalry in Technical Progress: The Effect of Patent Scope Decisions." New York: Columbia University, May 1991.

Metcalfe, J. S. "The Economic Foundations of Technology Policy: Equilibrium and Evolutionary Perspectives." University of Manchester, November 1992. Unpublished manuscript.

Miller, Merton H. "The Modigliani-Miller Propositions after Thirty Years." *Journal of Economic Perspectives* 2 (Fall 1988): 98–120.

Milward, A. S. *The Economic Effects of the Two World Wars on Britain.* London: MacMillan, 1970.

Mohnen, Pierre. "New Technology and Interindustry Spillovers." *Science/Technology/Industry Review* 7 (1990): 131–47.

Mokyr, Joel. *The Lever of Riches.* New York: Oxford University Press, 1990.

Mokyr, Joel. *Twenty Five Centuries of Technological Change: An Economic History.* Forthcoming.

Mørck, Randall, Andrei Shleifer, and Robert W. Vishny. "The Conflict between Managers and Shareholders." *NBER Reporter.* Cambridge, Mass.: National Bureau of Economic Research (Fall 1989): 8–10.

Mowery, David C., ed. *International Collaborative Ventures in U.S. Manufacturing.* Cambridge, Mass.: Ballinger, 1988.

Mowery, David C., and Nathan Rosenberg. *Technology and the Pursuit of Economic Growth.* Cambridge: Cambridge University Press, 1989.

Murphy, Kevin J., Andrei Shleifer, and Robert Vishny. "The Allocation of Talent: Implications for Growth." Chicago: University of Chicago, 1990. Manuscript.

Nadiri, M. Ishaq. "Contributions and Determinants of Research and Development Expenditures in the U.S. Manufacturing Industries." In *Capital, Efficiency and Growth.* George M. Von Furstenberg, ed. Cambridge, Mass.: Ballinger, 1980.

Nadiri, M. Ishaq. "Innovations and Technology Spillovers." New York University, Unpublished manuscript. September 1991.

Needham, Joseph. "Mathematics and Science in China and the West." *Science and Society,* 20 (1956): 320–43.

Needham, Joseph. *The Development of Iron and Steel Technology in China.* Cambridge: W. Heffer, 1964(b).

Needham, Joseph, ed. *Science and Civilization in China.* Cambridge: Cambridge University Press, 1964(a).

Needham, Joseph. *Science in Traditional China.* Cambridge, Mass.: Harvard University Press, 1981.

Nef, John U. "The Progress of Technology and the Growth of Large-Scale Industry in Great Britain, 1540–1640." *The Economic History Review* 1 (October 1934): 3–24.

Nelson, Richard R. "Capitalism as an Engine of Progress," *Research Policy* 19 (June 1990): 193–214.

Nelson, Richard R. "Schumpeter and Contemporary Research on the Economics of Innovation." New York: Columbia University, 1992.

Nelson, Richard, and Sidney Winter. *An Evolutionary Theory of Economic Change.* Cambridge, Mass: Harvard University Press, 1982.

North, Douglass C., and Robert Paul Thomas. *The Rise of the Western World: A New Economic History*. Cambridge: Cambridge University Press, 1973.

Olson, Mancur. *The Rise and Decline of Nations*. New Haven: Yale University Press, 1982.

Ordover, Janusz A. "A Patent System for Both Diffusion and Exclusion." *Journal of Economic Perspectives* 5 (Winter 1991): 43–60.

Ovitt, George, Jr. *The Restoration of Perfection: Labor and Technology in Medieval Culture*. New Brunswick: Rutgers University Press, 1987.

Painter, S. *William Marshal*. Baltimore: Johns Hopkins University Press, 1933.

Pearce, D. "Renegotiation-Proof Equilibria: Collective Rationality and Intertemporal Cooperation." Cowles Foundation Discussion paper no. 855. New Haven: Yale University, 1987/1990.

Peltzman, Sam. "An Evaluation of Consumer Protection Legislation: The 1962 Drug Amendments." *Journal of Political Economy*, Vol. 81, no. 5 (September–October 1973): 1049–91.

Petit, Maria-Luisa, and Boleslaw Tolwinski. "Learning By Doing and Technology Sharing in Asymmetric Duopolies." In *Annals of Dynamic Games*, Vol. 1, 1993.

Philip, Cynthia Owen. *Robert Fulton: A Biography*. New York: Franklin Watts, 1985.

Ping-Ti Ho. *The Ladder of Success in Imperial China, 1368–1911*. New York: Columbia University Press, 1962.

Porter, Michael E. *The Competitive Advantage of Nations*. New York: Free Press, 1990.

Posner, Richard A. "The Social Costs of Monopoly and Regulation." *Journal of Political Economy* 83 (August 1975): 807–27.

Postlethwayt, Malachy. *Universal Dictionary of Trade and Commerce*. London: 1751.

Postner, H. H., and L. Wesa. *Canadian Productivity Growth: An Alternative (Input-Output) Analysis*. Study prepared for the Economic Council of Canada, Ministry of Supply and Services, Ottawa, 1983.

Ram, Rati. "Education and the Convergence Hypothesis: Additional Cross-Country Evidence." Working paper. Normal: Illinois State University, May 1991.

Rapp, R. T. "The Unmaking of the Mediterranean Trade Hegemony: International Trade Rivalry and the Commercial Revolution." *Journal of Economic History* 35 (September 1975): 499–525.

Reynolds, Terry S. *Stronger than a Hundred Men: A History of the Vertical Water Wheel*. Baltimore: Johns Hopkins University Press, 1983.

Robinson, Joan. *The Economics of Imperfect Competition*. London: Macmillan, 1933.

Romer, Paul. "Increasing Returns and Long Run Growth." *Journal of Political Economy* 94 (October 1986): 1002–37.

Rosenberg, Nathan. *Perspectives on Technology*. Cambridge: Cambridge University Press, 1976.

Rosenberg, Nathan. *Inside the Black Box: Technology and Economics*. Cambridge: Cambridge University Press, 1982.

Rosenberg, Nathan, and L. E. Birdzell. *How the West Grew Rich*. New York: Basic Books, 1986.

Rostow, Walter W. *The Stages of Economic Growth*. Cambridge: Cambridge University Press, 1960.

Rubinstein, W. D., ed. *Wealth and the Wealthy in the Modern World*. London: Croom Helm, 1980.

Sallop, S. C., and L. J. White. "Economic Analysis of Private Antitrust Litigation." *Georgetown Law Journal* 74 no. 4 (April 1986): 1001–64.

Samuelson, Paul A. *Foundations of Economic Analysis*. Cambridge, Mass: Harvard University Press, 1947.

Say, Jean-Baptiste. *Traite de Economie Politique*. 1st ed. Paris: Deterville, 1803; 6th ed., 1829.

Say, Jean-Baptiste. *A Treatise on Political Economy*. Rev. American ed. Philadelphia: 1834 (based on the French edition, 1819) Reprint. New York: Augustus M. Kelley, 1971.

Schama, Simon. *Citizens: A Chronicle of the French Revolution*. New York: Knopf, 1989.

Scherer, Frederic M. *Industrial Market Structure and Economic Performance*. 2d ed. Chicago: Rand McNally Publishing Co., 1980.

Scherer, Frederic M. *Innovation and Growth: Schumpeterian Perspectives*. Essay 2, 8–31. Cambridge, Mass.: MIT Press, 1986.

Scherer, Frederic M. "Corporate Takeovers: The Efficiency Arguments." *Journal of Economic Perspectives* 2 (Summer 1988): 69–82.

Schmitz, James A., Jr. "Technological Integration, Communication Infrastructure and Long-Run Growth." Research paper no. 302. Stony Brook, N.Y.: Department of Economics, State University of New York at Stony Brook, 1988.

Schmookler, Jacob. "Inventors Past and Present." *Review of Economics and Statistics* (August 1957): 321–33.

Schmookler, Jacob. *Invention and Economic Growth*. Cambridge, Mass.: Harvard University Press, 1966.

Schumpeter, Joseph A. *The Theory of Economic Development*. 1911. Cambridge, Mass.: Harvard University Press, English translation, 1936.

Schumpeter, Joseph A. *Capitalism, Socialism and Democracy*. New York: Harper and Row, 1942.

Shleifer, Andrei, and Robert W. Vishny. "Value Maximization and the Acquisition Process." *Journal of Economic Perspectives* 2 (Winter 1988): 7–20.

Shleifer, Andrei, and Lawrence H. Summers. "Breach of Trust in Hostile Takeovers." In *Corporate Takeovers: Causes and Consequences*. Alan J. Auerbach, ed., Chicago: University of Chicago Press (1988): 33–56.

Shughart, William F. "Private Antitrust Enforcement, Compensation, Deterrence, or Extortion." *Regulation* 13 (Winter 1990): 53–61.

Smith, Adam. *The Wealth of Nations*. 1776. New York: Random House, 1937.

Solow, Robert M. "Technical Change and the Aggregate Production Function." *Review of Economics and Statistics* (August 1956): 312–20.

Stapleton, Darwin H. *The Transfer of Industrial Technologies to Early America*. 177. Philadelphia: Memoirs of the American Philosophical Society, 1987.

Stone, Lawrence. "The Bourgeois Revolution of Seventeenth Century England Revisited." *Past and Present* 109 (November 1985): 44–54.

Summers, Lawrence, and David Cutler. "Texaco and Penzoil Both Lost Big." *New York Times*, February 14, 1988, sect. 3, p. 3.

Summers, Lawrence, and Alan Heston. "Improved International Comparisons of Real Product and Its Composition, 1950–1980." *Review of Income and Wealth* series 30 (June 1984): 207–69.

Summers, Lawrence, and Alan Heston. "A New Set of International Comparisons of Real Product and Price Levels: Estimates for 130 Countries." *The Review of Income and Wealth* 34 (March 1988): 1–25.

Summers, Lawrence, Irvin B. Kravis, and Alan Heston. "Changes in the World Income Distribution." *Journal of Policy Making* 6 (May 1984): 237–69.

Taylor, C. T., and Z. A. Silberston. *The Economic Impact of the Patent System*. Cambridge: Cambridge University Press, 1973.

Teece, David J. "Technology Transfer by Multinational Firms: The Resources Cost of Transferring Technological Know-How." *Economic Journal* 87 (June 1977): 242–61.

Terleckyj, N. *Effects of R&D on the Productivity Growth of Industries: An Exploratory Study*. Washington, D.C.: National Planning Association, 1974.

Terleckyj, N. "Direct and Indirect Effects of Industrial Research and Development on the Produtivity Growth of Industries." In *New Developments in Productivity Measurment and Analysis* J. Kendrick and B. Vaccara, eds., Chicago: University of Chicago Press (1980): 359–77.

Thirsk, Joan. "The Restoration Land Settlement." *Journal of Modern History* 26 (December 1954): 315–26.

Tilton, John E. *International Diffusion of Technology: The Case of Semiconductors*. Washington, D.C.: Brookings Institution, 1971.

Tullock, Gordon. "Efficient Rent Seeking." In Buchanan et al.

Tullock, Gordon. "Do Economic Institutions Affect the Wealth of Nations?" 1986. Unpublished.

Tullock, Gordon. *The Economics of Special Privilege and Rent Seeking*. Boston: Kluwer Academic Publishers, 1989.

Ursprung, H. W. "Schumpeterian Entrepreneurs and Catastrophe Theory." In Bös, Bergson, and Meyers.

Varian, Hal R. "Measuring the Deadweight Costs of DUP and Rent Seeking Activities." *Economics and Politics* 1 (Spring 1989): 81–95.

Veblen, Thorstein B. *The Theory of Business Enterprise*. New York: Charles Scribner's Sons, 1904.

Veblen, Thorstein B. "Economics and Evolution." *The Place of Science in Modern Civilization.* New York: Viking Press, 1919.

Veblen, Thorstein B. *Absentee Ownership and Business in Recent Times.* New York: B. W. Heubsch, 1923.

Veyne, P. "Vie de Trimalcion." *Annales: Economies, Societés, Civilisations* 16 (March–April 1961): 213–47.

Von Hippel, Eric. *The Sources of Innovation.* New York: Oxford University Press, 1988.

White, Lynn, Jr. *Medieval Technology and Social Change.* Oxford: Clarendon Press, 1962.

Whitin, Thompson M. *The Theory of Inventory Management.* Princeton, N.J.: Princeton University Press, 1953.

Williamson, Jeffrey G. "Why Was British Growth So Slow during the Industrial Revolution?" *Journal of Economic History* 44 (September 1984): 687–712.

Williamson, Oliver E. *The Economic Institutions of Capitalism.* New York: Free Press, 1985.

Wolff, Edward N. *Growth, Accumulation, and Unproductive Activity.* New York: Cambridge University Press, 1987.

World Intellectual Property Organization. *Industrial Property Statistics 1988.* Part 1: Patents. Geneva: WIPO, 1989.

Young, Alwyn. "Substitution and Complementarity in Endogenous Innovation." Cambridge, Mass.: Sloan School of Management, Massachusetts Institute of Technology, March 1992.

Index